TRUTH MATTERS

Essays in Honor of
Jacques Maritain

American Maritain Association Publications

General Editor: Anthony O. Simon

Jacques Maritain: The Man and His Metaphysics
* Edited by John F.X. Knasas, 1988, ISBN 0-268-01205-9 (out of print)

Freedom in the Modern World: Jacques Maritain, Yves R. Simon, Mortimer J. Adler
* Edited by Michael D. Torre, 1989, Second Printing, 1990, ISBN 0-268-00978-3

From Twilight to Dawn: The Cultural Vision of Jacques Maritain
* Edited by Peter A. Redpath, 1990, ISBN 0-268-00979-1

The Future of Thomism
* Edited by Deal W. Hudson and Dennis Wm. Moran, 1992, ISBN 0-268-00986-4

Jacques Maritain and the Jews
* Edited by Robert Royal, 1994, ISBN 0-268-01193-1

Freedom, Virtue, and the Common Good
* Edited by Curtis L. Hancock and Anthony O. Simon, 1995, ISBN 0-268-00991-0

Postmodernism and Christian Philosophy
◆ Edited by Roman T. Ciapolo, 1997, ISBN 0-8132-0881-5

The Common Things: Essays on Thomism and Education
◆ Edited by Daniel McInerny, 1999, ISBN 0-9669226-0-3

The Failure of Modernism: The Cartesian Legacy and Contemporary Pluralism
◆ Edited by Brendan Sweetman, 1999, ISBN 0-9669226-1-1

Beauty, Art, and the Polis
◆ Edited by Alice Ramos, 2000, ISBN 0-9669226-2-X

Reassessing the Liberal State: Reading Maritain's Man and the State
◆Edited by Timothy Fuller and John P. Hittinger, 2001, ISBN 0-9669226-3-8

Faith, Scholarship, and Culture in the 21st Century
◆ Edited by Alice Ramos and Marie I. George, 2002, ISBN 0-9669226-5-4

Jacques Maritain and the Many Ways of Knowing
◆Edited by Douglas A. Ollivant, 2002, ISBN 0-9669226-4-6

Truth Matters: Essays in Honor of Jacques Maritain
◆Edited by John G. Trapani, Jr., 2004, ISBN 0-9669226-6-2

* Distributed by the University of Notre Dame Press
◆Distributed by The Catholic University of America Press

TRUTH MATTERS

Essays in Honor of Jacques Maritain

Edited, with an Introduction
by
John G. Trapani, Jr.

AMERICAN MARITAIN ASSOCIATION

Distributed by The Catholic University of America Press
Washington, D.C. 20064

Library of Congress Cataloging-in-Publication Data

Truth matters : essays in honor of Jacques Maritain / John G. Trapani,
Jr., editor.
    p. cm. — (American Maritain Association publications)
Includes bibliographical references and index.
  ISBN 0-9669226-6-2 (pbk. : alk. paper)
  1. Maritain, Jacques, 1882-1973. I. Maritain, Jacques, 1882-1973. II.
Trapani, John G. III. Series.

  B2430.M34T78 2004
  121—dc22
                        2003018387

To my parents

Margaret K. and John G. Trapani, Sr.

… by the model of your loving and virtuous lives,
you show that Goodness also matters …

Contents

Editor's Note

Truth Matters. The ambiguity of the title of this book is intentional. On the one hand, those two words can mean that the truth of things makes a difference; given the relation between theoretical principles and the practical consequences that follow from them, what one holds to be true matters, particularly in the realm of lived experience. Regardless of the specific branch of knowledge, whether it be the various disciplines of philosophy, the experimental or social sciences, education or political theory, the arts, or theology, the affirmation of one theory or principle to the exclusion of its contrary has practical consequences for ordinary, common experience. This claim itself, however, is not without consequences of its own: by making the claim that it does, it implies that indeed there is such a thing as "the truth of things" and, although certain qualifications would be necessary, it at least initially also implies that post-modern skepticism, as a thoroughgoing human epistemology, is false.

The second meaning of the title may be seen more clearly when written: truth-matters, that is, when it refers to those various branches of knowledge previously mentioned as those subject-areas or subject matters about which questions of truth are indeed an issue. As one might expect, here too there are qualifications to be made, and paramount among them is Aristotle's sage comment that it is the mark of the educated person that he or she not expect any more truth from a particular subject matter than that subject matter itself will allow. The failure to understand these discipline-specific limitations is often the seedbed of skepticism: should one fail to understand these limitations, one might be tempted to draw the false conclusion that truth is always equally difficult to attain no matter what the subject matter. Thus, while truth matters generally, it may also matter in different ways or degrees (concerning the significance of its consequences) in the various disciplines or subject matters that might fall under consideration.

xi

The Introduction to this volume seeks to clear up many of the confusions that so often occur in both epistemology and the metaphysics of truth. The collection of essays in this book, written in honor of Jacques Maritain (and as such, reflecting his position of philosophical realism), all apply these various insights and distinctions in various ways and in various disciplines, some theoretical, some ethical, and some practical – that is, they address the truth-matters about which truth matters!

Concerning the publication of this book, there are certain things that I know to be true: without the help of many people, this project would never have come to completion. First and foremost is Anthony O. Simon, the man who has been the Secretary/Treasurer of the American Maritain Association since it began more than twenty-seven years ago, and who is also the General Editor of the series of books of which this present volume is but the most recent. At the very outset of this project, Tony gave these Shakespearean words of sage advice ... they have served as a constant lodestar: you must "screw your courage to the hitching post," he counseled; trust your instincts and do not be afraid to act forthrightly when certain editorial decisions need to be made. From Tony, I have learned a great deal and I am glad to have the opportunity to express my gratitude in print.

I also received so much invaluable assistance from both Dennis Wm. Moran, Managing Editor of *The Review of Politics*, who did the compositing, and from Cathy Whalen, secretary to the Division of the Humanities at Walsh University, who was always as cheerful and tireless as she is competent. Richard Jusseaume, President of Walsh University, also has given much appreciated institutional and personal support to both my work and to that of the American Maritain Association itself.

I am also grateful to iconographer and Maritain scholar Katharine Osenga, whose original drawing of Jacques Maritain provides the art work for the cover of this book. Since Maritain himself loved the beautiful arts and shared friendships with so many artists who were rising stars in their day, I am confident that he would have been pleased to have the work of such a fine, young artist as Ms. Osenga, gracing the cover of a book dedicated in his honor.

Aristotle said of metaphysics that it was the least necessary but most important; what he didn't say, but perhaps should have, is that a good family is both most necessary and most important: to my mother and father, Margaret and John, you have blessed me with your unconditional love and unfailing support, and you have shown, by the model of your virtuous lives, that goodness, as well as truth, matters; to my children, Lia, Josef, Rachel, and Lauren, you have been my source of greatest pride and inspiration, and you have helped me to understand that we are not loved because we are worthy, but that we are worthy because we are loved; and finally, to my wife, Sherry, you have shown me the true meaning of sacramental love – you are my lover, my friend, my life.

"The Blind Men & the Elephant" Understanding the Secret to Epistemological Realism

John G. Trapani, Jr.

Introduction

Long ago, Aristotle identified the existence of certain *aporia*, philosophical puzzles or "knots" that can only be resolved or "untied" when the perplexed find and make the right distinctions: when we do, the problem is solved, the knot untied; when we do not, the problem remains and we may conclude that no resolution is possible, or we may develop vast and complex systems as ways of explaining the phenomena, systems which in their way complicate the very puzzle they were intended to resolve in the first place. Just as ancient astronomers developed more and more elaborate and complex explanations of planetary motion (for example, Ptolemy's deferent-epicycle scheme), so too the human mind, from simple, common experience to increasing degrees of intellectual puzzlement, may be led to formulate theories of all kinds in the attempt to resolve these puzzles. Making the right distinctions will spare us the intellectual contortions that, often brilliant in their cleverness or creativity, yield more confusion than clarity and light. No one, with sufficient reflection either in his or her own life or upon the history of thought, can fail to identify examples of this: from common sense "knots," the solutions of which one may fail to see until another points out their simplicity "right under our nose," to the "eureka" of scientific puzzles like those resolved by the Copernican revolution or the discovery of the double helix -- the answers all seem so simple after the fact! Of course, the reality is there all along; it is human discovery and understanding that may be long and slow.

Aristotle was also correct when he understood that the basic laws of logic and reasoning are, like the heavens, part of the fixed structure of reality. Reasoning depends upon first principles (for example, the logical principles of identity or non-contradiction); should those who endeavor to communicate rationally fail to agree on these first principles, then all communication becomes impossible since reasoning about ideas cannot go backwards infinitely. Starting points (the first principles) are either both shared and agreed to, or communication and progress are ultimately impossible. This insight is as true for human thought in general as it is concerning the first principles of and within specific disciplines.

Taken together, these two insights of Aristotle's provide the point of departure for this introductory essay. The philosophy of Jacques Maritain, the philosopher in whose honor the essays in this book are assembled, is the position of philosophical realism. As such, it embraces certain philosophical starting points that may be different from the starting points of other philosophical positions. It is these that need to be clearly articulated and examined if philosophical dialogue is to proceed. They are, moreover, as so many threads of classical philosophical knots. Recalling and enumerating these foundational distinctions may avoid countless intellectual convolutions and provide that clarity of understanding that human intelligence naturally desires.

In a book of essays, therefore, about truth and the importance of truth for the consequences that may follow from it, it is necessary to articulate the basic underlying assumptions or starting points concerning three essential factors: human knowledge, reality, and human nature. The following pages articulate a collection of these realist epistemological assumptions. If one agrees with them and they are observed and applied, puzzles may be resolved, knots untied. If one does not agree with them, then consequent epistemological discussions would need to focus either on these principles themselves in order to gain agreement or, if that proves futile, then the interlocutors can at least agree to disagree and end their philosophical discussion thereby sparing themselves the agitation and frustration that naturally occur when puzzles go unresolved.

Truth And Epistemological Realism: Seven Distinctions

Distinction #1: The first distinction involves the use of the term "knowledge" itself. Today, we use this term in a wide variety of ways and as a result, we create an *aporia* concerning the term itself. The ancient Greeks however, used the term "knowledge," *episteme*, in a very restricted sense: for them, it referred to that state of mind that concerned those things that were absolutely certain and unchangeable. On this reckoning, *episteme* (or certain knowledge) applies to proportionately very few things in our world of lived experience, things such as the self-evidence of the first principles of logic, tautologies, and the like. What the Greeks referred to as *doxa*, however, covers a wide diversity of states of mind, some of which **we** call "knowledge" in a loose or broad sense, and some of which we more rightly call "opinion." Not surprisingly, this ambiguity accounts for a great deal of puzzling misunderstandings, resulting in modern day *aporia*.

If indeed distinctions are the way out, then the following categories may be helpful: at one end of the epistemological spectrum, there is "knowledge" in the strict and restrictive sense of *episteme* indicated above, "knowledge in the hard sense." At the opposite end of the spectrum is the vast range of things that constitute personal opinions in the sense of preferences, prejudices, predilections, biases, or beliefs. These latter are entirely subjective and as such involve no truth-claims beyond those that are purely subjective or fatuously "true for me." In expanded or extended versions, this may become historical, geographical, individual or cultural relativism, that is, the belief that truth is relative to a particular time, place, individual or culture.

If these extremes were the only ones available to us, we might find ourselves in trouble indeed. Fortunately, that is not the case. In between these extremes resides the vast realm of "knowledge in the soft sense." While still a form of *doxa* (since it is not absolutely certain nor unchangeable), it is nonetheless real knowledge. This time, however, it is knowledge that is 1) testable by reference to empirical evidence that is objective and publicly verifiable, 2) subject to the rigors of logical reasoning and rational criticism, and 3) either corrigible and rectifiable, or falsifiable.[1]

The disciplined pursuit of truth concerns knowledge in this soft sense; knowledge in the hard sense (*episteme*) involves self-evidence, while "knowledge" in the subjective sense is really more properly called opinion or *doxa*

---

1. Mortimer J. Adler, *The Conditions of Philosophy* (New York: Atheneum, 1965), pp. 23-29.

in the hard sense. The important thing that distinguishes hard *doxa* from soft *doxa* or knowledge in the soft sense is that the judgments in the latter are refutable; opinions that are not refutable are mere opinions or hard *doxa*. Thus the first distinction is definitionally crucial; it involves three states of mind, all of which may permit further precisions but in general, it establishes three epistemological categories which are surely different and which need to be kept in mind as such. They are:

hard or strict *episteme*	soft *episteme*/soft *doxa*	hard or strict *doxa*
knowledge in the hard sense	knowledge in the soft sense	mere opinion

Distinction #2: A second distinction that helps to clarify the first concerns the distinction between "matters of truth" and "matters of taste." The former are objective, public, and subject to those criteria of evidence, rational criticism, and verifiability or falsifiability, while the latter are subjective, private, and as such, are not open to the criteria of evaluation. The former (such as the experimental and social sciences, mathematics, history, and philosophy) are transcultural, while the latter are not since they are individually or culturally relative. Moreover, the former, as the arena of "soft" knowledge, admits progress through addition, replacement, and correction, and is necessitated by the mass of evidence and the weight of reason—in it *de veritate disputandum est* (truth is disputable), while the latter, deriving from individual predispositions and/or cultural history and conditioning, do not—in it *de gustibus non disputandum est* (taste is not disputable).[2]

Distinction #3: The third distinction helps to clarify #2. Here we must distinguish "logical truth" from "poetic truth." The former involves a distinction of its own: descriptive or factual judgments (the correspondence between what is said or thought and the observed phenomenon of reality) on the one hand, and prescriptive judgments (the correspondence between what is said or thought and "right desire"[3]) on the other hand. Since they involve reality and/or human nature, judgments of logical truth are exclusionary, that is, two contradictory propositions cannot both be true. Poetic truth on the other hand, involving as it does the good of

2. Mortimer J. Adler, *Six Great Ideas* (New York: Collier Books/Macmillan, 1981), pp. 58-61.
3. See Mortimer J. Adler, *Ten Philosophical Mistakes* (New York: Macmillan Company, 1985), p. 123.

works made (regardless of whether these be the good of objects made according to the useful arts or the fine arts), is non-exclusionary, that is, the works of art or skill themselves do not compete with each other concerning "truth."[4]

Distinction #4: A subtle but important fourth distinction concerns propositions considered in themselves ("propositions entertained") vs. propositions about which judgments have been made ("propositions judged"). The truth or falsity of the former is absolute: for example, in the proposition "O.J. Simpson committed murder," considered in itself, this proposition is either true or not; it cannot be both. Concerning "propositions judged," however, the truth or falsity of the human judgments made are this time relative and revisable—a judgment deemed true at one time may be changed at a later time because of new evidence or different standards of evaluation. Thus the former concern logic and what-is-the-case objectively, while the latter concern the limitations of knowledge and fallible judgments. Salutary *doxa* or knowledge in the soft sense, if it is understood rightly, depends upon this distinction; failure to do so results in the claims of subjective relativism (something is true for *me* but not for *you*—for example, I think it is true that O.J. committed murder but you do not), and/or historical relativism (something was not true *then* but it is true *now*—for example, it was not true that O.J. committed murder according to the verdict of the first trial, but it may be discovered to be true in the future).[5]

Distinction # 5: Following right on the heels of this last distinction comes yet another. Since "propositions judged" involve the limitations of human knowledge and the fallibility of judgments, we must also distinguish those judgments that are certain "beyond the shadow of a doubt," from those judgments which have varying degrees of probability, i.e., from those that are more probable ("beyond a reasonable doubt") to those that are considered less probable ("by a preponderance of the evidence"). The two O.J. Simpson trials provide a good case in point: the outcome of the first trial was different from the outcome of the second because the "standard of evidence" was different in each trial. For "propositions judged" this uncertainty and mutability is perfectly acceptable; for "propositions entertained," contradictory conclusions or judgments cannot both be true: objectively, either O.J. committed murder or he did not.[6]

---

4. Mortimer J. Adler, "The Logic of Truth," *Truth In Religion* (New York: Collier Books/Macmillan, 1990), pp. 11-12.

5. Ibid., pp. 12-13.

6. Ibid., p. 16.

Distinction #6: Judged propositions are thus evaluated by different and various tests concerning our ability to determine their truth or falsity. The first test is the falsification test—a proposition can be falsified by experience and/or new and better evidence. The second test is the rational test—an argument can be shown to be in error on account of faulty reasoning or logic. The third test would be a combination of the two: new and better evidence *and* better reasons and/or better reasoning.[7] Thus we see that, concerning human judgments that are subject to doubt (i.e., knowledge in the soft sense), there are basically two questions to ask: first, is a particular statement or proposition a matter of fact or a matter of taste? (Recall that degrees of probability about matters of fact are possible—and hence they are matters for dispute, while this is not the case for matters of taste.) The second question arises only in matters of fact, namely: what are the grounds of evidence and/or rational arguments upon which a particular claim depends?

Distinction #7: In contrast to matters of fact (or truth), matters of taste, since they are not arguable or disputable, are most properly the subjects for the appreciation of diversity, pluralism, and multiculturalism. Herein lies yet another important distinction: tolerance and appreciation for the diversity of ideas are appropriate in matters of taste or poetic truth, not in matters of fact. While everyone ought always to honor, value, and treat with justice and respect those individuals whose ideas (or tastes) differ from his or her own, this is not true concerning the proper regard for the (factual) ideas themselves. Rather, the logic of the pursuit of truth demands that we seek and follow the truth wherever it may be found. In other words, we must distinguish, on the one hand, tolerance for all-those-whose-ideas-differ, from the lack of such tolerance concerning the competing or contradictory ideas themselves, on the other hand.[8] In his essay "Truth and Human Fellowship," Jacques Maritain makes this point clear: tolerance properly applied concerns the regard we ought to extend to all **persons** whose ideas may differ widely in both matters of fact as well as matters of taste. For error or falsehood, however, (technically found in matters of fact alone), tolerance, rightly extended to persons, does not extend to **ideas** (as matters of fact) themselves. Here, the truth (of ideas) alone matters, not only for its own sake, but also for the consequences that may, whether we are consciously aware of it or not, follow from it.[9]

---

7. Mortimer J. Adler, *Ten Philosophical Mistakes*, pp. 104-105.

8. Adler, *Truth In Religion*, pp. 5-6.

9. Jacques Maritain, "Truth and Human Fellowship," *On the Use of Philosophy* (Princeton, New Jersey: Princeton University Press, 1961), pp. 21-23.

"The Blind Men and the Elephant"
Presumptions About Reality

At the beginning of this introductory essay, three factors that impact the way we come to understand "truth" were mentioned: these involve assumptions about 1) knowledge itself, 2) extra-mental reality, and 3) human nature and human intelligence. The seven distinctions above help to avoid errors about knowledge and to unravel some of the strands of classical epistemological knots. It is now time to examine the contrasting philosophical assumptions about reality and about human nature. Reflection upon the parable of "The Blind Men and the Elephant" makes evident these contrasting assumptions.

The original purpose of the story is to make clear the need for all of us to develop a sensitivity to the perspectives of others. In the story, several blind men encounter an elephant. One touches the elephant's leg and remarks about how much an elephant is like the trunk of a tree. Another encounters the elephant's ear and likens it to a huge hanging carpet, while yet another, feeling the elephant's side, describes it as similar to a wall. And so it goes with the other blind men, each, being blind, has a different experience of what an elephant is: each perception is an incomplete, partial, and limited perspective; no one can be called wrong, no perspective false—the "reality" of the elephant in itself goes beyond the limited perspectives of the blind men taken individually or collectively. As the allegory attempts to show, our contact with reality is like that of blind men and women also: each has his or her own perspective of reality; each is unique, private, and, as our own perspective, each is beyond the critical judgment of another who may seek to tell us we are wrong or our perspective incorrect.

The story, however, is of course, its anecdotal attraction notwithstanding, thoroughly Kantian: the elephant, as a *ding an sich* unknowable in itself, is perceived by each of the blind men differently according to the experience of the various parts or aspects of the animal experienced. While the story does have its useful and valuable applications, its Kantian implication should not be missed since it implies particular conclusions about reality and human intelligence.

Specifically, the allegory involves two underlying presumptions. The first concerns reality itself. On the one hand, the Kantian presumption is that reality is not intelligible in itself. Rather its intelligibility is a function of the limits of human knowledge. This position has been reaffirmed over the past several centuries by those who have developed epistemologies that have either sought to expand Kant's limits in many and various ways or to articulate more conclusively the consequences of its fundamentally skeptical starting point. This position is reinforced by those, for example, who might argue that a dog's, reptile's, or worm's perception of its reality is a function of its perceptual power just as ours is for us; since dogs can hear sounds inaudible to the human ear, they would see this as an example of reality's noumenal character and of each species' inherent epistemological limitation.

The claims of the realist position differ in significant ways. Maritain would argue that the universe is intelligible *in itself* because of its causal dependence upon a Supreme Being who is intelligence itself. As a result, created things, Maritain writes, "… are not only what they are. They ceaselessly pass beyond themselves, and give more than they have because from all sides they are permeated by the activating influx of the Prime Cause."[10] The universe is thus flooded with intelligibility and as such, it is not merely limited in its knowability by the exclusively sense abilities of the various creatures that inhabit it; rather, the universe is supremely intelligible and its true nature can only be penetrated by intelligent creatures. Human understanding may indeed be limited, but it is the limits of our intellectual mode of gaining knowledge that imposes the restriction, not the limits of our sense powers alone nor any inherent limitation in the intelligibility of the universe itself.

In both metaphysical pictures, the Kantian and the Realist, reality is intelligible. The difference is that the Kantian limitation is in the noumenal, exclusively sensible nature of reality on the one hand, and in the limits of human intelligence on the other. By contrast, in the realist position, the sensible dimension of reality is only one dimension; the intelligible dimension of the universe, inherent in the universe itself, is the other. The intelligibility of the universe is not a function of human intellectual construction alone but rather a function of our unique human nature which is also different than the Kantian understanding of it.

"The Blind Men and the Elephant" Presumptions About Human Nature

The second underlying presumption of both the story and the Kantian understanding of the human mind's role in the explanation of knowledge is that they are both confined to and limited by a sensory experience of reality and as such, they are fundamentally blind to knowing reality in itself. The

10. Jacques Maritain, *Creative Intuition in Art and Poetry* (New York: Pantheon Books Inc., 1953), p. 127.

influence of this assumption is pervasive; the perspective of the experimental sciences, for example, yields one interpretation of reality (the table before me is mostly molecules whirling about in empty space) while common sense provides another perspective (the table is solid and stationary). Similar examples of seemingly irreconcilable perspectives may be found in and among other disciplines constitutive of present-day academia.

This modern Kantian-to-Postmodern epistemology that postulates the blindness of the human mind is, however, only one explanation of the human mind. Jacques Maritain, arguably the foremost realist philosopher in the tradition of Thomas Aquinas in the twentieth century, supplies another. Maritain acknowledges that all human knowledge is indeed rooted in sensory experience. However, for Aquinas, Maritain, and others in the Thomist/realist tradition, human nature is characterized and distinguished by its unique possession of a spiritual intellect. And it is precisely "the activity of intellect which extricates from sense experience—and raises to the white heat of immaterial visibility *in actu*—objects which the senses cannot uncover in things and which the intellect sees."[11] Herein lies the key to understanding the secret of epistemological realism: the intellect *sees*! "If I am a Thomist," Maritain writes, "it is in the last analysis because I have understood that the intellect sees, and that it is cut out to conquer being."[12] Of course, Maritain's claim cannot be understood without the help of analogical thinking—the two statements: "do you see the table?" and "do you see what I mean?" entail analogous uses of the verb "to see." Both are legitimate and correct usages, and the latter, as a metaphysical application of analogical thinking, ought not be confused with metaphor. In fact, Maritain cites three things or categories that the intellect "sees" and the senses cannot: 1) "being and its properties;" 2) "the mystery of abstractive intuition" ("the essential structures and intelligible principles seizable in the light of being"); and 3) "the mystery of analogical intellection" ("the intellect knows, without seeing them directly, the transcendental objects which are not contained in the world of sensory experience").[13]

The first modern philosopher to attempt a refutation of the Kantian limitation of human intelligence and human knowledge was Maritain's teacher and mentor, Henri Bergson. Bergson's criticism advanced the notion of intuition as a necessary complement to the limited, static, rational or conceptual account of reality that is the cornerstone of modern

11. Jacques Maritain, "On Human Knowledge," *The Range of Reason* (New York: Charles Scribner's Sons, 1952), p. 9.
12. Ibid.
13. Ibid.

epistemology. In his first book, *Bergsonian Philosophy and Thomism*, Maritain agreed that Bergson's philosophy offered a legitimate criticism of the limitation of modern epistemology, but he went on to assert that Bergson's philosophy itself did not go far enough since it had failed to understand adequately the true power and capacity of the human intellect. According to Maritain, the intellect is a superior, intuitive, immaterial knowing power which operates together with the instrumentality of the senses in a diversity of ways, and, having being itself as its proper object, puts us in direct and immediate contact with the intelligible dimension of reality itself.[14] Although he remained grateful and respectful of Bergson's inspiration, Maritain defended the Thomistic notion of intellect as a metaphysical fact of human nature.

Centuries earlier, Thomas Aquinas summed up the relation between the admittedly limited seeing power of the human intellect and the diaphanous inherent intelligibility of the created universe by using a metaphor of a night owl endeavoring to see the sun by day—we are limited not because we are blind or because reality is too opaque. Rather, the fullness of reality is **so** luminous and intelligible that **it** may be blinding to human intelligence as an abundance of light is to the eye. Thus Aquinas, with a reference to Aristotle, writes, "It may well happen that what is in itself the more certain may seem to us the less certain on account of the weakness of our intelligence, 'which is dazzled by the clearest objects of nature; as the owl is dazzled by the light of the sun' (*Metaph*. ii.lect.i)"[15] Thus our sight, and our capacity for grasping and attaining truth, may be limited by the abundance of the radiant intelligibility of reality, but not by any inherent blindness in the intellect itself. Our understanding of reality may need work—intellectual seeing can be improved by hard thinking in a way that our physical seeing, unaided by some optical instrument, cannot. Thus the human capacity for intellectual understanding ("sight") may grow beyond "the owl's" limitation to the extent that we as humans naturally transcend the limitations of a purely sensory encounter with material reality, and develop our intellectual capacity to such an extent that we approach the clear and more splendid light of radiant intelligibility manifest throughout all creation.

---

14. See Jacques Maritain, *Bergsonian Philosophy and Thomism* (New York: Philosophical Library, 1955), p. 145.

15. Thomas Aquinas, *Summa Theologica* (New York: Benziger Brothers, Inc., 1947), I.I.A5.Ad.1 (p. 3.)

Conclusion

The reader may appreciate knowing the assumptions or starting points of the editor and author of this Introduction and of the essay contributors concerning the three factors, mentioned at the outset, that impact the way we come to understand "truth." As opposed to the positions of Idealism, Kantianism, or Postmodernism, all here assembled embrace the realist position concerning these three factors: concerning reality, all affirm the existence of an inherently intelligible extra-mental reality; secondly, concerning human nature, all affirm that human beings are capable of genuine knowledge of reality because of the agency of both our sense powers and the power of the human intellect working together; and thirdly, concerning human knowledge itself, all hold that knowledge is not merely a construction of the human mind but rather, is a combination of both our sense knowledge of the material dimension of the universe as well as an intellectual understanding of those intelligible objects of knowledge that are both perceptible (like table or dog) and imperceptible (like truth, justice, or being).

The essays in this book share these realist assumptions. And if indeed truth is possible, even if disputable, then there is all the more reason and justification that we need to engage in discussions about truth in speculative, ethical, and practical matters. For not only is the pursuit of truth in these matters of the utmost importance in itself but also because truth-claims function as principles or starting points of reasoning that have far-reaching consequences of their own, as seen in the topics of discussion found in this collection. These essays provide ample witness to the claim that infuses this volume with purpose and proudly inspires it to be offered in honor of Jacques Maritain, a man whose whole life was dedicated to the pursuit and proclamation of truth: Truth Matters.

On the Prospect of Paradise on Earth
Maritain on Action and Contemplation

James V. Schall, S. J.

To wish paradise on earth is stark naïveté. But it is surely better than not to wish any paradise at all. To aspire to paradise is man's grandeur and how should I aspire to paradise except by beginning to realize paradise here below? The question is to know what paradise is. Paradise consists, as St. Augustine says, in the joy of the Truth. Contemplation is paradise on earth, a crucified paradise.
—Jacques Maritain, "Action and Contemplation," 1938[1]

The order of human virtues come to completion demands that practical action in the world and on the human community superabound from contemplation of truth, which means not only contemplation in its pure forms but, more generally, intellectual grasping of reality and enjoyment of knowledge for its own sake.
—Jacques Maritain, "Thomist View on Education," 1957[2]

Going out into the deep does not just mean that the Church is to be *much more a missionary Church*, but above all it says that she is to be more intensely contemplative.... Certainly, to contemplate *does not mean to forget the earth....* *Christian contemplation does not take us away from our earthly commitments.*
—John Paul II, Address to Extraordinary Consistory, 2001[3]

I

The operative motto of the Dominican Order is St. Thomas's famous expression, *contemplata tradere* ("to hand on what is contemplated"). Things that are to be handed on are, first, things that are personally, interiorly considered, pondered, known, indeed, enjoyed. This short phrase already contains the remarkable realization that the truths that we know and behold somehow are not merely ours, even in being ours; they are likewise to be passed on. Truth, as such, is free in the sense that no one owns it even if everyone is obliged to acknowledge it, freely. In a very real sense, it is better to hand on what we know than merely to keep it ourselves, even

1. Jacques Maritain, "Action and Contemplation," *Scholasticism and Politics* (Garden City, New York: Doubleday Image, 1960), p. 182.
2. Jacques Maritain, "Thomist View on Education," *The Education of Man: The Educational Philosophy of Jacques Maritain*, ed. Donald and Idella Gallagher (Garden City, New York: Doubleday, 1962), p. 56.
3. John Paul II, Address to Extraordinary Consistory of Cardinals, Ascension Thursday, May 24,2001, *L' Osservatore Romano*, English edition, 30 May 2001, #1, 8.

though we must first attend to it ourselves, an attention in which there is indeed much delight.

The issue was already present in the Cave Myth in *The Republic* of Plato, over the question of whether the philosopher, on beholding the good, ought subsequently to return to the cave and enlighten the citizens held there in darkness, a dangerous mission for the philosopher, as it turned out. But the fact was that in the good that he beheld, the philosopher saw its relation to those who did not know it.

Moreover, nothing Hegelian or collectivist can be found in this Thomistic notion of *contemplata tradere*, as if somehow its subject was some great inner-worldly being that transcended the personal reality that is given to each of us to make us what we are and not something else. The object both of creation and of redemption always remains individual persons, albeit in that very social nature given to them because their minds can, properly speaking "know all things." The Dominican motto has the implication that we need to set aside much time and effort to know the order of being, of *what is*. But within it, there is also a very vivid feeling that, welling-up within us, is a joy that wants truth to be known, a realization that what is indeed properly "for us" is also "for others."

Not to be outdone, the early Jesuits have their own, less well-known, motto that comes, I believe, from Jerome Nadal, one of Ignatius' early and most brilliant companions. It reads: each one is to be *in actione, contemplativus* (contemplative in action). This motto is not conceived to be in opposition to the Dominican tradition or to bypass it or, even less, to surpass it. Rather, *in actione, contemplativus* spells out something implicit in *contemplata tradere*. Without the *contemplata tradere*, there could be no *in actione, contemplativus*, no contemplative in action. One of the striking things about Christianity, in contrast to the Greek notion of contemplation, something Maritain often notes, is that it is, without ceasing to be contemplative, action oriented. The fullness of the virtues superabounds into action. The knowing of the truth always leads to doing something: the cup of water, the teaching all nations, the observing the commandments, the clear statement of the truth.

The Jesuits were not designed to be a contemplative order in the classical monastic sense, but no one could be Christian without some fundamental contemplative orientation. In the end, in both our theology and our liturgy, we are beholders, not doers. Hence, the Jesuit emphasis presupposes the contemplative. But in addition to the contemplative theological understanding that we find in St. Thomas's *Summa Theologiae* that ought to stand at the root of any Christian contemplation or action, we can, following theses also found in St. Thomas himself, look to the divine governance and providence as they work their way out in the world of nature and human history. There we see that what actually goes on in human worldly affairs, including in our own lives, is not apart from an active presence of God in being and in redeeming.[4] This is what St. Ignatius's famous "Contemplatio ad Obtinendum Amorem" ("Contemplation for Obtaining Love") that ended the Spiritual Exercises was all about. Thus, in all we do, no matter how secular, even, paradoxically, no matter how sinful, we can discern, if we are attentive, the presence of God's will and grace leading us, if we choose, even out of evil to that end for which we are created in the first place. This is the contemplative part of our action.[5]

The philosophical and theological traditions of both the East and West have been concerned with the relation of philosophy and politics, of action and contemplation, and their order to each other, to their proper objects. Religious orders, even nations and religions, exist because of differing positions taken on the priority and relation of action and contemplation, on the relationship of truth and fellowship, on the truth of practical things and the truth of speculative things. The place of science in modern culture is, at bottom, a question of the relative worth of action and contemplation. Indeed, if we follow certain theories of modern enlightened liberty and rationalism, we can easily arrive at a view that there is nothing in the universe to contemplate. Either we can know nothing but what we make or we deliberately design what we make to replace what is said to be from nature, as if the latter had no prior order or purpose.

Hence, the contemplations in modernity are mostly our self-formulated operative or artistic ideas presupposed to nothing but themselves or other exclusively humanistic sources. The only action is to carry out what our ideas are, whatever they are. The drama of prudence, the relation between what we ought to do and what we do do, is largely missing. We make little effort to judge what we think and do against *what is*. All of this brings us face to face with the following question rooted in classical contemplative theory or metaphysics: is what we are ourselves a product of design, of a

---

4. This in part is what St. Thomas's question on "Eternal Law" (I-II, 93) is about.

5. Robert Sokolowski points out that the philosophic act is one of making distinctions about differences found in things so that we can simply know *what is*. Thus, there is a contemplative moment in all we do. "The activity of making distinctions always has something contemplative about it. Whenever we make a distinction, we become somewhat disconnected from whatever practical or rhetorical activity we may be engaged in" (Robert Sokolowski, "The Method of Philosophy: Making Distinctions," *The Review of Metaphysics* 51 [March 1998], p. 524).

certain order and hence of an intelligence that makes us already better than any alternative that we might propose from our own minds? This is not to forget that in classical thought, our freedom is directed precisely to what we ought to be, from nature. The actions that lead to the virtues are themselves part of human nature even though they must be known and chosen, must be put into effect freely.

II

In 1938, Jacques Maritain gave a series of lectures in the United States published under the title of *Scholasticism and Politics*. One of these lectures was devoted to "Action and Contemplation," a consideration that seemed appropriate to present in the United States because it seemed at the time, as it probably still so seems, to be the nation that puts more emphasis on action as a central element in its cultural make up than it does contemplation. Maritain was aware of the tradition of American philosophical pragmatism. He recalled Whitman's poems as examples. Nonetheless, he thought, unexpectedly, that America had great reserves and possibilities for contemplation.[6] How so?

Maritain's approach to this topic naturally follows the classic discussion of the primacy of contemplation or theory among the Greeks and the relation of Word and Act as those ideas appear in Christian theology—"in the beginning was the Word," "do unto others as you would have them do unto you." But what was striking about Maritain's remarks on American pragmatic activism was his suspicion that "the activism which is manifested here assumes in many cases the aspect of a remedy against despair." Hectic action can distract us from the abyss that we suspect lies under our spiritual surface. This despair would suggest that what is missing from action is any inner content or purpose or coherence that would make it something more than its passing, historical reality. Action for action's sake, a theme we find in someone like Camus, also as a remedy for despair, assumes that reality itself has no inner order or purpose.[7] Human action thus takes its glory not from its meeting or not meeting eternal norms but from the creative power of the will to do whatever it wants. A despair would arise from the realization that ultimately what was done, however well or furiously, bore no transcendent meaning or sign. We lived precisely "in vain," to use Aristotle's phrase. Thus Maritain continued, "to my mind,

6. Maritain, *Scholasticism and Politics*, p. 182.
7. Albert Camus, *The Rebel: An Essay on Man in Revolt* (New York: Vintage, 1956).

if in American civilization certain elements are causing complaints or criticisms, those elements proceed definitely from a repression of the desire, natural to mankind, for the active response of the soul breathing what is eternal."[8] Hence, the misunderstanding or rejection of our being and purpose cannot but leave us with a feeling that our personal existence has no meaning beyond itself.

Maritain divides his essay into five sub-headings: 1) Greek Philosophy, 2) Christianity, 3) Superabounding Contemplation, 4) the Call to Contemplation, and 5) Orient and Occident. In the discussion of Greek contemplation, he devotes himself principally to Aristotle. He distinguishes between transitive activities which have their perfection in the thing made or in another being and immanent ones that remain in the one contemplating. He makes the remarkable observation that "people who exercise philanthropy as a transitive activity need the poor to help if they want to be helpful, sinners to preach to if they want to be preachers, victims whose wrongs they can redress. They need *patients.* "[9] This is why, ironically, things like help of the poor and needy, or opposition to war, have in the modern world themselves often become ideological substitutes for God. Obviously, there seems to be some radical limitation to such activity that must use its object for its own perfection. The poor clearly resent those whom they sense are "aiding" them primarily for essentially selfish motives.

Maritain maintains, however, that Aristotle also understood "immanent activity" which he did not confuse with transient activity, nor did he think all transient activity bad. This contemplative activity is the "characteristic activity of life and the spirit." The acts of knowing and loving, however, remain within the soul as their perfection. They are for the soul "an active superexistence, as it were, superior to the merely physical act of existence. Thus the soul, when it knows, becomes thereby something that it is not, and when it loves, aspires toward what it is not, as to another self. This action as such is above time." It is to be noted, in these reflections, how often Maritain comes back to the notion of "superabounding" or "superexistence" to describe the fullness of what goes on in human and divine relationships.[10] It is precisely because of this superabounding contemplation that our relation to others is not merely transitive, why it is not simply in need of objects to prove its own worth.

8. Maritain, *Scholasticism and Politics*, p.182.
9. Ibid., p.164.
10. See James V. Schall, "The Law of Superabundance," *Gregorianum* 72, no.3 (1991), p. 155ff. This essay treats Maritain's overall position on superabundance.

Aristotle held that this immanent action was more perfect than an act of the will or any transitory act. St. Thomas on this basis held that intelligence is "nobler than will" but only when considering the degree and nature of the immanent act itself. Maritain quickly points out that the Greeks, while understanding the intrinsic superiority of the contemplative life on the grounds stated, erroneously concluded from that position that "mankind lives for the sake of a few intellectuals."[11] Ironically, in one way or another, this notion that the rest of mankind lives for certain elites is rather widespread today. The Greeks for this reason maintained that ordinary human life in the case of politicians, artisans, and businessmen, while properly human, was something inferior to the contemplative or philosophic life. Indeed, these latter lives, including the political one, were considered to be servile.

III

The confrontation of Christian revelation with Greek philosophy took as its most obvious problem the question of the worthiness of ordinary life. St. Joseph was a carpenter, as was Christ. The Apostles were fishermen. St. Paul was something of a rabbi but he was also a tent-maker. The problem was twofold, since it was not only a question of dealing with the Greek and Roman view of the eternal status of slaves, but also with the Hebrew idea of the difference between Jews and Gentiles, with universalism, in other words. Christianity held that love was higher than knowledge, a position that St. Thomas reconciled with the truth of the Greek position by arguing that the object of love is higher than the internal contemplative activity of the knower or lover.

Maritain explained the point in this way: "considering the things we know and love, these things exist in us by knowledge according to the mode of existence and the dignity of our own soul, but by love they attract us to them according to their own mode of existence and their own dignity, and therefore it must be said that to love things that are superior to man is better than to know them. It is better to love God than to know him."[12] Following St. Albert the Great, Maritain differentiates Christian and Greek contemplation, the latter looking to the good of the contemplator, while the former seeks the reality of what is loved. Maritain cites the famous medieval Latin phrase, "Ubi amor, ibi oculus"—where is thy eye, there is thy

11. Maritain, *Scholasticism and Politics*, p. 165.
12. Ibid., p. 166.

love.[13] These two positions, of course, can be reconciled. The beatific vision remains primarily contemplative, in some sense, by grace, a possession of what is loved.

Maritain wrote "Action and Contemplation" before the reflections of Josef Pieper on leisure and work appeared, but he treats of many of the same issues, though, like the present pope, Maritain is more prone to use the word work to include intellectual activities than is Pieper.[14] Maritain first recalls that we must distinguish between craft or artistic production, which would have continued without a Fall, and the labor or sweat connected with work that is a consequence of the Fall. The point serves to enhance the dignity of manual activity as such. "Man's labour in its first and humblest state is a co-operation with God the Creator, and Christianity's rehabilitation of labour in the moral order is bound up with revelation, in the dogmatic order, of creation *ex nihilo*."[15]

Maritain sees the basis of labor ethics in this teaching that man is a co-creator. He recognizes that industry can be made into an idol, but "work has a value of natural redemption; it is like a remote prefiguration of the communication of love." Maritain points out that everyone instinctively recognizes that work is not just for its own sake, but ought to have a purpose for some good. If someone is told to dig ditches and fill them up, even at the highest of wages or salaries, and to continue to do so all one's life, most people would soon go mad because they see the futility of it all.[16]

This sense of the orientation of work is related to Maritain's notion of Christian contemplation overflowing into the good of real beings. Man is thus "both *homo faber* and *homo sapiens*, and he is *homo faber* before being in truth and actually *homo sapiens* and in order to become the latter."[17] Maritain sees the consequence of this dignity of work to be the implicit rejection of the erroneous Greek practice of slavery. This spiritual understanding of work had to be accomplished long before any purely political rejection of it was possible.

Maritain, however, does not in fact deny the essential point of the Greek position on contemplation among Christians.

13. See James V. Schall, "*Ubi Amor, Ibi Oculus,*" *Idylls and Rambles: Lighter Christian Essays* (San Francisco: Ignatius Press, 1994), pp. 195-99.
14. See Josef Pieper, *Leisure: The Basis of Culture*, trans. G. Malsbary (South Bend, Indiana: St. Augustine's Press, [1948] 1998).
15. Maritain, *Scholasticism and Politics*, p. 167.
16. Ibid.
17. Ibid.

It is true that contemplation itself is not work, not a thing of utility. It is a fruit. It is not ordinary leisure; it is a leisure coinciding with the very highest activity of the human substance. According to the profound views of St. Thomas Aquinas, following Aristotle, those who go beyond the socio-temporal life achieve in themselves the supra-social good to which the social tends as to a transcendent term, and by that very act are free from the law of labour. There remains no more for them but Thee and I, Him whom they love, and themselves.[18]

The priority given to contemplation is rooted in the fact that, precisely as an immanent activity, it superabounds. In this sense it is a "protection and a benediction to society." It is not itself a work or something of utility. Nonetheless, the very seeing of the relation of all things cannot but overflow into a realization of the worthiness of all things, especially all human things.

IV

Maritain next deals with this very notion of superabundant contemplation, which turns out to be a key to his understanding of both Greek philosophy and Christian revelation. The priority is not ultimately on action, however legitimate action is and however much theoreticians need to revert to action when something needs to be done in the world. Obviously, the understanding of what goes on in Christian contemplation means that the capacities or powers to do what is asked of Christians in revelation is not solely under their own power; as Maritain puts it, it is "beyond anything that the energies of human nature, left to themselves, can achieve."[19]

This position is, no doubt, hard doctrine for moderns who are told not only that autonomous humanism is not enough, but that in addition to grace, they need also the gifts of the Holy Spirit. Even in pious circles, we hear more of the active needs and obligations than we do of grace and the gifts of the Holy Spirit needed to achieve them. But the logic behind these teachings is pretty clear. Man is in fact called, through Creation, Incarnation, and Redemption, to an end higher than might be expected from his essential ontological condition. If he is to see God face-to-face, something that he can at least imagine on philosophical grounds to be something he would want, it is clear that no finite being can by his own powers experience something of the divine goodness or essence. The reality of revelation is addressed to human culture at this very point.

18. Ibid., p. 169.
19. Ibid., p. 170.

Maritain, interestingly, anticipates the current discussion in *Dominus Jesus* ("Christ and His Church," cited below #20) about how salvation outside the confines of Christianity is to be understood. The Document of the Congregation for the Doctrine of Faith explains the contemplative traditions found outside of Christianity.

> [Contemplation] can be called Christian in a different sense, ontological or metaphysical, since it lives by the grace of Christ. In that sense it can even be found, —substantially the same, whatever the difference of mode, degree, purity, or human setting, —in eras or lands where Christianity is not professed. It is the supernatural contemplation of the Old Testament and the New, of Moses and St. Paul, such as is exercised by the living faith and supernatural gifts. The existence of these divine gifts is taught us by Christian revelation, but they are alive in all who have the grace of Christ, even when not belonging visibly to His Church (for instance, some of the Jewish Hassidim whose story was told by Martin Buber, or that great Mohammedan mystic Al Hallaj, whom Louis Massignon has studied).[20]

Notice that Maritain, in "Action and Contemplation," has kept the essential point that if there is true supernatural contemplation outside Christianity, as there may well be, it is not caused by itself, but through the grace of Christ, even operative outside Christian confines for the general purposes of the one redemption in Christ.

There is a natural aspiration to contemplation that supernatural contemplation, in its turn, achieves and completes. Natural knowledge of the highest being no doubt can spark a desire for its reality. Yet, Maritain sees that in some sense all that we do, whether it be work, study, or natural contemplation, can and does prepare us for supernatural contemplation without directly causing it. This natural contemplation itself makes one open to and curious about what it does not know.[21]

How is action directed to contemplation? "The contemplation of the saints is not a proper and direct end of the political life," Maritain acknowledges. The same would be true of economic or other cultural activities. To answer the question of how human activities can be preparatory to contemplation, Maritain recalls the classical notion that the end of work is not just a kind of cessation of physical labor or a preparation to go back to work. Relaxation is a good thing in itself but "human work, even on the plane of social terrestrial life, must be accomplished with a view to an

20. Josef Cardinal Ratzinger, "Christ and His Church: Unique and Necessary for Salvation," Declaration of the Congregation for the Doctrine of the Faith, 6 August 2000, in *The Pope Speaks* 46 (January/February, 2001), pp. 33-52.
21. Maritain, *Scholasticism and Politics*, p. 171.

active and self-sufficient rest, to a terminal activity of an immanent and spiritual order, already participating in some measure in contemplation's supertemporality and generosity."[22]

Maritain does not think that the leisure provided by the good civil order that enables the highest of things to be considered is supernatural contemplation. Yet, it is, at even a higher level, preparatory to it. What is at stake here is the gift status of the things of revelation in the light of which all else is illuminated. The natural leisure of which Aristotle speaks, then, is a worthy and helpful thing, indeed it is that to which everyone in society ought to attend. It is not only professional philosophers who contemplate. "If in this kind of leisure, instead of shutting up human concerns in themselves, man remains open to what is higher than himself, and is borne by the natural movement which draws the human soul to the infinite, all this would be contemplation in an inchoate state or in preparation."

V

Maritain next turns to St. Thomas concerning the intrinsic superiority of the contemplative life. Contemplation is not an instrument of the active life or a tool for the acquisition of moral virtues. Rather it is "the end to which those things have to be directed as means and dispositions."[23] Christian contemplation is not confined to the intellect alone but in faith it is the fruit of love; it can enter "the sphere of action, in virtue of the generosity and abundance of love, which consists in giving oneself. Action then springs from the superabundance of contemplation." The Lord thus can use any instrument for His purposes. Maritain thinks that it is this superabundance in contemplation that makes it tend to practical, and not merely to theoretical, considerations. That is, the objects of contemplation through love's tendency are seen also in their own needs and purposes. Hence, the direction of the supernatural contemplative life is not transient or selfish, but in fact rooted in something seen, something capable of moving and worthy of being moved even within contemplation. Time also is redeemed, to cite St. Paul.[24]

22. Ibid., p.173.
23. Ibid.
24. Ibid., p.174.

The "gift" nature of Christianity has been a constant theme of the present pope.[25] Maritain's reflections on the difference between transitive action and Christian contemplation are related to the notion of gift and that theology that relates to the Holy Spirit and the inner life of the Trinity itself. Action is redeemed because it can, through contemplation, also be seen and carried out as a gift. Christian philosophy is not merely a philosophy of being but of "the superabundance of being." Maritain notes that in the Hindu philosophy of being, reality tends to be absorbed into contemplation, the very opposite of the Christian idea of secondary causality, of the goodness and permanence of *what is*. This is how Maritain states the difference:

> Immanent activity is 'generous,' because, striving to be achieved in love, it strives to achieve the good of other men, disinterestedly, gratuitously, as a *gift*. Christian theology is a theology of divine generosity, of that superabundance of divine being which is manifested in God Himself, as only revelation can tell us, in the plurality of Persons, and which is also manifested, as we could have discovered by reason alone, by the fact that God is Love, and that He is the creator.

The Redemption is itself an expression of what God did not have to do. God, Maritain teaches us, is a God of risk. He has given us "His Truth."[26] Amusingly, Maritain cites Nietzsche's admonition that we should "live dangerously." To which Maritain responds that this is merely a "pleonism." "One is out of danger only when one is dead," replies Maritain. But this leads him to discuss the classic question of whether we should pray for supernatural contemplative graces. Maritain thinks that there is a growing consensus among theologians that "all souls are called, if not in a proximate manner, at least in a remote one, to mystical contemplation as being the normal blossoming of grace's virtues and gifts."[27] This is what the notion of "gifts of the Holy Ghost" meant. St. Thomas even says that such gifts are necessary for salvation because by ourselves we could not avoid all sins.

Maritain remarks, furthermore, that three of the gifts, Counsel, Force, and Fear concern action while Intelligence and Wisdom refer to contemplation. The body of the faithful will display these gifts in different degrees in different lives. As the variety of such gifts will correspond to the human

25. See John Paul II, *Gift and Mystery* (New York: Doubleday, 1996); see Michael Waldstein, "Pope John Paul II's Personalist Teaching and St. Thomas Aquinas: Disagreement or Development of Doctrine?" (The Thomas Aquinas College Lecture Series; Santa Paula, California: Thomas Aquinas College, 2001).

26. Maritain, *Scholasticism and Politics*, p. 176.

27. Ibid.

condition of man in which, as Aristotle said, the contemplative life is divine while the active life is human, we can expect this variety of gifts of action or contemplation to be distributed proportionately.[28] Maritain acknowledges that the language in which we speak of gifts and contemplation is oftentimes difficult and confusing so that Aquinas, John of the Cross, or St. Theresa may describe the same thing in different ways.[29]

VI

Maritain finally comes back to the question of civilization in the East and West. At the time, he was particularly concerned about the effort to create in the West a purely activist culture, one fraught with great dangers because the very civil community "became the soul of a dynamism which is purely activistic, industrial and warlike, and mobilizes for that active end both science and thought."[30] But again, Maritain sees that this enthusiasm for an activist culture is what happens to a "truly great thing" led astray.[31] In the East, he sees the search for a liberation of the soul led by techniques and formulas of meditation that is subtle but somehow is apart from "the testimony that God expects from mankind."

Maritain sees that the resolution of this active-contemplative discussion to be found in St. Thomas when he points out that the Incarnation, in its reality and symbolism, gives the concrete basis of both the meaning of the gifts of the Holy Ghost and the meaning of a Christian contemplation that superabounds out of love for its object so that it includes others in their lives of action. This dynamism is not from the bottom up, but, as it were, from the top down. We may be seeking God, but He is certainly seeking us. In this sense, the descending movement, that is, God coming to man, is more important than the ascending movement, man searching for God in philosophic contemplation, however much this in principle remains good in itself. As members of Christ's body, the "divine plenitude superabounds within us in love and activity."[32]

Maritain saw the crisis of the West to be centered in its not seeing the importance of the descending element in contemplation, that element that made its tendency to activity one of love and not of servitude

28. Ibid., p. 178.
29. Ibid., p. 179.
30. Ibid., p. 180.
31. Ibid., p. 181.
32. Ibid.

or self interest. Of the East's tendency to contemplation, Maritain thought it was too philosophical and hence veered in the same inner direction as the Greek philosophers to the neglect worldly conditions. The sanctification of the profane depends on the "law of contemplation superabounding in action."[33]

It is at this point that we come to the passage in Maritain, cited in the beginning of this reflection, and to which the whole of these considerations has been directed. This is the question of, as it were, "paradise on earth." In one sense, following scholars like Eric Voegelin, we can legitimately interpret the whole of modernity as a gigantic effort to, as he called it, "immanentize the *eschaton*."[34] This is but another way of seeking to make the Kingdom of God to be on earth at the expense of any transcendent purpose.[35] Voegelin, as Maritain, saw a certain despair in Christian peoples, especially intellectuals, about the slowness of the coming of the Kingdom of God. Voegelin himself considers this effort towards making the Christian religion to be exclusively of this world to be caused largely by Christian men who lack the faith to believe in the reality of the supernatural destiny spelled out for them in revelation.[36]

Maritain, for his part, recognizes that the effort to place the kingdom of God on earth is itself "naive." However, following his earlier remarks about excessive activism being something of a cover for a despair that does not see the truth of the transcendent order, Maritain actually defines paradise, following St. Augustine, simply as "the joy of truth." That is a remarkable phrase; paradise is the joy of truth. That is to say, paradise is primarily a contemplative happiness, even when it overflows to inspire action as it does in the Christian notion of gift and superabundant contemplation. The good and its source are really found in existing things, particularly human persons, however much these finite things are not God. The role of the philosopher in society, in Maritain's view, is precisely a contemplative one to keep alive the sense of the priority of the transcendent order.[37]

33. Ibid., p. 182.

34. Eric Voegelin, *Science, Politics, and Gnosticism* (Chicago: Gateway, 1968), p. 89. See Ellis Sandoz, *The Voegelinian Revolution: A Biographical Introduction* (Baton Rouge: Louisiana State University Press, 1981), pp. 108-11.

35. See James V. Schall, "From Catholic Social Doctrine to the 'Kingdom of God on Earth,'" *Communio*, III (Winter, 1976), pp. 284-300: "The Altar as Throne," in *Churches on the Wrong Road*, ed. Stanley Atkins and T. McConnell (Chicago: Gateway-Regnery, 1986), pp. 193-238.

36. Voegelin, *Science, Politics, and Gnosticism*, p. 109.

37. See James V. Schall, "On the Political Importance of the Philosophic Life," *Jacques Maritain: The Philosopher in Society* (Lanham, Maryland: Rowman and Littlefield, 1998),

Rather than completely ridiculing this notion of the Kingdom of God on Earth in a political or worldly sense, however, Maritain is rather inclined to see it as just another manifestation for man's natural desire to know and imitate the good. Indeed, from any fair reading of what Scripture tells Christians to do in this world, that is precisely what they should do. In this sense, Maritain's theoretical position about the manner in which Christian contemplation, by remaining contemplative, still superabounds into action and puts back together in a surprising way action and contemplation in the descending order, as it were. That is, what is contemplated includes not only what the philosophic mind, both practical and theoretical can know, but also what the mind infused by revelation receives. The graces and gifts of revelation descend to illuminate and respond to those questions and issues that seem to be unable to be answered by natural contemplation and action alone.[38]

What Maritain's essay on "Action and Contemplation" does, in conclusion, is to defend the truth in the classical Greek (and Eastern) notions of contemplation. It also explains the erroneous consequences often drawn from this position. It shows how the Christian notion of contemplation and its superabounding gift-nature expands contemplation to include all the beings who themselves can have an inner spiritual and contemplative life even while seeing the seriousness of the projects of the world. We can, following Maritain, call this latter effort, if we see it merely as a finite effort to put the good revealed to us in our own temporal world, a "paradise on earth." But this is something that is generally not seen or even begun to be carried out without revelation's emphasis on the sanctity of each person and the transcendent destiny for which he was created and redeemed. The joy of the truth, given to each of us in precisely supernatural contemplation, that contemplation is not merely illuminated by our own inner powers but proceeds, as Maritain put is, from grace and the gifts of the Holy Ghost.

pp. 39-58; see also Josef Pieper, "The Purpose of Politics," *Joseph Pieper: An Anthology* (San Francisco: Ignatius Press, 1989), pp. 121-23.

38. This is the argument that I have tried to spell out in *At the Limits of Political Philosophy: From "Brilliant Errors" to Things of Uncommon Importance* (Washington, D.C.: The Catholic University of America Press, 1996).

Truth and Friendship: The Importance of the Conversation of Friends

John A. Cuddeback

Introduction

Most will readily grant that friendship is helpful in philosophy, the pursuit of wisdom. Indeed, as Aristotle and Aquinas understand it, true or virtuous friendship is clearly *helpful* for most any worthy goal that a person pursues. Beyond that, however, is the question: is friendship *necessary* for being a good philosopher? Or in other words, is friendship necessary for success in the pursuit of wisdom? Two views in response to this question are possible: one is that it is too obvious a point to even require a proof, and the other is that it is too difficult a point to even attempt a proof. But perhaps the truth is somewhere in between. Upon considering the common stereotype of the philosopher as someone who pursues private, intellectual projects in an ivory castle, it becomes clear that this is more than just a stereotype. For many of us, it is an accurate portrayal of how we pursue wisdom. So much for the necessity of friendship being too obvious. As for the difficulty of proving it, let us proceed to consider the matter itself.

St. Thomas Aquinas distinguishes two ways that a thing may be "necessary" for some end. In the first way, a thing is necessary if without it, the end simply cannot be attained. Thus food is necessary for the maintenance of human life. In the second way, a thing is necessary if with it, an end "is attained better and more conveniently" than without it. Thus a horse is necessary for a long journey.[1] It is in this second sense, I will argue, that

---

1. Thomas Aquinas, *Summa Theologiae*, trans. Fathers of the English Dominican Province (New York: Benziger, 1948), III, 1.2c [*ST*].

friendship is necessary for the successful pursuit of wisdom. Here is another way of stating this thesis: one can only be as good a philosopher as he or she is (and has) a good friend.

When Aquinas considers those things that are "required" for happiness, he includes friendship. In asserting that friendship is necessary for happiness in this life, he explains: "For in order that man may do well, whether in the works of the active life, or in those of the contemplative life, he needs the fellowship of friends."[2] What Aquinas asserts here remains largely unheeded, and perhaps especially by those who have devoted their lives to philosophy.[3] Why, in order to do well in the works of the contemplative life, which surely are those works leading to wisdom, does a man need the fellowship of friends? Aquinas's point can be explained and defended through the following syllogism: Good conversation is essential to the pursuit of wisdom. Friends are most capable of good conversation. Therefore, friends are most capable of the pursuit of wisdom. Let us commence with the minor premise by considering the conversation of friends, and then proceed to the major premise by considering why this conversation is so critical for the pursuit of wisdom.

The Conversation of Friends

We should start by reminding ourselves of a key insight in Aristotle's notion of friendship. Persons can be true friends, i.e., friends in the proper sense of the term, to the extent that each a) pursues and lives the virtuous life, and b) desires to pursue and live that life *together with* the friend.[4]

Now, what most characterizes the conversation of friends? It seems that the *telos* of conversation between friends is simply this: to pursue the truth together. But perhaps we should not say "simply," for this *telos* is two-fold: it is a pursuit of truth, and it is done *together*. In other words, in conversation, friends seek both the discovery or contemplation of truths, as well as the sharing of their lives. These two things should not be separated, but they can be distinguished. We enter into many conversations that aim at conveying, learning, or considering some truth, but in which we do not seek to share our lives with the interlocutor. In friendship on the other hand, there is always the added element of the common life: beyond the

---

2. *ST*, I-II 4.8c.
3. A welcome exception is a new book by David Burrell, C.S.C., *Friendship and Ways to Truth*, (Notre Dame, Indiana: University of Notre Dame Press, 2000).
4. See Aristotle *Nicomachean Ethics* 1156b6ff.

immediate object of the conversation itself, we are consciously doing something *together*.[5]

Given that seeking truth together is the *telos* of the conversation of friends, what are some of the properties of this conversation? There are at least two that deserve mention: simplicity and depth. The word "simplicity" captures the crucial fact that the conversation of friends is marked by the lack of concern for *appearances*, i.e., the appearances of the self in conversation. One of the great hindrances to fruitful conversation is the tendency to reflect more upon how we our presenting ourselves, than upon the topic of the conversation. With friends, we can simply be ourselves. We need not be concerned with impressing, or with being misunderstood, since our friends know us for who we are. And since our friends love us, we can count on being supported and on being given the benefit of the doubt. This allows for a great freedom and focus in conversation: friends can attend to the matter at hand without self-consciousness, distraction, or fear.

The property of "depth" is closely related to simplicity. Friends are most able to converse about "matters of moment." Those things that are most serious and weighty are the ones that friends tend to share with one another, and often only with one another. In describing how the apostle John was privileged above all the other apostles in his relation with the Lord, Aquinas asserts this principle: secrets are revealed to friends.[6] St. John was made privy to truths that others would not be, and perhaps could not be, by virtue of his friendship with the Lord.

Good Conversation and the Pursuit of Wisdom

In a consideration of wisdom, it is important to distinguish between the natural, intellectual virtue of wisdom, and the wisdom that is a supernatural gift of the Holy Spirit. The focus in this paper is on the natural virtue; it is more straightforward to speak of the "pursuit" of this virtue, than of the pursuit of the supernatural gift. It is also important to distinguish between speculative wisdom, the habit of considering the highest, unchanging truths,

---

5. In Book IX of the *Nicomachean Ethics*, Aristotle gives a gem of an argument as to why even the supremely happy man needs friends. He says that just as a man enjoys the perception of his own existence, so too he wants to enjoy the perception of the existence of his friend, who is his "other self." And he has this perception through conversation, "for this is what living together would seem to mean in the case of man, and not, as in the case of cattle, feeding in the same place" (Aristotle, *Nicomachean Ethics*, ed. Richard Mckeon [New York: Random House, 1941], 1170b10-13).

6. Thomas Aquinas, *Lectura super Joannem*, prologue, #11.

and practical wisdom, or prudence, which is the habit of applying reason to moral action in specific cases. The considerations here will focus on speculative wisdom, although they are applicable to practical wisdom also.

Now in order to distinguish wisdom from the other speculative, intellectual virtues, Aquinas makes the distinction between truth that is known through itself, called a principle, and truth that is known as the term of reason's inquiry. As regards the latter, he distinguishes between that which is the term, or last, in some particular genus and that which is "the ultimate term of all human knowledge." He proceeds to explain:

> And, since "things that are knowable last from our standpoint, are knowable first and chiefly in their nature," (*Physics*, I,1.) hence that which is last with respect to all human knowledge is that which is knowable first and chiefly in its nature. And about these is there "wisdom, which considers the highest causes," as stated in the *Metaphysics*, (I, 1,2).[7]

If one thing is clear in Aristotle and Aquinas's understanding of wisdom, it is that wisdom is a *bonum arduum*, an arduous good. To understand reality through understanding the highest causes of reality: this is the heart of wisdom ... and sadly, something that even philosophers often lose sight of. We truly succeed in the pursuit of wisdom only inasmuch as we are able to come to see the first causes, and all else through these first causes. Insight into the first causes themselves is difficult for at least two reasons: (a) as the highest realities, they are related to our intellect, as the sun is to our vision,[8] and (b) they are reached as the term of an extended line of inquiry which entails, among other things, sustained and even heroic effort. It should come as no surprise that Aristotle suggests that youth are ill suited for doing philosophy.[9]

But what is the basis for this assertion? Why are there even many "philosophers" for whom many years have yielded a paltry harvest of wisdom? Surely, there is no simple answer to this question. One answer, however, might be that what Aristotle and Aquinas call virtuous friendship is necessary to doing what must be done to succeed in the pursuit of wisdom. Since the essence of true friendship is the communal striving toward the good life—the life of virtues both intellectual and moral—there are many different approaches we could take to this matter. Several connections between the conversation of friends and the pursuit of wisdom might prove helpful.

7. *ST*, I-II, 57.2c.
8. See Aristotle *Metaphysics* 993b10, and *ST*, I, 1.5ad1.
9. See *Nicomachean Ethics* 1142a12-17. Aristotle notes that it is commonly held that neither practical wisdom nor speculative wisdom is to be found in the youth.

Conversation between friends provides the natural context for pursuing wisdom. Friends, first of all, make one another more aware of what the human good is. In "living together" or being together with a friend, each is drawn, indeed inspired, to focus on what is most important. Who has not had the experience, particularly when actually engaged in conversation with a friend, of being inspired by that friend to be better? What we might not do for ourselves, or do as well for ourselves, we will do or do better because of our friends. Now this certainly applies in the case of pursuing insight into the highest things. Thus friends inspire one another to pursue wisdom, *and* encourage one another when the road seems long. How many times would we have turned back, in this as in other pursuits, if it were not for their encouragement?

But what about the speculative project itself? It goes without saying that in formulating correct principles and reasoning well from them, the human intellect needs the assistance of other intellects, both in its formative stages and in its mature exercise. Yet here one can reasonably ask: need it be assistance from a *friend*? It is obvious that many of those who help along the speculative journey need not be and are not friends. For instance, in the early stages of the intellectual life, such as in schooling, teachers are not friends in the full sense to students, due to their inequality. And in the case of the mature intellectual, it might seem that there is no pressing need for friends, as long as the person has another to help work through problems.

A response can be made first as regards the young. Does not experience reveal that the best teachers are those who bear themselves toward their students, as though they were friends? While not actually being a friend in the full sense to a student, the good teacher is always first concerned with the true good of the student—just as a friend would be. In other words, the teacher plays the role now that later, in the student's maturity, will be played by a friend.

The case of the mature intellectual bears a little more investigation. Here the point about the "simplicity" of the conversation of friends is crucial. Friends are able to look at reality together with the power of *two intellects*. Since friends are truly "other selves,"[10] their intellectual powers can function as though one, with no intervention of selfish or vain concerns. Two intellects focus together on discerning the truth.

Beyond the superiority of two intellects rather than one alone, there is the inestimable benefit of the corrective influence of the friend concerning

10. See *Nicomachean Ethics* 1170b7.

the acquisition of insight and the pursuit of demonstrative arguments. Anyone who has earnestly trodden the path of the intellectual life realizes how many times he or she has been preserved from error or fallacy through the watchful eye of another. Now certainly non-friends can correct a thinker when he or she errs; but it is the correction of friends that is usually most thoughtfully given, *and* most fruitfully received.

At the beginning of the fifth book of the *Republic*, Socrates gives expression to the spirit of the pursuit of wisdom among friends. Glaucon, trying to encourage Socrates to explain his position on the difficult problem of holding children in common, says: "Then don't hesitate, for your audience isn't inconsiderate, incredulous, or hostile." Socrates responds with the question: "Are you trying to encourage me by saying that?" He continues:

> Well, you're doing the opposite. Your encouragement would be fine, if I could be sure I was speaking with knowledge, for one can feel both secure and confident when one knows the truth about the dearest and most important things and speaks about them among those who are themselves wise and dear friends. But to speak, as I'm doing, at a time when one is unsure of oneself and searching for the truth, is a frightening and insecure thing to do. I'm not afraid of being laughed at—that would be childish indeed. But I am afraid that, if I slip from the truth, just where it's most important not to, I'll not only fall myself but drag my friends down as well.[11]

Of course, Socrates is convinced by his friends to proceed and give his argument. His attitude here illustrates the inspiration, the confidence, and the cautious attentiveness that animate the conversation of friends. This particular example also indicates how certain questions are so vexing or sensitive that one only feels comfortable discussing them among friends.

Now a *Christian* philosopher has a unique insight into the importance of friendship in the pursuit of wisdom. Consider that Aquinas speaks of wisdom as a virtue that exercises *judgment*. After he explains in the text quoted earlier that wisdom considers the highest causes, he proceeds to note: "Wherefore it [speculative wisdom] rightly judges all things and sets them in order, because there can be no perfect and universal judgment that is not based on the first causes."[12] Aquinas distinguishes between two ways that one can be of good judgment: through the proper use of reason, or through *connaturality* or sympathy with the subject being

---

11. Plato, *Republic*, trans. G. M. A. Grube and C. D. C. Reeve (Indianapolis, Indiana: Hackett, 1992), 450d-451b.
12. *ST*, I-II, 57.2c.

judged.[13] He uses this distinction to explain that the supernatural gift of wisdom bestows the ability to judge well of divine things by a connaturality with them through supernatural charity,[14] which is a supernatural friend-ship with God. Thus it turns out that in the supernatural order, as well as the natural, friendship is the key to wisdom.

It is particularly noteworthy that the Christian also understands that the ultimate object of contemplation is itself a person (or a Trinity of Persons). For Aristotle, friendship belongs to the ultimate end itself only inasmuch as friends, having grown together in virtue, contemplate the highest objects together; united in love, they look outward together at the first causes. Friendship takes on a whole new importance when the First Cause itself is a person, with whom one can have a friendship. Aware that in this most special way a person's end *is* friendship, the Christian philosopher can see that human friendship provides a basis for a natural ability to judge of the end by a kind of connaturality. Indeed, how can one comprehend a call to divine friendship without some lived experience of true friendship? This point, however, certainly does not exclude the possibility of grace making up for deficiencies in nature. In other words, it is not absolutely necessary that one experience human friendship in order to appreciate divine friend-ship; recall Aquinas's teaching that God's gratuitous offer of supernatural beatitude is the "*communicatio*," or shared-good, upon which is based the truly supernatural friendship of charity.[15] At the same time, we would do well to appreciate the importance of human friendship as a natural prepara-tion for divine friendship, both for comprehending it and exercising it.

Conclusion

An insight from Maritain's essay, "Truth and Human Fellowship," provides a fitting conclusion for this discussion. Maritain argues that, contrary to a popular opinion, there is not an essential connection be-tween a) claiming to know truth, and b) feeling bound to impose that truth on others. He explains:

> In reality it is through rational means, that is, through persuasion, not through coercion, that the rational animal is bound by his very nature to try to induce his fellow men to share in what he knows or claims to know as true or just. The

---

13. Maritain gives an excellent treatment of the notion of connaturality in *The Range of Reason* (New York: Charles Scribner's Sons, 1952), pp. 22-29.

14. *ST*, II-II, 45.2c.

15. See *ST*, II-II, 23.1c.

metaphysician, because he trusts human reason, and the believer, because he trusts divine grace and knows that "a forced faith is a hypocrisy hateful to God and man," as Cardinal Manning put it, do not use holy war to make their "eternal truth" accessible to other people; they appeal to the inner freedom of other people by offering them either their demonstrations or the testimony of their love.[16]

This is a helpful distinction of two ways of appealing to others to bring them to see what you see: by rational demonstrations or by the testimony of love. *It is friends who are in the position to do both of these at the same time, and in a most excellent manner.* The conversation of friends always has the character of being a testimony of love, and is, once again, the natural context for a common consideration of demonstrations.

Friendship, then, is "necessary" for the pursuit of wisdom, necessary in the same way that a horse is for a long journey. If it is possible for a person to attain some wisdom without true friendship, it is only because others have acted "as friends" along the way. We have focused on that action most characteristic of friendship: conversation. It is no accident that an age marked by paucity in virtuous friendships, is marked also by a loss of the art of conversation. If the thesis of this paper stands, it is then also no accident that there is a dearth of men and women reaching to the heights of wisdom. Maritain remarked, "The fact that philosophical discussions seem to consist of deaf men's quarrels is not reassuring for civilization."[17] Indeed it is not. Maritain rightly saw that there is no simple remedy to this problem. We should not suggest: why can't we all just be friends. Indeed, if Aristotle and Aquinas have anything to teach us about friendship, it is that the main reason we *can't* be friends is that our appetites are not ordered to the true good. If philosophers' discussions are to consist of more than deaf men's quarrels, more of us need to see moral virtue and friendship as necessary parts of the pursuit of wisdom.

---

16. Jacques Maritain, "Truth and Human Fellowship," *On the Use of Philosophy* (Princeton, New Jersey: Princeton University Press, 1961), pp. 20-21.
    17. Ibid., p. 25.

The Sine Qua Non of Love:
A Pluralism Within

Gregory J. Kerr

> I have known many happy marriages, but never a compatible one. The whole aim of marriage is to fight through and survive the instant when incompatibility becomes unquestionable. For a man and a woman, as such, are incompatible.
>
> —G. K. Chesterton, *What's Wrong with the World*

Probably never in the history of humanity has there been more emphasis on pluralism, diversity, multiculturalism, and difference. And just as assuredly, there has never been a time when we more expected generic and homogenized similarity. We are shocked at the quote above and we are shocked at the idea of other people being incompatible with us. Equally certain, on the other hand, as Allan Bloom noted so well in the *Closing of the American Mind*, people in our modern world are very wary of affecting the lives of others for fear of appearing intolerant; after all, we are all so different and unique! We fear that we will impose our personal preferences upon others and that our differences will limit them. We will inhibit their personal growth as unique human beings. Who are we, we ask, to affect their lives? Notice how Bloom puts it:

> [T]oday's students ... do not, in what were once called love affairs, say "I love you," and never, "I'll always love you." [A]s to dreams about the future with a partner, they have none. That would be to impose a rigid, authoritarian pattern on the future.... A serious person today does not want to force the feelings of others.

The same goes for possessiveness. When I hear such things, all so sensible and in harmony with a liberal society, I feel that I am in the presence of robots.[1]

What is surprising about the contemporary liberal vision of pluralism is this: since we are "tolerant," we wish to be pluralists but with one caveat: no one's view of reality can really be true. No one's view can be better than the others. This means that while you are affirmed in your right to come up with your own theory or believe your own religion, you can never claim it to be true. The result, of course, is that we never feel free to think or believe anything. It is not surprising that for Bloom, students no longer say "I love you" for they do not want to impose themselves on others. According to their view, they are all too biased and limited in their views. Only God would have the knowledge required! The popular contemporary writer on love, M. Scott Peck, author of *The Road Less Traveled*, believes that to tell others what is good for them is indeed like playing God. And, for Peck, if we are going to be genuinely loving, that is exactly what we have to do! We need to play God![2]

Even though Karol Wojtyla (Pope John Paul II) will say that no one can think for us and no one can will for us,[3] still we can show, without claiming divine inspiration, that it is meaningful to talk about loving human beings and assisting their growth in a positive way. There are truths in this area and through an analysis of the necessary elements involved in human discourse we can arrive at certain central truths about our humanity and about how to love others.

First, all human beings desire to communicate with one another. Second, as Jacques Maritain observes, this desire can only be accomplished when our words and ideas comply with the transcendental principles of the one, the true, the good, and the beautiful. He writes: "The moment one touches a transcendental, one touches being itself.... It is remarkable that men really communicate with one another only by passing through being or one of its properties."[4] This is true because people cannot communicate with one another if their ideas and words are logically incoherent (lack

1. Allan Bloom, *The Closing of the American Mind* (New York: Simon and Schuster, 1987), pp. 123.

2. M. Scott Peck, M.D.,*The Road Less Traveled: A New Psychology of Love, Traditional Values and Spiritual Growth* (New York: Touchstone, 1978). "Love compels us to play God....," pp. 154-5.

3. Karol Woltyla, *Love and Responsibility* (San Francisco: Ignatius Press, 1993), p. 24.

4. Jacques Maritain, *Art and Scholasticism and the Frontiers of Poetry*, trans. Joseph Evans (Notre Dame, Indiana: University of Notre Dame Press, 1974), p. 32.

unity), intend no relationship to reality (not true), intend no value (i.e., intend no worth to the other), or do not address the beauty of the existentially unique and concrete situation that they are in. Third, if human beings are communicators who must rely upon the transcendental principles, then these principles must be fundamental aspects of human nature itself. If to be human is to know and communicate through the transcendentals, then love will be those thoughts, feelings, and actions that contribute to the growth of our or another's abilities to do this better. To love others is to help them develop their ability to learn about the true and to have a unified vision of the whole of reality, to help them to become more free to respond to what is truly good and valuable, and to help them to be able to appropriate themselves aesthetically and existentially as unique human beings.

Paul J. Wadell, C.P. says "A human being is a creature of appetites, of powerful, perduring tendencies. A human being is one whose very nature is appetite, whose whole being is a turning toward all those goods which promise fullness of life. We are hungry for completion..."[5] To do this, however, we must love the right things in the right way. In part, this can be translated into saying that the human being has a natural appetite for truth, goodness, and beauty, and, to truly love is to nurture one's own or another's intellectual and moral virtues that regulate these appetites towards the true, the good, and the beautiful.

Contrary to much of current educational theory, the growth of these abilities is not automatic. These abilities, like muscles, do not flourish but atrophy when left alone. People—parents, friends, and lovers—don't help the beloved when they only leave them alone to decide and learn for themselves all the time. To develop virtue, according to Aristotle, we must endure some degree of pain or discomfort in attempting to repeatedly hit the mean between two extremes by aiming away from the extreme that hitherto has brought us inappropriate pleasure. People love when they, through time, effort, and guidance, help themselves or others build virtues or good habits along these transcendental lines.

But there is a catch, a problem: these lines often are in tension with each other. Each appetite, each aspiration, each type of knowing has a blind spot[6] towards the value of the others. There can even be fighting among them. As Maritain wrote in his essay "Concerning Poetic Knowledge:"

5. Paul J. Wadell, C.P., *The Primacy of Love: An Introduction to the Ethics of Thomas Aquinas* (New York: Paulist Press, 1992), pp. 81-2.
6. The "blind spot" idea was first suggested to me by Thomas Nagel in his work, *The View From Nowhere* (New York: Oxford University Press, 1986), p. 126ff.

The fact is that all these [human] energies, insofar as they pertain to the transcendental universe, aspire like poetry to surpass their nature and to infinitise themselves.... Art, poetry, metaphysics, prayer, contemplation, each one is wounded, struck traitorously in the best of itself, and that is the very condition of its living. Man unites them by force."[7]

Theories of love face the same problems. In attempting what might be called a transcendental analysis of certain theories of love and friendship, we will explore them in the light of the different transcendental aspirations of humanity. Many of the problems concerning theories about love stem from the fact that they are themselves built on, and in turn focus upon, a particular transcendental. This causes them to have blind spots towards the value of the other transcendental approaches and perspectives. Maritain noticed a similar and analogous problem concerning philosophical theories in "Truth and Human Fellowship" where he writes:

The more deeply we look into these controversies, the more we realize that they thrive on a certain number (increasing with the progress of time) of basic themes to which each newly arriving philosopher endeavors to give some kind of place— however uncomfortable, and though acquired at the price of consistency—in his own system, while at the same time, more often that not, his overemphasis on one of the themes in question causes his system to be at odds with those of his fellow-competitor—and with the truth of the matter. The greater and truer a philosophy, the more perfect the *balance* between all the ever-recurrent basic themes with whose *discordant* [emphasis mine] claims philosophical reflection has to do.[8]

Maritain's notion of themes can be related to these fundamental transcendental aspirations. The word "balance" takes ever greater meaning here when one reflects upon the internal conflicts between these aspirations within each human being. A classic example of this occurs in Maritain's *Peasant of the Garonne* where he describes the radical difference in approach and vocabulary between the theologian and the saint, the speculative and the practical thinker, concerning their knowledge based upon the "true" and their knowledge based upon the "good." He writes:

The real does not appear in the same light in both cases. The theologian declares that grace perfects nature and does not destroy it; the saint declares that grace requires us to make nature die to itself. They are both telling the truth. But it would be a shame

7. Jacques and Raissa Maritain, *The Situation of Poetry* (New York: Kraus Reprint Co; Philosophical Library, 1968), p. 56.
8. Jacques Maritain, "Truth and Human Fellowship," *On the Use of Philosophy: Three Essays* (New York: Atheneum Reprint, Princeton University Press, 1961), pp. 29-30.

to reverse their languages by making use in the speculative order of formulas which are true for the practical order, and vice versa.... Let us think of the 'contempt for creatures' professed by the saints.... For the philosopher and the theologian it would mean: creatures are worth nothing in themselves; for the saint: they are worth nothing for me.... The saint sees in practice that creatures are nothing in comparison with the One to whom he has given his heart and of the End he has chosen.[9]

As we explore theories of love, we will show how theorists tend to favor one transcendental aspiration for knowing and then become blind to the others. It will be shown that there are those like Plato, and M. Scott Peck, who focus upon the *good* and practical nature of love but are blind to the bodily *truth* about human nature and of the guidelines it provides. As will be made evident, there are those like C.S. Lewis who focus upon the truth about friendships and provide brilliant insight into genuine friendship but diminish its moral element. There are others, like Montaigne, Kierkegaard, and Marcel, who take an existential or aesthetic approach but then leave no possibilities for any natural guidelines or principles at all. All of these theorists want to preserve and value something that is truly worthwhile, but they neglect other valuable aspects of love in doing so.

The solution to this difficulty involves a kind of pluralism ... not a pluralism concerning truth, but a pluralism within. It involves affirming that while there is indeed one reality, there are different and incommensurable ways of accessing it. To love ourselves and others means to affirm these important but conflicting aspirations within all human beings. It means to affirm the unity of reality with the plurality of the ways of knowing it. To love, then, is at least this: to nurture the growth of these natural but conflicting, and yet interdependent, aspirations and appetites within us all.

Notwithstanding certain interpretations of Plato, no one can be at ease with the speed with which he guides our minds to love that which is invisible, eternal, form-like, and divine. Even in the earthy *Symposium*, where there is much talk of bodily love, Socrates' major contribution is to provide us with a ladder out of that. He goads us on to ascend to the form of beauty! Thus, the ultimate love is not that of other persons but that of a reality that is out of this world and impersonal. For Plato, the true is fused into the good and, as with Augustine, there is an impatience with the material aspects of truth in reality. The great insight of this Platonic view lies in the highlighting of the special nature and dignity of the human soul as it rises in its partial freedom from matter. The error is the identification of the

---

9. Jacques Maritain, *The Peasant of the Garonne: An Old Layman Questions Himself About the Present Time* (New York: Holt, Rinehart and Winston, 1968), p. 44.

soul with the real self and the forgetting our bodies and the spirit-incarnate whole that we really are.

Perhaps no contemporary writer has had more of an effect upon contemporary society than M. Scott Peck. Through years of providing therapy, Dr. Peck has come to define love as "the will to extend one's self for the purpose of nurturing one's own or another's spiritual growth."[10] Peck tells us that this implies choice and effort. Having given us a necessary condition of love, Peck, in subsequent pages, tells us that feeling, romantic love, and affection are not genuine forms of love. In doing so, he clearly wants to steer his patients away from unhealthy, delusional, codependent, and abusive relationships. He, like life management theorist Stephen R. Covey, wants to assert the importance of the idea that "love is a verb." Perhaps Dr. Covey illustrates the logic of this position best in his *Seven Habits of Highly Effective People* by retelling a conversation with a seminar participant:

> "Stephen, I like what you're saying. But every situation is so different. Look at my marriage. I'm really worried. My wife and I just don't have the same feelings for each other we used to have. I guess I just don't love her anymore and she doesn't love me. What can I do?"
> "The feeling isn't there anymore?" I asked.
> "That's right," he reaffirmed. "And we have three children we're really concerned about. What do you suggest?"
> "Love her," I replied.
> "I told you, the feeling just isn't there anymore."
> "Love her."
> "You don't understand. The feeling of love just isn't there."
> "Then love her. If the feeling isn't there, that's a good reason to love her."
> "But how do you love when you don't love?"
> "My friend, love is a verb. Love—the feeling—is a fruit of love, the verb. So love her. Serve her. Sacrifice. Listen to her. Empathize. Appreciate. Affirm her. Are you willing to do that?"[11]

Both Covey and Peck make excellent cases for why love should be considered a verb. This is love considered from the point of view of the good, of what ought to be the case, rather than the true, what is already the case. There are great advantages to this, of course, the primary one being that if we conceive of love in this fashion we can be responsible and proactive in loving others rather than being at the mercy of other people's agendas, circumstances, and physical and/or psychological environments.

---

10. Peck, *The Road Less Traveled*, p. 81.
11. Stephen R. Covey, *The Seven Habits of Highly Effective People: Restoring the Character Ethic* (New York: Fireside, 1989), pp. 79-80.

However, again, there are problems. We may tend to overlook real psychological and cultural forces as well as miss the value of the natural forms and structures that these loves take. Peck, for instance, thinks that feelings, romance, and affection are not forms of love at all. For him, all of these have suspicious ties to biology. He says about falling in love that it is "a genetically determined instinctual component of mating behavior," "a trick that our genes pull on our otherwise perceptive mind to hoodwink or trap us into marriage," and a "regression to infantile merging and omnipotence."[12]

Another grave problem is the neglect of the body. For Peck, love is the fuel for spiritual growth and since the aim of life is spiritual growth and since spiritual growth is, for Peck, the same as mental growth, there turns out to be absolutely no real role for the body. This results in a view that allows, for Peck, open marriages and, although rare, therapeutic sex with clients.[13] The bottom line is, if it has to do with the body, it has very little to do with love.

Some authors consider certain forms of love from the vantage point of the true. Take C.S. Lewis's classic, *The Four Loves*, for example. The reader relishes in Lewis's description of the natural gifts of affection, friendship, and romantic love, all given freely to be enjoyed for what they are. We can enjoy all of them without worrying if they are bringing us spiritual growth or making us better. Friendship, like philosophy or art, is for itself and not for some other purpose.[14]

While we might expect some place for the "good" or for ethics within the natural structure of friendship from this Christian Neo-Platonist, we find none. "Friendship," according to Lewis, "is an affair of disentangled, or stripped, minds." "*Eros*," Lewis continues, "will have naked bodies; friendship naked personalities. Hence (if you will not misunderstand me) the exquisite arbitrariness and irresponsibility of this love."[15] Lewis goes on to say that friendship has no duties. He talks about how it is neutral in the school of virtue: "Friendship (as the ancients saw) can be a school of virtue; but also (as they did not see) a school of vice. It is ambivalent. It makes good men better and bad men worse."[16]

Although Lewis does claim that friendship, like affection and romantic love, do need the "good" of charity in order to survive and not go bad on us,

12. Peck, *The Road Less Traveled*, p. 90.
13. Ibid., p. 93, 175-76.
14. C. S. Lewis, *The Four Loves* (New York: Harcourt Brace Jovanovich, 1960, 1988), p. 71.
15. Ibid., pp. 70-71.
16. Ibid., p. 80.

still, it is remarkable that he sides with Montaigne rather than Aristotle and Plato both of whom argue that morality is constitutive of genuine friendship. Finally, there are those who stress the existential/aesthetic dimension of love. This is the realm of beauty. Michel de Montaigne in his essay, "Of Friendship," begins with a reference to painting. He quotes Cicero that "Love is the attempt to form a friendship inspired by beauty." He continues, "If you press me to tell why I love him, I feel that this cannot be expressed, except by answering: Because it was he, because it was I."[17] Indeed, for Montaigne, there is no explanation of, and no moral elements in, a friendship. The "union of such friends, being truly perfect, makes them lose the sense of such duties, and hate and banish from between them these words of separation and distinction: benefit, obligation, gratitude, request, thanks, and the like."[18]

Kierkegaard, in his *Works of Love*, also stressed the existential nature of love. In particular, he highlights the existential nature of the Christian's obedience to Christ's command to "love your neighbor." According to Kierkegaard, Christ's command excludes consideration of any formal structures of the natural loves as well as any form of love being good for, or suitable to, the human "form" or nature. For Kierkegaard, we are simply to follow the command of Christ. There are no truths or conditions that must be in place. There is nothing good or fulfilling to be sought. We are simply to do it! To love otherwise is "poetic" love and that is based upon personal preferences and inclinations and, because there is no truth about humanity, no human nature, all choices based upon the self must be understood as "selfish." There is no time here to make distinctions or to define love. He writes:

> Just because Christianity is the true ethic, it knows how to shorten deliberations and cut short prolix introductions, to remove provisional waiting and preclude all waste of time.... Love to one's neighbor is therefore eternal equality in loving, but this eternal quality is the opposite of exclusive love or preference.... Equality is just this, not to make distinctions.... Exclusive love or preference, on the other hand, means to make distinctions.... Christianity is in itself too profound, in its movements too serious, for dancing and skipping in such free-wheeling frivolity of talk about the higher, highest, the supremely highest.... [And] If you think to come closer to this highest by the help of education, you make a great mistake.[19]

17. Excepts from Montaigne: *The Complete Essays of Montaigne*, trans. Donald M. Frame (Board of Trustees of the Leland Stanford Junior University, 1958) in *Other Selves: Philosophers on Friendship*, ed. Michael Pakaluk (Indianapolis, Indiana: Hackett, 1991), pp. 192ff.
18. Ibid., p. 194.
19. Søren Kierkegaard, *Works of Love*, trans. Howard and Edna Hong (New York: Harper and Row, 1962) in Pakaluk's *Other Selves*, pp. 239, 245-46.

What matters for Kierkegaard is one's relationship and obedience to God. He will not listen to the Socratic demand in the *Euthyphro* for a form. He is beyond Plato's forms. And if we don't notice it here, we can always remember his view of Abraham and of his famous teleological suspension of the ethical.[20]

Another philosophy of love that is built on existence but perhaps in a more positive manner is that of Gabriel Marcel. Marcel talks about the mystery of love, and as a mystery, it is one of those philosophical problems where the one who investigates it is a part of the problem, and so cannot be objective about it. Human love cannot be separated out for an objective analysis.[21] Love is not, as the derivation of the word "objective" suggests, "thrown in front of me." Love is a force that creates us, develops us, and is not simply a tie between already constituted human beings. It is beyond the problematical, beyond criteria, and exists among unique people and relationships and thus cannot be universalized. It is, in a sense, more than I am. It is creative. Marcel's notion of creative fidelity is unlike anything else we have discussed here. Now the emphasis is not upon activity or effort in doing something, but on one's being available, being permeable and open to others, a kind of active passivity, an attention to the other as an unique human being. Marcel writes, "Creative fidelity consists in maintaining ourselves actively in a permeable state; and there is a mysterious interchange between this free act and the gift granted in response to it."[22] Rather than considering two autonomous human beings making a connection to one another, Marcel insists on a notion of *co-esse* or a "being with." We exist with others, and this is an important part of reality.

But then, if love remains a mystery, we might ask Marcel the following questions: first, must we say that there are no rules, principles, or universals? Second, are there no already constituted human natures required for such *co-esse*? While Marcel gives us brilliant insights, he does so at a cost. Perhaps, this is a necessary cost, but it is a cost. Perhaps this is similar to the deformation, the transformation, and the indifference to the 'true" and the "good" that Maritain claims for the artist *qua* artist.

What is it then that provokes us to enlist in one of these camps— either of the true, of the good, or of the existential/aesthetic—and to take

20. See Soren Kierkegaard's "Problem 1," in his masterpiece *Fear and Trembling*.
21. Gabriel Marcel, "On the Ontological Mystery," *The Philosophy of Existentialism* (Secaucus, New Jersey: The Citadel Press, 1956, Philosophical Library), p. 19.
22. Ibid., p. 38.

sides? These views are all valuable but they are incommensurable. Are they contradictory? I would argue no, no more than the statements of the Theologian and the Saint mentioned above. They belong to different paradigms; paradigms of the good, the true, and the beautiful. As Karol Wojtyla has said, "Inner life means spiritual life. It revolves around truth and goodness."[23] For Wojtyla, these are two foci for humanity, but are those two alone sufficient? Might we add others, beauty or existence perhaps, as well?

Like Chesterton's idea that "The whole aim of marriage is to fight through and survive the instant when incompatibility becomes unquestionable," this dilemma of the incompatibility of the different kinds of knowledge cannot be resolved in thought but only in actual human existence, for each kind of knowledge will wish to reign over the others and reduce them to a kind of slavery. It is in living that we know that we must see not with one eye but two (or more). The reality of love demands all our ways of knowing. Ultimately, these ways can be shown to be interdependent, but that is only after they have been distinguished and appreciated as independent. We are told to love God with our whole heart, soul, mind, and strength, and that Jesus calls himself, "the way, the truth, and the life." St. Paul tells us how to accomplish this through faith, hope, and love. Indeed, the different loves do not see eye to eye, that's why we distinguish them! There is a pluralism of loves, really different ways to know and love the world. It is in our actual living and loving that we unite them. Perhaps we can reflect upon what Kierkegaard said,

> The true is no higher than the good and the beautiful, but the true and the good and the beautiful belong essentially to every human existence, and are unified for an existing individual not in thought but in existence.[24]

And to repeat what Maritain has said,

> Art, poetry, metaphysics, prayer, contemplation, each one is wounded, struck traitorously in the best of itself, and that is the very condition of its living. Man unites them by force."[25]

---

23. Woltyla, *Love and Responsibility*, pp. 22-23.
24. Søren Kierkegaard, *Concluding Unscientific Postscript*, trans. David Swenson, (Princeton: Princeton University Press, 1941), p. 311.
25. Jacques and Raissa Maritain, *The Situation of Poetry*, p. 56.

Maritain and the Idea of a Catholic University

Gavin T. Colvert

Jacques Maritain's essay "Truth and Human Fellowship" contemplates a simple but profoundly important conclusion: genuine intellectual cooperation among persons with differing points of view requires a shared commitment to the pursuit of truth.[1] The repudiation of truth as a goal of inquiry in the name of toleration, on the other hand, destroys the basis for mutual cooperation. This conclusion generates an apparent paradox. Truth does not admit compromise, yet it is imperative that we cooperate for the sake of the common good.[2] If truth precludes cooperation, then the search for truth and human fellowship appears hopeless. In response to this apparent paradox, Maritain offers a compelling account of how different traditions can appropriate each other's insights without discarding respect for truth.

The purpose of this essay is to examine Maritain's proposal and to show that it can provide a useful model for thinking through the current predicament in North American Catholic higher education. His account of cooperation offers a vision of shared intellectual life that many scholars at Catholic institutions can embrace. Yet, it is not so toothless as to be indiscriminately acceptable to all. Maritain's position reposes upon his

1. Jacques Maritain, "Truth and Human Fellowship," *On the Use of Philosophy: Three Essays* (Princeton, New Jersey: Princeton University Press, 1961), pp. 16-43.
2. Ibid., p. 25.

metaphysical and epistemological realism, which will be unacceptable to more radical "post-modern" intellectuals. While some may regard this feature of his approach as a weakness, we will demonstrate that the boundaries of intellectual discourse Maritain embraces offer a healthy but manageable challenge to Catholic institutions and their members to fulfill their missions more effectively.

A comprehensive study of Maritain's critical realism would be helpful for this task, but that is beyond the scope of the present analysis.[3] Our purpose is to situate Maritain's view with respect to the available approaches to the intellectual life at Christian institutions of higher education. The survey of these approaches does not pretend to be comprehensive; rather two representative positions are considered: the high theological model of Cardinal Newman, and the quasi-accommodationist view of George Marsden's *The Outrageous Idea of Christian Scholarship*. Maritain's account of cooperation falls in between these two, offering more latitude than Newman's idea of a university, but affirming a solid commitment to truth as the basis for free inquiry. George Marsden rightly calls attention to the marginalization of Christian scholars within the academy, but he appears perilously close to giving up the principles of truth and objectivity that Maritain so eloquently defends in his essay.

Maritain points out that one often encounters "people who think that not to believe in any truth, or not to adhere firmly to any assertion as unshakably true in itself, is a primary condition required of democratic citizens in order to be tolerant of one another ...."[4] He counters that this sort of attitude is self-destructive to democracy and will eventually result in the replacement of liberty by coercion. This is the position of many radicalized intellectuals in the academy today, who vigorously defend the principle of free inquiry as incompatible with the mission of Catholic higher education. The widespread endorsement of this viewpoint in the academy represents the principal stumbling block to the acceptance of Maritain's model of intellectual cooperation. Commitment to the pursuit of truth is the only firm and lasting basis for intellectual collaboration and mutual respect.

---

3. Principles necessary for the present discussion will be deployed in course. For further details, the reader is encouraged to consult *Distinguish to Unite; or, The Degrees of Knowledge* (New York: Charles Scribner's Sons, 1959).

4. Ibid., p 18.

Newman's Idea of a University

No attempt to examine the nature of Catholic higher education could be complete without a discussion of John Henry Newman's *The Idea of a University*.[5] As one critic of Newman's lectures puts it, "No work in the English language has had more influence on the public ideals of higher education."[6] Frank Turner makes this observation, despite his sense that Newman's thought is at odds with the mainstream of North American educators.[7] Newman's model of liberal education requires a cohesive vision of liberal studies unified under theology, a vision that is practically impossible on a large scale in the present intellectual climate. Some Christian academics like George Marsden, recognizing this reality, have attempted to salvage a space for the integration of faith and learning within the secular pluralistic model that predominates.[8] Their vision differs significantly from Newman's precisely because they give up the integrity of truth that is so pivotal for his argument. A viable solution to this predicament, offering a sort of middle ground, is found in Maritain's idea that human fellowship can coincide with the vigorous pursuit of truth. His vision is less cohesive than Newman's, and therefore more adaptable to the present situation, but more demanding than Marsden's. It can therefore provide a golden mean that larger, more pluralistic Catholic institutions should be seeking.

At the beginning of Discourse II in *The Idea of a University*, Newman identifies two principal questions he wishes to consider: 1) whether theology can appropriately be excluded from a university education, and 2) whether students should be guided to pursue vocational and professional studies or the liberal arts.[9] He answers that the liberal arts have value in themselves, beyond the utility value of professional studies, and should therefore be preferred.[10] Theology is a form of knowledge, equal in value to

---

5. John Henry Newman, *The Idea of a University*, ed. Frank M. Turner (New Haven: Yale University Press, 1996).

6. Frank M. Turner, "Newman's University and Ours," *The Idea of a University*, p. 28.

7. Ibid., p. 283. A thorough and scholarly presentation of the contemporary situation within American Catholic colleges and universities can be found in: James Tunstead Burtchaell, *The Dying of the Light: The Disengagement of Colleges and Universities from their Christian Churches* (Grand Rapids, Michigan: William B. Eerdmans, 1998). Observations in this chapter about the current climate in Catholic academia are drawn from the author's own experience; they are corroborated by this excellent resource.

8. See George Marsden, *The Outrageous Idea of Christian Scholarship* (New York: Oxford University Press, 1997).

9. Newman, *The Idea of a University*, p. 25.

10. This is the subject of Discourse V, ibid., pp. 76ff.

the other arts and sciences, so theology cannot be excluded from the university curriculum. As Newman puts it, "A University ... by its very name professes to teach universal knowledge: Theology is surely a branch of knowledge ...."[11] He adds that the goal of knowledge is truth, truth is of facts and their relations, and all facts and relations are tied together in a single web of reality.[12]

Newman uses this conclusion about the unity of truth to argue, in the third Discourse, for the claim that theology is not only one of the sciences, but it also provides these others with their unity and purpose.[13] The various sciences study portions of reality forming "various partial views or abstractions."[14] As such, each is sovereign within its own subsphere, but imperfect and needing completion when viewed concretely as part of the whole of reality.[15] This completion comes from theology, since theology aims at knowledge of the divine being, and God is the source of all reality. Furthermore, by providing integration to the other sciences, it also directs them to their final end. Newman concludes, "... how can any Catholic imagine that it is possible for him to cultivate Philosophy and Science with due attention to their ultimate end, which is Truth, supposing that [theology] ... be omitted from among the subjects of his teaching? In a word, Religious Truth is not only a portion, but a condition of general knowledge."[16]

Current Practice

On the surface, it would appear that many Catholic institutions of higher education follow Newman's model, since they do include theology in their curricula and most have maintained a professed commitment to liberal education, despite the growth of professional programs on their campuses.[17]

11. Ibid., p.25.
12. Ibid., p. 41.
13. Ibid., p. 41.
14. Ibid., p. 42.
15. Ibid., p. 51.
16. Ibid., p. 57.
17. Burtchaell (*The Dying of the Light*) documents the case of several Catholic institutions that had varying degrees of success in preserving their commitment to liberal arts education and the inclusion of theology in their curricula. Perhaps the worst case is that of the College of New Rochelle, whose programs of continuing education and professional studies rapidly overtook the traditional liberal arts (pp. 657-59). Like many other institutions at the time, CNR converted its theology program into "Religious Studies." Other institutions experienced a more gradual diminution of their classical curricula and commitment to the teaching of theology.

The apostolic constitution *Ex Corde Ecclesiae* seeks to enhance the Catholic character of these institutions. The document contemplates a substantive renewal of the Catholic intellectual life penetrating every constituency in the institution, thus effectively reaching towards Newman's vision of "Education ... on a theological principle."[18] Many Catholic colleges and universities, however, have tended to focus their energy on resisting the document's modest juridical norms for the theology faculty.

Thus, the appearance of a commonality between Newman and contemporary Catholic education remains a surface resemblance. Institutions have moved to drop required courses in Catholic theology or to eliminate their requirements *de facto* by creating a range of courses, some of them quite non-theological in scope, which satisfy the requirement.[19] Furthermore, "theology departments" have often been transformed into faculties of "religious studies." This name change is more than merely cosmetic. Occupants of those departments have begun to conceptualize their work in new and different ways. Religious studies can be looked upon not as a body of knowledge or important truths about God, but as an empirical, phenomenological or literary study of religious behaviour and discourse. Even if individual scholars remain committed to the possibility of studying theological truths, religious studies, as a discipline, becomes a particular research unit within the academy rather than a place for the study of truths that unify the curriculum.

Some measure of the "success" of these changes aimed at domesticating theology in the university can be discerned from the fact that many students and faculty regard the Catholicity of their university education in terms of affective experiences with campus ministry programs, not cognitive work in theology.[20] Religion has been privatized on Catholic campuses, in much the same way as it has been in broader American culture. Newman foresaw this tendency and vigorously opposed it. According to him, it was an unfortunate feature of certain strains of Protestant thinking about religious faith, that faith was thought to consist, "not in knowledge, but in feeling or sentiment."[21] Instead, he preferred the Catholic view that "faith was an intellectual act, its object

---

18. Newman, *The Idea of a University*, p. 20.

19. Burtchaell documents this trend at three major Catholic institutions: Catholic University, St. John's University and Boston College (Burtchaell, *The Dying of the Light*, p. 627).

20. See e.g. ibid., p. 625, quoting Fr. Neenan, S.J. at Boston College. Students and colleagues have frequently responded to the author with precisely the same assessment of the identifiable features of Catholic education.

21. Newman, *The Idea of a University*, p. 30.

truth, and its result knowledge."[22] For Newman, the role of theology in a university is predicated upon the unity of truth and its complementarity with religious faith.[23] Any attempt to preserve his view of the place of theology in a liberal education that undermines his understanding of the unity of truth, eviscerates the core of this position. We shall see below that George Marsden's effort to secure a space for Christian scholarship in academia tends in this direction.

Catholic colleges and universities might be thought to fare better on the whole with respect to Newman's second essential characteristic of university education, its liberal character. After all, while they may have lost their commitment to specific doctrinal claims, many institutions have tried to shore up their Catholic character and traditions by appealing to the moral value of liberal education for the formation of character. Jesuit institutions especially have found this direction attractive, espousing the Ignatian ideal of service to others and the preferential option for the poor. Liberal education then becomes a sort of seminary for peace and social justice, which is seen as more central to a person's development than professional training. In this way, the moral dimension of a liberal arts education is seen to be synonymous with an institution's Catholic identity. Indeed, the focus of many Catholic religious studies departments has been to replace theological requirements with courses concerned with social justice issues.

This approach fails doubly to meet with Newman's idea of a university education. While he was by no means insensitive to the corporal works of mercy, he had a healthy respect for the reality of human sinfulness and the real limitations of higher education. It is worth quoting his thoughts more fully here:

> Knowledge is one thing, virtue is another; good sense is not conscience, refinement is not humility, nor is largeness and justness of view faith. Philosophy ... gives no command over the passions, no influential motives, no vivifying principles. Liberal Education makes not the Christian, not the Catholic, but the gentleman ... [The qualities of a gentleman] are no guarantee for sanctity or even for conscientiousness.[24]

If he were a contemporary observer, Newman probably would say that Catholic institutions of higher education demand both too much and too little from the concept of liberal education. On the one hand, they ex-

---

22. Ibid.
23. It would appear that St. Ignatius shared the same view, although many of his latter day confreres do not (Burtchaell, *The Dying of the Light*, p. 628).
24. Newman, *The Idea of A University*, p. 89.

pect it to provide moral character formation that it cannot be expected to do. Furthermore, they have mistakenly deprived knowledge and truth of its intrinsic value by subordinating it as a mere means to the achievement of certain moral ends. On the other hand, they have despaired of the unity of truth and theology's role in the quest for it. The attempt to yoke Catholic identity solely to a program of character formation is a direct concomitant of the collapse of the conception of the unity of truth.

Assessing the Viability of the High Theological Model

Since contemporary practice in American Catholic higher education is quite distant from Newman's 'high theological' vision of a university, it is natural to ask whether his proposal is feasible or impractically utopian. Newman himself confessed in his lectures to having doubts about its practicality.[25] The present analysis takes the view that Newman's model can be successful, but only under certain controlled conditions. Careful reflection demonstrates that the success of the high theological model depends very much upon the sort of institution one intends to create. For Newman the unity of truth is what justifies the inclusion of theology in the curriculum, not ultimately a moral vision or historical tradition. Furthermore, theology provides a purpose in light of which the other elements of a liberal education can be organized and given meaning. An integral consensus about truth is therefore pivotal for Newman's vision. Without that consensus, it is not only theology that will be without justification, but the broader purpose of a university education. This leads inexorably to the conclusion that his model requires a single theological system at the core of the curriculum. It is not a plurality of faiths within the university community that is unmanageable, but the loss of an integrating rational principle. Thus, even though Newman rightly indicates that the arguments in the lectures are not based upon authority but philosophical reflection, his model presupposes that Catholic theology will unify the institution. This model has concrete implications for the type of institution one can create. It is incompatible with schools in which the Religious Studies Department views theology as merely another research enterprise alongside many others. Furthermore, where theology is the integrating final cause of a curriculum, there can hardly be a war within the theology faculty, or even among other faculty within the institution as they relate to the discipline of theology. The integrity of truth must penetrate deeply, so that it can serve as the animating spirit of a place.

25. Ibid., pp. 20-21.

Conscientious faculty must be honest with students. Otherwise, they cannot model the appropriate respect for truth that is essential to inculcating a love of learning. If faculty members are deeply ambivalent about the integrating final cause of the curriculum, they will either deceive their students or ultimately pass that ambivalent and fragmented view on to them. This will undermine the whole educational process, not merely the study of a particular subject. Moreover, it is unimaginable that faculty could carry off this enterprise in good conscience without a considerable degree of theological sophistication in addition to their own particular professional competencies. The high theological model thus requires an extraordinary unity of purpose from its faculty, and an uncommon level of training, especially considering the typical pattern of postgraduate education today.

All of these constraints upon the choice of faculty and the organizational structure of the institution point to a single conclusion. Like Aristotle's *polis*, Newman's university will be relatively small, and it will require good friendships among persons possessing the intellectual, moral and theological virtues. Furthermore, like Aristotle's conception of friendship, Newman's university will be remarkably stable but rare. Attempts to expand such a university beyond very modest boundaries will inevitably result in a collapse of its unifying principle and the remarkable model of liberal education Newman envisioned. It should be no surprise that Catholic universities (many of which were founded by closely knit religious communities) that grew rapidly in size after World War II, have fallen upon hard times and are struggling with their Catholicity. Newman's vision of a Catholic liberal arts education is by no means impossible, but it is difficult to execute successfully. It will be unavailable to most larger and mid-sized Catholic institutions today, which have very pluralistic faculties and less homogenous student populations. Whether these institutions can retain enough of an authentically Catholic character without strict adherence to the Newmanian model, we shall consider shortly.

One clear vision of how to implement Newman's original model of liberal education in a world where lay scholars are going to serve as the faculty is articulated in the founding document of Thomas Aquinas College.[26] Some features of that document are worth noting. First and foremost is the fact that it explicitly repudiates the principle of free inquiry as the basic axiom of academic life.[27] This repudiation is neither a rejection of

26. Ronald P. McArthur, et al., *A Proposal for the Fulfillment of Catholic Liberal Education: The Founding Document of Thomas Aquinas College* (Santa Paula, California: Thomas Aquinas College, 1993).

27. Ibid., pp. 17ff.

intellectual freedom nor the search for truth. Rather, the document co-
gently argues in logical fashion that the pursuit of truth can only be made
possible by the possession of certain rational first principles that are accepted as undeniable.[28] Furthermore, it takes the view that acquiring and
abiding in the truth is necessary for genuine intellectual freedom. In our
case, where human rationality is limited and imperfect, reason can only
attain its ultimate purpose with the assistance of faith. Free inquiry is an
important means of attaining wisdom where there is controversy and doubt,
but it is not the end in itself. This is perfectly understandable in light of
Newman's view that theology is not just one of the fields of human knowledge, but the unifying element in the university curriculum. This leads to an
important and potentially startling conclusion in the document. Only the
religious university, where the pursuit of truth serves under the light of
faith, can offer the fullness of a liberal education.[29] So far as it goes, this is
a coherent model for a Catholic liberal arts education.

The Search for Alternative Models

The high theological model of a Catholic college or university, with its
specific emphasis upon the unity of all the sciences and arts under theology
and the light of faith, has much to offer. Students will receive a solid grounding in the traditional liberal arts and sciences that is free from the corrosive
effects of post-modern fragmentation upon the curriculum. In order to
carry off this pedagogical plan successfully, there must be extraordinary
unanimity among the various faculty members, and a corresponding ability
to present the liberal arts as unified in this manner. While many Catholic
educators aspire towards the unity of truth, the state of their particular
fields of expertise is not at that goal. Practically speaking, it would be very
difficult to achieve the sort of consensus required by the high theological
model at most larger and mid-sized Catholic colleges and universities because the integrity of truth is so foreign to contemporary culture.

Without denigrating the extraordinary service these institutions provide to the community, it is necessary to ask whether a different model
for a Catholic institution of higher education, one more thoroughly in the
earthly city, but still authentically Catholic, can be articulated. There are
three principal advantages to pursuing this line of inquiry. First, Catholic
institutions have a duty not only to provide formation for their students,

28. Ibid., p. 24.
29. Ibid., p. 39.

but also to engage in fruitful dialogue with the contemporary world in order to contribute to the common good. This can only happen if Catholic scholars and students work together closely with other people of good will. Without sacrificing intellectual rigor or the principles of the faith, competent scholars must engage the contemporary world in dialogue, on mutually agreeable terms. Second, we must face the current situation within the Catholic community forthrightly. An entire generation of the faithful know so little about their own faith and are often alienated from it in such a way that they will be disinclined to choose what the high theological model has to offer. Third, and most relevant from the point of view of Maritain's essay on intellectual cooperation, we must face the fact that many faculty at the vast majority of Catholic institutions of higher education find themselves in an ambivalent or even hostile relationship to their institution's Catholicity. There has been well justified skepticism in recent years concerning whether many Catholic colleges and universities have traveled so far down the road to secularization that they are incapable of serving their Catholic mission. While such doubts are justified, it remains incumbent upon us to ask whether or not some institutions can retrieve their authentic Catholicity within the real boundaries of their institutional potentialities and resources.

The fact is that it is possible for some to do so, but that the predominant approach many Catholic institutions are adopting is bound to fail. They embrace radical pluralism at the heart of their curricula, while attempting to preserve "Catholic identity" as one of a series of special perspectives or interest groups. Perspectivalism rests upon the very kind of relativism that, Maritain warns, threatens to undermine their institutional integrity.[30] Furthermore, the pursuit of truth is replaced by a series of procedural arrangements. Some disconcerting aspects of the current crisis in Catholic higher education are relatively uncontroversial. Many of these institutions have begun to regret the loss of their Catholicity and the dissolution of their core curricula. Faculty, administrators and students wonder aloud about the integrity and purpose of a liberal education. Efforts to correct the course have been made by placing renewed emphasis upon mission statements that articulate institutional identity. Numerous institutions have revised or reinstituted a core curriculum.[31] Pedagogical consensus among the faculty, however, is harder to achieve in an age of professional specialization and post-modern fragmentation.

30. Maritain, "Truth and Human Fellowship," p. 23.
31. See e.g. *Conversations on Jesuit Higher Education*, Spring 1999: 15. The entire issue is devoted to the revitalization of core curricula.

The situation has become so extraordinary that many Catholic colleges and universities now contemplate the creation of centers for "Catholic Studies" alongside other specialized programs such as gender studies, peace studies, and environmental studies. Their goal is to preserve a legitimate space within the life of the institution for the Catholic character of the place, while frankly acknowledging that the institution as a whole can no longer sustain the effort. When sympathetic faculty members join together to discuss what a "Catholic Studies" program should be, however, rancorous argument may ensue. No common understanding exists about the content of such a program of study or what it must aim to produce. This should not come as a surprise when we recall that the Newmanian model of the integral curriculum has been set aside. Social scientists, literature and art history specialists, philosophers, and theologians all have very different discipline-generated conceptions of a desired curriculum. These troubles are merely symptoms of a deeper difficulty. The effort to preserve the Catholic character of such an institution has sacrificed the foundation for the sake of certain manifestations. As Maritain put it in *Education at the Crossroads*, education has lost sight of the end for the sake of certain means:

> This supremacy of means over end and the consequent collapse of all sure purpose and real efficiency seem to be the main reproach to contemporary education. The means are not bad. On the contrary, they are generally much better than those of the old pedagogy. The misfortune is precisely that they are so good that we lose sight of the end.[32]

A Catholic studies program is a prime example of a fundamental transformation in the way that education is conceptualized. Instead of an institution's Catholicity being integral to its animating spirit, it is rather viewed as one of a series of incompatible perspectives that must be represented in order to meet the demands of equity. Larger and mid-size Catholic institutions cannot go back to a simpler time when smaller faculties and student bodies could allow for the implementation of Newman's ideal. We must ask whether Catholic education must either accommodate itself to the contemporary academy or take up a kind of monastic isolation within society? Let us look briefly at the case for accommodation.

---

32. Jacques Maritain, *Education at the Crossroads* (New Haven: Yale University Press, 1943), p. 3.

George Marsden's Defense of Christian Scholarship

One must be cautious not to dismiss prematurely the idea of Catholic Studies programs. They are often the result of a genuine desire to do something constructive about an institution's Catholicity. Ivory tower speculation aimed at casting doubt upon realistic though imperfect efforts to fix a problem would not be helpful. Centers of Catholic thought at large secular institutions have been well established for some period of time. Furthermore, serious and thoughtful minds, like the Christian historian George Marsden, have endorsed these sorts of programs. Marsden has spent a great deal of time reflecting upon how faith and learning can continue to co-exist in the academy. As a Protestant Christian who has taught at Catholic, Protestant and secular universities, he has experience of the widest variety of efforts to preserve religious intellectual culture in the academy. In order to understand why such programs will ultimately prove unsuccessful in Catholic higher education, we should take a brief look at Marsden's work.

In his 1994 study *The Soul of the American University*, Marsden documented the secularization of mainstream American universities over time.[33] While this process came later for Catholic institutions, the pace of secularization has accelerated in recent years. At the end of his book, Marsden made a modest proposal for the return of religious scholarship to the academy that generated a firestorm of criticism. In response to this reaction, he wrote a second book: *The Outrageous Idea of Christian Scholarship*. The aim of this book was to defend the case for Christian scholarship as a respectable enterprise on secular academic grounds. While Marsden's book is not specifically about Catholic institutions and is more concerned with scholarship than pedagogy, the thesis it puts forward has been inspirational for many who are concerned about secularization among religious institutions of higher education. Marsden endorses the idea of centers or institutes within Catholic universities as a way of preserving their Catholic identity.[34]

At first glance the argument of Marsden's book is an ingenious one. He maintains that by its own current criteria of scholarly merit, pluralism, and equitable treatment, the secular post-modern academy no longer has any reasonable basis for excluding religious perspectives.[35] We immediately notice a significant difference between Newman's justification and Marsden's.

---

33. George Marsden, *The Soul of the American University: From Protestant Establishment to Established Non-Belief* (New York: Oxford University Press, 1994).
34. Marsden, *The Outrageous Idea of Christian Scholarship*, pp. 103-104.
35. Ibid., p. 33.

For Newman, theology belongs in the curriculum because it is a unifying form of knowledge. For Marsden, the justification is extrinsic and moral. Religious perspectives merit a place in the academy as a matter of fairness or equity to all groups.

The relevance of this argument to Catholic institutions may not seem evident until we recall that the faculties of these institutions have become as pluralistic and diverse as many of their secular counterparts. Groups within these institutions agitate against "Catholic identity" as a form of exclusion and unfairness. Marsden's point is that the pendulum has swung in the other direction and it is time for academia to grant religious perspectives their rightful place within the curriculum. Since this argument is made on the basis of equity, its rhetoric does not permit a repossession of the center of the curriculum. Rather, equity takes the form of endowing a center or institute, or even a number of chairs to promote "Catholic identity" along-side various other interdisciplinary and co-curricular initiatives.

Marsden's equity argument to the post-modern academy is made on the following grounds. The original reason for the disestablishment of religion in the academy depended upon an Enlightenment conception of rationality that has now been discarded.[36] According to that conception, only empirically verifiable statements are meaningful. Scientific and social scientific research aims at truth. Religion is discredited as a source of wisdom, because its knowledge-claims depend upon blind faith. It constitutes an emotional and aesthetic commitment that one is entitled to hold as a subjective matter of freedom of conscience, but it ought not to intrude upon the objective matter of academic scientific inquiry. Furthermore, religious doctrine is by its very nature divisive. Religious perspectives are not only unproductive of a body of knowledge; they are positively hostile to the cooperation required for the advancement of human understanding. Therefore, they are to be excluded from the academy and reserved to the home and church, synagogue, mosque or temple.

Since the Enlightenment, however, a new consensus has emerged. Here Marsden refers to the increasing awareness of the historical and so-ciological conditioning of human thought. He alludes to the example of Thomas Kuhn's *The Structure of Scientific Revolutions*.[37] No longer does the academy regard scientific knowledge as free-floating from a back-ground intellectual context. Drawing upon the work of Reformed epistemologist Nicholas Wolterstorff, Marsden points to the idea that all

36. Ibid., pp. 25-26.
37. Ibid., p. 27.

theorizing happens in the context of certain control beliefs.[38] These control beliefs do not free us from the evidential and justificatory standards of academic research. But, we are increasingly aware that research is shaped by assumptions and preconditions that can even be opaque to the researcher him or herself.

Marsden points to recent work in Marxist and feminist studies that call attention to the idea that our gender, race and ethnicity are part of our identity in such a way as to have a fundamental impact upon our scholarly commitments and research programs.[39] He concludes that "religious commitments" are no different. In fact, they shape our identity in ways even more fundamental and far-reaching than some of these other categories. This use of "identity politics" as a way to make the case for Christian perspectives has important consequences. One cannot engage in the rhetoric of perspectivalism without embracing it in other areas. Once the notion of "Catholic studies" is adopted as a vehicle to preserve Catholic identity, one must give up making more universal claims about the scope of Christianity and the curriculum.

Marsden uses the displacement of the Enlightenment conception of rationality in order to make the case for Christian scholarship. There is an important paradox in his presentation of his case that reveals the difficulty with his adoption of the accommodationist model. One of the reasons why Christian perspectives can claim to make a substantive contribution to the academy, and therefore why they should be given a place at the table, is their anti-relativist character. Marsden essentially endorses Newman's model of the integrity of truth.[40] That is, Christian perspectives can provide a welcome contribution to the academy because they offer first principles that help us reclaim the idea of wisdom. But, these first principles militate against the perspectival view. Marsden is well aware of the apparent paradox of defending Christian perspectives by appealing to contemporary relativist practice in the academy. He notes:

> Christians and other believers who reject the dominant naturalistic biases in the academy would be foolish to do so in the name of postmodern relativism. What they should be arguing is that the contemporary academy on its own terms has no consistent grounds for rejecting all religious perspectives.[41]

38. Ibid., p. 50.
39. Ibid., pp. 51-54.
40. For his discussion of Newman, see ibid., p. 76.
41. Ibid., p. 30.

This is an ingenious idea, if it can be carried through. Marsden wants Christian scholars to maintain a perspective external to the cultural relativism in the academy, while using the language internal to that domain in order to affect a political outcome. There are several serious problems with this idea, however, the first of which is a potential charge of hypocrisy. This is a special problem for the Christian who claims not to conceptualize truth in pragmatic terms. It is analogous to the problem Socrates faced in trying to defend himself at his trial. While his accusers were willing to perjure themselves in order to secure a conviction, he could not consistently espouse untruths about his case in order to defend against a series of unjust charges.

The situation of the Christian academic is similar. We cannot isolate our discourses into separate compartments. If we find the rhetoric of relativism unacceptable for internal dialogue among ourselves, it would be unreasonable to engage in these external polemics. If the reader finds this argument impossibly Utopian or naïve, consider the case of a group of academics who, for practical purposes, mount such an argument in order to fund a Catholic Studies Program. They will have to relinquish Newman's idea that theology provides a unifying final cause for the whole curriculum, and with it the integrity of truth. They can shift back and forth between language games for political purposes, but this action will speak louder than any words they may write or say in defense of truth against post-modern fragmentation.

In addition to the problem of hypocrisy, cultural relativists express the concern that Christian scholarship is intolerant.[42] Christians are certainly capable of toleration in the original sense of the term. As we will see shortly, genuine toleration constitutes the impetus towards a middle way between Newman and Marsden that is central to Jacques Maritain's philosophy of intellectual cooperation. Toleration in this original sense is a virtue having to do with respect for seeking the truth. We tolerate views that we do not agree with because we believe that pursuit of truth is a supreme goal of human activity, and we recognize as philosophical realists in the Maritainian sense that everyone is capable of error.

This does not satisfy cultural relativists, who repudiate these claims about truth. Marsden quotes a remark by Stanley Fish, who asserts that Christianity is dangerous to the liberal academy because all "'genuine religion' must subvert liberalism, rather than accommodate itself to the latter."[43] Marsden argues to the contrary that "some believers have no interest in

---

42. Ibid., pp. 31-32.
43. Ibid., p. 44.

destroying the pluralistic academy."[44] Fish's comments are revealing, however. Post-modern academicians do not see Christianity as just another perspective among many. The Christian viewpoint, by its very existence, threatens to undermine the principles that preserve the current political situation. Newman's vision of the integrity of the curriculum cannot be tolerated because it challenges the core of both Enlightenment scientism and post-modern pluralism.

Marsden and many other Christian intellectuals have failed to appreciate fully the force of this argument. When it is combined with a second important point, we can begin to see why the strategy of embracing the rhetoric of post-modern relativism in order to build Catholic institutes within Catholic universities is bound to fail. The modern academy does not have the same attitude towards truth and justice that Marsden has. His argument that religious perspectives must be accepted at the academic table does not appear compelling to his opponents. Intellectuals who repudiate a commitment to truth as the goal of inquiry in Marsden or Newman's sense will never be compelled by arguments about equity and consistency. Once a Catholic institution cedes its commitment to universal truth as a goal of inquiry, it sets in motion a struggle between adversaries in the academy that cannot reach an amicable form of co-existence. The problem is not fundamentally one of orthodoxy or specifically Catholic truth, but of the very idea of truth as the goal of scholarship and teaching. To the opponents of Catholic tradition in the university, there is a political problem with which fairness and justice are not involved. Furthermore, tacit or explicit acknowledgment of post-modern fragmentation provides one of the most potent theoretical and political tools for further fragmenting the curriculum. Catholic Studies programs may very well be, contrary to the fervent hope of their supporters, the final nail in the coffin of Catholicity at Catholic colleges and universities.

Maritain and Intellectual Cooperation

At this point, we are faced with an apparent dilemma. On the one hand, Newman's idea of a university, which requires the unity of the arts and sciences under theology, is impractical as a model for larger and mid-size Catholic colleges and universities. On the other hand, Catholic institutions that seek to preserve their Catholicity by acknowledging the fragmentary character of their curricula and creating a Catholic center within the institution seem bound to fail. Short of writing off the majority of Catholic

44. Ibid., p. 45.

institutions of higher education in the country as having grown too large and too diverse to continue serving their missions, the question arises whether a middle road can be found. Is there a model for Catholic education in the midst of the earthly city that will allow existing institutions to preserve enough of the vision of Catholic liberal education in order to serve their missions? Two of Jacques Maritain's works, "Truth and Human Fellowship," and *Education at the Crossroads* point the way toward an imperfect but worthy solution. Like Aristotle's second-best city, Maritain's vision of intellectual cooperation provides us with the very best alternative for institutions that are staffed by a pluralistic group of faculty members. It is also best for students who are not from the outset suitably disposed towards the integral vision of a Catholic education that a select few of the smaller Catholic Colleges can offer.

In a move that seems prescient, Maritain begins his essay on intellectual cooperation with a vigorous critique of pragmatism and relativism. As he points out, some intellectuals clamor for the need to get rid of "zeal for truth" in the name of liberal toleration.[45] Their idea is that true believers, who seek universal truth, are the source of fanaticism and persecution. On the contrary, Maritain asserts that pragmatism and relativism turn out to be the real source of intolerance, especially intolerance towards truth.[46] Those who seek truth are not above engaging in intellectual persecution of their peers, but Maritain thinks that "humility together with faith in truth" is the only viable alternative.[47]

Relativists must "cut themselves off from truth," otherwise they become committed to imposing their particular beliefs on everyone else. For them, authentic democracy requires that we discard truth as a goal of inquiry and replace it with acceptance by the majority of our peers. Maritain argues that this view is deadly because it removes its own support from under itself. The common commitment to belief in such truths as the value of freedom, the sacred character of justice, and the necessity of the rule of law, all can be called into question. We can see this trajectory in relativism when we recall that Marsden's argument in defense of the rights of Christian scholarship in terms of equity fails to find traction with his opponents.

Maritain concludes the first section of his essay with an argument for the view that genuine toleration can only proceed from the absolute com-

---

45. Maritain, "Truth and Human Fellowship," pp. 16-17.
46. Ibid., p. 18.
47. Ibid., p. 17.

mitment to the possibility of attaining truth.[48] This argument springs from the deep sense of awareness Maritain has, as a philosophical realist and a Christian, of the transcendence of the world. For the relativist, the universe runs out no farther than our own conceptual schemes provide. For the realist, on the other hand, the world transcends our grasp of it, and yet it is available to us. In *Education at the Crossroads*, Maritain observes: "thinking begins, not only with difficulties but with *insights*, and ends up in insights which are made true by rational proving or experimental verifying, not by pragmatic sanction."[49] As he puts the point in *The Degrees of Knowledge*, "the mind, from the very start, reveals itself as warranted in its certitude by things and measured by an *esse* independent of itself ...."[50] Confidence about the possibility of attaining truth, rather than closing the mind off to other ideas, enforces upon it a sense of humility.[51] With our awareness of the world's transcendence of our conceptual schemes, must also go the awareness that we can be mistaken about our worldview. Coupled with love of the truth and zeal to attain it, humility provides the basis for loving the truth-seeking capacity in our fellow human beings. This is the pivotal source of intellectual cooperation.

Maritain and Liberal Education

Maritain's philosophy of education takes its point of departure from the rejection of pragmatism and the importance of learning to love wisdom. In *Education at the Crossroads*, he argues that we have lost our way in education, placing educational means above ends, which leads to a loss of appreciation for the intrinsic value of truth and a focus upon increasing specialization. Our sense of what matters has been transformed into a focus upon the cultivation of particular kinds of technical expertise. In order to recover the basis of genuine liberal education, we must focus not only upon making young people proficient in certain specific disciplines and skilled in the mental gymnastics of reason and argument; rather, we must teach them to delight in the beauty of truth.[52] Not surprisingly, Maritain's vision of the end of liberal education is quite similar to Newman's. The purpose of liberal education is not to induce a special skill in the student or even the special appreciation for a particular field, but to help the student

48. Ibid., p. 24.
49. Maritain, *Education at the Crossroads*, p. 13.
50. Maritain, *The Degrees of Knowledge*, p. 74.
51. Maritain, "Truth and Human Fellowship," p. 24.
52. Maritain, *Education at the Crossroads*, p. 52.

take hold of the beauty of truth in each of the fields of human endeavor.[53] At the pinnacle of this process, liberal education must allow the student to attain knowledge of first principles, since these are the basis of wisdom. This includes training in philosophy and theology as the underpinning and goal of the educational process.[54] He quotes with approval Newman's statement that a university "is a place of teaching universal knowledge."[55]

It is clear that Maritain's idea of a university shares with Newman's a commitment to the unity of truth as the goal of inquiry, which was the crucial premise that Marsden was forced to lay aside by embracing perspectivalism in his bid to preserve religious identity and tradition. At this point, however, Maritain's narrative of liberal education takes a significant turn. As he observes, although good philosophy attains truth and contradictory philosophical positions cannot both be true, the reality of the human situation is that philosophers themselves "are bound to hold philosophical positions that differ widely."[56] Somehow, we must continue to provide a liberal education to our students despite these differences, and without descending into the fragmentation of relativism. But, how can it be done? This would seem to be a generalized version of the problem which many North American Catholic institutions of higher education face today.

Maritain's answer to this question is that we must understand how it is possible for philosophers to cooperate, not merely to tolerate or respect each other's differences. The case of philosophy is typical of the wider problem of liberal education in the sense that the search for truth "admits of no compromise."[57] The solution to the problem of philosophical cooperation is not to be found in the ubiquitous pseudo-virtue of openness, vigorously criticized by Allan Bloom in *The Closing of the American Mind*.[58] Rather, we must somehow manage genuinely to appreciate other intellectual systems with which we vigorously disagree and even regard as thoroughly incorrect. Maritain offers two key insights into how this inherently difficult task may be accomplished. These provide the rudiments of a plausible guide as to how Catholic universities may conceptualize their mission in such a way as to do justice to the integrity of truth and the plurality of their

---

53. Ibid., p. 63.
54. Ibid., pp. 71ff.
55. Ibid., p. 76.
56. Ibid., p. 72.
57. Maritain, "Truth and Human Fellowship," p. 25.
58. Allan Bloom, *The Closing of the American Mind* (New York: Simon and Schuster, 1987), pp. 25-43.

faculties. None of what Maritain proposes will be easy to achieve. It will depend upon the cultivation of certain civic virtues in the academic community and it is notoriously difficult to legislate the virtues. Still, the achievement of intellectual cooperation is not an impossible goal and Catholic institutions that shepherd carefully the process of choosing and supporting their faculties can achieve this goal.

First, Maritain argues that it is possible to love the truth-seeking capacity and desire in one's neighbor, even if one disagrees with the direction that aptitude takes in this person.[59] As a good realist, he insists that this love is possible, in part, because even in erroneous philosophical positions, there is still attainment of truth.[60] Realism begins with the capacity for the knower to access truths about reality. Even erroneous worldviews begin from a large stock of correct opinions and fundamental insights about the world, and they have a desire to solve certain real difficulties. This leads to a second insight, namely that it is possible from this loving point of view to become imaginatively engaged with another conceptual system foreign to our own.[61] We can do this in two ways. First, we take the external point of view, looking at the conceptual scheme of the other as an internally coherent network of concepts. Second, we take the internal point of view, attempting to understand the "central *intuition*" or core insight of the other system.[62] Maritain insists that the basic insight expresses a truth about reality and displays a conceptual scheme's beauty and power. Difficult as it is to imagine, Maritain contends that this insight provides us with "the *place* which each system could, according to its own frame of reference, grant the other system as the legitimate place the latter is cut out to occupy in the universe of thought."[63] Catholic intellectuals must therefore make a constant effort to deepen their appreciation of truth by engaging in serious dialogue with other intellectual traditions. Furthermore, scholars who will bring a healthy dialogue to Catholic institutions must share a commitment to truth as a goal of inquiry, and have the ability to enter imaginatively into the Catholic tradition's core insights, recognizing their beauty and power.

59. Maritain, "Truth and Human Fellowship," p. 29.
60. Ibid., pp. 27-28.
61. Ibid., p. 26.
62. Ibid., p. 28.
63. Ibid., p. 27.

Catholic Education and Intellectual Cooperation

These observations drawn from Maritain's philosophy of education and intellectual cooperation provide us with several lessons concerning the future of Catholic higher education. First, the Catholicity of an institution will not be preserved by retreating into a fortress of Catholic "identity" within the larger shell of what was once a Catholic university. The unity of truth as the goal of inquiry is an indispensable purpose for all faculty members at such institutions. Treating the core insight of Catholic education as a fragmentary matter of "identity" or tradition historicizes it in such a way as to render it useless. It will also deprive students of the proper end of liberal education, causing them to focus entirely upon the discipline specific means to knowledge. This will only engender confusion and skepticism in the minds of the students. Catholic institutions need not seek for all of their faculty members to be orthodox Catholics, or even believing Christians, in order to avoid this fragmentation. Indeed, a diverse faculty can represent a truthful picture of the struggle for understanding and a salutary reminder of the need to deepen one's grasp of the roots of his or her tradition. But, prospective faculty members must share the sense that they are engaged in a collective enterprise of truth-seeking, that such an enterprise is not futile or ill-fated, and that truth is ultimately one. They must also have the capacity to appreciate the beauty and truth of the Catholic view with which they may vigorously differ. Finally, one would expect that a Catholic institution that sees itself as engaged in the pursuit and teaching of integral truth will want to hire and nurture Catholic faculty members who can do the very best job articulating it.

While these requirements might appear toothless, they are in fact not. Minimally, intellectuals who adopt the position of post-modern academics that truth is not a goal of inquiry, or who espouse a kind of irreducible perspectivalism cannot, in good conscience, meet these conditions. Furthermore, Maritain's philosophy of intellectual cooperation demands more than just lip service to truth or respect for an historical tradition. If we say that we are genuinely engaged in the pursuit of truth, we cannot merely tolerate other conceptual systems or historical traditions. Faculty members at Catholic institutions who remain genuinely hostile to the Catholic intellectual tradition fail to find that place from which they can enter imaginatively into the Catholic vision of truth. This is not another way of saying that secular academics must provide in equity a place for Catholic scholarship at the academic table. It demands much more than that. If one is to make teaching at a Catholic institution his or her life's work, there should be an interest in and zeal for understanding the place from which the Catholic vision of reality can attain truth, even if one cannot fully assume the point of view internal to that vision. Thus, a faculty member who regards the Catholic view as merely an emotional affectation or pure folly, and who is committed to the pursuit of truth, but can see no intellectual place for the Catholic position within that search, cannot in good conscience serve the mission of a Catholic college or university.

On the other hand, none of what Maritain says about intellectual cooperation is inconsistent with a faculty member subjecting the tradition to vigorous intellectual scrutiny and even criticism. This is part and parcel of the zeal for truth and the love of truth-seeking capacities in our fellow human beings. Correction in the spirit of genuine intellectual friendship can be among our highest moral duties as scholars. Practically speaking, what is the difference between sheer hostility to the mission of a Catholic liberal arts institution and the attempt to engage imaginatively with it through respectful criticism cannot be expressed in a simple algorithm or recipe. This requires prudential judgment. In concrete cases, however, it is quite possible to judge this from experience. One should think that it would be manifested minimally in a desire to support vigorous examination of the Catholic vision of truth at all levels and in all areas of the curriculum, and in the desire to enter into discussion about these matters with one's colleagues. Faculty members who are willing to tolerate the Catholic intellectual life at a Catholic college so long as it is constrained to the chapel, to a building or program, or it is made someone else's responsibility either misunderstand their role or have failed to enter imaginatively into the tradition.

A Fellowship Founded on Truth: The History of the Saint Ignatius Institute

Michael D. Torre

At the climactic moment of the great German war film *Das Boot*, the submarine is under attack, as it tries to run the Straits of Gibraltar on the surface. Its captain gives the desperate order to dive, as the only means of saving it from being destroyed. The submarine goes into an uncontrolled descent and ends on the bottom of the Mediterranean, with its engines severely damaged. As they work against time to fix it, the submarine slowly fills with their carbon dioxide, and the captain finally despairs of being able to get off the bottom. At that very moment, the Chief Engineer comes to make his report: the engines have been fixed. The submarine is still on the bottom, and we remain uncertain as to whether it can rise again, but there is hope. The captain talks softly to himself: *"Gute leute muss man immer haben. Gute leute"* ("One must always have good people. Good people."). Indeed, this we have already seen in the film: what makes the submarine so powerful, and so successful, is not so much its state-of-the-art metal hull, but the crew within her.

On January 19th of 2001, the Saint Ignatius Institute at the University of San Francisco came under attack. It, too, lies submerged. Like that of the German U-Boat, its secret lay in its personnel. Certainly, it had a unique and distinguished program of Catholic higher education. But it was the people involved in it that made it especially great. In this essay, and in honor of its glorious 25 years, I wish to tell its story. In addition to its curriculum—an exemplary model of Catholic higher education—it was also an example of what Maritain speaks about in his essay, "Truth and Human Fellowship:" "the basis of good fellowship among men of different creeds is not of the order of the intellect and ideas, but of the heart and love. It ... is not a fellowship of beliefs, but the fellowship of men who believe."[1] I will tell the story, first of its program and personnel, and then of the mortal attack it has sustained.

I remember well my first experience of the Institute. I had just graduated with a Ph.D. in Systematic and Philosophical Theology. I was in the midst of my first teaching assignment, a one year sabbatical replacement, and in search of work. I had applied to teach part-time in the program in the following year, had sent in my Curriculum Vitae, and was now coming for an interview. As I entered the office, Raymond Dennehy was in the midst of telling a sparkling joke. As he finished, Erasmo Leiva started howling with his wonderful laugh, one which erupts from deep within and makes anyone who hears it glad. Such was my first taste of what had been advertised to me as an "up-tight" conservative program. To my delight, I found instead that I was on a Chaucerian pilgrimage.

My next surprise came soon after. I expected to have a polite interview, and be told that they would get back to me (and I'd probably never hear from them again). Instead, the Associate who was then in charge—John Galten, another layman—began talking to me as though I were obviously going to be teaching for them in the Fall. This turned out to be the case: they were already ready to hire me, sight unseen. I wondered at this for quite a while, and one day received my answer. One of the people I had put down as a referent was deeply respected by John Galten. His word was enough. The Institute was looking for people, not credentials. Who I was counted for more than what I had or, at this early stage of my career, had not accomplished. My degree and background were important, but my person and my likely effect upon undergraduates in the classroom were far more important to them than my professional academic success.

I realized with something of a shock that I was here encountering a different understanding of undergraduate education, one that used to be quite common in Catholic colleges and universities, but that had become virtually obsolete. The Institute was unpretentious. It knew it was in the business of teaching undergraduates. It was seeking to give young men and women a formation for life, not for a profession. It was thus looking for teachers who would inspire them with a love of the truth, and a conviction that finding it was not an impossible task. It knew that its education was for the student's whole person, including his or her faith; it likewise understood quite clearly that this commitment yielded a very different set of priorities than educating for a profession.

My final surprise came when I encountered the "dread director," one Fr. Joseph Fessio, S.J. What quickly endeared him to me was his humanity. Although he, too, enjoyed laughing, he also did not mind acknowledging that he had causes, books, and people that he particularly loved. He had the sobriety common to many Jesuits—a virtue I have only slowly come to admire—but it was not excessively controlled nor unduly rational, but balanced by his own temperament, personality, and courage. I also was delighted to learn that he was not overbearingly authoritarian. Every Institute teacher was free to teach as he or she saw fit. I never once was told how or what to teach. The clear principle at work was the teacher's integrity and a commitment to the program's vision.

The story of that vision—what the Saint Ignatius Institute was and how it came into being—touches in many ways on the history of Catholic education in the last quarter century. It used to be that every student of most American Catholic colleges and universities was required to minor in Thomistic Philosophy. There was a set of seven or eight required courses—on average, one a semester—and there was a comparable number of courses required in Catholic Theology. This was the formative element of the students' General Education, and the goal was frankly apologetic: it prepared them to appropriate their Catholic Tradition and to be an active participant in an Enlightenment and Protestant culture that was perceived as broadly hostile to it.

At the Jesuit University of San Francisco and elsewhere, that tradition of Catholic education began to change in the 1960s. Such a heavy dose of Philosophy and Theology was judged excessive and unduly defensive. The general requirements in these subjects were halved, to four each. Then, in 1970s, these requirements were halved again. Students were required to take only two courses in Philosophy and two in Theology. These courses thus became part of a General Education "grid" that featured a similar number of requirements in other subjects of the undergraduate curriculum. They ceased to be the *formative* element of a student's education.

As this was occurring, a group of teachers at The University of San Francisco—mostly lay men and women, but some Jesuits—decided that what was best in the older *ratio studiorum* ought to be preserved ...

specifically, the traditional requirements in Philosophy and Theology. After much talk and prayer (and a memorable pilgrimage to Our Lady of Guadaloupe), Fr. Joseph Fessio, S.J., put together a first blueprint of the idea, one which was then duly approved by the university's Curriculum Committee. Thus was the Saint Ignatius Institute conceived and brought forth.

From its inception, the program was original and innovative in at least two respects. First, it was a program that fulfilled the student's General Education requirements; it was not a Major. Thus, students—on average about 40 in each entering class—came from all majors and schools: premed Chemistry majors and nurses, those seeking a degree in business, and those in more typical liberal arts majors: English, History, Philosophy. Its students were not isolated from the rest of the University, and they partook of all its offerings and rich diversity. Second, the Institute chose to combine the Jesuit *ratio studiorum* with Great Books seminars, modeled on Great Books programs that were in place at St. Mary's College (just twenty miles away, across the San Francisco Bay), at St. John's University in Maryland, and at the University of Notre Dame. The program was organized historically: students moved through four periods, Ancient, Medieval, Modern, and Contemporary. There was a seminar in each semester, with an equal number devoted to literature, philosophy, and theology.

Another unique feature was the way these seminars were paired with lecture courses. As examples, the freshman seminar on ancient philosophy was paired with a lecture course on ethics, and a junior seminar on medieval philosophy and theology was paired with a lecture course on metaphysics. The program uniquely and consciously combined the pedagogies appropriate to each type of education. Thus, students were free to range through the great classics of the Western (and later, in the senior year, the Eastern) Tradition: the accent in the seminars was on their own interpretation, discussion, and personal appropriation of the texts. The lectures then balanced this more subjective accent with a systematic and objective development of their chosen subject matter. Thus, the Institute maintained something of the "apologetic" spirit that had shaped the earlier *ratio studiorum*, but it balanced this with the more "open and diverse" spirit proper to Great Books seminars. This balance was unique and crucial to its success.

The aim of the entire program was to place the riches of Catholic faith and culture into positive conversation with the rational and scientific spirit of the West, and with the complexities of contemporary life. It maintained the centrality of philosophy and theology in the Catholic tradition. In philosophy, it was committed to the tradition of Thomistic realism. In theology, it was expressly and staunchly supportive of the authority of the ordinary *Magisterium*, as a crucial and necessary touchstone for interpreting Scripture and the whole Tradition. Thus, one of its first public acts was to sponsor a conference in 1978 celebrating the tenth anniversary of *Humanae Vitae*: an action that, in those heady "days of dissent," was quite counter-cultural.

Besides Great Books seminars, and courses in philosophy and theology, the program included courses in history, science, and fine arts that fulfilled the university's General Education requirements. It also included electives that enriched its offerings: a course on Catholic spirituality, another on the Catholic literary revival of the 20th century, and, most recently, a course on Pope John Paul II's view of marriage and the family. Faculty frequently offered reading courses and even organized a summer tour of Europe.

Since the Institute's aim was to educate the whole person, it expressly combined its intellectual program with matters social and religious. As freshmen and sophomores, students lived on common floors in the dormitories. There was an orientation retreat for freshmen at the start of the year, and social activities planned throughout its course. There was daily Mass, First Friday nights of adoration, and Ignatian retreats each semester. Students were actively engaged in the campus newspaper, in social outreach to the city's poor, and in the pro-life movement. Yet all these activities were entirely optional. Since there were always a certain number of non-Catholic students in the program (a percentage that grew with the passing years), students participated as they judged best.

Those who put together this program recognized that the pluralism of the American scene tended to produce students who were not only tolerant, but skeptical or relativistic in their basic outlook, especially when it came to matters of faith and morals. It sought deliberately to counter this spirit with the one that Maritain advocates in his essay: "there is a real and genuine tolerance only when a man is firmly and absolutely convinced of a truth or of what he holds to be true, and when he at the same time recognizes the right of those who deny this truth to exist and to contradict him and to speak their own mind."[2]

Having taught for 17 years in the program, I can claim with certainty that it bore rich fruit in the lives of its students. The Institute did what Catholic education had commonly sought to do: it gave students an intellectual formation for life based upon the integration of faith and reason, a

2. Ibid., p. 24.

cornerstone of the proud history of Catholic education. It gave them a way of appropriating for themselves the riches of the Catholic Tradition and of bringing together the life of faith and the life of the mind. This was not to occur in any one course, but was to be the cumulative effect of many courses and professors, all co-operating in a common project, with a common, shared vision for it. It worked. Evidence of this can be found in the vocations to which it gave rise: numerous priests, numerous sisters. This was due, more than anything else, to the spirit that pervaded the program: the love of Christ and His Church, and the conviction that in it was to be found the plenitude of God's grace. Its love of learning produced as many Ph.D.s as it did priests. And it also led to a number of Catholic marriages and families. The Spirit was palpably at work in the hearts of so many of its students!

It is important to note that the Institute was the creation of faculty, not the administration. Indeed, it was conceived as an *alternative* to the General Education that the administration was sponsoring and that most of the University's faculty supported. It remained committed to a more traditional educational program and vision, in the face of a growing liberal and pluralistic culture that characterized the University of San Francisco.[3] Here, again, the Institute succeeded in finding a solution to the difficult problem of unity and diversity. While it frankly recognized that it could not maintain itself unless a crucial core of faculty "owned" its whole vision, especially in philosophy and theology, it was happy to welcome others of different views and faiths as colleagues. Thus, for example, last year it could count Protestant, Jewish, Hindu, and non-believing faculty members, as well as non-practicing Catholics. The only requirement was that faculty had a recognition of and a respect for what the Institute was centrally about; that they had a willingness not to oppose or attempt to undermine its vision. It in fact attracted some of the best non-Catholic faculty, for they could see it *stood* for something—that it was *serious* about its educational ideal and *forthright* in its defense of that ideal ... and that it attracted some of the University's finest students. Besides, it is just hard to pass up an opportunity to be part of a Chaucerian pilgrimage!

---

3. That tendency has continued at the University of San Francisco, so that its latest proposed General Education curriculum reduces Philosophy and Theology to one course each (plus Ethics), and its latest Mission Statement drops all reference to God, Christ, or the Church. The 1992 Mission Statement included declarations such as these: "As Catholic, the University affirms its close relationship and commitment to the educational mission of the Roman Catholic Church...[it]affirms the ultimate grandeur of the world as created, loved, and redeemed by God." (*University of San Francisco General Catalogue*, 1991-1993, p. 2). A decade later, all such references—to God, redemption, or the Church—were deliberately dropped.

The central core of the Institute was truly one of what Maritain calls "little teams and small flocks,"[4] and, overall, it was an incarnation of that ideal of truth and human fellowship to which he gave eloquent testament. Above all, it was characterized by friendship. When faculty members were of diverse faiths, that friendship might not be entirely "comfortable," but it was authentic and good. From its inception, the Institute was blessed with a faculty that not only enjoyed intellectual exchange and the shared life of faith, but also the pleasures of life. It had a markedly Chestertonian spirit.

Unfortunately, as Maritain reminds us, "truth always makes trouble,"[5] and the Institute was a living testament to that rule. From its inception, it was a "sign of contradiction" and met with strong opposition, since its vision of Catholic intellectual life and theology was more traditional than what suited many members of the Theology Department. The Institute had insisted that good theological method required assent to the acknowledged authorities of its field, and in particular to the authority of the ordinary *Magisterium*. Thus, it opposed public dissent to that authority. It also insisted that Catholic theologians who thought differently, and who could not support its staunch defense of that *Magisterium*, did not share the Institute's vision and thus should not teach in it. Predictably, this stand angered its opponents.

When the challenge came, it came swiftly and violently. A liberal Jesuit theologian demanded to teach a course in his field of Catholic spirituality. When the Director refused, the theologian brought suit against the University, on the ground that its programs had to employ full-time faculty over the part-time faculty that were being used. On contractual grounds, he won his suit. The Director, however, went out and hired Fr. Louis Bouyer, C.O., a renowned expert, to teach this course, and so the suit went nowhere.

This outcome, however, only served to embitter its liberal opponents, and their efforts to torpedo the program never ceased. They regarded the Institute's insistence that its theology professors share its position of support for the teaching of the *Magisterium* as narrow-spirited and an insult to the professional competence of its tenured theologians. In the words of one of its most embittered members, the Theology Faculty needed "to continually apply to teach SII courses until it had control"[6] of its theological

---

4. Jacques Maritain, *The Peasant of the Garonne* (New York: Holt, Rinehart and Winston, 1968) pp. 170-73.

5. Maritain, "Truth and Human Fellowship," p. 21.

6. Francis Buckley, S.J., then Chair of the Theology Department, as quoted in the Official Minutes of the Theology Department Meeting, November 16, 1994.

vision. For them, and for many Jesuits of the California Province, the Institute represented a fifth column. It was a thorn in their side and an embarrassment. They had the Institute subjected to outside reviews, but these tended to laud the program, rather than criticize it.[7] The pressure on the program to alter its character nevertheless remained unrelenting. The first Director was ultimately fired and his replacement (another Jesuit) finally grew weary of the tension with his brother Jesuits and resigned. Intolerant liberals in my experience are more persistent than their conservative counterparts, for they are most unwilling to recognize that they are sinning against their own self-defining virtue of tolerance.

In the Fall of 2001, the University of San Francisco acquired a new President, a Jesuit who was known to be a committed opponent of the Institute. He was swift to take action against it. He first quietly secured the Trustees' support, and then he summarily fired the directors, one of whom (John Galten) had worked for the University for twenty-five years, and both of whom were in their early sixties. They were told to clear their desks and be off campus at the end of the next working day. In their place, he put an untenured faculty member who had twice taught one course in the program. He did this without consulting either the Institute's faculty or Advisory Board. When asked why he did not consult with either of these groups, or why he did not appoint a senior faculty member with more experience of and commitment to the program, he said they would not have shared his vision of where he wished the program to go.[8] Also, there

7. The first report (to the President) was assigned to Michael Scriven—an agnostic philosopher then Director of the Evaluation Institute in the University's School of Education. Here is a rather telling excerpt from his report: "SII does not represent itself as a theology department or a department of religious studies. Those areas are already covered on campus. Is there to be no room for an Asian Culture department or center which treats of Eastern religions, even advocates them, on the USF campus? Is USF tied by charter to "liberal" Catholicism? It is obvious that the answer is negative in each case, and the position of the critics (on this point) is, as far as we could discover, far more narrow-minded than that they project onto SII. An outsider might have wondered whether USF needed an enclave of "conservative" theology until one saw the attacks on SII (over this point) which showed more clearly then catalogs that liberalism has become the new orthodoxy and hence that a stronger foundation for presenting the alternative was indeed desirable." (Michael Scriven, *The St. Ignatius Institute: A Report to the President of the University of San Francisco*, September, 1979, Section 6.7, p. 18).

8. Specifically, the President is quoted as having said that the ousted directors were "not the people who are going to take the program in the direction that I want to go.... We are trying to integrate the Institute into the life of the University. It was too isolationist." (Quoted in *Campus*, the publication of the Intercollegiate Studies Institute), vol. 13, no. 1, Fall, 2001, p. 10.

was little point to consulting them, since they only would have protested, and he intended to move in his direction, regardless of what they said. Later, he indicated to students just where that direction lay: "he would no longer allow" the Institute, he told them, to "eliminate" those (liberal) theologians who opposed its vision.[9]

At the heart of the dispute between the parties in question lies precisely the issue Maritain addresses in his essay. The liberals who oppose the program favor a tolerance that requires that one not stand for any particular, defining truth. For these men, as for the President who crafted it, a Mission Statement absent any reference to God, Christ, or the Church makes sense, since it provides a "level-playing field," where all will feel equally welcome. As Maritain might have said, they are looking for a "comfortable friendship between believers of all denominations," and, to ensure this, they favor "a kind of transcendent liberal indifference with respect to any definite creed."[10] The Institute, from its inception, was opposed to this position in its very soul: to undermine its theological stand was to damage irreparably its life-giving form.

For those faculty who had, for 25 years, offered an alternative to such an educational vision, it was clear that this firing of the director signaled an end to tolerating the Institute as a traditional Catholic educational program. The only recourse the senior faculty had in this situation was to resign in protest. At the lunch where this decision was reached, the sentiment was unanimous. This was even more surprising given that, for most, the Institute had been their only reason for being at the University and had been a source of unalloyed joy: a grace-filled program and academic experience.

Meanwhile, at present, the new director is going ahead with changes to the program itself. His first decision was (ironically) to require no seminar in non-Western literature. He is also revamping the program so that, as of the fall of 2002, it will include no courses in systematic (Thomistic) philosophy. Conserving these was possibly the main reason the Institute was originally founded. At the President's suggestion, he also hired an ex-priest and ex-Jesuit to teach philosophy in the spring of 2002: a bio-ethicist with liberal views on euthanasia, human cloning, and fetal-tissue banks. These changes, among others, signal the new direction the President and new director are imparting to the Institute.

Such, then, is the story of the original Saint Ignatius Institute, a program that, for 25 years, was a living instance of the ideal of which Maritain

9. These words of the President are taken from a taped interview of a conversation he had with some students on March 1, 2001.
10. Maritain, "Truth and Human Fellowship," p. 39.

spoke. As one who was given grace upon grace through it, I can bear witness not only to that ideal being good, but of its being possible. The basic model of its education can be adapted to the General Education requirements of any university. What is needed is a core faculty of good people deeply committed to maintaining its vision and an administration willing to support it, even against possible opposition. I also wish to bear witness to the need to fight for this ideal, even if it means suffering hard defeats, and even its death. We were privileged to live Maritain's ideal, and it is deeply good. The very best of God's work is great, and worth dying to defend.

In *Das Boot*, the Chief Engineer reported back to the captain that the ship was fixed. It should be ready to rise. Yet, even with that report, the crew remains in doubt. Will the system function as it was intended to? Will it truly rise from the bottom, to a new breath of fresh air? The atmosphere is thick with carbon dioxide, and time has just about run out. It had been a gallant fight to put it back into trim, even if it would not rise. A prayer was thus in every heart and on every lip of the submarine's crew; so it is with the former faculty of the Saint Ignatius Institute, *"gute leute"* all, who worked in a model program of Catholic education for the good of its students, and *ad majorem dei gloriam.*

Truth or Consequences?
Maritain and Dewey on the Philosophy of Education

Timothy S. Valentine, S.J.

We have all observed theories that, while they may seem compelling in principle, fail when one applies them to real life. Something like this happened during my student days at Teachers College, Columbia University, where, one might add, no one believes in God, but everyone lights votive candles to John Dewey.

A classmate in the philosophy and education program, a mother of two, was a disciple of the American pragmatist philosopher, and subscribed to his theory of "progressive" education, which rejects the idea of authority imposed, as it were, "from above," preferring instead the "cultivation of individuality."[1] In practical terms, this means allowing the interests of the students, not the teacher, to drive the activities of the classroom. Recalling the activities that grabbed my attention at age seven—more along the lines of watching "Batman" than exploring the process of photosynthesis—I raised some objection, but to no avail. My classmate had embraced the progressive model and dismissed my concerns as those of one locked into the "traditional," that is, a "teacher-centered" or authoritarian approach to learning.

Despite our ideological differences, my colleague and I were good friends, and after class we walked together to the telephone booths to call

---

1. John Dewey, *Experience and Education* (New York: Macmillan, 1963 [1938]), p. 19.

our respective homes. Before long, I could not help overhearing an increasingly heated conversation, in which my friend tried to convince her nine-year-old son to stop playing Nintendo and clean his room before she got home. At one point, most of the people in the room heard the infamous retort that ends discussion between parent and child: "because I'm the *Mom*, that's why!" So much for the child's interests dictating the course of action! I recalled the wag who once remarked: "The only problem with pragmatism is that *it doesn't work.*"

Jacques Maritain was the kind of thinker who could recognize the strengths of contemporary educational methods, while at the same time anticipating their problems. I could find no evidence that he ever met John Dewey when he was a visiting professor at Columbia University in the early 1940s, after the still productive Dewey had retired.[2] Yet it would be remarkable had they not met, for not only does Maritain call the American philosopher a "great thinker,"[3] but he understood the implications of secular and progressive theories like those Dewey advocated.

This paper will explore the way in which the epistemological starting points of these philosophers influence their educational priorities. For all man's power to think and act deliberately, he remains, according to Dewey, a natural being whose concerns go no further than adapting to, and surviving in, a "purely mechanical physical world."[4] It follows, then, that human existence is for Dewey a "problem" that calls out for a solution; education is simply the means of furnishing human beings with what they need in order to eradicate the ills afflicting society.

Although Maritain acknowledges and praises the advantages of pragmatic theories of education, he insists that ultimately, "thinking begins, not only with difficulties but with *insights*, [and] without trust in truth, there is no human effectiveness."[5] This conviction makes room for the entire range of human endeavor: survival of course, but also man's spiritual and axiological concerns. The question facing educators, therefore, involves what comes first: the practical use of knowledge in order to solve problems, or a speculative passion for truth, independent of its application?

2. Alexander Leitch, *A Princeton Companion* (Princeton: Princeton University Press, 1978), p. 313.

3. Jacques Maritain, *Education at the Crossroads* (New Haven: Yale University Press, 1943), p.115.

4. John Dewey, *Democracy and Education* (New York: Free Press, 1966 [1916]), p. 285.

5. Maritain, *Education at the Crossroads*, p. 13. See also Deal W. Hudson and Matthew J. Mancini, *Understanding Maritain: Philosopher and Friend* (Macon, Georgia: Mercer University Press, 1987), p. 277.

In *Education at the Crossroads*, Maritain expresses his admiration for the American emphasis on scientific method, the instrumental value of knowledge, and the need for democracy. Nevertheless, he finds problematic those methods of inquiry that identify truth solely with the empirically verifiable, the idea that the pragmatic application of knowledge is paramount, and the notion that democracy can flourish apart from a spiritual ideal. He therefore challenges his American students "to be as courageous in the field of intellect and reason as in the battles of land and sea and air."[6] These particular concerns make for a fruitful conversation with the thought of John Dewey, whose principles had enormous influence on American education in the twentieth century. This paper will examine the respective views of Maritain and Dewey by noting their points of agreement, their differences concerning reason, faith, and morality, and some concrete implications for education.

Points of Agreement

It would be inaccurate to claim that Maritain's humanistic views constitute a wholesale rejection of Dewey's pragmatic approach. Rather, while Maritain praises the concrete innovations this method seems to have yielded, he is concerned that its underlying principles might eventually overstep their legitimate sphere of competence. This runs the risk, he implies, of the educational process becoming intellectually narrow, spiritually sterile, and morally bankrupt.

For one thing, both Dewey and Maritain agree that education must have "aims." This might seem obvious, but it is not. Conversations with new teachers often reveal that they are quite voluble when discussing curriculum design, or classroom management, or methods of assessment, and yet if asked precisely *why* they do what they do, they become not so much laconic as uncommunicative. This would be distressing to both Dewey and Maritain. The true educator, they maintain, must direct classroom activity toward a terminus. Thus Dewey distinguishes between a mere "result," for example, the aftermath of a strong wind blowing sand in every direction, and an "end," when worker bees methodically build and maintain the hive to ensure the survival of the species. The former is merely the random effect of energy expended on matter; the latter, although not the result of conscious deliberation, is yet an instance of activities performed in continuity that finally reaches "completion."[7] Maritain, for his part, notes that

6. Maritain, *Education at the Crossroads*, p. 117.
7. John Dewey, *Democracy and Education*, p. 101.

while new methods of education often surpass what he calls the "old pedagogy," they concentrate on skills, but have no organizing principle. To dramatize his point, he compares the teacher with great technique but no clear objective to the brilliant physician who contents him or herself with a brilliant diagnosis, but lets the patient die for lack of a cure. In improving the means, one must not neglect the end.[8]

One also finds consensus between Dewey and Maritain regarding scientific method, both as a source of knowledge and as a tool for social progress. Dewey stresses, indeed to the point of excess, the notion of scientific method as the arbiter of truth, that science is ultimately "the friend and ally of man," for the simple reason that it makes possible "the control of nature."[9] According to Maritain, the truths of science combine with those of other disciplines to form a "symphony" with both complicated structure and internal unity. In his view, the sciences should form an integral part of both the secondary school "quadrivium" and collegiate study.[10]

A third point of convergence between Dewey and Maritain concerns their mutual regard for action in education. Not surprisingly, Dewey the pragmatist thinks action—for instance, building a bridge or curing a disease—is the ultimate mark of "truth" in an academic subject or even in philosophy itself, a term he uses to indicate a "generalized theory of education ... to be tested in action."[11] So integral is activity to human cognition that he claims they are virtually inseparable.[12] Although Maritain adopts a less exalted view of action, he also recognizes the advantages that accrue to an education that involves activity.[13] Action, as young people today might put it, is what "keeps it [the official school curriculum] real."

Metaphysical and Epistemological Differences

A deeper examination of these philosophers, however, reveals some striking dissimilarities between them. Of course, Dewey occasionally uses the terms "truth" and "epistemology," although he thinks that they tend to

8. Maritain, *Education at the Crossroads*, p. 3.
9. John Dewey, *Individualism Old and New* (New York: Minton, Balch and Company, 1930), p. 151.
10. Maritain, *Education at the Crossroads*, pp. 5, 47, 57, 67-68.
11. Dewey, *Democracy and Education*, p. 331.
12. Ibid., pp. 137-138. "(M)ind and intelligent or purposeful engagement in a course of action into which things enter are identical."
13. Maritain, *Education at the Crossroads*, p. 43. The teacher must be ready "with the lessons of logic and reasoning that invite to action the unexercised reason of youth."

create "a gulf between the knowing mind and the world," so much so that the two become "wholly separate from one another."[14] Thus, instead of "epistemology," he prefers the more dynamic sounding "theory of inquiry," and instead of "truth," he favors the term "warranted assertibility." Dewey's criteria for making a "warrantably assertable" statement include five things: a difficult situation in which people find themselves, the articulation of the "problem," the proposal of a "solution," the activity of "reasoning"(that is, the analysis of options about what must be done), and finally, the procurement of resources for the project.[15] If limited to the sphere of science, this could be a defensible position, although it is debatable whether one can only acquire knowledge within a "problem" situation. The much more disturbing notion is the idea that natural or empirical science is the ultimate judge of truth statements. In *A Common Faith*, Dewey states: "There is but one sure road of access to truth—the road of patient, cooperative inquiry operating by means of observation, experiment, record and controlled reflection."[16] This is a truly breathtaking claim, and its context is significant. Dewey is describing what is for him a "revolution" regarding "the seat of intellectual authority." He maintains that, up to this point, human beings have looked to religion for the answers to the ultimate questions of human existence. This is no longer the case, he contends; indeed, the well being of society depends upon the elimination of such a dangerous idea.[17] Instead, Dewey suggests that inasmuch as an idea can be empirically proven, analyzed, defined, and used for some practical purpose, it is "true." It is therefore not surprising that Dewey identifies science and religion as "rival" systems that make opposing claims. To hold a different conception of truth is, according to him, to operate under the mistaken premises that thought is separable from activity, and that moral principles transcend action.[18] Bizarre ideas such as these, according to Dewey, have exercised a stranglehold over western civilization for the past two millennia.

14. Dewey, *Democracy and Education*, p. 293.
15. John Dewey, *Logic: The Theory of Inquiry* (New York: Irvington Publishers, 1982 [1938]), pp. 105-19.
16. John Dewey, *A Common Faith* (New Haven: Yale University Press, 1934), p. 32.
17. Ibid., p. 31.
18. John Dewey, *The Quest for Certainty* (New York: Minton, Balch and Company, 1929), pp. 43-44. Dewey rejects the ideas "that knowing is independent of a purpose to control the quality of experienced objects ... [and] that values are authentic and valid only on condition that they are properties of Being independent of human action; [and] that their right to regulate action is dependent upon their being independent of action."

One might therefore ask, however, whether Dewey accurately represents the "traditional" religious position or, at any rate, the position of Christian philosophy in its Thomistic form. As Maritain points out in *The Degrees of Knowledge*:

> The scholastics said that the relation between the soul that knows and the thing known is a real relation (because it puts something new in the soul) but [this] ... relation of reason ... does not in any way affect or change the thing known. The thing and the mind are not two things in the act of knowing ... [they] are not only joined, they are strictly *one*.[19]

Clearly, Thomism recognizes a dynamic relationship, indeed a unity, between the mind and an object of knowledge, yet it does so without implying that in the absence of a mind to know it, a thing ceases to be. In this sense, Dewey is guilty of the error Maritain detects in modern philosophy, namely, the failure to distinguish between the thing in itself, that exists independently of my mind possessing "extramental" existence, and the thing as object of knowledge, that is, the thing *for me*.[20] Ultimately, the danger of scientific positivism for education is that it bases its claims upon what Maritain calls a "spurious metaphysics ... deprived of ... philosophical insight ... without which education ... becomes the training of an animal for the utility of the state."[21] Perhaps it is easier to understand a purely scientific view of the world that only recognizes the empirically verifiable as "real." Perhaps it is less troublesome to avoid questions that concern the origin, nature, and end of human existence.[22] And yet, does not a position such as this drain life of its deepest meaning, its beauty, its sense of purpose? Maritain concedes that there is a struggle between a purely scientific explanation of the world, which explains "how matter behaves," but not "what matter is," and the philosophical/religious explanation that seeks the "wisdom for which the human mind thirsts."[23] Properly understood, science can perform an invaluable service to mankind, but educators must be aware of its scope and its limitations. Moreover, to be true to its own principles, science must recognize at least the possibility of phenomena that cannot be explained with the tools it currently possesses.

19. Jacques Maritain, *The Degrees of Knowledge*, trans. Gerald B. Phelan (New York: Charles Scribners Sons, 1959), p. 87.

20. Ibid., p. 91.

21. Maritain, *Education at the Crossroads*, p. 6.

22. Ibid., p. 4.

23. Jacques Maritain, *Man's Approach to God* (Latrobe, Pennsylvania: The Archabbey Press, 1960), p. 3.

Differences Regarding Faith and Its Object

Given the metaphysical and epistemological abyss separating Dewey and Maritain, their views on the subject of religious and moral education are predictable. Dewey esteems what he calls the "religious" attitude. Its roots, he maintains, are in the imagination, and it compels an individual to undertake, not surprisingly, an *activity* for the sake of an "ideal end," even in the face of opposition or intimidation.[24] As Dewey understands it, this disposition is consistent with, because it is subject to, a purely scientific view of the world. He compares the religious attitude with "religion," that is, a collection of beliefs and ideas regarding "unseen powers" that elicits myriad expressions of devotion and obedience, and that for the lack of any intellectual rigor and moral cohesion, is responsible for many of history's darkest hours.[25] "Faith," for Dewey, is the stance one adopts toward religion, by which one merely accepts various unproven beliefs as true; it is "a *substitute* for knowledge,"[26] and therein lies its danger. One assents to a number of ideas, says Dewey, not because they are intellectually plausible, but because they are imposed by an external authority that sometimes compels its adherents to do deplorable things. The responsibility of genuinely religious people today is to disengage religious or "mystic" experience from its moorings in the realm of the supernatural, which historical religions established long ago.[27]

Yet if there is an ideology that dominates contemporary human thought, Maritain suggests that it is not the religious view, but the purely scientific one.[28] He does not mean that revealed religion and science are antithetical *per se*. Indeed, for Maritain they are compatible and complementary, inasmuch as they represent different kinds of truth to which the mind gains access through different methods. If anything, Maritain implies that extreme scientism is inadequate, not because its ambitions are too great, but precisely because it settles for so little. To say that "truth" is no more or no less than what is "entirely verifiable in sense-experience"[29] is not only to deny that an ordinary encounter points beyond itself to the transcendent, but indeed it is to overlook what precedes natural knowledge. Even before acquiring information

---

24. Dewey, *A Common Faith*, pp. 23, 27.
25. Ibid., pp. 4-6.
26. Ibid., p. 20. Italics mine.
27. Ibid., pp. 2, 6, 30, 65, 73.
28. Maritain, *Man's Approach to God*, p. 2.
29. Maritain, *Education at the Crossroads*, p. 4.

about the world, one undergoes what Maritain calls a series of "intellective leaps." The first of these is the "prime intuition of Being," that is, awe at the very fact of existence, that every creature *is* "in its own way ... completely independent from *me*." This gives way to the potentially terrifying awareness that although I actually exist, I need not. In turn, contingent being itself implies "some absolute, irrefragable existence, completely free from nothingness and death."[30] Thus, without denying scientific truth or the method for attaining it, indeed without invoking the name of God, Maritain argues that there is more to reality than what we can observe.

Moreover, Maritain recognizes that faith yields an imperfect knowledge, but only because of the subject's limitations. Unlike Dewey, Maritain adds that the object of faith surpasses finite beings, whose existence and qualities can be perceived and measured.[31] Indeed, faith exceeds knowledge of the material world, which merely points to the source of all being and perfection.[32] For Maritain, genuinely religious people recognize that the realities they accept through faith are not impossible or absurd; on the contrary, they lie above and beyond the grasp of reason. Accordingly, human beings talk about the divine, not by means of language in its literal sense, but by way of analogy.[33]

Differences Regarding Moral Education

Concerning morality, once again Dewey criticizes the traditional view that conceives of truth as a fixed body of ideas to which one gives unquestioning intellectual assent. According to him, an individual finds the criteria for ethical judgment, not in generalized concepts about human nature, but only "in consequences."[34] Morality on the collective level, in turn, is largely a matter of balancing interests between parties. While Dewey at times criticizes what he calls the "practical failure of utilitarianism," his own views are not altogether unlike it.[35] Whereas utilitarians,

30. Maritain, *Man's Approach to God*, pp. 8, 9, 11.
31. Ibid., p.24.
32. Ibid., pp. 26-27. Faith "dwells in the divine fountainhead itself. In contrast, merely rational and natural knowledge of God dwells in the created world, and from there gazes—without seeing it in itself—at the inaccessible source toward which all perfections of created things converge."
33. Ibid., pp. 24, 31.
34. John Dewey, *Ethics*, rev. ed. (New York: Henry Holt and Company, 1932), p. 363.
35. John Dewey, *Characters and Events* (New York: Henry Holt and Company, 1932), p. 813.

such as Bentham and Mill, are concerned with the greatest good for the greatest number, Dewey is concerned with how a group settles its differences. Democracy, which he calls "organized intelligence," is the most effective method of articulating and balancing individual interests to serve those of "the great majority."[36]

The pertinence of all this to education lies in Dewey's conviction that the school is, for all practical purposes, not so much preparation *for* democracy as democracy in miniature.[37] At the same time, education is the institution through which "the mature, the adult, gradually raise the helpless to the point where they can look out for themselves."[38] It does so by "simplifying, purifying, and balancing" the social environment. This means transmitting society's valuable habits and mental dispositions to the young, and eliminating undesirable ones, while enabling individuals gradually to become members of a larger group.[39] Yet precisely how this happens Dewey does not explain, and it does not help when he states that groups exercise "a formative influence"—that is, they *impose themselves*—upon their younger members. Although Dewey employs a euphemism about "nurturing the capacities of the immature," the distinction between genuine moral development and manipulation of the young ultimately remains unclear.[40]

Maritain's approach to moral education, by contrast, integrates many of the positive elements of Dewey's thought, without either minimizing the importance of faith or suggesting a veiled form of social control. If Dewey accuses institutional religion of projecting natural values "into a supernatural realm for safe-keeping and sanction,"[41] Maritain offers a different explanation for the link between ethics and religion. For him, morality is one of the three "pre-philosophic approaches" to God, the others being awe at existence, and aesthetic experience. It is not that adherents of religion blindly follow a set of static, preconceived moral regulations. Rather, the personal experience of moral goodness arouses within the human being

---

36. John Dewey, *Liberalism and Social Action* (New York: Minton, Balch and Company, 1935), p. 77. Democracy settles "conflicting claims ... to the interests of all—or at least of the great majority. The method of democracy—insofar as it is that of organized intelligence—is to bring these conflicts out into the open ... where they can be discussed in the light of more inclusive interests than are represented by either of them separately."

37. Dewey, *Democracy and Education*, p. 360.

38. John Dewey, *Reconstruction in Philosophy* (New York: Henry Holt and Company, 1920), p.184.

39. Dewey, *Democracy and Education*, pp. 19-21.

40. Ibid., pp. 21, 22.

41. Dewey, *A Common Faith*, p. 73.

a yearning for Goodness Itself.[42] Like the desire for meaning and beauty, moral intuition is yet another example of the human capacity to detect the transcendent within the ordinary. Indeed, as George Steiner insists, the very attempt to convey meaning of any kind "is, in the final analysis, underwritten by the assumption of God's presence."[43]

Moreover, Maritain explicitly rejects as one of the great misconceptions of modern education, the goal of "adapting" the individual to the conditions of social life. To do so is to put the cart before the horse. Why? Because if the social environment is toxic, that is, immoral, then "adapting" the young to it is simply another term for *corrupting* them.[44] One of the great weaknesses of Dewey's system is that, for all its talk of "aims," it lacks a clear, unified goal that holds true for all human beings. According to Maritain, by contrast, education develops people's God-given intellectual and moral capacities in order that they might understand and evaluate the cultural legacy of which they are heirs.[45] He does not envision morality as a matter of group habits imposed on individuals, but rather as the exercise of a uniquely human process through which people achieve their end. Maritain's argument, unlike Dewey's, is genuinely teleological.

Implications/Conclusion

As we have seen, the aforementioned differences between the educational theories of Maritain and Dewey are significant in three areas: intellectual, religious, and moral. For Maritain, pragmatism is a poor basis for education because its "aims," however well intentioned, are set very low. Intellectually, is education simply the process of training people to solve problems, and of helping them to learn how to adapt to their environment, as Dewey claims? Is it true that education is merely "one with growing, having no end beyond itself?"[46] Or is the aim of education, instead, to

42. Maritain, *Man's Approach to God*, pp. 19-20. "[W]hen a man experiences ... the impact of the moral good, and is thus awakened to moral existence, and directs his life toward the good for the sake of the good, then he directs his life, without knowing it, toward the absolute Good."

43. George Steiner, *Real Presences* (Chicago: The University of Chicago Press, 1989), p. 3.

44. Maritain, *Education at the Crossroads*, p. 15.

45. Ibid., p. 10; See also pp. 9, 42. "The aim of education is to guide man in the evolving dynamism through which he shapes himself as a human person—armed with knowledge, strength of judgment, and moral virtues—while at the same time conveying to him the spiritual heritage of the nation and the civilization in which he is involved."

46. Dewey, *Democracy and Education*, p. 53.

"provide one with the foundations of real wisdom," and thus to liberate the human person, as Maritain claims?[47]

Concerning religion, there is growing evidence that Dewey's prediction of the eclipse of religion's role in the life of a nation, and the rise of a purely secular society, has been discredited. *The New York Times* even admits that the forecast of Dewey, a so-called "intellectual giant," may have been premature. It notes, for instance, the undeniable influence of religious principles in debates about public policy, from bioethical issues (stem cell research, abortion, and euthanasia) to matters of family life (gay marriage/adoption), and from educational controversies (prayer in public schools and school vouchers) to just war with Iraq.[48] Indeed, as Maritain points out, the lessons conveyed through participation in religious activities, which are usually extra-curricular, often "exert an action which is more important in the achievement of education than education itself."[49]

And finally, regarding moral education, Dewey's pragmatic convictions focus on consequences and the balance of interests, not on universal principles. He explicitly rejects the notion of natural law, and for that matter, any system of morality that claims "universal validity," precisely because it implies a religious or comprehensive world view.[50] His idea is echoed frequently by students who understand morality as only a "socially constructed," historically conditioned, phenomenon. When asked, for example, whether slavery is morally objectionable, they respond, "To us, here and now, yes, but not to people one hundred and fifty years ago." The unspoken presumption, of course, is that one may not condemn any practice in principle, however heinous, because to do so smacks of "intolerance," and one must not seem intolerant of anything ... except, of course, intolerance itself! Yet in this case, the idea of "tolerance" becomes itself a generalized attitude claiming universal validity.

Furthermore, understanding personal morality strictly in terms of consequences can be disastrous, not only because the absence of principle prevents one from seeing the larger context, but because it is not always possible to predict long-term consequences accurately. A perfect example of this is the "one-child-per-couple policy" that China has enforced by means of forced sterilization and abortion. The practice was originally

---

47. Maritain, *Education at the Crossroads*, pp. 48, 71, 100.
48. Felicia Lee, "The Secular Society Gets Religion," *The New York Times*, 24 August 2002, p. B 7.
49. Maritain, *Education at the Crossroads*, p. 25.
50. Dewey, *Characters and Events*, pp. 476-78.

intended to reduce the population and raise the standard of living, but the actual result is that today men outnumber women in China by about forty million. This has created what one writer calls a "demographic nightmare that threatens China's stability and endangers prospects for greater political freedom." The disparity between the number of men and women is linked to a rise in "forced marriages, girls stolen for wives, bigamy, visiting prostitutes, rape, adultery ... homosexuality ... crime," and even the specter of war.[51]

Not surprisingly, it is in the context of a discussion of collective morality that Maritain mentions Dewey by name. While Maritain declares his admiration for Dewey as a person, he faults him for justifying democracy on a merely pragmatic basis, and for not recognizing the "spiritual" power that ought to motivate it. Of course, for Maritain, democracy is preferable to other systems. Yet this is not simply because democracy serves the interests of the majority; instead, it is because democracy is born of "the will to justice and brotherly love," that it originates from the moral human urgency that yearns for Goodness Itself.[52]

Ultimately, Maritain's thought on the relationship between truth and education is distilled in his advice to young people at the end of *Education at the Crossroads*. According to him, education has many important features, but its first concern is, and must be, truth, that is, the conformity of the mind to reality. Everything else—the acquisition of knowledge, the control of the environment, or practical success—is secondary. Only when human beings are equipped with a passion for truth, can they "show the world how human action may be reconciled with and permeated by an ideal which is more real than reality, and why it is possible and right to die for liberty."[53]

---

51. Paul Wiseman, "China Thrown Off Balance as Boys Outnumber Girls," *USA Today*, 19 June 2002, p. A 1.

52. Maritain, *Education at the Crossroads*, p. 115.

53. Ibid., p. 117. "What your intellect and reason have to win is something which is not to be measured or manipulated by scientific tools but grasped by the strength of rational insight arising from what your eyes see and your hands touch; a universe of realties which make your thought true by virtue of their very being, and not merely as a result of successful action. This is the universe of intelligible being and of the sacred character of truth as such."

Becoming Oneself: Maritain on Liberal Education

Anne M. Wiles

As the values of an increasingly materialistic society are more and more reflected in institutions of higher learning, we need to remind ourselves of the nature and purpose of liberal education, a purpose that Jacques Maritain so clearly articulates, an education the value of which Maritain himself is an exemplar *par excellence*.

As teacher, philosopher, and disciple of Aristotle and Aquinas, Maritain thought and wrote extensively about education. From the early work, *Education at the Crossroads*[1] through his latest works *On the Church of Christ*[2] and *The Peasant of the Garrone*,[3] his concern for the education of the person is evident.

Even Maritain's theoretical works, for example, *Man and the State*,[4] *The Degrees of Knowledge*,[5] and *Creative Intuition in Art and Poetry*[6] have

1. Jacques Maritain, *Education at the Crossroads* (New Haven, Connecticut:Yale University Press, 1943).

2. Jacques Maritain, *On the Church of Christ* (Notre Dame, Indiana: University of Notre Dame Press,1973).

3. Jacques Maritain, *The Peasant of the Garonne* (New York: Holt, Rinehart and Winston, 1968).

4. Jacques Maritain, *Man and the State* (Chicago: The University of Chicago, 1951).

5. Jacques Maritain, *The Degrees of Knowledge*, (New York: Charles Scribner's Sons, 1959).

6. Jacques Maritain, *Creative Intuition in Art and Poetry* (New York: Pantheon Books, 1953).

at their core an interest in the perfection of the person through love and knowledge, i.e., in liberal education.

Maritain's writings on education range from the practical to the metaphysical. In *Education at the Crossroads*, he examines the practical aspects of education in the schools of America and Europe during the crises of the Second World War and its aftermath, and he makes specific recommendations for the practice of education at various levels, including the undergraduate college curriculum.[7] In the same work, as a foundation for these curricular recommendations, he articulates a philosophy of education that centers on the nature of man and the nature of education.[8] Although Maritain never abandons the fundamental principles he sets out in this early work, his later writings add depth and nuance not explicit in the earlier articulation. Concerning the aims of education, Maritain observes that, " the prime goal of education is the conquest of internal and spiritual freedom to be achieved by the individual person...."[9] This quotation gives rise to two interrelated questions that form the structural framework of this essay: What is the nature of the human person? And, in what way does education liberate the person?

What is the Nature of the Human Person?

There are no doubt multiple and complex reasons for the widespread and largely modern view that human intelligence differs only in degree and not in kind from intelligence in an orangutan. The view is so well entrenched that to raise doubt about the validity and scope of one of its main supports—Darwinian evolutionism—is to invite the criticism implicit in the labels, "reactionary," "unscientific," "fundamentalist," or "creationist," even, perhaps especially, from non-philosophical scientists.

Empiricism and materialism, sometimes quixotically coupled with epistemological relativism or, more often, with a thoroughgoing skepticism about the ability of the human mind to know any "absolute" truths, provide the epistemological and metaphysical basis for the claim that human intelligence does not differ essentially from animal intelligence. The confusion reflected in this position is partly a result of the illegitimate extension of "scientific method" to areas where the method is inappropriate and inadequate (i.e., to the rise of scientism), but the root cause of the errors

7. Maritain, *Education at the Crossroads*, pp. 64-84.
8. Ibid., pp.1-28.
9. Ibid., p. 11.

concerning human nature and the distinctiveness of human intelligence, as well as of scientism itself, is an inadequate philosophical or liberal education and the resultant self-perpetuating ignorance bolstered by Cartesian, Humean, Kantian and pragmatic theories of truth and knowledge.

The Aristotelian-Thomistic tradition provides a means to correct these errors, including conceptual tools for making the appropriate distinctions, and an epistemology adequate to accommodate truths other than the merely scientific. Moreover, those steeped in the western classical tradition, beginning with Homer, have an extraordinarily rich literature which testifies by its existence and content that humans are more than animal, and, while far less than God, are yet something divine.

The scientific view of man finds early expression in Descartes' mechanistic view; the humanistic view is expressed in the philosophical perspective of Aristotle and Aquinas. The purely scientific idea of man emphasizes measurable and observable data without considering essence or being. This view avoids such questions as: does man possess free will which allows self-direction, or is he determined by psychological and social factors over which he has no control? On the other hand, the philosophical idea of the human person is an ontological idea, "not entirely verifiable in sense-experience, though it possesses criteria and proofs of its own, and it deals with the essential and intrinsic, though not visible or tangible characters, and with the intelligible density of that being we call man."[10] The purely scientific idea of man has no reference to ultimate reality and thus cannot provide the fundamental principle necessary for human education, namely, an adequate ontological account of the nature and *telos* of the human person. Distinguishing the nature of the human being from that of other animals is not merely a theoretic or purely academic matter; it is of central and controlling importance if education is to be something other than the training of an animal for the utility of the state.

A human person does not exist merely as a physical being, but as one who has a richer and nobler existence through knowledge and love. Although dependent on the slightest accident of matter, the human person yet has a wholeness, independence and integrity that is formed by the substantial, integral union of spirit or soul with a material dimension. "It is this mystery of our nature," Maritain notes, "which religious thought designates when it says that the person is the image of God."[11] Education is

10. Ibid., p. 5.
11. Ibid., p. 8.

primarily concerned with the person, not with the material individual *per se*, which, nonetheless, cannot be ignored.

The Aristotelian-Thomistic understanding of human nature, clarified by Maritain, reveals the inadequacies of a purely materialistic, naturalistic, or animalistic conception of human nature. It also counters the tendency to treat others as disembodied intellects, or bundles of emotions. A smile is more than the expansion of the lips. Cheshire cats, present or not, don't smile and hyenas don't laugh. These activities belong to a universe of meaning, participation in which is open only to persons. Maritain makes clear that psychophysical habits, conditioned reflexes, sense memorization, etc, are related to the material individual, not to what is specifically or uniquely human. He marks this distinction in a memorable phrase, "Education is not animal training. The education of man is a human awakening."[12]

Some care must be taken here, for even activities referred to as "training," whether they be physical or mental, or the rudiments of etiquette and morals in children, are still *human* activities and as such, differ specifically from the training of a cat or monkey; such activities, "can be intrinsically improved and can outstrip their own immediate practical value through being *humanized* ... by understanding."[13] This implies, as a prelude to liberal education in the full sense, that even in early education, the dignity and promise of the child can be respected, for example, by providing an explanation that he or she can understand for any work required.[14] Preparation for liberal education begins in an appeal to reason that allows for autonomy appropriate to the age and circumstances of the child. The danger for the older student and the adult, is that the utilitarian aspect of education (i.e., job training) might, in the thinking of the prevalent culture, displace or overshadow the essential aim of a truly *liberal* education. As Maritain notes, "The overwhelming cult of specialization dehumanizes man's life."[15]

---

12. Ibid., p. 9.

13. Ibid., p.10.

14. I have a vivid recollection of my fourth grade teacher saying, "This year you will learn to take notes as someone speaks or reads. You will need this skill when you go to college." Though the readings were from American history, not of especial interest to at least one ten-year old girl, I was filled with desire to accomplish the skill. I suppose, in part, because I admired Miss Walden who represented in her person all that I imagined of adult womanhood and college—and because she said "when," not "if" you go to college. I do not know whether she had read Maritain, St. Thomas, or Aristotle, but in that one statement she recognized the dignity of her students as persons. She strengthened not only my skills, but also the expectation of my becoming what I could be.

15. Maritain, *Education at the Crossroads*, p.19.

In What Way Does Education Liberate the Person?
Techné and Wisdom

Heraclitus is reputed to have said that much learning does not make one wise. In Plato's *Apology*, Socrates distinguished between knowledge of a craft (*techné*) that the artisans he questioned did have, and wisdom, a perfection of the intellect they lacked. For his part, Aristotle identified three broad uses of the human intellect: 1) the productive use, directed towards the creation of some artifact, 2) the practical use, the purpose of which is to determine what should be done and what should be desired, and, 3) the speculative use, the *telos* or purpose of which is the discovery of truth for its own sake, and for no end beyond itself.[16]

The productive use of the intellect is necessarily directed toward and bound by the limitations of the external matter on which it works. The corresponding excellence is essentially a *techné* and is evidenced in the object produced. The excellence of the practical intellect, concerned with action and desire, remains within the person as a moral excellence or virtue. The intellect is most free in its speculative use since the sole object is truth, and it willingly follows wherever truth leads. The excellence of the speculative intellect is also a perfection of the person. Every perfection of the intellect is a good, but the Greek tradition places greater value on the practical and especially the speculative uses of the intellect with the resulting emphasis on the moral and intellectual virtues that are the perfections of these habits. Human perfection or happiness is activity in accordance with the moral and intellectual virtues. The good man is the happy man.

The essential aim of liberal education is based on the nature of the human person and his deep natural aspirations, the most fundamental of which, Maritain says, is the aspiration to freedom. By 'freedom,' Maritain does not mean "free-will;" he means "that freedom which is spontaneity, expansion or autonomy" of the person, and which we have to gain through constant effort and struggle."[17] Aristotle recognized the independence and freedom achieved by the exercise of the moral and intellectual virtues, but Maritain credits the Gospel with raising human perfection to an even higher level by showing that it consists also in the perfection of love. Setting out the main goal of education, Maritain embraces both the Greek and Christian views of the perfection of the person, "the prime goal of education is the

16. Aristotle *Nicomachean Ethics* 1138 b18-1141 b27.
17. Maritain, *Education at the Crossroads*, p.11.

conquest of internal and spiritual freedom to be achieved by the individual person, or, in other words, his liberation through knowledge and wisdom, good will and love."[18]

The freedom of which Maritain speaks is not an aimless unfolding of potentialities. Spiritual activities are intentional, by nature tending towards an object that will measure and rule them, not by bondage, but by liberty.[19] The intellect searches for, and is freed by knowing truth; and, "truth does not depend upon us, but upon what is."[20]

In addition to the moral and intellectual virtues, the role and importance of intellectual intuition should not be underestimated. It, too, plays a vital part in a truly liberal education. Unfortunately, intuition, as a direct and immediate knowledge, has generally received a bad press among philosophers outside the Aristotelian-Thomistic tradition, especially following the radical empiricism of Hume. The failure to appreciate the role of intellectual intuition, even in respect to scientific knowledge, has resulted in a narrow understanding of truth, knowledge, and the process of learning and teaching. Consequently, the prevalent understanding of what liberal education is and how it should be engendered is also adversely affected.

Many university students today are exceedingly skeptical that there is such a thing as intuition as a process of the intellect that is reliable and productive of truth. Because they either have not read (or if they have read, have not understood) the classical western literature, they tend to think of intuition as some irrational "hunch," that is not really "scientific" and hence, not really knowledge. It should come as no surprise that students have and express these views since many of their professors in the modern university have not themselves enjoyed a truly liberal education and are also equally imbued with the attitude of scientism.

As Aristotle pointed out, the first principles of demonstration, necessary for scientific knowledge are known by intuition.[21] Since they are the starting points of demonstration, they cannot themselves be proved, yet they are not "irrational" or "merely assumed;" they are supportable by reason. One who understands such a principle recognizes it as self-evident. Examples of these principles are the principle of identity, of sufficient reason, and of finality; they are the principles that are presupposed by all of the sciences.

18. Ibid.
19. Ibid.
20. Ibid., p. 12.
21. Aristotle *Nicomachean Ethics* 1140 b30-1141 a19.

That first principles can be identified and articulated is often rejected because the principles are taken too narrowly. First principles, known by intellectual intuition, are best thought of as formal principles that function as constraints on our thinking and action. The principle of non-contradiction, for example, acts as a formal constraint on what can be coherently thought and said. Unless such principles are recognized as self-evident, and, in the way described above, as directive of thinking, acting and willing, then neither truth, objective moral standards, nor a correct understanding of the nature and aims of education is possible. Misunderstanding the nature and importance of intellectual intuition, students often think an objective (absolute) moral standard is a statement on the order of "never lie," i.e., a statement with highly specified content. They also generally believe that statements verifiable by the scientific method are the best available model of "truth," and, since they accept that such "truths" may be false tomorrow, they consequently also think there are, in fact, no absolute truths, or at least none worth knowing. So what, if all men by nature desire to know? For them, knowledge is about information, not truth.

The other role of intuition that Aristotle identifies is the recognition of particulars as being instances of a certain kind or class.[22] This recognition, when articulated, may function as the minor premise of the so-called practical syllogism. For example, if one knows that "Red salmon is a healthful food one ought to eat" [major premise], to reach the conclusion, "Let me eat this salmon," one must know the minor premise, "This fish on my plate is red salmon." The minor premise is known by intuition, i.e., by recognizing that the fish is of a certain kind, namely, red salmon. Recognition of a particular as a certain kind occurs in or through sense perception, but is not itself a sense perception. It is a higher intellectual function requiring a conceptual framework, a universe of meaning.

In *Creative Intuition in Art and Poetry*, Maritain draws attention to yet another role, or perhaps another type of intuition. Creative or poetic intuition arises from the preconscious life of the intellect. This spiritual preconscious is not the Freudian unconscious of instincts, repressed desire or images, and traumatic memories.[23] Rather, Maritain sees it as a spiritual or musical preconscious that underlies not only specifically mystical or aesthetic experiences, but also the ordinary and everyday function of intelligence as it understands or discovers something new. Drawing upon

22. Ibid., 1143 a32- b17.
23. Maritain, *Education at the Crossroads*, p. 40.

the Thomistic philosophy of human nature, Maritain depicts the spiritual unconscious or preconscious as a rich intellectual, though non-conceptual, activity involving the intellect, imagination and intuitive data from external sensation,[24] springing from "a root activity in which the intellect and the imagination, as well as the powers of desire, love, and emotion are engaged in common ... stirred and activated by the light of the Illuminating Intellect."[25] Poetic knowledge (as Maritain uses the expression) grasps the nature of things and their interconnections through creative intuition or connatural knowledge. Since every person is capable of intellectual intuition, it is in this very apprehension that one has the potential to become aware of one's own self. Poetic intuition may issue in and perfect an external work, though it need not. The spiritual activities of the will and the intellect, on the other hand, stay within and may perfect the person. Such activities are purposive and seek an object which will measure and rule them, spiritually, not by force, and thus the object loved or known may become a part of the loving and knowing person.[26]

Maritain characterizes human thinking as a vital energy of knowledge or spiritual intuition *into* and not *about* its objects. Such intuition is not confined to poetic knowledge, since all human thinking begins with insights and ends in insights "made true by rational proving or experimental verifying...."[27] As a result of this spiritual intuition, "... human thought is able to illumine experience, to realize desires which are human because they are rooted in the prime desire for unlimited good, and to dominate, control, and refashion the world. At the beginning of human action, insofar as it is human, there is truth, grasped or believed to be grasped for the sake of truth. Without trust in truth, there is no human effectiveness." [28]

Liberal teaching and learning, tending as they do toward the perfection of the person require both love and knowledge, respect for the uniqueness of the person and for the universality of the truth. Truth is concerned with what *is*, not what the individual would like to *think* is. Maritain writes, "Truth is an infinite realm—as infinite as being—whose wholeness transcends infinitely our powers of perception, and each fragment of which must be grasped through vital and purified internal activity. This conquest of being, this progressive attainment of new truths, or the progressive realization of the ever-growing and ever-renewed significance of truths

24. Maritain, *Creative Intuition in Art and Poetry*, p. 94; also, see diagram on p. 108.
25. Ibid., p.110.
26. Maritain, *Education at the Crossroads*, pp. 11-12.
27. Ibid., p. 13.
28. Ibid.

already attained, opens and enlarges our mind and life, and really situates them in freedom and autonomy".[29]

In the *Phaedo,* Plato emphasized that all learning takes place within the learner, through the activity of the learner. Respecting this fundamental truth about learning, the teacher, much like the physician, can only cooperate with nature. Both education and medicine are *ars cooperativa naturae,* arts of ministering and subservient to nature.[30] While both the mind's natural activity on the part of the student and the intellectual guidance of the teacher are dynamic factors in liberal education, Maritain notes that, "the principal agent in education, the primary dynamic factor or propelling force, is the internal vital principle in the one to be educated."[31] On the other hand, the teacher is a real cause and agent, "a real giver whose own dynamism, moral authority and positive guidance are indispensable."[32]

The teacher who would help another to "become what he is" must have "knowledge into," or love of, the absolute uniqueness of the other person. The uniqueness of the person, as a particular individual, is grasped by intuition. Intuition springs from what Maritain has termed the "preconscious of the spirit," and yet, since this preconscious is a rich mixture of what the person has read, thought, seen and experienced, it differs greatly from one person to another. One person may, by various means, help enrich the preconscious and conscious intelligence of another, and enrich himself at the same time, for example, by reading great literature together, visiting art galleries, seeing plays, opera, talking, traveling, etc. Finally, with reference to the "preconscious spiritual dynamism of human personality,"[33] one may aid in the liberal education of another by keeping in personal contact, for this gives to the "mysterious identity of the soul" the "comforting assurance of being recognized by a human personal gaze, inexpressible either in concepts or words."[34]

29. Ibid., p. 12.
30. Ibid., p. 30.
31. Ibid., p. 31.
32. Ibid., p. 33.
33. Ibid., p. 41.
34. Ibid., p. 41. Maritain is here speaking of the relation between a teacher and pupil, but the point has general application. The exact quotation is: "It is with reference to this preconscious spiritual dynamism of human personality that keeping personal contact with the pupil is of such great import, not only as a better technique for making study more attractive and stimulating, but above all to give to that mysterious identity of the child's soul, which is unknown to himself, and which no techniques can reach, the comforting assurance of being in some way recognized by a human personal gaze, inexpressible either in concept or words."

A Tribute to Rev. Gerald B. Phelan: Educator and Lover of Truth

Desmond J. FitzGerald

Monsignor Gerald Bernard Phelan (1892-1965) was a priest from Halifax, Nova Scotia. After studies in the local seminary of Halifax, he was ordained in 1914. Fr. Phelan went to the Catholic University of America for his first graduate work and received a S.T.B. from there in 1915. In 1924, he received a Ph.D. from the University of Louvain, followed by the *Agrégé en Philosophie* in 1925 from the same institution. In this way, he was part of that generation of Thomists who, having studied at Louvain, brought the enthusiasm of the Thomistic Revival to Canada. Interestingly, his Louvain dissertation concerned the experimental psychology of feeling and its modalities, and it was as a professor of psychology that Fr. Phelan came to St. Michael's, University of Toronto, in 1925.

Fr. Phelan was thus at the University of Toronto when the Basilian Fathers, especially Fr. Henry Carr, C.S.B., began planning an institute for medieval philosophy that, at the suggestion of Etienne Gilson, eventually becoming a Pontifical Institute of Mediaeval Studies when it received its papal charter from Pope Pius XII in 1939. Working as co-director with Gilson, Fr. Phelan undertook the work of assembling a library suitable for medieval research, collecting microfilms of manuscripts, the originals of which existed in a number of European libraries. Fr. Phelan also developed a working relationship with the Dean of the graduate school of the University of Toronto, whereby it came about that the courses in philosophy given in the Pontifical Institute would count for credit towards graduate degrees of the University of Toronto, even though the Institute remained an independent academic entity. Fr. Phelan served as President of the Pontifical Institute of Medieval Studies from its inception until 1946.

The Institute gave an intensive three-year course leading to the Licentiate of Mediaeval Studies (L.M.S.) degree in a range of medieval topics: history, theology, canon law, medieval literature, as well as philosophy. There was also the more rarely earned doctor of medieval studies. In the 1940s, American students would take the L.M.S. and then the Ph.D. in philosophy from the University of Toronto before embarking upon their teaching careers.

Fr. Phelan was especially close to Jacques Maritain, who first came to North America to lecture at Toronto in the early 1930s at the suggestion of Gilson (who himself had come to Toronto from Harvard where he was a visiting professor of Medieval philosophy in the 1926-1927 academic year). When Maritain lectured in English and paused for the right word, he would often give his thought in French and Fr. Phelan, sitting in the first row, would suggest the English phrase Maritain was seeking. In fact, one of Fr. Phelan's first books was entitled *Jacques Maritain*,[1] an expansion of a lecture he had given in New York in 1936. Thus it was only fitting that when the American Catholic Philosophical Association came to present the Cardinal Spellman Aquinas Medal to Jacques Maritain in 1951, it was Fr. Phelan who delivered the citation that honored Maritain. Some eight years later, in 1959, when Fr. Phelan himself was the recipient of the medal, it was Jacques Maritain who this time gave the citation that honored his friend. On that occasion, Maritain said:

> ... I hope I may be able to express today in a not too inadequate manner both my admiration for the riches of his philosophical wisdom and the magnitude of the debt that Christian philosophy and Catholic higher learning owe to his exceptional talents and lofty activities, in which the light of superior and genuine scholarship is quickened by the most attentive and delicate charity.... I also profoundly admire the total self-giving with which he put his time and energy at the service of his colleagues and of the students, helping them, illuminating them in invaluable conversations, spending hours and hours directing innumerable theses. It is with the same selfless generosity that he gives his French friends a uniquely precious assistance when they are confronted with the ordeals of translation.[2]

These last few lines of Maritain's citation bring out several special qualities of Fr. Phelan that cannot be documented in publication. Everyone who

1. Gerald B. Phelan, *Jacques Maritain* (New York: Sheed and Ward), 1937.
2. *Proceedings of the American Catholic Philosophical Association*, vol. 33, (1959), pp. 9-10.

knew him in that period of the Institute's development spoke of his won-derful conversation. While his publishing record is not in the same league as Maritain's or Gilson's, he nonetheless made his impact on the Thomistic revival by directing a number of dissertations, and by his teaching and expositions on Thomistic metaphysics. Although he was very knowledge-able on a wide range of subjects from St. Thomas's writings, he had a special interest in Aquinas's *De Veritate*. Additionally, Fr. Phelan also partici-pated in the translation of Maritain's *Existence and the Existent*,[3] as well as supervising the translation of the fourth edition of *Distinguish to Unite*, better known as *The Degrees of Knowledge*.[4] He also translated a little known work of Jacques Maritian's wife, Raissa, *The Prince of this World*,[5] published by the Institute in 1933.

In 1946, Fr. Phelan moved to the University of Notre Dame to found their Institute of Medieval Studies; he remained there until the 1950s. He subsequently returned to Toronto where he died on May 30, 1965. Shortly after his death, a member of the Basilian community, Fr. Arthur G. Kirn, put together a number of papers that Fr. Phelan had presented during his teach-ing career.[6] Amongst the selections was the noted Aquinas Lecture of 1941, "St. Thomas and Analogy." This lecture was one of the earliest in the Marquette University series (just after those given by Mortimer J. Adler, Anton C. Pegis, and Yves R. Simon), and it was considered the standard reference work on this fundamental topic of metaphysics until the later, more detailed studies of George P. Klubtertanz, S.J. and Ralph McInerny. Fr. Kirn's collection also included Fr. Phelan's reflections on "The Concept of Beauty in St. Thomas Aquinas," and a paper that Fr. Phelan wrote just after World War II when existentialism was attracting attention in North America, "The Existentialism of St. Thomas." Some of these papers origi-nally had been presented at meetings of the American Catholic Philosophical

3. Jacques Maritain, *Existence and the Existent*, translated from the French by Lewis Galantiere and Gerald B. Phelan (New York: Pantheon Books, Inc. 1948, and New York: Doubleday and Company, Inc. Image Books, 1957).

4. Jacques Maritain, *Distinguish to Unite or The Degrees of Knowledge*, translated from the fourth French edition under the supervision of Gerald B. Phelan (New York: Charles Scribner's Sons, and London: Godfrey Bles, 1959).

5. Raissa Maritain, *The Prince of this World* (Toronto: The Institute of Mediaeval Studies, 1933). The biographical material on Phelan was largely based on the obituary written by Anton C. Pegis in *Mediaeval Studies*, Vol. 27 (1965) and the history of the Institute owes much to Laurence K. Shook, *Etienne Gilson* (Toronto: The Pontifical Institute of Mediaeval Studies, 1984).

6. G. B. Phelan: *Selected Papers*, edited by Arthur G. Kirn, C.S.B. (Toronto: Pontifical Institute of Mediaeval Studies, 1967).

Association, an organization founded in 1926 with Fr. Phelan as a pioneer member. Fr. Kirn's anthology also included Fr. Phelan's very important essay, "*Verum Sequitur Esse Rerum*." In the 1950s, when epistemology was a required subject in most Catholic colleges and universities, this essay was considered a classic reading and was included in such anthologies as Roland Houde and Joseph Mullally's *Philosophy of Knowledge*, a widely used textbook for epistemology classes in the 1960s.

In "*Verum Sequitur Esse Rerum*,"[7] Fr. Phelan, following a quotation from St. Thomas, notes that, while truth properly relates to our knowledge, it is ultimately based on the being of things. That is, truth is the relationship between what we know and the way things are, and we achieve truth in our knowing when we accurately grasp things as they are in reality. This is what is meant by the traditional definition of truth as the *adequatio rei et intellectus*,[8] the agreement between knowledge and things. In this essay, Fr. Phelan is not trying to be original in any creative sense. Rather, he sought to be faithful to the thought of Aquinas, particularly the *De Veritate*.

Specifically, Fr. Phelan emphasized the point that truth is achieved in the act of judgment, when the intellect, having grasped the essences of several things, puts them together or separates them according as they are together or separated in reality. The presupposition of this exposition is a metaphysical and epistemological realism which affirms that we are capable of knowing things as they are, and that we are able to verify our judgments. As Fr. Phelan affirms, "sense experience and first principles are not only the starting point of knowledge but the ultimate tests of the truth of judgments."[9] In expounding on the way that knowledge achieves its completion in the act of judging, Fr. Phelan continues,

> Knowledge ... is not complete until the mind sees the identity of the essence existing in two different modes and thus achieves truth, i.e., recognizes that what is possessed in knowledge is identical with what is held in the physical existence by the thing itself. The fullness of knowledge is therefore, only achieved when the mind reaches on to the *esse* of its object as a physical being.[10]

Thus Phelan is affirming that in our act of judging, the judgment completes knowledge. The knower has put together in the intentional order what is in fact together in the physical, extra-mental order. As imperfect

7. *G. B. Phelan: Selected Papers*, pp.133-54.
8. Aquinas, *Summa Theologiae*, I, 16, 2c.
9. *G. B. Phelan: Selected Papers*, p.148, n. 48.
10. Ibid.

knowers, we take real things apart, as it were, when we know them—we grasp in different acts of understanding, the different aspects of the things; we grasp the substance and its accidents in distinct concepts. But finally, we put it all together in the operation of composing and dividing in which we achieve truth. Thus it is in the judgment that there is truth when we come to know things as they are. And it is from this fact that Fr. Phelan derives his essay's title, "*Verum Sequitur Esse Rerum*," "truth follows from the being of things."

But what of error, one might fairly ask? If knowing goes as it should, we ought to achieve truth every time since our knowledge proceeds directly from our experience of things. Unfortunately, that is not so simple for human beings, since we are possessed of only the lowest grade of intelligence; we know things in a piecemeal fashion, as it were, and we must put what we know in a fragmented way, back together through a series of intellectual judgments. As Fr. Phelan explains:

> knowledge of what is comes to us piecemeal. Now we see this aspect, now that. Each separate aspect … comes to us distinct from the rest. We must gather them up—assemble them as manufacturers of automobiles might say—and restore them to their unity in the thing by asserting that all these aspects which have come to us separately and which, by our judgment we have combined in the unity of mental existence, actually exist unseparated within the thing, which is the object of our knowledge, in the unity of its act of physical existence. This is, alas! a long, tedious laborious task, for, in the last analysis it is nothing less than the whole business of acquiring knowledge…. Because the objects of our knowledge are themselves very complex; because our intellectual insight is too weak to penetrate the real in its full, rich content (for, are we not in the lowest range of the hierarchy of intelligent beings?); because we cannot understand anything but the simplest objects without a multiplicity of concepts, errors inevitably arise. Our effort to put things together in judgments is much like trying to solve a jigsaw puzzle. The danger of error is always imminent. So many parts look alike when they are not alike; we are constantly putting the wrong parts together and we have to watch attentively each step we take; sometimes we do not detect our mistakes until we have finished the picture and find we have some pieces left over.[11]

This paper was originally published in 1939 in Volume I of *Mediaeval Studies*, the annual publication of the Pontifical Institute. It came after the controversies of the early 1930s amongst the so-called neo-scholastics who were asking whether or not Thomism could embrace elements of Cartesianism or Kantianism. Fr. Phelan's position, as expressed in his essay, is solidly in the traditional Thomist camp of Gilson and Maritain in this

11. Ibid.

controversy.[12] It provides a sample of the rich analysis Fr. Phelan gives to his study of the knowing process in this exposition of Aquinas's theory of the metaphysics of truth. Without attempting to present a *précis* of Fr. Phelan's paper, some of the topics that are developed in the original paper include an important section on the notion of intentional existence, and he includes a repudiation of the idealist's statement of the epistemological problem ... there is no "how does the mind go from thought to things;" rather, he provides a strong re-affirmation that our knowledge is always a knowledge of things, and that truth is always the conformity between the mind and things.

My purpose for penning this tribute to Fr. Phelan is to present to a new generation of Thomists an introduction to one of the great teachers in that first generation of the Thomistic Revival in the 20th Century, scholars that included Maritain, Gilson, DeKoninick, Yves R. Simon, and Mortimer Adler. Fr. Phelan was the teacher of a number of outstanding second generation Thomistic scholars who studied under him in Toronto in the late 1930s and 1940s. Some of that second generation included such masters as Anton C. Pegis, Vernon Bourke, James Anderson, Robert Henle, George Klubertanz, Leo Sweeney, Robert W. Schmidt, Joseph Owens, Armand Maurer and so many more. They in their turn, having earned their Ph.D. from Toronto or the Pontifical Institute, went on to educate future generations of students who carry on the tradition of a love for truth that characterizes the Thomistic Revival that began in the twentieth century and still continues today.

12. Desmond J. FitzGerald, "Etienne Gilson: From Historian to Philosopher," *Thomistic Papers II*, ed. Leonard A. Kennedy and Jack C. Marler (Houston, Texas: Center for Thomistic Studies, 1986).

Darwin and Design: Exploring a Debate

Peter A. Pagan Aguiar

An intense passion for truth, especially religious truth, is often regarded as a key source of intolerance and civil conflict in pluralistic societies. Exploring this issue in his essay, "Truth and Human Fellowship," Maritain argues at length in support of the conclusion that "genuine human fellowship is not jeopardized—quite the contrary!—it is fostered by zeal for truth, *if only love is there.*"[1] The addition of love is a vital qualification, and, as his essay makes clear, at the heart of his notion of love is the divine Word sought in humility.[2] Interestingly, this essay is followed immediately by "God and Science," an essay of comparable importance. In the latter essay Maritain observes that the modern scientific approach to truth and reality has taken center stage in Western culture, although the "old notion of a basic opposition between science and religion is progressively passing away."[3] He adds: "[T]he relation of modern science to man's knowledge of God—demands a rather delicate, sometimes complicated analysis."[4]

It is certainly true that the putatively necessary conflict between religion and science is a myth no longer as commonly promulgated in academic

---

1. Jacques Maritain, "Truth and Human Fellowship," *On the Use of Philosophy* (Princeton, New Jersey: Princeton University Press, 1961), p. 43 (emphasis added.)

2. Ibid., pp. 17, 41.

3. Ibid., pp. 44-45.

4. Ibid., p. 45. Considering Maritain's scientific background, he was in a position to appreciate the complexity of the analysis involved. On Maritain's background in science, see Stanley Jaki, "Maritain and Science," *Chance or Reality and Other Essays* (Lanham, Maryland: University Press of America, 1986), pp. 41-62.

circles as it once was,[5] although the myth is far from dead.[6] Today the scholarly debate has shifted to the question of whether the genesis of modern science depended essentially on Judeo-Christian revelation. For instance, according to David Lindberg and Ronald Numbers,

> the exact relationship between ... Christianity and science [remains elusive]. All too often those who have argued that Christianity gave birth to modern science—most notably the Protestant historian Reijer Hooykaas and the Catholic priest-scientist Stanley L. Jaki—have sacrificed careful history for scarcely concealed apologetics. From the fact that modern science developed in Christian Europe they have tended to conclude, without further demonstration, that there was a causal connection between Christianity and science. ... [A new breed of scholars] demonstrated that neither 'conflict' nor 'harmony' adequately captured the complex interaction between Christianity and science.[7]

A similar view informs two works by John Hedley Brooke.[8] Inasmuch as shades of historicism color Brooke's stimulating analyses, one may wonder whether his historiographical assessment of prior conceptions of the origin and development of science vis-à-vis religion is any less applicable to his own historical narrative. And Lindberg and Numbers's *ad hominem* dismissal of Jaki's contribution to the history of science may elicit doubts as to whether the purity of the motives inspiring their own historical vision of the genesis of modern science surpasses the integrity of Jaki's scholarly endeavors.[9]

Recently, however, a number of prominent Christian and non-Christian thinkers have been waging a rather contentious battle of words over whether natural science can disclose and identify in a definitive way the unique

5. Compare Ian G. Barbour, *Religion and Science: Historical and Contemporary Issues* (New York: HarperCollins Publishers, 1997); Gary B. Ferngren, ed., *Science & Religion: A Historical Introduction* (Baltimore, Maryland: Johns Hopkins University Press, 2002); John F. Haught, *Science & Religion: From Conflict to Conversation* (Mahwah, New Jersey: Paulist Press, 1995).

6. See Ronald L. Numbers, *The Creationists: The Evolution of Scientific Creationism* (Berkeley: University of California Press, 1992), pp. 158-83, *passim*.

7. David C. Lindberg and Ronald L. Numbers, eds., *God and Nature: Historical Essays on the Encounter between Christianity and Science* (Berkeley: University of California Press, 1986), pp. 5-6.

8. John Hedley Brooke, *Science and Religion: Some Historical Perspectives* (New York: Cambridge University Press, 1991); John H. Brooke and Geoffrey Cantor, *Reconstructing Nature: The Engagement of Science and Religion* (New York: Oxford University Press, 1998).

9. Compare Stanley Jaki, *The Savior of Science* (Grand Rapids, Michigan: William B. Eerdmans, 1988; reprint, 2000), pp. 215-16.

fingerprints of a divine Architect.[10] This issue is more complex than might initially appear, as one finds Christians and non-Christians on both sides. Indeed, some of the more caustic quarrels obtain among Christians who are otherwise united in their opposition to philosophical materialism.[11] William Dembski provides an example of what I have in mind:

> *Design theorists are no friends of theistic evolution.* As far as design theorists are concerned, theistic evolution is American evangelicalism's ill-conceived accommodation to Darwinism. ... When boiled down to its scientific content, theistic evolution is no different from atheistic evolution. ... As far as design theorists are concerned, theistic evolution is an oxymoron.[12]

The Van Till-Johnson exchange offers another illustration:

> If biological evolution is, as far as Johnson can see, inextricable from the presuppositions of naturalism, and if evolutionary naturalism is radically opposed to the existence of a supernatural Creator, then how is it possible for a person to be what Johnson calls a 'theistic naturalist'? How could one possibly be an authentic Christian theist—one whose worldview is built on belief in the Creator God—and at the same time a proponent of naturalism? Isn't 'theistic naturalism' an oxymoron of the highest order? It would seem so, and this appears to be precisely the kind of conclusion that Johnson would have the readers of *First Things* reach. As he defines it, theistic naturalism is a transparently incoherent stance that no rational or intelligent Christian could possibly take. Hence, to be a proponent of such (Johnson offers Diogenes Allen, Ernan McMullin, and myself as prime examples), it would appear that one must give up either rationality, or intelligence, or authentic Christian faith.[13]

Johnson's "apologetic" reply includes the following: "Obviously I offended Van Till with that phrase 'theistic naturalism.' In a way I am sorry for that." Johnson, however, stresses that "theistic naturalism is ultimately incoherent," and he is evidently convinced that theistic evolutionists endorse theistic naturalism, which "limits God's freedom by the dictates of naturalistic philosophy." Battles

10. See Richard F. Carlson, ed., *Science and Christianity: Four Views* (Illinois: InterVarsity Press, 2000); Phillip E. Johnson, "The Rhetorical Problem of Intelligent Design," *Rhetoric & Public Affairs* 1, no. 4 (1998), pp. 587-91; Robert T. Pennock, ed., *Intelligent Design Creationism and Its Critics* (Cambridge, Massachusetts: MIT Press, 2001).

11. See Phillip E. Johnson, Denis O. Lamoureux, et al., *Darwinism Defeated? The Johnson-Lamoureux Debate on Biological Origins* (Vancouver, Canada: Regent College Publishing, 1999); Edward T. Oakes, S.J., et al., "Edward T. Oakes and His Critics: An Exchange," *First Things* 112 (April 2001), pp. 5-13.

12. William A. Dembski, "What every theologian should know about creation, evolution, and design," http://www.origins.org/articles/dembski_theologn.html.

13. Howard J. Van Till and Phillip Johnson, "God and Evolution: An Exchange," *First Things* 34 (June/July 1993), pp. 32-41.

of this sort do not tend to promote human fellowship over social discord. From a Thomistic standpoint, it seems fair to say that these debates touching on "the relation of modern science to man's knowledge of God" accentuate the need for more penetrating philosophic analyses in an age dominated by modern science. In what follows, I explore the conflict-ridden topic of design theory vs. evolutionism and underscore some theoretical difficulties in the positions advanced by writers on each side. We will hardly find ourselves in a situation conducive to fruitful dialogue unless these philosophic lacunae are properly understood and overcome.

Genesis vs. Evolution?

In the PBS eight-hour television documentary, *Evolution*, an impressive array of today's most outspoken neo-Darwinists, including Dr. Kenneth Miller, a Roman Catholic and professor of biology at Brown University, were featured. Billed as "one of the most important series in PBS history," the documentary was aired originally in September 2001, and its central idea is explored further in Carl Zimmer and Stephen Jay Gould's 384-page companion book—*Evolution: The Triumph of an Idea.*

Evolutionary theory, which touches on fundamental anthropological and theological questions, is often presented in public schools as if it were an absolutely indisputable scientific fact. And the PBS documentary, regarded by some as an example of thinly disguised propaganda, reinforces this doctrinaire view. In the eyes of many, such presentations suggest an antireligious bias in public education. The question of God, often declared to be a private matter of conscience, is excluded from the curriculum, while the apparent conflict between evolutionary theory and religious faith is "resolved" by asserting that natural science is agnostic with respect to the question of God's existence, or by distinguishing between the realm of empirical facts (science) and the realm of personal values (religion). But the mere assertion that natural science can neither prove nor disprove God's existence does not explain *how* evolutionary theory and biblical faith are to be reconciled. Likewise, the fact/value distinction stressed in Stephen J. Gould's NOMA (nonoverlapping magisteria) principle seems to exclude God from the realm of extramental reality, an exclusion no orthodox Christian would countenance.[14]

---

14. See Stephen J. Gould, "Nonoverlapping Magisteria," *Intelligent Design Creationism and Its Critics*, pp. 737-49. In a note (p. 749), Gould asserts that Pope Pius XII violated the NOMA principle if he actually rejected polygenism as "incompatible with the doctrine of original sin. ... I would declare him out of line for letting the magisterium of religion dictate

Champions of design theory,[15] such as Phillip Johnson and William Dembski, deserve credit for their efforts in drawing attention to ambiguous aspects of evolutionary theory as presented in the typical biology course. For instance, it is often asserted that God need not be introduced to explain the origin and development of life, from the simplest life forms to the most complex organisms. Various writers[16] seem to believe that physical or natural laws alone suffice as the ultimate basis for the desired web of explanations.[17] This approach to the problem seems to render God superfluous as an explanatory principle.[18] Why turn to religion when science can supply the answers? Even the belief in miracles strikes many people today as a quaint survival of premodern cultures, a product of religious mythology. Yet design theorists maintain that science properly understood can reveal the existence of an intelligent Designer operating throughout the world of nature.[19] Unlike many of their opponents, design theorists have no reservations about bringing God into the science lab. Design theorists, like many others, are disturbed by the secularist policy of excluding God from the public square, including state-sponsored education. And this exclusionary policy typically assumes the form of a state-mandated silence imposed in the name of tolerance and cultural diversity, although,

a conclusion within the magisterium of science." This indicates clearly that, for Gould, the domain of theological faith is subordinate to that of empirical science. Gould's NOMA principle is discussed in Phillip Johnson, *The Wedge of Truth: Splitting the Foundations of Naturalism* (Illinois: InterVarsity Press, 2000), pp. 95-102.

15. Michael Denton, *Evolution: A Theory in Crisis* (Bethesda, Maryland: Adler and Adler, 1986), cited by Numbers, *The Creationists*, p. 435, n. 35, contributed in a significant way to the initial development of design theory, one of the more sophisticated branches of scientific creationism. Denton, however, is not an advocate of scientific creationism. Cf. Michael J. Denton, "The Intelligent Design Movement: Comments on Special Creationism," in *Darwinism Defeated?*, pp. 141-54.

16. E.g., Richard Dawkins, "Science Discredits Religion," in *Philosophy of Religion: Selected Readings*, 2/e, ed. Michael Peterson et al. (New York: Oxford University Press, 2001), pp. 509-12.

17. "[A]lthough atheism might have been *logically* tenable before Darwin, Darwin made it possible to be an intellectually fulfilled atheist." Richard Dawkins, *The Blind Watchmaker* (New York: W. W. Norton and Company, 1986), p. 6. The views of a number of these authors are discussed in Kenneth R. Miller, *Finding Darwin's God: A Scientist's Search for Common Ground between God and Evolution* (New York: HarperCollins Publishers, 1999), chaps. 6 and 7; Robert T. Pennock, *Tower of Babel: The Evidence Against the New Creationism* (Cambridge, Massachusetts: MIT Press, 1999), pp. 171, 202, 245, 333-34, 336.

18. Compare Thomas Aquinas, *Summa theologiae*, I, q. 2, a. 3, obj. 2.

19. E.g., William A. Dembski, "Not Even False? Reassessing the Demise of British Natural Theology," *Philosophia Christi*, Series 2, vol. 1, no. 1 (1999), pp. 17-43.

in effect, the imposed silence on religious matters favors a secularist mentality. In view of the widespread and openly hostile attitude toward religion in the public square—an attitude shared by agnostics and others in positions of political influence—various believers seek any available means to resist the tide of secularism.[20]

On October 10 Zenit News Agency reported that during a speech the previous day to the Synod of Bishops, Josef Cardinal Ratzinger pointed out that the "marginalization of God" helps to explain the crisis now confronting the Catholic Church.[21] And many are convinced that our society cannot but continue to decline culturally as long as it refuses to recognize the Creator's absolute centrality. As some appreciation of the universality of divine providence seems essential to the sound moral and spiritual development of human souls, many would agree that our public schools should welcome, rather than exclude, references to God within the context of classroom instruction.[22] And some, including leading design theorists such as William Dembski, are of the opinion that genuine empirical science can definitively establish the reality of an intelligent cosmic Designer, whose unmistakable signature can be deciphered through an open-minded investigation of the extraordinary complexity of DNA, for example.

Design Theory: Boon or Bane?

In "Not Even False? Reassessing the Demise of British Natural Theology," Dembski maintains that design theory is empirically testable inasmuch as it possesses "empirical content." For Dembski, a theory has empirical content "if it entails or renders probable a proposition P that has empirical content," that is, a proposition that "rules out certain possible observations."[23] Dembski maintains, moreover, that from the standpoint of eighteenth-century British natural theology it was hardly controversial to assert the claim that the existence of a super-intelligent cosmic Designer is demonstrable within the proper boundaries of natural science. But the truth of this claim was eventually obscured, according to Dembski, by two critical developments.

20. Consider the September 2000 televised debate at Franklin and Marshall College between Alan Keyes and Alan Dershowitz on the role of religion in society. Available at http://www.c-spanstore.com/159474.html.

21. Zenit News Agency, http://www.zenit.org/english/visualizza.phtml?sid=11119 (October 10, 2001).

22. The issue of divine providence will surface again in the latter half of this paper.

23. Dembski, "Not Even False?" p. 21, n. 8.

The first development concerns a shift in conceptual emphasis within British natural theology.[24] During the initial stages of British natural theology's evolution, writers such as William Paley, William Derham, and Thomas Reid relied heavily on the idea of contrivance in crafting their arguments for the existence of a divine Designer as the ultimate source of the order observed throughout nature. This cosmic Designer was commonly understood to be intimately involved in the progressive unfolding of the natural world. As British natural theology continued to evolve conceptually, however, writers such as Charles Babbage abandoned the idea of contrivance as a sign of intelligent order in favor of the idea of natural law to explain the order observed in the natural world. These writers considered the idea of natural law superior to that of contrivance from the standpoint of natural theology and of God's infinite dignity. God was deemed capable of achieving His goals by means of natural laws without directly intervening regularly in the countless events of an evolving universe. This conceptual shift also seemed to harmonize better with a more sophisticated, modern scientific understanding of the physical universe.

Dembski proceeds to argue that an unintended consequence of this problematic shift was a more or less subtle but fundamental revision of natural theology along deistic lines. In view of the new emphasis on the laws of nature in explaining the order of the cosmos, many came to regard as unnecessary the concept of God as an intimately involved cosmic Designer. That seemingly primitive theistic concept was supplanted by a more erudite concept of God as divine Legislator. Now, however, God as divine Legislator appeared far more distant and much less immediately involved in the daily unfolding of the natural world. In consequence, the updated natural theology seemed less consistent with theism than with deism.[25]

The second development, according to Dembski, concerns the rise of a distorted conception of science in the nineteenth century.[26] The cultural dominance of this new, positivist conception of natural science led to the *a priori* dismissal of the possibility of empirical scientific proofs of the existence of a divine Designer. In Dembski's view, the new positivist conception of science ultimately resulted in the demise of deism and, with the aid of secularists such as Thomas Huxley, the triumph of agnosticism. In response to what they deem to be a methodologically deformed conception of natural science, Dembski and other design theorists wish

24. Ibid., pp. 22-27.
25. Ibid., pp. 23, 25, 27.
26. Ibid., pp. 27-30.

to introduce what, in their view, would constitute a more adequate and less biased scientific methodology, one that is not *necessarily* agnostic vis-à-vis *intelligent* design.

Many would find Dembski's analysis rhetorically compelling; nonetheless, his analysis is inconclusive. Perhaps the most objectionable aspect of Dembski's project is that design theory appears to grant excessive credit to natural science and, in consequence, detracts from philosophical theology.[27] His approach suggests that philosophical theology cannot stand without the support of natural science. No doubt the discoveries of modern science can be especially useful to those engaged in the activity of philosophical theology. But it is a mistake to infer that the value and viability of philosophical theology depends essentially on this or that scientific theory. In their endeavor to redraw and expand the boundaries of natural science, design theorists such as Dembski blur the line of demarcation between empirical science and philosophical theology. This endeavor results in a controversial amalgamation known as "physico-theology,"[28] which historically has not had a favorable impact on religion.[29] As certain critics have observed, physico-theology might be able to provide a strong argument for the existence of a finite deity, an extremely powerful secondary cause, but nothing beyond that.[30] While stressing the immanence of God, Dembski and other design theorists do not seem to appreciate fully the infinite magnitude of God's omnipotence and transcendence.

Natural science and philosophical theology are distinct and autonomous modes of inquiry, and their proper independence cannot profitably be sacrificed on the altar of disciplinary integration. Like other proponents of design theory, Dembski does not seem to give sufficient attention to the essential difference between philosophical naturalism and methodological naturalism. The meta-scientific assertion that there are no causes other than strictly natural (non-divine) causes reflects the stance of philo-

27. On the granting of theological purchase to natural science and attendant difficulties, cf. Brooke, *Science and Religion*, pp. 192-225.

28. See Ernan McMullin, "Natural Science and Belief in a Creator: Historical Notes," in *Physics, Philosophy, and Theology: A Common Quest for Understanding*, ed. Robert J. Russell, William R. Stoeger, S.J. and George V. Coyne, S.J. (Vatican City: Vatican Observatory, 1988), pp. 49-79; Michael J. Buckley, S.J., "The Newtonian Settlement and the Origins of Atheism," in *Physics, Philosophy, and Theology*, pp. 81-102.

29. See Michael J. Buckley, S.J., *At the Origins of Modern Atheism* (New Haven: Yale University Press, 1987).

30. Compare James Collins, *God in Modern Philosophy* (Chicago: Henry Regnery Company, 1959; reprint, 1967), pp. 355-61; Edward T. Oakes, S.J., "Newman, Yes; Paley, No," *First Things* 109 (January 2001), pp. 48-52.

sophical naturalism, not that of methodological naturalism.[31] When used illicitly to support philosophical naturalism, the practice of natural science ceases being authentic science and becomes scientism, an ideology that contradicts metaphysical and theological truth. Scientism is nothing but an inverted metaphysics. Unlike philosophical naturalism, methodological naturalism demands only that properly scientific explanations, not meta-scientific explanations, be restricted to the order of purely natural causes, and it does not deny the epistemic legitimacy of meta-scientific, that is, philosophic and theological, explanations. Thus, when founded on methodological naturalism, natural science seeks to explain observed patterns and natural phenomena by reference to natural causes exclusively, without thereby implying that there are no causes other than finite natural causes. According to methodological naturalism properly understood, a cause which transcends the realm of material being is beyond the investigative competence of natural science; the investigation of intelligent immaterial causes pertains to other domains of speculative inquiry. One might add that the possibility of these higher domains of speculative inquiry is suggested by implicit "boundary questions" that surface at the methodological perimeter of natural science.[32]

Evolution Within Neo-Darwinian Boundaries?

On the other side of the divide, there are evolutionary theorists such as Kenneth Miller. His 1999 book in defense of neo-Darwinism, *Finding Darwin's God: A Scientist's Search for Common Ground Between God and Evolution*, has received high praise. Consider Jacob Neusner's comment on the book's dust jacket:

> Religion's answer to Stephen Jay Gould's scientific atheism, Kenneth R. Miller, Brown's superstar in biology and religion, here shows "not only why Darwinian evolution does not preclude the existence of God, but how remarkably consistent evolution is with religion." Written with sharp wit and in pungent prose, his book redefines the entire debate by showing the true meaning of the science represented by the name of Darwin. Had William Jennings Bryan read Miller's book, he would

31. Regarding philosophical naturalism, see Mariano Artigas, *The Mind of the Universe: Understanding Science & Religion* (Pennsylvania: Templeton Foundation Press, 2000), pp. 117-18, 214-16.

32. See Mariano Artigas, "The Mind of the Universe: Understanding Science and Religion," in *Faith, Scholarship, and Culture in the 21st Century*, ed. Alice Ramos and Marie I. George (Washington, D.C.: The Catholic University of America Press, 2002), pp. 116-18; *The Mind of the Universe*, pp. 13-20, 111.

have not botched the Scopes trial—but then, there'd not have been such a trial to begin with.

Acknowledging the basic distinction between philosophical naturalism and methodological naturalism, Miller rejects the former in favor of the latter.[33] He also believes that Darwin espoused methodological naturalism, not philosophical naturalism. Accordingly, Miller opposes both design theorists, including Phillip Johnson, William Dembski, and Michael Behe, and proponents of evolutionary theory based on philosophical naturalism, including Edward O. Wilson, William Provine, Daniel Dennett, and Richard Dawkins. As a Roman Catholic, Miller attempts to show that there is no essential conflict between theistic belief and neo-Darwinism properly understood. In fact, he is convinced that neo-Darwinism sets the stage for a more mature and subtle understanding of God.[34]

Finding Darwin's God may obtain a favorable reception among various readers with religious proclivities. For, unlike the typical neo-Darwinist, Miller challenges those who maintain that the neo-Darwinian theory of evolution undercuts traditional monotheistic religions. A close examination of *Finding Darwin's God*, however, reveals that the gift Miller offers unwary readers is nothing more than a Trojan horse, although he himself seems unaware of the dangers involved.

A particularly controversial aspect of *Finding Darwin's God* is the notion of God that it seeks to defend. The impact of that notion is apparent in various parts of Miller's work. For instance, he appears to endorse the view that "the physical world has an existence independent of God's will."[35] This view, of course, is not the common teaching of leading theologians within the Catholic intellectual tradition, namely, that all finite beings depend absolutely upon God's creative power exercised through His di-

33. Miller articulates this key distinction in terms of absolute and scientific materialism. Cf. *Finding Darwin's God*, pp. 27-28; 192-219. Robert T. Pennock, another leading critic of design theory, also stresses the importance of this distinction in *Tower of Babel*, pp. 189-96. Unfortunately, this distinction does not help Pennock secure a firm grasp of the ontological difference between human persons and non-rational animals (ibid., pp. 114-15), nor does it help him differentiate sound from unsound conceptions of God, as he seems to defend doctrinal pluralism against Phillip Johnson (ibid., p. 192). Johnson, in contrast, seems guilty of an illicit leap in reasoning. Compare Edward T. Oakes, S.J., above, notes 11 and 30. *Pace* Pennock, a sound philosophical theology can eliminate at least some religious conceptions he appears to regard as legitimate theological options, but it does not yield nearly as much as Johnson suggests by his sudden transition from the domain of natural theology to that of revealed theology *(Wedge of Truth*, chap. 7).

34. Miller, *Finding Darwin's God*, pp. 233-45, 260-92.

35. Ibid., p. 234.

vine will.[36] Miller suggests that he accepts, on the basis of religious *faith*, the Judeo-Christian doctrine that God created the physical universe. "The existence of the universe is not self-explanatory, and to a believer the existence of every particle, wave, and field is a product of the continuing will of God."[37] From the standpoint of scientific *reason*, however, he holds that it is impossible to establish that matter is not self-caused.

Either there is a God, and the big bang [sic] dates the moment of His creation of the universe, or there is a tendency of matter to create itself from nothingness. If that is the case, the big bang [sic] merely marks the moment of that self-creation or the latest oscillation in a grand series of cosmic cycles. ... If cosmology provided us with a way to distinguish between these two extreme alternatives, we might then wait for the scientific word from on high on the status of the Almighty. Unfortunately, it doesn't, and we can't.[38]

It is not evident how one might reconcile such an opinion with any sound *integration* of faith and reason, and it is unclear whether Miller truly appreciates the importance of such integration, in which theological faith is understood as a perfection of natural reason, and not vice versa.

Concerning the scientist's assertion that it is conceivable that matter might be able to create itself *ex nihilo*, one could object that such an assertion involves an intrinsic contradiction. It would not suffice to reply that, since there is no intrinsic contradiction in the scientific claim that the material universe may have originated via quantum tunneling or a vacuum fluctuation,[39] matter's self-creation *ex nihilo* is not logically impossible. The reason this reply would not suffice is that such origination is not, strictly speaking, identical to creation *ex nihilo*. A vacuum fluctuation involves a change from one state to another, whereas creation *ex nihilo* falls completely outside the category of change.[40]

36. For instance see Aquinas, *Summa theologiae*, I, q. 9, a. 2, *corp.*; q. 19, a. 4; q. 44, a. 1; q. 104, a. 1.

37. Miller, *Finding Darwin's God*, p. 241.

38. Ibid., p. 226. On the question of self-causation, others have expressed a similar view: "There had once been an interfering God who made all things. But now there was a God so much wiser who could make things make themselves" (Brooke and Cantor, *Reconstructing Nature*, pp. 161-62). Here Brooke and Cantor are referring to Charles Kingsley, a clergyman sympathetic to Darwin's theory. Even if one provides a benign interpretation of the ambiguous statement about things making themselves (in kind), the anthropological question regarding the production of human souls remains. This question will resurface later.

39. Compare William E. Carroll, "Aquinas and the Big Bang," *First Things* 97 (November 1999), pp. 18-20.

40. See Aquinas, *Summa theologiae*, I, q. 3, a. 8, *corp.*; q. 45, a. 2, ad 2 & 3; a. 3, *corp.*; *Summa contra gentiles*, Bk. II, chaps. 16-18. Artigas, *The Mind of the Universe*, pp. 112-15.

Here one might ask whether a vacuum fluctuation is significantly different from creation *ex nihilo* if, contrary to the law of conservation of mass-energy,[41] the total mass-energy sum of the subsequent state exceeds that of the initial state. If the sums differ, however briefly, one would naturally seek a causal explanation for the increase. In that case, the question would be whether the ontological difference, however small, could be explained without reference to a transcendent efficient cause of being (*ens*) qua being (*esse*). And if, in explaining the relevant ontological difference, one refuses to acknowledge the reality of a transcendent efficient cause from whom the cosmos ultimately receives its proper order and participated intelligibility, it is unclear how one could avoid the anti-metaphysical (and, consequently, antiscientific) stance of writers such as Hume and Kant, who do not recognize the intrinsic order and rational intelligibility of the cosmos.[42] Thus, the assertion that human reason left to itself cannot know that matter's self-creation *ex nihilo* is absolutely impossible is not credible, for unaided reason can grasp the metaphysical truth that what does not actually exist cannot serve as an efficient cause of anything.[43]

Such reasoning, however, would not persuade Miller. According to his way of thinking, scientists would be compelled by the force of logic to conclude that God created the material world if it were possible to demonstrate that matter could not create itself *ex nihilo*; however, science cannot prove the existence of God. Ergo, since matter is not uncreated but mutable, no logical absurdity would be implied were scientists to entertain seriously the scientific hypothesis that matter created itself *ex nihilo*. The problem with this line of reasoning is that an empirical scientific proof of God's existence does not follow logically from the recognition that matter's self-creation *ex nihilo* is absolutely impossible. If one remains strictly within the proper methodological boundaries of empirical

41. See Jaki, *Savior of Science*, pp. 123-29; *The Road of Science and the Ways to God* (Chicago: The University of Chicago Press, 1978), pp. 148-50.

42. Compare Charles A. Hart, *Thomistic Metaphysics: An Inquiry Into the Act of Existing* (Englewood Cliffs, New Jersey: Prentice-Hall, Inc., 1959), pp. 293-95; Jaki, *The Road of Science and the Ways to God*, pp. 96-127, 153-54; *Chance or Reality*, p. 31; *The Only Chaos and Other Essays* (Lanham, Maryland: University Press of America, 1990), pp. 205-7, 230; Joseph Owens, C.Ss.R., "This Truth Sublime," in *Towards a Christian Philosophy* (Washington, D.C.: The Catholic University of America Press, 1990), p. 193.

43. See Aquinas, *Summa theologiae*, I, q. 2, a. 3, *corp.*; *Summa contra gentiles*, Bk. I, Chap. 22, §6; James F. Anderson, *The Cause of Being: The Philosophy of Creation in St. Thomas* (St. Louis, Missouri: B. Herder Book Co., 1952), pp. 3-4; Charles A. Hart, *Thomistic Metaphysics*, pp. 262-64, 267-68; George P. Klubertanz, S.J., *Introduction to The Philosophy of Being* (New York: Appleton-Century-Crofts, Inc., 1955), pp. 130-35.

science, the most one could infer from the absolute impossibility of matter's self-creation *ex nihilo* is that, from a causal standpoint, the existence of matter has no *scientific* explanation.

Here one might pause to ask why consideration of a plausible alternative has been omitted, namely, the classical Greek view that matter is without temporal beginning and, hence, is not created *ex nihilo*. There are two reasons why the insertion of this classical view would not help to advance the present discussion. The first reason is that even if one were to concede that the material world is without temporal beginning, it would not follow necessarily that the existence of this world does not presuppose a transcendent efficient cause of being. It is necessarily the case, of course, that if a thing has a beginning in time, then it depends for its existence upon an efficient cause. But the negation of the consequent does not follow logically from the denial of the antecedent, unless antecedent and consequent are identical, which is not the case in this instance.[44] The second reason is that the question at issue here is whether matter qua matter is its very own *raison d'être* or whether it presupposes an extrinsic cause of its existence. In other words, is the matter of a corporeal being (*ens*) identical to its being (*esse*), or are matter and being (*esse*) really distinct? If the former, then, in effect, we are left with philosophical materialism, which may or may not be philosophically coherent.[45] If the latter, then matter qua matter is not its very own *raison d'être*, and one must search elsewhere for the efficient cause of being (*id quod est*) qua being (*id quod est*).[46] In either case, the question is not scientific but metaphysical in nature.

One might add that Miller's position as an empirical scientist would be compromised if he were to concede that matter is, *per impossibile*, self-caused *ex nihilo*. For if matter could create itself *ex nihilo*, then the meta-scientific principle of efficient causality,[47] according to which an effect necessarily depends on an actual, not purely imaginary, efficient cause, would no longer obtain. Without benefit of this meta-scientific principle, however, the naturally intelligible foundation of empirical science, along

44. See Aquinas, *Summa theologiae*, I, q. 44, aa. 1 & 2; q. 45, a. 4; *On the Eternity of the World*, 2/e, trans. Cyril Vollert, S.J., et al. (Milwaukee, Wisconsin: Marquette University Press, 1984); Anderson, *The Cause of Being*, pp. 51-112; John F. Wippel, *Metaphysical Themes in Thomas Aquinas*, (Washington, D.C.: The Catholic University of America Press, 1984), pp. 191-214.

45. See Aquinas, *Summa theologiae*, I, q. 3, a. 1, *corp.*; a. 8, *corp.* & ad 3; q. 44, a. 2, *corp.*

46. See Gerald B. Phelan, *G. B. Phelan: Selected Papers*, ed. Arthur G. Kirn, C.S.B. (Toronto: Pontifical Institute of Mediaeval Studies, 1967), pp. 63-66.

47. See Robert J. Kreyche, *First Philosophy: An Introductory Text in Metaphysics* (New York: Holt, Rinehart and Winston, Inc., 1959), pp. 224-43.

with every other form of knowledge, would be undermined.[48] For the practice of empirical science presupposes an active search for proximate (natural,
not supernatural) causes of known effects, but if the natural cause is removed, the properly scientific quest for causal explanations would be in
vain. And this exposes a certain irony in Miller's line of thought. The irony
is that his position ultimately lends support to the approach of scientific
creationists if the meta-scientific principle of efficient causality presupposed by empirical science is not universally applicable. For, in searching
for causal gaps within the natural order, scientific creationists attempt to
climb above the realm of purely natural causes investigated by modern
science in order to raise the empirical curtain on the supernatural.[49] As it
turns out, Miller does reject the universality of the principle of causality
within the natural order of things when he abandons this principle at the
atomic level of quantum events:

> [M]atter in the universe behaves in such a way that we can *never* achieve complete
> knowledge of any fragment of it ... [hence] the breaks in causality at the atomic level
> make it fundamentally *impossible* to exclude the idea that what we have really
> caught a glimpse of might indeed reflect the mind of God.[50]

Miller appears to labor under the assumption that (the Copenhagen interpretation of) Heisenberg's principle of uncertainty is needed to secure a
coherent defense of human freedom.

> [I]f [natural] laws were to run all the way down to the building blocks of matter,
> they would also have denied free will. [But these laws do *not* apply at the level of
> quantum systems.][51]

> [A] strictly determined chain of events in which our emergence was preordained,

---

48. Compare Jaki, *The Road of Science and the Ways to God*, pp. 202-209.
49. Such endeavors detract from a proper understanding of the transcendent creative
act of the primary cause operating through the actions of secondary causes while
simultaneously preserving their status as *genuine* secondary causes in accordance with
their natures. (See Aquinas, *Summa theologiae*, I, q. 8, aa. 1 & 3; a. 2, *corp.*) In effect,
such endeavors bolster fideism, which has no use for metaphysical principles (or
metaphysical *preambula fidei*) as it leaps toward the Supernatural. (Compare Ralph
McInerny, *Characters in Search of Their Author* [Notre Dame, Indiana: University of
Notre Dame Press, 2001], pp. 23, 61-68; Pope John Paul II, *Fides et ratio*, nos. 48, 52-
3, 55, 61, 63, 83-4, 88.)
50. Miller, *Finding Darwin's God*, pp. 213-14; also compare p. 230.
51. Ibid., p. 251.

would require a strictly determinant [sic] physical world. In such a place, all events would have predictable outcomes, and the future would be open neither to chance nor independent human action. A world in which we would *always* evolve is also a world in we [sic] would *never* be free.[52]

In a certain respect Miller's assumption would make sense if one were operating with an anthropology rooted in philosophical materialism,[53] and his anthropology appears to fit such a description.[54] Unfortunately for Miller, his understanding of quantum uncertainty (of the Copenhagen variety)[55] does not yield the freedom he thinks it does, but only a counterfeit.[56] Like meaning and morally significant acts, genuine freedom does not stem from anything but an immaterial principle,[57] which is altogether beyond the purview of empirical science.[58] And the intellective principle of free choice could not exist apart from the primary and universal efficient cause that is also the ultimate and universal final cause—the unparticipated good.[59] The defense of spiritual freedom, then, must proceed along *meta*physical lines; natural science alone will not suffice to accomplish the task.[60]

If one turns to consider the proper integration of the deliverances of divine faith and those of natural reason—an integration not evident in Miller's work—one may also note that if neo-Darwinism admits the assertion that matter could create itself *ex nihilo*, and if the claim concerning matter's self-creation *ex nihilo* contradicts metaphysical truths presupposed by Judeo-Christian doctrine, then neo-Darwinism and Judeo-Christian doctrine are mutually inconsistent. But Judeo-Christian

52. Ibid., p. 273.

53. See Artigas, *The Mind of the Universe*, pp. 216-21.

54. In a moment I will return to this point.

55. See Jaki, *The Road of Science and the Ways to God*, pp. 197-213.

56. One may wonder whether the attempt to defend freedom of choice on the basis of the Copenhagen interpretation of Heisenberg's principle of uncertainty is but another instance of that implicit fideism which eschews the activity of philosophic inquiry enriched by metaphysical principles.

57. Compare Aquinas, *Summa theologiae*, I, q. 83, a. 1, corp. & ad 5; a. 3, corp.

58. Apparently Miller thinks otherwise: "*In biological terms*, evolution is the only way a Creator could have made us the creatures we are—*free* beings in a world of authentic and *meaningful moral* and *spiritual choices*" (Miller, *Finding Darwin's God*, p. 291; emphasis added).

59. Compare Aquinas, *Summa theologiae*, I, q. 6, a. 3; q. 82, aa. 1 & 2; q. 83, a. 1, ad 3; q. 105, a. 4.

60. On the perennial question of human freedom, one valuable study is Vernon J. Bourke's *Will in Western Thought: An Historico-Critical Survey* (New York: Sheed and Ward, 1964).

61. See note 67 below.

doctrine presupposes the metaphysical truth that no entity can be its own efficient cause of existence.[61]

Moreover, the trajectory of Miller's thought appears to presuppose a meta-scientific theory, namely, philosophical materialism, that conflicts with traditional Abrahamic faiths. For instance, consider the following:

> We could ... hold up the origin of life itself as an unexplained mystery, and find in that our proof of God at work. Since neither I nor anyone else can yet present a detailed, step-by-step account of the origin of life from nonliving matter, such an assertion would be safe from [scientific] challenge—*but only for the moment.*[62]

Given that the demonstration of the existence of immaterial substance exceeds the competence of natural science, Miller's statement appears to imply that an ontologically inferior cause (e.g., inert matter) may be sufficient *per se*, apart from a higher (immaterial) cause, to explain an ontologically superior effect (e.g., rational animals). In other words, he implies that an effect may possess a good or perfection, for example, intelligence, which the total efficient cause of the effect does not possess in any respect, whether univocally or otherwise.[63] This, of course, is consistent with the view that matter could create itself *ex nihilo*. For the effect (the matter created *ex nihilo*) would possess a good or perfection, namely, the act of existence, not possessed by the efficient cause of the matter that was created *ex nihilo*. Not surprisingly, ortho-dox neo-Darwinism proceeds on the assumption that an effect can possess a perfection not possessed in any way by the effect's proper efficient cause.

The foregoing suggests a related difficulty. Neo-Darwinists seek to explain the origin of the human species by reference to natural causes alone, thereby advancing the view that the human person, body *and* mind, can in principle be explained exclusively in terms of material causes. Such a view cannot but yield a radically truncated anthropology.[64] For the metaphysical difference between man and non-rational animals is regarded as nothing more than a difference in degree.[65] According to this view, the human mind is believed to emerge, in some yet-to-be-explained fashion, from self-organized matter, or it is reduced to an epiphenomenon of highly

---

62. Miller, *Finding Darwin's God*, p. 276; emphasis added. This is consistent with an earlier assertion: "Any idea that life requires an inexplicable vital essence, a spirit, an *élan vital*, has long since vanished from our lives and laboratories, a casualty of genetics and biochemistry" (ibid., p. 214).

63. On the contrary, see Thomas Aquinas, *Summa theologiae*, I, q. 4, a. 2, *corp.*; q. 2, a. 3, *corp.* (*Quarta via*); q. 65, a. 1, *corp.*

64. Compare Artigas, *The Mind of the Universe*, pp. 216-21.

65. Compare Jaki, *The Savior of Science*, pp. 140-41, 230-31.

developed cerebral tissue. In either case, human phylogenesis is conceived strictly in terms of material causes. The essential nature of man, however, is found in the hylomorphic composition of *material* body possessing life in potency and *spiritual* soul, the first act of an organic body.[66] And just as act, absolutely speaking, cannot be posterior to potency,[67] so a spiritual soul cannot be derived ontologically from a material body possessing life in potency without violating the philosophic truth that the perfection of a metaphysically superior principle (e.g., form, finite spirit) cannot be explained causally by a metaphysically inferior principle (e.g., matter, organic body having life in potency).[68] Darwin and contemporary champions of Darwinism do not appreciate this fundamental truth,[69] as the metaphysical

66. Compare Aquinas, *Summa theologiae*, I, q. 75, a. 4; a. 5, ad 3 & 4; qq. 76, 90 & 91. Note that Question 91, which explores the formation of the first human body, does not preclude a properly evolutionary explanation, although not in the manner understood by Miller. For, unlike Aquinas (*Summa theologiae*, I, q. 91, a. 4, ad 1), he does not accept the teleologically sensitive view that the physical universe was created for man's sake. Nor would Miller agree with Aquinas that natural causes are directed by the supernatural primary cause (*Summa theologiae*, I, q. 2, a. 3, *corp.* & ad 2; qq. 22 & 103). Here one should stress that Aquinas's understanding of the divine ordering of secondary causes (*Summa theologiae*, I, q. 105, aa. 5 and 6, for instance) is other than the view held by modern and contemporary advocates of physico-theology, in which the cosmic Designer is conceived as an extremely powerful *external* (not to be confused with *extrinsic*) cause. Unlike the latter view, Aquinas's understanding of efficient causality rests on the doctrine of the analogy of being. (Compare Phelan, *G. B. Phelan: Selected Papers*, p. 121; Hart, *Thomistic Metaphysics*, pp. 271-91, 293.) This helps clarify why *any* biological theory of evolution founded on naturalism, whether philosophical or methodological, must be targeted as dangerous by proponents of physico-theology, inasmuch as they presuppose a *physical*, not *metaphysical*, theory of efficient causality. From the perspective of a properly metaphysical theory of efficient causality, however, scientific theories of biological evolution based on *methodological* naturalism pose no real threat to revealed truths of faith. Of course methodological naturalism should not be confused with scientism, which *is* incompatible with religious truth. Compare John Paul II, *Fides et ratio*, no. 88.

67. Compare Aquinas, *Summa theologiae*, I, q. 3, a. 1, *corp.*; a. 8, *corp.*; q. 2, a. 3, *corp.*; q. 4, a. 1, ad 2; q. 9, a. 1, *corp.*; above, note 43. For some probing discussions of the issues involved in the priority of act to potency, see James A. Weisheipl, O.P., "The Principle *Omne Quod Movetur Ab Alio Movetur* in Medieval Physics," in *Nature and Motion in the Middle Ages*, ed. William E. Carroll (Washington, D.C.: The Catholic University of America Press, 1985), pp. 75-97; Joseph Owens, C.Ss.R., "Actuality in the 'Prima Via' of St. Thomas," in *St. Thomas Aquinas on the Existence of God*, ed. John R. Catan (Albany: State University of New York Press, 1980), pp. 192-207.

68. Compare Aquinas, *Summa theologiae*, I, q. 3, a. 2, *corp.*; q. 4, a. 2, obj. 3 & ad 3; q. 44, a. 2, ad 2; Robert E. Brennan, O.P., *General Psychology: An Interpretation of the Science of Mind Based on Thomas Aquinas* (New York: The Macmillan Company, 1937), pp. 73-6, 480.

69. Not all natural scientists fail to appreciate the anthropological difficulties involved. Compare Brooke and Cantor, *Reconstructing Nature*, pp. 161-62.

hierarchy of being[70] lies beyond the scope of the reductionist boundaries of the materialist philosophy behind Darwin's evolutionary theory.[71]

Thus, it would appear that a strictly neo-Darwinian explanation of man's origin cannot logically be reconciled with a fully developed Christian anthropology, a point stressed indirectly in Pope John Paul II's October 1996 address to the Pontifical Academy of Sciences:

> If the human body takes its origin from pre-existent living matter, the spiritual soul is immediately created by God. Consequently, theories of evolution which, in accordance with the philosophies inspiring them, consider the spirit as emerging from the forces of living matter or as a mere epiphenomenon of this matter are incompatible with the truth about man. Nor are they able to ground the dignity of the person.[72]

It would seem, then, that the philosophic vision behind the neo-Darwinian theory of evolution cannot supply an adequate and complete etiologic grasp of human nature, particularly since the Darwinian emphasis on the *blind* mechanism of natural selection[73] operating on purely *random* variations sets aside the idea of global teleology or universal final causality.[74] This becomes apparent elsewhere in Miller's book:

---

70. On the metaphysical hierarchy of being, see Hart, *Thomistic Metaphysics*, pp. 143-69.

71. Compare Stanley L. Jaki, *Angels, Apes, and Men* (Peru, Illinois: Sherwood Sugden and Company, 1983) pp. 51-53, 56-59. Also see above, note 45.

72. John Paul II, Message to the Pontifical Academy of Sciences (October 22, 1996), no. 5. Reprinted in *First Things* 71 (March 1997), pp. 28-29. See Dennis Bonnette, *Origin of the Human Species* (Amsterdam/Atlanta, Georgia: Editions Rodopi, 2001), pp. 69-74.

73. One might note that the explanatory power of the idea of natural selection is more limited than some of its advocates suppose. "Natural selection...we now know is the explanation for the existence and apparently purposeful form of all life" (Dawkins, *The Blind Watchmaker*, p. 5). Neo-Darwinians explain biological evolution in terms of the "causal mechanism" of natural selection preserving favorable genetic mutations which occur randomly and are transmitted reproductively to subsequent generations. Natural selection operating on random genetic variations, however, does not explain the *original* reproductive mechanism by means of which genetic information is transmitted to offspring. For the neo-Darwinian process of natural selection could not have begun without the original reproductive mechanism. This point is made by Peter Geach, "An Irrelevance of Omnipotence," *Philosophy* 48 (1973), p. 330. Also see Bonnette, *Origin of the Human Species*, pp. 1-2; Brooke and Cantor, *Reconstructing Nature*, p. 162. Thus, the *origin* of self-replicating life forms stands in need of an explanation beyond the compass of the neo-Darwinian synthesis, although not necessarily outside the purview of natural science. Compare Brooke and Cantor, p. 162.

74. Concerning global teleology, see Aquinas, *Summa theologiae*, I-II, q. 1, a. 2; *De veritate*, q. 5, a. 2, *corp.*

[E]volution admits to no obvious purpose or single goal, just like human history. History, like evolution, seems to occur without divine guidance. ... [M]ankind's appearance on this planet was *not* preordained, ... we are here not as the products of an inevitable procession of evolutionary success, but as an afterthought, a minor detail, a happenstance in a history that might just as well have left us out.[75]

Evolution is a natural process, and natural processes are undirected. Even if God can intervene in nature, why should He when nature can do a perfectly fine job of achieving His aims all by itself? ... The notion that God had to act ... directly to produce us [human beings] contradicts not only the scientific evidence of how our species arose, but even a strictly theological reading of history.[76]

New [human] individuals do not spring, like Athena, from the minds of gods ... our origins as individuals come *entirely* from the materials of life.[77]

Miller sees no reason for concern on the part of Christians, for he dismisses the classical religious doctrines of divine providence and fore-knowledge as essentially incompatible with human freedom.[78] *Pace* Miller, however, learned Christian scholars have affirmed these classical doctrines without denying the truth of free will; they admit no logical incompatibility between these doctrines and human freedom.[79]

What is one to infer from the foregoing? At the very least, it is not obvious how Miller can reconcile his Catholic faith with his repudiation of divine providence. Belief in a *finite* deity, of course, would lend considerable support to Miller's confident rejection of the classical religious doctrine of divine providence.[80] The alleged incompatibility between that doctrine and the affirmation of human freedom, however, is hardly confirmed in the light of a sound philo-

75. Miller, *Finding Darwin's God*, pp. 237, 272. Also see ibid., pp. 238-39. Compare Brooke and Cantor, *Reconstructing Nature*, pp. 163-64.

76. Miller, *Finding Darwin's God*, p. 244.

77. Ibid., p. 250 (emphasis added).

78. Ibid., pp. 233-39, 241. On Darwin's rejection of divine providence in favor of natural selection, see F. F. Centore, "Faith and Biological Reductionism: Darwin as a Religious Reformer," in *Science and Faith*, ed. Gerard V. Bradley and Don DeMarco (South Bend, Indiana: St. Augustine's Press, 2001), pp. 50-67.

79. For instance, David B. Burrell, "Jacques Maritain and Bernard Lonergan on Divine and Human Freedom," in *The Future of Thomism*, ed. Deal W. Hudson and Dennis Wm. Moran (Notre Dame, Indiana: University of Notre Dame Press, 1992), pp. 161-68; above, note 66; below, note 87. What Miller needs is a properly metaphysical understanding of the analogy of causality, which can address both primary and secondary causes. A physical theory of efficient causality will not suffice.

80. For a concise articulation of this doctrine, see Aquinas, *Summa theologiae*, I, q. 22; Maurice R. Holloway, S.J., *An Introduction to Natural Theology* (New York: Appleton-Century-Crofts, Inc., 1959), pp. 362-80.

sophical theology in which God is conceived as pure, Self-subsistent Act.[81] It is not my intention to suggest that the philosophic problem of human freedom vis-à-vis divine providence and eternal foreknowledge is easily resolved, particularly since much has been written on this fundamental question.[82] I simply wish to point out that Miller's facile dismissal of the classical religious doctrines of divine providence and eternal foreknowledge is objectionable on various grounds, and it exposes a dearth of philosophic and theological erudition, the sort of erudition evinced in the Thomistic corpus.[83]

In the last analysis, Miller's conception of God is a rather curious hybrid. On one level, the level of ordinary experience, his quest for the divine terminates in deism, which allows no place for the providential Creator and Father affirmed within the Judeo-Christian tradition. On another level, however, the level of subatomic phenomena, Miller's conception of God is the product of process theology, a conception in which omnipotence and eternal foreknowledge are not counted among the divine attributes.

> If all power is on God's side, what powers are assignable to humanity? ... But if omnipotence is defended, and everything that happens is God's will, then God is responsible for evil and suffering and God's goodness is compromised.[84]

If one embraces the traditional faith of Christian thinkers such as Augustine of Hippo, Anselm of Canterbury, or Thomas Aquinas, one will find the

---

81. Aquinas, *Summa theologiae*, I, q. 3, a. 1, *corp.*; a. 4; q. 75, a. 5, ad 4.

82. See, for instance, Wippel, *Metaphysical Themes in Thomas Aquinas*, pp. 243-70. This problem cannot but appear logically insoluble apart from a sound philosophic conception of divine causality, although developing such a conception is an arduous undertaking.

83. For example, Aquinas, *Summa theologiae*, I, q. 13, a. 7; q. 14, a. 13; q. 19, a. 8; q. 22, a. 4; q. 105, a. 4.

84. Miller, *Finding Darwin's God*, p. 241. This passage is a quotation taken from Barbour, *Religion and Science*, p. 308. Compare Brooke and Cantor, *Reconstructing Nature*, pp. 162-65. The view that "God might have deliberately set limits to omnipotence by choosing to work through natural agencies rather than override them" (*Reconstructing Nature*, p. 165) misses the mark, for it assumes a physical theory of causality. On the contrary, the *universal* operation of the primary cause in secondary causes exhibits and perfectly accords with God's omnipotence. Compare Aquinas, *Summa theologiae*, I, q. 105, a. 5.

85. A far more exalted notion of God is articulated in, for instance, the magisterial work of Michael Dodds, O.P., *The Unchanging God of Love* (Fribourg, Suisse: Editiones Universitaires, 1986). This critical study provides an incisive analysis of the concept of God espoused by proponents of process theology. Also see Robert Sokolowski, *The God of Faith and Reason: Foundations of Christian Theology* (Washington, D.C.: The Catholic University of America Press, 1982; reprint, 1995), pp. 1-30.

terminus of Miller's search for God disappointing.[85] Moreover, Miller's failure to achieve a convincing integration of faith and reason in *Finding Darwin's God* should hardly be surprising in view of his questionable subordination of religion to science. Readers interested in finding a wholesome integration of faith and reason at the boundaries of natural science and theology would do well to search elsewhere.[86]

Conclusion

While Dembski does not seem to grasp clearly God's absolute transcendence, Miller does not fully appreciate the immanence of God's omnipresent power in both natural processes and human freedom.[87] Ironically, although these two Christian writers consider themselves to be on opposite sides of the religious and scientific debate over God and evolution, Dembski and Miller share a basic but problematic assumption. In different ways, both writers conceive of God in terms of an extremely powerful but finite (secondary) cause.[88] The identification of this secondary cause with the omnipotent God of the Judeo-Christian tradition, however, is not without profound consequences. Miller, of course, would not retain the doctrine

86. For instance, in addition to the works of Mariano Artigas and Stanley Jaki cited above, see William E. Carroll, "The Scientific Revolution and Contemporary Discourse on Faith and Reason," in *Faith and Reason*, ed. Timothy L. Smith (South Bend, Indiana: St. Augustine's Press, 2001), pp. 195-216; Charles J. Chaput, "Alpha and Omega: Reconciling Science and Faith," in *Science and Faith*, pp. 1-11; Pierre Conway, O.P., *Faith Views the Universe: A Thomistic Perspective*, (Lanham, Maryland: University Press of America, 1997); Stanley L. Jaki, *Bible and Science* (Front Royal, Virginia: Christendom Press, 1996). Readers interested in a much broader treatment of the question of integration of faith and reason may wish to consult John Paul II, *Fides et ratio*, http://www.ewtn.com/library/ENCYC/JP2FIDES.HTM (September 14, 1998), or the collection of essays edited by David Ruel Foster and Joseph W. Koterski, S.J., *The Two Wings of Catholic Thought: Essays on Fides et Ratio* (Washington, D.C.: Catholic The University of America Press, 2003).

87. On the integration of the notions of primary and secondary causality within the natural order, see Aquinas, *Summa theologiae*, I, q. 105, aa. 1-7; Artigas, "The Mind of the Universe: Understanding Science and Religion," pp. 118-21; *The Mind of the Universe*, pp. 145-56, 324-34. For a concise but interesting historical account of competing views of causation, see John Henry, "Causation," in *Science & Religion: A Historical Introduction*, pp. 130-41. One might add that the failure to see that the creative agency of the primary cause is simultaneously immanent and transcendent is not uncommon. "Darwin, to his credit, had sharpened up the choice: it was a question now of all or nothing. God was an active participant, immanent in the world, or completely absent" (Brooke and Cantor, *Reconstructing Nature*, p. 165). Of course the divine transcendence should not be construed along deistic lines of thought, which presupposes a physical theory of causality (see above, note 66).

88. See above, note 66.

of divine omnipotence, for he does not see how it could be reconciled with the affirmation of human freedom.[89] But eliminating the divine attribute of omnipotence is not obviously consistent with retaining the metaphysical distinction between primary and secondary causality, a distinction implied by the metaphysical and theological doctrine of creation *ex nihilo*, as no natural cause could serve as the universal efficient cause of being (*id quod est*) qua being (*id quod est*).[90]

What writers like Dembski and Miller need to develop is a sound and robust philosophical theology.[91] In the light of such a theology, Dembski might begin to reconsider the scientific merit of design theory, and Miller might begin to appreciate that any evolutionary theory compatible with classical theism as propounded within the traditional Abrahamic faiths is poorly served by any neo-Darwinian theory based on philosophical materialism. If we devote sufficient time to the development of an adequate philosophical theology fundamentally different from the inherently problematic physico-theology favored by proponents of design theory, and if we strive to avoid the error of reducing evolutionary theory to neo-Darwinism—an error that permeates the content of the PBS documentary on evolution and that is perpetuated in countless schools throughout the country[92]—we will thereby find

89. Miller's difficulty arises from an understanding of divine omnipotence based on a physical theory of efficient causality, a theory reflected in his view of divine action and influence at the level of quantum events. A metaphysical theory of efficient causality, however, is presupposed by any adequate defense of the good or perfection of *participated* freedom of intelligent secondary causes (compare Aquinas, *Summa theologiae*, I, q. 4, a. 2, *corp.*). The spiritual freedom possessed by these participated agents, who are images of the primary (or unparticipated) cause (*Summa theologiae*, I, q. 93, a. 1), could not be sustained on the basis of a finite divine exemplar. And, if Miller is correct, God is nothing more than a finite divine exemplar.

90. See James F. Anderson, *The Cause of Being: The Philosophy of Creation in St. Thomas* (St. Louis, Missouri: B. Herder Book Co., 1952). Apart from the doctrine of creation *ex nihilo*, one cannot develop an adequate metaphysical doctrine of the One Who Is—Self-subsisting *Esse*. Various writers have discussed the conception of God I have in mind. E.g., Sokolowski, *The God of Faith and Reason*, pp. 8-10, 41-51; David B. Burrell, *Knowing the Unknowable God* (Notre Dame, Indiana: University of Notre Dame Press, 1986), pp. 19-34, 92-108. Compare Aquinas, *Summa theologiae*, I, qq. 3 and 44.

91. In pursuing this goal, one might begin by consulting the 1999-2000 Gifford Lectures delivered by McInerny, *Characters in Search of Their Author*.

92. Consider, for instance, the following remark: "Darwin's vision has expanded to encompass a new world of biology in which the links from molecule to cell and from cell to organism are becoming clear. *Evolution* prevails, but it prevails with a richness and subtlety *its originator* may have found surprising, and in the context of developments in other sciences he could not have anticipated" (Miller, *Finding Darwin's God*, p. 290; emphasis added). Despite such imprecise locutions, Miller is aware that neo-Darwinism is but one

ourselves better situated to overcome the unnecessary conflicts that frequently surface at the boundaries between scientific and theological discourse.
We can then begin to strengthen the cultural bonds of social intercourse in
the hope of attaining a more fruitful union of minds in pursuit of an increasingly profound understanding of the truth of participated beings and their
metaphysically simple efficient cause.[93]

(currently dominant) species of evolutionary theory. One should avoid eliding the distinction
between species and genus, especially in this case. For the failure to distinguish between neo-
Darwinism and evolutionary theory is partly to blame for the hostile attitude of many
toward *any* theory of biological evolution.

93. See Aquinas, *Summa contra gentiles*, Bk. I, chap. 18.

Maritain, Augustine and Liberalism on "Judge not!"

James G. Hanink

"[P]hilosophers are naturally intolerant, and genuine tolerance among
them means a great victory of virtue over nature..."[1]
—Jacques Maritain, "Truth and Human Fellowship"

Puzzles

To be liberal, we are told, is to be open-minded. It is to be inclusive. In
particular, it is to eschew judging one's fellows. Such tolerance ranks in the
first tier of liberal virtues. And why should it be otherwise? After all, "Judge
not!" (Mt 7:1) is a scriptural command, and one which liberals are fond of
citing—if only to confound the friends of (non-liberal) dogma.

Yet herein lies a puzzle. Jacques Maritain, peasant of the Garrone, and
long before him St. Augustine, Bishop of Hippo, did indeed judge their
fellow citizens. They did so with full knowledge of the biblical injunction
"Judge not!" True, both Maritain and Augustine confessed to being sinners; yet neither included offenses against liberal tolerance among their
sins. But why not? Might not their omissions point to a laxity of conscience?

Before we address this question, let's turn to another, and more dis-
criminating, ideal. Christians, we are told, should embrace sinners and yet

Christopher Kaczor and Carroll Kearley read an earlier version of this essay. The
former, more than once, helped me to clarify my discussion. The latter encouraged me to
pursue it.
1. Jacques Maritain, "Truth and Human Fellowship," *On the Use of Philosophy* (Princeton:
Princeton University Press, 1961), p. 31.

hate their sins. Since the Christian knows himself to be a liar if he claims to be without sin, he (pardonably) hopes that others will respond in kind. Such charity ranks in the first tier of Christian virtues. How could it be otherwise? Scripture has it that Jesus loved us while we were yet sinners (Rom 5:8). It is a text that Christians are fond of citing—if only to confound merely liberal optimists *and* merely conservative pessimists.[2]

Herein lies a second puzzle. It is in acting that we write the story of our lives; the diurnal drama of good and evil is the forge of character.[3] But this interplay of act and agent should give us pause. If in acting evilly I become evil, why should you hate my acts and yet love *me*? Or if in acting evilly you become evil, why should I hate your acts and yet love *you*? If we are to judge at all, ought not our judgments be coherent? Why on earth, or elsewhere, should we judge acts but not the agents shaped by these same acts? After all, we become who we are by acting as we do. Consider, for example, a topical case. Imagine that one is a critic of secular liberalism and has set out to unravel the covering of tolerance that is among its chief virtues. In this enterprise is there not also a duty to indict those who clothe themselves in such *ersatz* finery?

Solutions

Puzzles call for solutions, and the pair of puzzles before us is no exception. We can express the first puzzle as follows: how is it that both Jacques Maritain and St. Augustine can honor Scripture's injunction "Judge not!" and yet fail to confess their offenses against the liberal's trademark tolerance? To be sure, this question points to a prior question. Did both Maritain and Augustine offend against liberal tolerance?

The answer, in a word, is yes. Here we might note, if not detail, Augustine's support for coercive strictures against the Donatists.[4] He also affirmed the

2. The prophet, moreover, confounds tyrants of every stripe. The Liturgy for the Nativity of John the Baptist cites *Isaiah* 49: 2: "He made my mouth like a sharp sword."

3. The stories of our lives, in turn, are the wellsprings of literature, and great literature reflects the drama between good and evil, as Allen Tate taught us. In *Exiles and Fugitives: The Letters of Jacques and Raissa Maritain, Allen Tate, and Caroline Gordon*, edited by John M. Dunaway (Baton Rouge and London: Louisiana State University Press, 1992), Tate refers to his *Essays of Four Decades* for indices of Maritain's influence.

4. See Peter Brown, *Augustine of Hippo* (Berkeley: University of California Press, 1967), especially chap. 21, pp. 233-43. For a recent account of Augustine's calibrated response to the Donatists, see John von Heyking's *Augustine and Politics as Longing in the World* (Columbia and London: University of Missouri Press, 2001). In chap. 7, "The Coercion of Heretics," pp. 222-57, von Heyking explains Augustine's restrictions on capital punishment.

grim necessity for judgment. Though even a just judge could mistakenly find an innocent man guilty, Augustine says that judges, in light of the wretchedness of man's estate, must exercise the duty of their office.[5]

We might note, too, though not detail, Maritain's dissent from Hans Kelsen's judicial rating of Pontius Pilate. For Kelsen, a legal positivist, Pilate is not only a just judge but also a *tolerant* one. How so? Because Pilate finds himself unable to discern the truth, he wisely appeals to the test of democracy.[6] Let the many decide! But to fault Kelsen's majoritarian sensibility, as Maritain does, offends against liberal virtue. Indeed, so maximal a tolerance as Hans Kelsen's counsels that even a judge forego judgement when radical pluralism is at issue ... and it finds nothing wretched in doing so. Better the rule of the majority, it warns, than the absolutism of a pretender to the crown of truth.[7]

With their offenses against tolerance on record, how might Augustine and Maritain justify themselves? Both find clear warrant for their judgments in a basic moral realism that teaches, minimally, that despite the wounds of original sin, and the resultant "twistiness of the human mind,"[8] we know the reality of our sin. But repentance is impossible unless we acknowledge what it is that we repent, and forgiveness requires that we identify what is to be forgiven. Thus any advance in charity, and even any order in civil life, *requires* that we judge both others and ourselves.[9] Here conscience comes into play, that conscience which is the last, best exercise of practical judgment. Not surprisingly, St. Thomas Aquinas finds that fraternal correction is a work of charity.[10]

5. Augustine, *The City of God*, ed. David Knowles (Baltimore, Maryland: Penguin Books, 1972), XIX, chap. 7, p. 860. Jean Bethke Elshtain calls our attention to this passage in her *Augustine and the Limits of Politics* (Notre Dame, Indiana: University of Notre Dame Press, 1995), p. 95.

6. See Maritain, "Truth and Human Fellowship," p. 21, for a sketch of Kelsen's stance.

7. But we must be fair. Helen Silving, whom Maritain cites on this matter, notes that Kelsen ignored his "epistemological relativism" in drafting the Austrian Constitution (after World War I) and produced a document that recognized civil liberties. See Helen Silving, "The Conflict of Liberty and Equality," *Iowa Law Review* 35, no. 3 (Spring 1950), pp. 357-92. At the same time, we should recognize the continuing allure of majoritarianism. Robert George has recently highlighted Justice Antonin Scalia's remarkable comment that "You protect minorities only because the majority determines that there are certain minority positions that deserve protection." See George's *The Clash of Orthodoxies: Law, Religion, and Morality in Crisis* (Wilmington, Delaware: ISI Books, 2001), p. 130.

8. The phrase, I recall, is Elizabeth Anscombe's.

9. To be sure, such judgment is consistent with a *measured* tolerance both of agents and their acts. In fact, a measured tolerance, as distinct from the tolerance of skepticism or indifference, presupposes a judgment of the malice in agents and the consequences of their acts—or else there is nothing to tolerate. Christopher Kaczor alerted me to this presupposition.

10. Thomas Aquinas, *Summa Theologica*, II-II, Q. 33, Art. 1.

But when in charity we correct one another, we are to judge what we *do*. God will judge who we *are*. Thus Augustine distinguishes the "duty" to denounce what is vicious from the folly of judging "the secrets of the heart."[11] Maritain, for his part, observes that we might fairly judge actions, character, temperament, and something of another's interior disposition. We dare not, however, judge "the innermost heart" of another.[12] In contrasting, then, the "judge not" of liberal tolerance and true fraternal correction, we can exculpate both Augustine and Maritain. Have they judged others? Do they teach that we are to judge one another? Yes—and yes, again. But we are to judge human acts, not human hearts. In their making and honoring this distinction, we can resolve any puzzlement we might have about how they can both obey the biblical injunction "Judge not!" and yet publicly judge, albeit in the liberal's sense, their fellow citizens.

But this resolution of our first puzzle seems to accentuate the force of our second puzzle. Consider, once more, Augustine's language. When he speaks of "secrets of the heart," he in effect distinguishes between what one does and who one is—on the inside.[13] Yet how tenable is this distinction between one's acts and the agent one inwardly becomes in acting? Augustine in part supports it on the basis that we cannot always read another's intention. Yet sometimes, as he notes, we *can* read another's intention, and he offers the case of blasphemy as an example.[14]

And consider, once again, Maritain's language. He, too, speaks of "the innermost heart." In doing so, he also distinguishes between what one does and who one is. The worry, once more, is that this is a distinction without a difference. Just who is one apart from one's actions, character, and temperament? Who is the self that remains apart from such qualities? What is left of *moral* significance?

I have argued, just now, that a basic moral realism grounds the judgment of fraternal correction. Such judgment, however, looks to the sin; God alone judges the sinner. So be it. But our earlier question returns, with its more pressing puzzle. If in acting one constructs the person one is, why

11. Augustine, *Commentary on the Lord's Sermon on the Mount with Seventeen Related Sermons*, trans. Denis J. Kavanagh, O.S.A. (New York: Fathers of the Church, Inc., 1951), p. 170.

12. Maritain, "Truth and Human Fellowship," pp. 35-6.

13. In this vein the *Catechism of the Catholic Church* speaks of the heart, in its biblical meaning, as "our hidden center, beyond the grasp of our reason and of others; only the Spirit of God can fathom the human heart and know it fully" (2563).

14. Augustine, *Commentary on the Lord's Sermon on the Mount*, p. 169.

should we judge actions but never their agents?[15] The answer to this second puzzle, I submit, lies in the personalism that both Augustine and Maritain exemplify. Broadly speaking, to be a personalist is to see the person as both the central reality of existence and the source of moral agency. As such, a personalist realism is the natural habitat of the moral realism critical to resolving the first of our puzzles. For only if the person is an irreducible reality, an agent able to freely choose either good or evil, does it make sense to speak of sin and being held responsible for one's sin.

With regard to the puzzle at hand, the personalist would argue that it is the sinner *as person*, as subject of inwardness, whom we cannot, and so dare not, judge. Augustine tells us as much in a striking, if indirect, way. "[W]hat [moral] harm," he asks, "did the injustice of the persecutors do to the martyrs? Nevertheless, it did great harm to the persecutors themselves."[16] Appearances, of course, would seem to tell a very different story; the persecutor lives and often seems to flourish.[17] The martyr, in whom (as in Jesus) there is no comeliness, dies and is seen no more. Surely this is so, insofar as we are able to see. But in truth the *person* of the persecutor is now in moral peril, though we cannot judge its resolution. The martyr, however, is in Abraham's bosom, and this we know not by our judgment but because of God's promise.

A close look at Maritain's account of the person ("Truth and Human Fellowship") as it bears on the grievous error of judging the person as such focuses on two particularly critical texts.

The first text comes in the course of a reference to natural mysticism. Such a mysticism, says Maritain, has for its object "that invaluable reality which is the Self, in its pure act of existing, immediately attained through the void created by intellectual concentration."[18] Note what this statement seems to suggest. It is only in mystical insight that one becomes present, as it were, to the core of one's own self. But such an insight as this can scarcely be produced at will to serve as the ground of self-judgment, much

---

15. With regard to the dynamic of self-construction, see my "Karol Wojtyla: Personalism, intransitivity, and character," *Communio* 23 (Summer, 1996), pp. 244-51.

16. Augustine, *Commentary on the Lord's Sermon on the Mount*, p. 172. Here Augustine echoes the Socratic Maxim that it is better to suffer evil than to do evil. For a discussion of this principle, see John Finnis, *Fundamentals of Ethics* (Washington: Georgetown University Press, 1983), pp. 112-16.

17. For a variant, so do "the sots and thralls of lust" in Hopkins's "*Justus quidem tu es, Domine*" in *Gerard Manley Hopkins*, ed. Catherine Phillips (Oxford: Oxford University Press, 1986), p. 183.

18. Maritain, "Truth and Human Fellowship," p. 43.

less—by way of a fanciful extrapolation from one's own case—the judgment of others.

The second text comes within a reference to the order of the heart and to love as the source of dialogue. "Love," observes Maritain, "does not go out to essences nor to qualities nor to ideas, but to persons," and in true friendship "it is the mystery of persons and of the divine presence within them which is … in play."[19] We find this same insistence on the person as the object of love, and more fully stated, in his *The Person and the Common Good*.

> Love is not concerned with qualities. They are not the object of our love. We love the deepest most substantial and hidden, the most *existing* reality of the beloved being. This is a metaphysical center deeper than all the qualities and essences which we can find and enumerate in the beloved.[20]

Thus it is love, and not the judgment of qualities, that becomes our avenue to the person. But only the lover rightly grasps the beloved's reciprocation of love. It follows that since sin is, at root, a turning away from God's love, only God can judge the sinner's failure to love. We, for our part, cannot judge the person at the very axis of his or her existence, that is, as a lover and a beloved of the Trinity of Love.

That in acting we become who we are is a truth we can hardly dismiss. But our deepest acts of self-constitution are those free acts of love, prompted by God's love, which open us to God's own life. These actions so decisively transcend the empirical that neither they, nor the self whom they help to constitute, can be the objects of exhaustive human judgment. Nor in reaching this conclusion are we left with an empty self, a self that is artificially detached from its identity and moral significance.

In discussing the often-neglected J. M. E. McTaggart, Peter Geach indirectly confirms the integrity of the selfhood of the lover and the beloved. Thus he affirms the thesis that (agapic) "[l]ove is for a person, not in respect of this or that characteristic, but just as this person."[21] This love is particular, not generic. It chiefly consists, he says, in "a desire for the life of the beloved and for union with the beloved."[22] Such love must be particular rather than generic, because, for every lover and every beloved, it is

19. Ibid., p. 35.

20. Jacques Maritain, *The Person and the Common Good*, trans. John J. FitzGerald (Notre Dame, Indiana: University of Notre Dame Press, 1966), p. 39.

21. Peter Geach, "Truth, Love, and Immortality," in *Truth and Hope* (Notre Dame, Indiana: University of Notre Dame Press, 2001), p. 12.

22. Geach, *Truth and Hope*, p. 12.

each act of love, and every distinct capacity for love, in contradistinction to any other quality or capacity, that ultimately individuates and morally distinguishes the lover and the beloved.

What, then, is the solution to the second of our puzzles? Why on earth, one might again ask, should we judge acts but not their agents? In summary, the answer is this: the person alone is love's true object; and the person is constituted by acts of love and by a capacity for love. Especially insofar as these acts are ordered to God, they uniquely transcend the empirical. Nonetheless, it is only in the relation of love that we could adequately judge a person. Thus God alone can rightly judge, since only God knows how, at the core of our inwardness, we reciprocate His love. Yet it is no abstract person that God judges but rather the heart of the person in his or her self-elected beauty or blight. If *we*, for our part, cannot judge persons as God does, neither can we love them as God does. Yet we love persons best in their metaphysical incommunicability rather than through the limited expressions of their empirical qualities.

Objections and Replies

Obviously my exegesis of "Judge not!," and the pair of puzzles to which it gives rise, faces objections. Here consideration of a single objection to each solution must suffice.

Augustine and Maritain find warrant for their judgments, and their offenses against a liberal tolerance, in a sturdy moral realism. Yet, as Jacques Maritain knew, many will dispute such realism squarely on moral grounds. The moral realist, so reads the liberal complaint, is congenitally arrogant. But this same complaint registers a moral judgment. Indeed, it suggests the same moral realism that it superficially impugns. ("So be it," says the misological postmodern. "Self-refutation is the hobgoblin of small minds!") In any case, as the liberal complaint further charges, congenital arrogance is an insurmountable objection to moral realism as a foundation for authentic morality.

Bluster as he might, the liberal critic cannot escape self-contradiction. Nonetheless, such blustering can be rhetorically effective. But whether or not the crowd applauds, the critic does us a service if we take this occasion to reflect on the role of humility. Both Augustine and Maritain are at the ready here. For Augustine, humility is the cornerstone of virtue. Thus he asks, "Are you thinking of raising the great fabric of spirituality? Attend first of all to the foundation of humility."[23] Maritain, in agreement, finds that

23. *Serm.* LXIX, I. PL 38, 441.

humility is the servant of truth. And would some forego truth out of a fear of arrogance? It is humility, he says, that tempers the quest for truth, and it is "truth, not ignorance, which makes us humble."[24]

Still, some will insist that an appeal to moral realism pays too steep a price. Moral realism, they note, underscores the distinction between the sinner and his sin. Yet that distinction is suspect if through our acts, whether vicious or virtuous, we forge our character. In reply, we can ourselves reaffirm and underscore the personalist view of the sinner as one whose defining core transcends, in love, the quotidian qualities which alone fall within the range of human judgment. But even so, as the debate advances, many will deny that there is such an "inner person." Perhaps even the majority within the academy will profess that, at least since Hume, any substantial self has become of largely historical interest.

Consider, for example, the quintessentially American and decently liberal William James. Looking inward, he finds that *"the 'Self of selves,' when carefully examined, is found to consist mainly of the collection of ... peculiar motions in the head or between the head and throat"* (emphasis in the original).[25] If this be candor, one might prefer dissimulation. Yet despite his own finding, he notes that stubborn "common-sense" remains sure that however variable one's stream of consciousness "it involves a real belonging to a real Owner, to a pure spiritual entity of some kind."[26] Undaunted, James presents himself as the tutor of mere commonsense.

But there is a revealing tension within William James's own thought that he does not seem fully to appreciate. On the one hand, he gives wholehearted assent to freedom of the will. Yet his (here) insouciantly materialist approach to the self at best ignores the existence of free will. But what is habitually ignored is in due time often denied. Ruefully, James comments that "most actual psychologists have no hesitation in denying that free will exists."[27] There is, in this tension, a lesson for us. If we deny the irreducibility of the person, we in practice deny free choice. But if we deny free

---

24. Maritain, "Truth and Human Fellowship," p. 24.

25. William James, *Principles of Psychology* (Cambridge, Massachusetts: Harvard University Press, 1981) vol. 1, chap. 10, p. 288.

26. Ibid., p. 320.

27. William James, *Psychology: Briefer Course* (Cambridge, Massachusetts: Harvard University Press, 1984), chap. 26, p. 392. Nor, it seems, do contemporary social scientists think differently. John Finnis finds that "almost all who write or teach political or social theory are ... refusing or failing to acknowledge the reality of free choice, and treating their subject-matter as if it were a natural substance or else a technique or product of technique." See his *Aquinas: Moral, Political, and Legal Theory* (Oxford: Oxford University Press, 1998), p. 22.

choice, we deny moral responsibility. If we deny moral responsibility, we move beyond moral good and evil. And in moving beyond good and evil, the liberal polity itself—which privileges liberal virtues—self-destructs as a moral desideratum.[28] Liberalism and materialism, once aligned, undermine both personhood and the quest for community. Whether, then, it is Hume or James (or some other thinker) who denies the self, to do so in the end compromises the intelligibility of human activity, including the doubtful forays of dismal reductionists.

Envoi

Let me close now with a postscript on the spirit of judgment. Well over a century ago, John Henry Newman opined that "It would be a gain to the country were it more superstitious, more bigoted, more gloomy, more fierce in its religion than it at present shows itself to be."[29] Bracing words, these, in the midst of our own culture wars. And frightening words, these, in the light of the defining events of 11 September 2001. Could such a judgment as Newman's, in any case, possibly be true?

Let us distinguish to discern. Superstition is always an evil, though perhaps sometimes a lesser evil than skepticism. Bigotry is always evil, though perhaps sometimes less so than indifference. A merely conservative gloominess is always mistaken, as is a merely liberal optimism; neither comports with reality.

But what about fierceness? *It* need not be mistaken at all. True, Dionysius teaches that while fierceness is natural in a dog, it ill befits a man. But to this St. Thomas replies, in *De Malo*, that we must distinguish between anger that prevails over reason and anger that serves reason.[30] Against the Stoics, he notes that the first is antecedent, while the second is consequent, to rational judgment. The first is a familiar enemy of reason; the second is a too little acknowledged friend. Consequent anger reflects the engagement of the rational will; it heightens the force of one's resolve. Insofar as the will is directed to the good of the person, this

---

28. John Rawls notes that although "political liberalism seeks common ground and is neutral in aim ... it may still affirm the superiority of certain forms of moral character and encourage certain moral virtues." See his *Political Liberalism* (New York: Columbia University Press, 1996), p. 194.

29. A. J. Conyers cites this recommendation at the outset of his *The Long Truce: How Toleration Made the World Safe for Power and Profit* (Dallas, Texas: Spence, 2001), p. vii.

30. Thomas Aquinas, *On Evil*, trans. Jean T. Oesterle (Notre Dame, Indiana: University of Notre Dame Press, 1995), Question XII, Article 1.

consequent anger can express love.[31]

Not only do we need more fierceness, of the right sort, in religion; we need it in philosophy and in public life as well. Without it we will be sorely tempted to tolerate the intolerable. There is a saying, often on the mark, that "As California goes, so goes the nation." In my own Los Angeles (or, as some have it, "Lost Angels"), our many and secular liberals hold court daily in the Public Square. Once assembled, they issue proclamations. One such document, issued by the City of Los Angeles Task Force on Family Diversity, is titled *Strengthening Families: a Model for Community Action.* Therein we find the following instructive passage.

> Recognizing human diversity is very different from making judgments about it. The Task Force did not engage in the endless academic debate over the relative merits of different lifestyles, personalities, relationships, or types of family structures. Instead, the Task Force focused on the importance of learning to live together and work together constructively to solve problems. In a world that mass communications and close urban living have made so small, alienating judgments do not better the quality of life for anyone.[32]

Such language is coded. An interpretation?

For a start, "[m]aking judgments," a defining mark of human intelligence, becomes suspect. Why? Because to do so leads to "endless academic debate." But if such debate is interminable, it is because it has become an index of emotivism.[33] Feeling has supplanted reason. And, insinuates the document, why bother to debate? After all, "lifestyles" and "relationships" are as idiosyncratic as "personalities!" Judgments about what a family actually *is* can only be "alienating." Conventional counsel is more comforting: let's go along to get along.

But this will never do. For such a counsel is a summons to chaos. In this case, it abandons the family, the singular school of love that an authentic state is to serve.[34] In every case, it sacrifices courage on the altar of comfort. Such folly, as Jacques Maritain taught us, is a defining mark of

31. For a helpful discussion of righteous anger, see Judith Barad's "Aquinas and the Role of Anger in Social Reform," *Logos: A Journal of Catholic Thought and Culture* 3: I (2000), pp. 124-44.

32. Cited by Jay Kohorn, "Insecurities are behind debate on homosexuality," *Daily Breeze* B4, 5 March 2001.

33. For a telling discussion of this link, see Alasdair MacIntyre, *After Virtue*, 2nd ed. (Notre Dame, Indiana: University of Notre Dame, 1984), p. 12.

34. As for the kind of primacy that the family retains over the state, we might recall Aquinas's point that "Human beings are by nature more conjugal than political" (*Ethics* VIII.12 n.19).

bourgeois liberalism.[35] Let us, then, carry on Maritain's struggle against this species of liberalism. Let us do so in a way that honors the humanity of the liberal but confronts the established, and liberal, disorder.

35. For an analysis of this malignity, see Maritain, *The Person and the Common Good*, pp. 91-103.

Truthfulness, the Common Good, and the Hierarchy of Goods

A. Leo White

An ongoing debate among natural law theorists concerns the way in which the various basic goods are related to each other. St. Thomas maintains that the ultimate good of human beings is the beatific vision. It follows that any action is good inasmuch as it leads one toward this goal, while an action is evil if it leads one away. Germain Grisez laments the way in which many post-Suarezian or "conventional" natural law theorists have used this understanding of the ultimate human end as a foundation for their natural law theory. According to Grisez, they have attempted to derive basic moral principles by combining a theoretical knowledge of human nature with the knowledge that God wills that we achieve the fulfillment of that nature.[1] By seeking to act in conformity with the natural purposes of one's faculties, one fulfills the divine will, and this in turn leads to the attainment of the beatific vision.

This attempt at natural law theory leads to an otherworldly attitude, says Grisez, for the goods of this life have all been instrumentalized for the sake of religion, that is, obedience to the will of God.[2] His own theory avoids this otherworldliness by claiming that each basic human good is

---

1. Germain Grisez, "The First Principle of Practical Reason: A Commentary on the *Summa Theologiae*, Question 94, Article 2," *Natural Law Forum* 10 (1965), p. 193; *The Way of the Lord Jesus*, vol. 1; *Christian Moral Principles* (Chicago: Franciscan Herald Press, 1983), p. 104.

2. Grisez, *Christian Moral Principles*, pp. 17, 25.

irreducible.[3] Hence while it may be true that religion is among the basic human goods, there are other ones as well, and their goodness is not deduced from their relation to the good of religion. Many Thomists have criticized Grisez for the way in which he puts the good of religion on the same level as that of play, another one of the basic goods in Grisez's scheme.[4] Hittinger, for example, points out important reasons for Aquinas's claim that religion "commands all other virtues."[5]

This paper goes beyond the discussion of how religion is related to other basic goods, proposing that one can see the interrelationships among *all* genera of goods once one has looked at them under the light of the common good. The term "common good" has a broader meaning in this essay than it does in St. Thomas's own writings. Aquinas's treatise on law in the *Summa Theologiae* correlates the common good with law. According to this treatise, every type of law—be it eternal, natural, human, or divine—has its corresponding common good or end. In fact, even the participation by non-rational creatures in the Eternal Law has God as their common good. What this article proposes, however, is that the correlates of the different kinds of law are not the only species of common goods, for virtuous self-love and friendship likewise aim at a common good. Only by looking at these as common goods are we able to discern how the various genera of goods are related to each other.

The argument proceeds in two stages. First, it establishes an essential, twofold link between each sort of common good and the pursuit and expression of truth. That is, truthfulness is always motivated by the desire to attain a common good of some sort; conversely one can attain each sort of common good only inasmuch as the seeker is truthful. For example, virtuous self-love requires self-honesty or authenticity, and friendship requires honesty toward others.

After looking at the various levels of common good and showing how each is essentially linked with some type of truthfulness, the paper examines how the various types of common goods are related to each other. It argues that for Aquinas the inclination toward a more *universal* common good encompasses and perfects the inclination toward a more *particular* common good. Consequently, the quest for God as the common good of the universe encompasses and elevates the desire to live in society as well

---

3. Ibid., p. 349.
4. Russel Hittinger, *A Critique of the New Natural Law Theory* (Notre Dame, Indiana: University of Notre Dame Press, 1987), pp. 124, 142.
5. Ibid., p. 170.

as all other desires. This broader application of the term "common good" thereby makes it possible for one to identify a hierarchy among basic human goods, while avoiding the sort of instrumentalizing of the lower good to the higher one that Grisez associates with conventional natural law theory.

Authentic Self-love

In his *Commentary on the Nichomachean Ethics* and in the *Summa Theologiae*, Aquinas echoes Aristotle's analysis of how a virtuous person is first of all a friend of his self.[6] Here we find a microcosmic analog to the common good. Consider how two friends share time together with each other and agree about what is painful and pleasant. These two characteristics are found in the self-love of a virtuous person as well. That is, he too enjoys spending time with himself inasmuch as he takes pleasure in reflecting upon his past, present and future. And just as two friends share joys and sorrows together, so too does a virtuous human find a kind of agreement between his sentient and rational appetitive principles.[7]

These two ways in which a virtuous person is a friend to himself seem to be interrelated. For the virtuous person distinguishes himself from the vicious one precisely by seeking the *good of his whole life*, and "whole life" here includes not only the events of his past, present and future, but also his sensory and intellectual operations. In fact, these two are interrelated: a life as a temporal whole and the whole of that life as formed by sense and intellect. In order to illustrate how they are interrelated, we should contrast the self-love of the virtuous person with the self-hatred that can be found in a particular kind of vicious person: one who is over-indulgent.

An over-indulgent person seeks what is sensually pleasing to the sense of touch while disregarding the relationship between pleasure and the rational good. He seeks the good *ut nunc* (as something to be had right now) rather than the good simply inasmuch as it is good, or *bonum simpliciter* (good without qualification). In this manner, he treats himself as if he were an animal.[8] It might be more accurate to say that he treats himself as if he were an imperfect animal, that is, one without memory or foresight. For even perfect animals (*i.e.*, those with memory and anticipation) do a better

---

6. Thomas Aquinas, *Summa Theologiae* [henceforth *ST*], II-II, q. 25, a. 7, c.; *In Decem Libros Ethicorum Aristotelis ad Nichomachum Expositio* [henceforth *In Nich.*] (Turin: Marietti, 1949), IX, lec. 9.

7. *In Nich.*, IX, lec. 4, pars. 1808-9.

8. *In Nich.*, IX, lec. 8, par. 1864.

job of managing pleasures than over-indulgent humans. Perfect animals engage in painful or at least non-gratifying behavior when they expect it to lead to some anticipated good. Even though higher brutes cannot grasp order as such, they are naturally guided by instinctive judgment and appetite to act in an orderly manner. But like Callicles in the *Gorgias*,[9] the over-indulgent person rejects order in his life. In seeking immediate gratification, the over-indulgent person avoids thinking about the past and future significance of his actions. That is, he refuses to think about his life as a temporal whole, seeking pleasure here and now instead.[10] And in refusing to go beyond the present moment in his considerations, he refuses to consider what is good *simpliciter*.

The self-controlled person, on the other hand, has learned to distinguish the good *simpliciter* from the good *ut nunc* as a result of thinking holistically. That is, by relating his present to his past and future he discerns that the good of sense is ordered toward the good of reason. In other words, a person with goodwill toward himself recognizes that the sensory inclinations are good only to the degree that they are ordered toward the good of his whole life. This recognition involves a special kind of truthfulness, which we could call "authenticity" or being honest to oneself. Only a person with this virtue of authenticity is able to integrate his sensory and rational appetite and thereby enjoy the good *simpliciter*.

Thus we see that there is a close relationship between truthfulness and the common good, broadly conceived. For the virtuous person seeks the truth about his own well-being precisely because he regards his whole life as a kind of common good which he wishes to possess.

Love between Friends

The *sine qua non* of friendship is goodwill, i.e., the wish that the other person live well. Friends not only have goodwill; they also consistently act to achieve each other's well being. One should not suppose, however, that each friend acts in a manner that is utterly altruistic or self-oblivious. That is, one who acts for the sake of a friend need not forget about his own well-being. On the contrary, one's own well-being is furthered through acts of friendship. But that is not to say that one benefits a friend for the sake of some consequence beneficial to oneself. On the contrary, friendship in the fullest sense of the term does not involve one's

9. Plato *Gorgias* 492a.
10. *In Nich.*, IX, lec. 4, par. 1816.

instrumentalizing the other person. Instead of either using the other or forgetting about one's own well-being, a friend identifies his own good *with* the good of the other.[11]

The core of the life of friendship seems to consist in what we might call collaboration or "cooperative ventures." That is, friendship germinates and grows only when friends act in concert in performing acts consonant with virtue. The goal of these collaborations typically seems to be some good other than friendship itself: friends who go skiing together, for example, enjoy the many things that happen during a skiing event as a concrete good enjoyed by both together. But we must add that the cooperation itself is a kind of common good, for both find it natural and enjoyable to act together. That is because the joint acts of friendship give one a chance to enjoy one's own excellence as reflected in one's friend. Furthermore, one enjoys one's own acts of self-generosity toward one's "other self."[12]

Aquinas points out that friends deliberate with each other.[13] I would argue that this remark is a bit of an understatement because deliberation is just one phase in practical reasoning, and friends seem to deliberate together only because they have already apprehended the same goal. Furthermore, they typically deliberate because they also anticipate collaborating on the ends they seek. It follows that not just deliberation but the entire spectrum of practical reasoning tends to overlap between friends. And this overlapping underscores how truthfulness is a necessary condition for the cooperation that lies at the core of friendship. For friends cannot act together for the same goal unless they think together, and they cannot think together unless they communicate honestly. The cognitive, affective, and operative unity achieved by friends in their common pursuits is therefore rooted in truthfulness. And since one enjoys friendship itself as a good only after having reflected on this unity, it follows that one enjoys friendship itself as a common good only inasmuch as one believes that, as friends, they have been truthful to each other.

We could summarize the relationship between truthfulness and friendship in the following manner: (1) the desire to attain a common good motivates friends to communicate in a truthful manner; (2) friends act as one only to the degree that there is truthfulness; and (3) one can enjoy the acts of friendship only to the degree that one perceives that both friends' interactions have been grounded in honesty.

11. *In Nich.*, IX, lec. 8 par. 1860, Aquinas describes friendship as a kind of oneness.
12. *ST*, I-II, q. 4, a. 8, c.
13. *ST*, I-II, q. 14, a. 3, ad 4.

Justice

Aquinas informs us that there is a parallel between the way in which the ability to think abstractly enables members of society to communicate with each other, and the way in which it enables them to work together for the common good. This parallel illustrates how truthfulness and the common good are interrelated at the societal level.

With animal communication, non-rational animals are guided by instinctive judgment. Although this instinctive judgment is a kind of participation in reason, these animals do not possess reason's grasp of what is universal. Therefore, they seek only particular goods at a particular place and time. Humans too seek particular goods, but they do so under a universal formality.[14] That is, they pursue particular goods *qua* participating in the universal good. This difference has consequences for the ways in which humans and other social animals communicate. Because brutes rely upon sentient cognition—which is concerned with the here and now—*they can only communicate with one who is present here and now*. But humans, as Aquinas points out in his *Commentary on Aristotle's De Interpretatione*, are capable of intellectual cognition, which abstracts from the here and now. This abstraction enables humans to consider future and distant objects. Aquinas says therefore that only humans resort to writing because only an animal capable of abstraction would bother to communicate with those who are remote in time and place.[15]

This ability to communicate with those who are absent, says Aquinas at the beginning of his *Commentary on the Politics*, is closely related to the human abilty to recognize what is just and unjust. That is, brutes can convey only how they feel here and now, while humans can talk about what is useful and harmful as such. Therefore, he concludes, humans and not brutes can thematize the good and the bad, the just and the unjust.[16]

The parochial way in which non-rational animals think and operate is most apparent in those cases in which an animal is hostile toward those that do not belong to its group, even though they may be of the same species. It is proper to non-rational animals *qua* non-rational to be friendly only towards those with whom they are familiar and hostile

---

14. *ST*, I, q. 80, a. 2, ad 2.
15. Thomas Aquinas, *In Aristotelis Libros Peri Hermeneias* (Turin: Marietti, 1955), I, lec. 2, par. 2.
16. Thomas Aquinas, *In Libros Politicorum Aristotelis* (Turin: Marietti, 1951), I, lec. 1, par. 29.

toward those with whom they are unfamiliar.[17] That is because brutes perceive only "this good" (e.g., the good of their "family") rather than the good as such.[18]

We can contrast the animal hostility toward the unfamiliar with the way in which just human beings work together with strangers at the cash register, in a government office, etc. Those who engage in the latter transactions may form a kind of friendship which Aristotle calls the friendship of utility.[19] One could argue, however, that this kind of friendship flourishes only within the context of a broader solidarity that exists among those who agree about justice. Consider how virtuous members of the same society whose personal interests are in competition with each other will show self-restraint in their pursuit of their particular, competing goals when they believe that it is just to do so. Just members of society will treat even competitors and adversaries in a fair manner. It should be noted that in certain situations, even friends may find their goals somewhat diverging from each other. In such cases, justice preserves friendship while injustice destroys it. In all of these scenarios, justice guides those who for some reason are not functioning as friends in the full sense of the term to act together for the common good.

From the above we can infer the relationship between truthfulness and the common good in society. A society is a living, cohesive whole only to the degree that those who are not necessarily familiar with each other wish to act in unison for a common good. This social cohesion requires communication that reaches beyond the here and now. It requires the ability to communicate both with those with whom one is on familiar terms as well as with strangers. Aquinas notes, therefore, that societies get along better when members speak the same language.[20] But more important than the commonness of a shared language are the shared beliefs that are communicated through speech and action. And the principle of all of these beliefs is that it is fitting that all members of this society (both the familiar and the stranger) share in the same common good. This belief animates all fruitful discussions about how to achieve justice.

---

17. Note that the implication here is that all animals that are *naturally* hostile to strangers of the same species are irrational. No claim is being made for the converse, i.e., that all irrational animals are hostile to strangers of the same species, for some animals are in fact friendly toward strangers of the same species.

18. "This good" signifies a particular good at a particular time and place, as opposed to "the good as such."

19. Aristotle *Nichomachean Ethics*, VIII, chap. 3.

20. Aquinas, *In Peri Hermeneias*, I, lec. 2, par. 2.

Two conclusions about a just society result: first, truthful communication with strangers is desirable precisely because one recognizes a common good which transcends one's immediate family or circle of friends. An honest person recognizes not only the good of his immediate family and acquaintances, but also that of society as a whole precisely by apprehending *the* good under a universal formality.

Secondly, one can achieve the common good of society only to the degree that there is truthfulness among its members. Aquinas points out that society would not be able to function if its members could not trust each other.[21] This claim is true on more than one level. First and most obviously, if members of society were to lie to each other frequently, eventually they would be unable to cooperate in the activities that constitute the life of a society. But on a deeper level, we could argue that the very act of lying immediately alienates the perpetrator from his listeners. One who lies in order to influence the actions of others is treating those whom he deceives like sub-human animals. And a government that acts in this manner may well be treating its citizens like cattle to be herded. Certain material benefits may accrue to citizens as a result of these manipulations, but it cannot be called a common good of rational beings.

Approaches to God

Let us now turn to the proposition that humans seek knowledge of God precisely inasmuch as they realize that God is the common good of the universe.

We may begin by defining what is meant by "common good of the universe." In Book III of the *Summa Contra Gentiles*, Aquinas uses the principle that every agent acts for the sake of a good to argue for the conclusion that God, as the highest good, is cause of the goodness of all things and is the end of all things. Aquinas calls God the common good of the universe in order to indicate that "the good of all things taken together depends on [God]."[22]

The claim that God is the common good of the universe plays a central role in Aquinas's theory of natural law. The eternal law, which consists of the divine ideas, is promulgated by God's giving each creature its natural inclinations. Each creature therefore participates in the eternal law by seek-

---

21. *ST*, II-II, q. 109, a. 3, ad 1.
22. Thomas Aquinas, *Summa contra Gentiles* [hereafter *ScG*], III, cap. 17, par. 6. See also *ST*, I-II, q. 94, a. 2, c.

ing its own good. And in seeking its own good, each creature in some sense seeks God.[23] Unlike sub-rational creatures, however, rational ones are cognizant of the good as such. That is, we seek particular things only inasmuch as we apprehend them as sharing in goodness.[24] It follows that happiness, which is the complete attainment of what rational creatures strive for, consists of the most complete possession of goodness that a rational creature could wish for. That is, the ultimate end of man is the beatific vision of God, i.e., an immediate cognitive union with God.[25]

Although every human is searching for happiness, certainly it is not clear to every human being that happiness consists of the vision of God. Aquinas acknowledges as much at the beginning of the *Summa* when he says that we have a general and confused notion of God planted in us by nature. That is, we naturally desire happiness but we do not necessarily have a clear idea of what constitutes happiness.[26] A key task here, therefore, is to describe how speculative wonder is essentially ordered toward the contemplation of God. We can do this by considering the stages through which a philosopher might come to recognize that knowing God constitutes our true and complete happiness.

Up to this point, we have examined truthfulness at it relates to the active life. That is, we have pointed out that friends and fellow members of society find it desirable to communicate truthfully at least inasmuch as doing so enables them to engage in transitive actions (*i.e.*, physical interactions with one's environment) through which they come to possess a common good. Truthfulness as it falls under this description pertains to practical rather than speculative reasoning. But there are other cases in which the *very* possession of truth seems to be the goal of human striving. These occur only when we seek to possess and share truths about *necessities*, that is, about realities and aspects of reality that cannot be changed by human action.

One may argue that a human being desires to know necessary truths because of a fundamental desire to understand the order that exists in the world as a whole. Consider how we may be struck with the desire to understand why one type of thing functions as it does. If our desire for knowledge is not merely subordinated toward transitive actions, then we will not be satisfied with looking at that object in an isolated fashion. In-

23. *SCG*, III, cap.17, par. 2.
24. *ST*, I, q. 80, a. 2, ad 2.
25. *ST*, I-II, q. 3, a. 8, c.
26. *ST*, I, q. 2, a. 1, ad 1.

stead, the quest for an adequate understanding of it will lead us to ask broader and broader questions until it develops into universal wonder. This tendency illustrates how the desire to understand the nature of this or that type of thing is animated by an inchoate desire to know how *all* of reality coheres or fits together. It seems, therefore, that the kind of wonder that drives speculative inquiry is *cosmic* in nature or it is not wonder at all. That is, speculative inquiry is fueled by the desire to understand what kind of order exists in the universe as a whole.

Our philosophical desire to understand the order that exists in the whole world is rooted in the awareness that our own well-being is tied to that order. We understand that our own being is better than that of non-cognizant things and that of non-rational animals. In fact, humans are the highest beings to be found in the material world, although there are higher, immaterial beings. Thus the degree of goodness that we possess fits into a kind of cosmic order. On the other hand, if there were no such order, then calling our life "good" would be a mere convention or a result of an anthropocentric perspective.

Of course, the order existing among the parts of the universe has an implicit reference to that which is best, i.e., to Goodness Itself. The desire to know order, therefore, is fulfilled only with the knowledge of God as the very Source of being of all creatures and hence their common good. Therefore, God as the Common Good of the universe is the ultimate object of speculative inquiry in this life. And to the extent that one understands that the best of all beings is a personal being (*i.e.*, one characterized by knowledge and will), one will regard the very existence of the universe as the result of a free, creative act on God's part. One will also regard this personal being as likewise capable of communicating with creatures. It may be natural for man to desire to communicate with and live in a kind of society with the Best of all beings. But since friendship presupposes equality among friends, some may consider it impossible to enter into friendship with God—impossible unless we somehow were enabled to share in the Divine Nature. Nevertheless, even such a person may at least wish for what he regards as impossible, so that the highest striving of mankind is for a kind of divinization that makes friendship with God possible.

The preceding remarks about God as the Common Good of the universe can be summarized with two conclusions. First: one engages in speculative inquiry because one desires to know the purpose of the universe. This inquiry may lead to the conclusion that God is the common good of the universe, which may in turn awaken a spiritual longing for unity with God. Secondly, the ultimate way in which we may attain union with God is through a cognitive union with God which Aquinas calls the beatific vision. Once again we attain a common good only inasmuch as truth is shared.

The Interrelations among Human Inclinations

Let us now examine how the various inclinations are related to each other. It can be argued that some common goods are more universal than others, and that the love of the more universal common good perfects one's love for the more particular. The key to arriving at an understanding of these interrelations is the following analogy: authentic self-love is related to the love for the common good one shares with a friend as the love for the common good that one shares with fellow members of one's society is related to the love for the common good of the universe. In other words, there is an analogy of proportionality among the pairs that we can construct out of these four terms. To put it in formal language, $A/B : B/C : C/D$, where A is the self-love; B is the love that animates friendship; C is the love that animates the virtue of justice;[27] and D is the desire to know the common good of the universe, which animates virtues such as philosophical wisdom and religion.

Each of the first terms in the above analogy is related to the second as the "particular" is to the "common." For example, self-love is concerned with what is particularly one's own, i.e., one's own well-being, while friendship focuses on the goods that human beings who know each other can share in common. Friendship is concerned with the good of those whom one has encountered within the confines of one's own particular place and time, while justice (at least inasmuch as it distinguishes itself from friendship) seeks to share a common good even with those who are outsiders, strangers, competitors, foreigners, etc. Finally justice is directed toward the common good of one's own particular society at a particular place and time, while wisdom and religion are directed toward the common good of the entire universe for all places and times.

27. The word "justice" in this section signifies principally the virtue that Aquinas calls "legal justice " (*iustitia legalis*). This virtue relates all moral virtues to the common good of society: see *ST*, II-II, q. 58, a. 5, c; q. 61, a. 5, ad 4; *In Nich.*, V, lec. 2, par. 13. For that reason Aquinas in *ST*, II-II, q. 58, a. 6, c. notes a parallel between legal justice and the virtue of charity. Yet the term "justice" in this section may also apply to the virtues of distributive and communicative justice inasmuch as these are motivated by goodwill. Through this goodwill one wishes the common good of society for particular individuals: *ST*, II-II, q. 61, a. 1, ad 4.

The above comparison helps us to see how the virtues and practices that perfect the inclinations toward more common goods influence the inclinations toward more particular goods. The minimal condition for loving oneself is for one to be concerned with one's own bodily existence. But friendship transforms self-love to something more profound than the mere will to survive. One who has friends desires not only to stay alive rather than die, but also to live with one's friends rather than be alone. In loving one's friends, one loves friendship as a good for oneself. Friendship therefore transforms and deepens one's self-love. Wishing to spend time with a friend is, if you will, a better way of loving oneself than merely wanting to stay alive.

The virtue of justice transforms and deepens friendship, for one who recognizes strangers as sharing in a common good is able to love one's own friends in a more perfect manner than one who fails to value the well-being of strangers and other outsiders. Furthermore, the love that animates justice deepens self-love, for a person guided by this solidarity with fellow citizens wants not only to live well with his family and friends but also to share in the life of a community that extends beyond the duration of his own bodily life. He is more clearly aware of the excellence of the best part of his soul (*i.e.*, the rational part), for he recognizes that he shares reason in common with all other humans. We should note in contrast that those who contribute to society for merely tribal reasons do not have a clear grasp of what is good about themselves. They fail to love the best part of themselves. We could say, therefore, that a just man loves himself more profoundly than those who show goodwill only toward those in their immediate circles.

One can argue that the virtues associated with knowledge of the common good of the universe transform all others. For example, devotion to God can transform goodwill toward fellow citizens into something greater than justice, for a person who loves God wishes the same transcendent good (*i.e.*, union with the divine) for his fellow finite rational beings as well as for himself.[28] Furthermore, the one who is devoted to God is able to enter into friendships in which the greatest degree of mutual love abounds, for the common good that religious friends share is greater than any other

---

28. *ST*, II-II, q. 25, a. 1, c. & a. 2, c. Note that this love for God may be either the natural love for God as creator and final end or common good of the universe, or the infused theological virtue of charity through which one loves God as the object of beatitude: *ST*, I-II, q. 109, c & ad 3. See also *ST*, I, q. 60, a. 5, c.

common good.[29] And since this person wishes the greatest good for him or herself, we might say that the one who loves God has perfect self-love.

In each of the above cases, the inclination directed toward a more universal good transforms the inclination directed toward a more particular good into something more excellent. That is, one who loves God is able to attain more perfectly all of the goods that one seeks through acts of justice; one who is just is able to attain more perfectly all of the goods that one seeks through acts of friendship; and one who is a genuine friend may attain more perfectly the goods that one seeks through self-love. It follows that the inclination to know the truth about God can transform all other inclinations. The virtue of religion, animated by the love of God, directs all other virtues by transforming them into something greater.

Conclusion

All human inclinations are rooted in the rational creature's natural love for the universal good. But one only gradually comes to recognize that God alone corresponds to this natural love. One starts with a more particular understanding of what is good, and after a process of making many comparisons, learns to distinguish what is more particular from what is more universal. For example, one becomes a good friend by recognizing that the same goods that one wishes for oneself can also be wished for those with whom one lives in close contact. And one becomes a good member of society by recognizing that the same good will that one has toward one's family members and close friends can also be had toward strangers. In making these and similar discoveries, one learns that the particular good is good only inasmuch as it is ordered toward the common good. Moral growth is therefore a process through which one comes to recognize the nature of the universal good more and more clearly.

Thus the discovery that only union with God, as the common good of the universe, can satisfy the longings of the human heart need not instrumentalize other goods. This discovery does not annul the goodness of all other things that one sought, so that they are now seen as worthless; rather, it intensifies our appreciation of their goodness, for one who acquires a theocentric moral perspective loves himself, his friends, and fellow members of society more deeply than before. There is no question here of instrumentalizing other goods for the sake of religion or for the

---

29. Note that Aquinas recognizes that in this life, contemplation requires friends: *ST*, I-II, q. 4, a. 8, c.

sake of attaining the beatific vision.

Moral philosophy attains the status of a science to the degree that it explains why specific actions are good, which it does by referring all particular goods to the universal good. For example, a philosopher can say that the enjoyment of friendship is good inasmuch as it is ordered toward the enjoyment of God. To say this, however, is not to regard friendship as devoid of intrinsic goodness other than its instrumentality toward the beatific vision. Rather, it is to recognize that friendship itself possesses an inner teleology that is fulfilled only inasmuch as it is permeated by our quest for and possession of the highest good. By showing that we are ultimately seeking to know God, the moral philosopher simply renders explicit what is implicit in our quest for happiness.

Aquinas, Maritain, and the Metaphysical Foundation of Practical Reason

Matthew S. Pugh

For the past thirty-five years or so, much of the debate in Thomistic ethics has concerned the following question: Can Thomas's moral philosophy be separated from Thomas's metaphysics? Stated more specifically, must the first principle of practical reason be grounded in a metaphysical apprehension of being, or is the first principle of practical reason simply the a priori starting point for an autonomous ethics? Certainly this is a most important debate, for if Thomas's moral philosophy can be separated from his metaphysics, that separation will have significant consequences not only for Thomistic ethics, but for the whole of Thomas's philosophy of the person and the common good as well. Specifically, Thomas's philosophy of the human person, which informs his understanding of the common good, presupposes a conception of practical reason grounded in a metaphysics of *esse* and participation. Thus, any separation of Aquinas's ethics from his metaphysics, by cutting the link between practical reason and the apprehension of being, would necessarily undermine, and consequently distort, Aquinas's notions of the person and the common good.

No neo-Thomist saw this more clearly than Jacques Maritain. According to Maritain, the notions of the person and the common good lie at the very heart of Aquinas's moral philosophy. And there can be no doubt that for Maritain, Thomas's moral philosophy is grounded in a metaphysics of *esse* and participation. Indeed, one could even claim that such works as *A Preface to Metaphysics*,[1] and *Existence and the Existent*,[2] which so forcefully emphasize the existential dimension of Thomas's metaphysics, lay the foundation for *The Person and the Common Good*.[3] Nevertheless, many Thomists who wish to defend the traditional view that Thomas's ethics is necessarily grounded in Thomas's metaphysics of being seem to have forgotten what Maritain knew and so effectively demonstrated—the metaphysics in question is first and foremost a metaphysics of being understood primarily as *esse*, not essence. And it is precisely this understanding that is most needed if the challenge posed by those who would remake his ethics, and thereby destroy it, is to be overcome. Of course some reformulators, such as John Finnis and Germaine Grisez, have well established and in a certain respect compelling reasons for rejecting the link that Aquinas makes between metaphysics and ethics. For example, they accept the fact/ value distinction, which holds that moral norms ("oughts") cannot be derived from nature ("is"), that one cannot draw evaluative conclusions from non-evaluative premises; to do so is to commit the naturalistic fallacy, which confuses an evaluative property, such as being good, with a natural property, such as being pleasant. As Grisez says, "If one supposes that principles of natural law are formed by examining kinds of action in comparison with human nature and noting their agreement, or disagreement, then one must respond to the objection that it is impossible to derive normative judgments from metaphysical speculations."[4] For Finnis, the only sense in which principles of right and wrong can be called "derived" is in the sense that they are derived from the pre-moral, but non-natural principles of practical reason. Since principles of right and wrong are not in that case derived from nature or facts, their derivation from the first principle of practical reason does not entail the naturallistic fallacy. For Finnis and Grisez, then, the first principle of practical reason is simply a pre-moral given, which is revealed whenever practical reason, through an act of non-inferential

---

1. Jacques Maritain, *Preface to Metaphysics* (New York, New York: Sheed and Ward, 1948).

2. Jacques Maritain, *Existence and the Existent*, trans. Lewis Galantiere and Gerald B. Phelan (Landham, Maryland: University of America Press, 1987, reprint).

3. Jacques Maritain, *The Person and the Common Good*, trans. John J. Fitzgerald (Notre Dame, Indiana: University of Notre Dame Press, 1985).

4. Germaine Grisez, "The First Principle of Practical Reason," in *Aquinas, A Collection of Critical Essays*, ed. A. Kenney, (Garden City, New York: Anchor Books, 1969), p. 382.

understanding, "grasps that the object of the inclination that one experiences is an instance of the general form of good."[5] These are undoubtedly serious objections. Unfortunately, what has come to be understood as the standard neo-Thomist interpretation of Aquinas's moral philosophy does not provide an adequate response. In that interpretation, practical reason seems to be a combination of theoretical-metaphysical apprehension plus will. There, natural law is identified with an order that lies deep within the being of things. Beneath the ought lies the is—the natural order. Practical reason simply sees what is, and then prescribes what ought to be. In this essentialist reading of Aquinas, one derives moral norms from a knowledge of natural kinds. Here the moral order is reduced to the order of nature, for the moral order arises from the very nature of things.

It is my contention, however, that this fundamentally essentialist interpretation of Aquinas, which the reformulators like Finnis and Grisez have uncritically accepted, misrepresents Thomas. Only an existentialist interpretation of Aquinas's metaphysics, like Maritain's, can avoid the problems that so concern Finnis and Grisez. For once the existential dimension of Thomas's metaphysics and its implications for ethics are truly understood, we see that there is in Thomas's moral philosophy no basis for a reduction of moral norms to nature, and therefore no possibility of committing the naturalistic fallacy. There is certainly, then, no need to separate ethics from metaphysics, or to undermine Thomas's notions of the person and the common good.

I

Specifically, Maritain's existential interpretation of Aquinas recognizes the importance that the real distinction between a being's essence and its act of being, or degree of perfection, has in linking speculative and practical reason. As all students of St. Thomas know, Thomas maintains that every being is made up of two metaphysical co-principles, namely, essence, which determines what a being is essentially, and *esse*, the act of being which makes a being actually what it is. Every being, in effect, forms a unity of essence and act of being. But in their interpretation of Aquinas's moral philosophy, many neo-Thomists have invariably given priority to essence rather than *esse*, for proponents of traditional Thomism have come to generally accept the idea that the morally good is derived from the specific nature of man. This essence, or nature, is thought to provide a goal

---

5. John Finnis, *Natural Law and Natural Rights* (Oxford: Clarendon Press, 1980), p. 34.

and therefore a measure of man's perfection. It is precisely this essentialism, however, that lays Thomas's moral philosophy open to the charge of committing the naturalistic fallacy.[6]

Yet many of the texts of St. Thomas, surprisingly, indicate that goodness, and consequently the whole moral order, is not grounded in being in this way. Indeed, these texts demonstrate that in Aquinas's view, the good is grounded in being principally by way of *esse*. Thomas makes this very clear, for example, in *De Veritate*, XXI, 1 and 2,[7] when he addresses, respectively, the questions, "Does Good Add Something to Being?" and "Are Being and Goodness Really the Same?" In response to the first question, Thomas avers that though the good does add something to being, it does not add anything real to being; the good adds to being a relation of reason only. But it is in his attempt to justify this position that Thomas's understanding of how the good is grounded in being truly comes to light. He begins by saying that something can add to another in three ways. In the first way, something adds to another a reality which is outside the essence of that other thing. This is how, for example, an accidental property like whiteness, which is extrinsic to the essence of body, adds to body. In the second way, something adds to another by limiting and determining the other, though in this case what limits and determines the other does not lie outside the essence of the other. Here Thomas uses the example of how man adds to animal in the sense that rational soul is contained actually in the essence of man, but only implicitly or potentially in the essence of animal. In the third way, something adds to another according to reason alone. Thomas says, "This is the case when something is of the essence of one thing which is not of the essence of the other, and this 'something' has no being in the nature of things but only in reason." [8] What Thomas has in mind here is what he calls a being of reason, such as blindness, which though a privation and not a being existing in nature, nevertheless adds something (blindness) to man. And, since not every man is blind, the privation in this case involves a restriction.

Of course, the good does not add to being in the first way, that is, by addition of something real, for no nature lying outside universal being could add to being something that was not already in being. But neither does good add to being in the second way, for though something can be added to

---

6. Anthony Lisska, *Aquinas's Theory of Natural Law: An Analtyical Reconstruction* (Oxford: Clarendon Press, 1996).

7. Thomas Aquinas, *De Veritate*, XXI, 1 and 2, trans. Robert W. Schmidt, S. J., as *Truth*, vol. 3 (Chicago: Henry Regnery Company, 1954), pp. 3-13.

8. Ibid.

being in a certain sense in this way (since the ten categories do add to being a determinate mode of existing rooted in the very essence of the thing), the good does not add to being in this way, precisely because the good, like being, is also divided into the ten categories. Thomas is here referring to the convertibility of being and goodness. Consequently, if the good does not add anything real to being, the good either adds nothing to being, or it adds to being according to reason alone. But the good must add something to being, for as Aquinas says, it is not nugatory to predicate good of being. Therefore, the good adds to being something pertaining to reason alone. Now something pertaining to reason is added to being either in the form of a negation, or in the form of an affirmative relation. The term "one," for example, adds to being a negation, for one means undivided being. The good (as well as the true) are said affirmatively of being, however, so they add a relation of reason to being. But a relation of reason exists when, of two *relata*, what does not depend is referred to its correlative. On the other hand, a real relation exists when, of two *relata*, there is a dependency of one *relata* on the other. Thus, in the relation obtaining between the knowable and knowledge, the relation of the knowable to knowledge is one of reason alone, since the knowable does not depend on knowledge. But the relation of knowledge to the knowable is a real relation, since there is a real dependency of knowledge on the knowable. To this observation, Thomas adds, "the knowable is said to be relative (or better, referable) not because it is itself referred to something else, but because something else is referred to it, and so it is with all other things that are related to each other as measure and measured, or as perfective and perfectible."[9] This is certainly a most significant observation, for it shows that for Aquinas the good, the perfective, signifies a real dependency of that which is perfected on that which perfects, though not of that which perfects on that which is perfected. In fact Aquinas goes on to say in the same article that it necessarily follows, then, given the nature of the relation according to reason alone, that the good (as well as the true) add "perfectiveness" to being. He then makes a very important distinction, for a being can be perfective of another being, either as regards the perfecting thing's specific intelligible nature, form, or essence, or as regards the perfecting thing's *esse*, its act of being. Insofar as a being perfects the intellect according to the perfecting being's form, it adds the true to being. However, because the being of the form is not present in the intellect according to its natural existence, the truth that is added to being is in the mind only. But insofar as a being perfects another

9. Ibid., p. 6.

according to the perfecting thing's *esse*, it adds the good to being. The very *esse* of the perfecting thing, then, is perfective of another's being. He is quick to add to this that that which perfects another by its very *esse* necessarily has the nature of an end. Thus the good adds to being final causality. He concludes with the following definition of goodness: "Goodness, then, is primarily and principally predicated of being as perfective of another in the manner of an end."[10]

For Thomas, then, goodness, like causality, is a relational term, and so only exists as such in reason, that is, as a non-real relation of reason, when considering how one thing is perfective of another's being.[11]

It should be noted at this point that Aquinas makes a further claim in *De Veritate*, XXI, 1, ad. 1, that though a thing's essence, absolutely considered, suffices for predicating being of it through that essence, *essence does not suffice as a ground for predicating goodness of a thing*, precisely because goodness adds to being a relation of final causality. *Considered from the standpoint of final causality*, beings are not good essentially, but participatively. This means that a being takes on the aspect of final causality, and hence is good, insofar as it is ordered as a secondary end to some ultimate, final end. As Thomas says, "But in the case of the creature's essence, a thing is said to be good only in relation to God, from which relation it acquires the aspect of a final cause. And thus in one sense it is said that the creature is not good essentially, but participatively."[12] In other words, a being's final causality, its goodness, is only made possible by its containment in a series or hierarchy of secondary final causes that is itself ordered to one, ultimate, final cause.

There can thus be no doubt that for Thomas goodness, which has the nature of an end, is grounded in being understood from the standpoint of *esse*, for though the good adds perfectiveness to being, it does so via the perfecting being's act of being, or *esse*, as final end, or cause.

10. Ibid., p.7.

11. Scott MacDonald makes a most interesting analysis of real and conceptual relations in his "The Metaphysics of Goodness and the Doctrine of the Transcendentals," in *Being and Goodness*, ed. Scott MacDonald, (Ithaca, New York: Cornell University Press, 1991), pp. 31-56. Though his purpose in that article is primarily to defend the Interchangeability Thesis for being and goodness, and in particular to clarify St. Albert the Great's understanding of that thesis, his analysis is actually quite relevant to this study, since Thomas's way of stating the distinction appears to be quite similar to the way St. Albert states it in *Super Dionysium De Divinis Nominibus*, IV. Yet as MacDonald asserts, Aquinas's views on the distinction between real and conceptual relations differ considerably from Albert's. By showing how Thomas's views differ from St. Albert's, MacDonald greatly clarifies Thomas's understanding of the difference between real and conceptual relations.

12. Aquinas, *De Veritate*.

However, in order to further clarify how goodness is grounded in being understood as *esse*, it is necessary to make another very important but subtle distinction that is central in Thomas's metaphysics. This distinction has to do with the difference between a being's act of existing (its brute existence), and a being's act of being (its degree of perfection, or actualization). *Esse*, in other words, must be distinguished from *existere*.

For example, in *De Veritate*, XXI, 1, Thomas says, following Aristotle, that "those defining the good in the most correct way declare it to be that which all things desire (or aim at)."[13] But we must ask how, given that Aquinas identifies goodness with final causality, and final causality with *esse*, *esse* can be that which all things desire if *esse* simply means existence, for any existing thing already exists. Any being might, however, desire its own actualization, which in turn would determine its degree of perfection. Furthermore, Thomas's comments about the nature of perfection in *De Veritate*, XXI, 2, no doubt presuppose the *esse-existere* distinction. In the body of that article, Aquinas claims that everything having the nature of an end has also the nature of goodness, since the essence of goodness is that something be perfective of another in the manner of an end. He goes on to say, however, that there are two things which characterize an end: 1) the end is what is sought after or desired by those who have not yet attained it, and 2) the end is desired, or is desirable to, those things which share in its possession. The first signifies a being's tendency to realize or possess its end, the second signifies a being's resting in its end. But these two things characterize *esse*. As Thomas says, "These two things belong to the very act of being."[14] And he adds to this, "The very act of being (*ipsum esse*) thus has the character of goodness."[15] *Esse*, then, has the nature of an end, but it cannot simply be identified with a thing's brute existence, for to say of an existing thing that its very act of existing (which it already has by virtue of the fact that it is), is that toward which it tends as something which it has not yet attained, is to say that it both does and does not exist—though we might well be able to say of a thing that it both does and does not have being, if *esse* is understood as a being's degree of perfection. A thing's *existence*, of course, does not admit of degrees—a being either exists or it does not exist. That Thomas is here making a distinction between being and existence is further indicated by this statement, "For those things which do not yet have this act (of being), tend toward it by a natural appetite."[16]

13. Ibid.
14. Ibid., p. 11.
15. Ibid.
16. Ibid.

Obviously, a being cannot tend toward anything unless it already exists. Consequently what such a being tends toward cannot be being meant as *existere*, but rather being meant as actualization, or degree of perfection.

Needless to say, this distinction has profound implications for the whole of Thomas's thought, for if the essence of goodness lies in final causality (a being is good insofar as it is perfective of another in the manner of an end), and if "end" is marked by tendency and rest, and these characterize the very nature of *esse*, then a being's *esse* is perfective not only of another, but also of itself. Yet because a being's *esse* must ultimately be viewed relationally, that is, in reference to the whole hierarchy of extrinsic ends through which it has received being, that being's *esse* must be understood participatively. The *esse* which perfects a being intrinsically cannot be disconnected from that which perfects the being extrinsically.

Now the consequence of viewing *esse*, and hence goodness, participatively, is to understand that goodness is at once perfective both extrinsically and intrinsically. Goodness/*esse* perfects extrinsically insofar as a contingent being is caused by another, that is, insofar as the former stands in a real relation to the latter as that which is perfective of the first in the manner of a final cause, and it perfects intrinsically insofar as a being's *esse* is perfective of it as an end, that is, insofar as there is an inner tendency in every being to actualize, perfect, fulfill, or realize its hidden potency.[17] Yet the *esse* that perfects intrinsically is *esse* received from something else, and ultimately from God Himself.[18] For Thomas, then, goodness is indeed grounded in being, though understood as *esse*, as a being's degree of

17. How, one might ask, can goodness be both extrinsic and intrinsic to a being, if Thomas's claims in *De Veritate*, XXI.1, are true? If goodness adds no reality to being, that is, if goodness is related to being only conceptually, rather than really, and if this relation is an extrinsic relation, how can goodness be intrinsic to any being? Doesn't this change the relation not only into an intrinsic relation, but a real relation as well? In fact it doesn't, as long as we keep two things in mind: (a) the intrinsic relation is nothing more than the restatement, so to speak, of the extrinsic relation within the being in question, which means that the end (*esse*) intrinsic to a thing is the relation given to the thing by that which perfects it as an end, (b) The relation can only be understood from the standpoint of participation, namely, the participation of *esse* in *esse*. In effect, the notion of the extrinsic end as *esse* cannot be separated in reality from the notion of the extrinsic end (the *esse* of the other, and indeed of all the others to which the *esse* of the being in question is linked) which perfects the being of the first.

18. We must emphasize, however, that this perfecting is not a coming-into-being of essence or substantial form (which, like a thing's existence, also already is), much less a coming-into-being of a thing's existence. *De Veritate*, XXI, 1, ad. 1 and 4; *Summa Theologiae*, Ia., 5, 1, and Jan Aersten, "Good as Transcendental and the Transcendence of the Good," in *Being and Goodness*, ed. MacDonald, pp. 56-73.

perfection, or realization. And since this means the *esse* of any contingent being is necessarily participated *esse*,[19] and since a thing perfects another in regard to the perfecting being's *esse*, then this also means that the goodness of a contingent creature is participated goodness. One thing's *esse* is perfective of another being, but some other *esse* is perfective of the first. All of these, though, are ordered to some final, or ultimate end, which is not itself ordered to any other being. And the importance of this cannot be overstated, for as we shall see, it has very significant implications for understanding the role of practical reason in Thomas's ethics. Here it is worth quoting Thomas in full.

> The influence of an efficient cause is to act; that of a final cause is to be sought, or desired. A secondary agent acts only by the efficacy of the first agent existing in it; similarly, a secondary end is sought only by reason of the worth of the principle end existing in it inasmuch as it is ordinated to the principle end, or has its likeness.
>
> Accordingly, because God is the last end, He is sought in every end, just as, because He is the first efficient cause, He acts in every agent. But this is what tendency to God implicitly means. For the efficacy of the first cause is in the second as the principles of reasoning are in the conclusions. But to reduce conclusions to their principles or secondary causes to their cause belongs only to the *power of reasoning*. Hence, only a rational nature can trace secondary ends back to God by a sort of analytic procedure so as to seek God Him self explicitly. In demonstrative sciences a conclusion is *correctly* drawn only by a reduction to first principles. In the same way the appetite of a rational creature is *correctly* directed only by an explicit appetitive tendency to God, either actual or habitual.[20]

Now as we have seen, for Aquinas a thing is good insofar as it has being, for the essence of goodness is that it be perfective of another in the manner of an end. To be an end, however, is to have the characteristics of tendency and rest. Since tendency and rest belong to the very act of being, to *esse*, any being, insofar as it has being, has the nature of an end, and hence is good. And this means, as we have also seen, that good-

---

19. As noted above, participation is the key to understanding how goodness is both extrinsic and intrinsic to any created being. But this requires that we specify exactly how Aquinas uses this term. A most insightful study of this problem is given in John Wippel's "Participation and the Problem of the One and the Many," in *The Metaphysical Thought of Thomas Aquinas* (Washington, D. C.: The Catholic University of America Press, 2000), pp. 94-132. In that article, Wippel attempts to address three questions concerning participation, all of which are relevant to our study. 1) What does Thomas mean by participation, specifically of beings in *esse*? 2) If beings participate in *esse*, is this meant primarily as *esse commune*, or subsisting *esse* (God)? 3) Does participation primarily mean composition or similitude? The important point to note is that the answers *to all three questions are unified by a notion of participation primarily understood as the participation of an effect in its cause.*

20. Aquinas, *De Veritate*, XXII, 2, pp. 41-2.

ness is both extrinsic and intrinsic to a being; extrinsic insofar as a being is perfected by another, and intrinsic, insofar as every being has *esse*. But if this is true, then a being is good not fundamentally by essence, but by participated *esse*. And this in turn means that the first end is in the secondary ends, both in the end extrinsic to a being and perfective of it as final cause, and in the end intrinsic to a being and perfective of it also as final cause, as its own act of being. What this implies, of course, is that the end is not only in the being that perfects another being extrinsically, but more importantly, is in the very *esse* of the perfected being. A being's *esse* thus participates not only the secondary *esse* or end which perfects it extrinsically, but also the first end which is in every end. Since a thing's being is both intrinsically perfecting and extrinsically perfected, every creature, in seeking its own being (*esse*, not *existere*) as an end, also, and necessarily seeks—given that all contingent *esse* is participated *esse*— what extrinsically perfects it as its end. In other words, in seeking its own being, every creature, in order to realize itself, also and necessarily seeks the highest end, or ultimate *esse*.

II

The foregoing considerations lay the groundwork for Thomas's moral philosophy as well as his conception of practical reason, and shows at once how the challenge posed by reformulators like Finnis and Grisez can be met. For as all students of St. Thomas know, though there is in every contingent being a real distinction of essence and act of being, every being nevertheless constitutes a unity. This unity, furthermore, is reflected in the intellect's act of knowing being. In other words, the intellect's act of knowing being reflects the unity of being itself. That is, corresponding to the unity of essence and *esse* in every being is a unity of speculative and practical reason in the one power of the knower. Thus, just as the true and the good are unified in being as two modes of perfection rather than distinct orders of being, so speculative and practical reason are unified as two *modes* of knowing, rather than distinct powers of knowing.[21]   In fact, Thomas even goes so far as to say that practical reason is simply an extension of speculative reason. Of course Thomas recognizes that speculative and practical reason differ in their objects, and refers speculative reason to its proper object which is truth, and

21. Aquinas, *Summa Theologiae*, I, Q. 79, art. 11.

practical reason to its proper object, which is the good. But he is quick to add that these objects are really one and the same, given their convertibility with being.[22]

The point is that the intellect, under its dual modes of knowing, knows being simultaneously as both true and good. Both speculative and practical reason know being. It's just that speculative reason knows being under the aspect of truth, while practical reason knows being under the aspect of goodness, and then directs what it knows to some operation. In effect, practical reason knows being from the standpoint of *esse*, that is, as perfective. And this means, of course, that practical reason also knows it as participated, and participating.

We see that here, then, there is no reduction of the order of the good to the order of being, for the good and being are one and the same. Being is good, and the good has being. Neither is the practical reduced to, nor derived from, the speculative. Speculative knowing is not prior to practical knowing, for both are simply two modes of one act of knowing. Thus there is for Aquinas no real separation of the evaluative and non-evaluative, for both spring from a basic unity, or source. It is only when the intellect reflects upon its own act of knowing that it sees that the unity of being reflected in that act simultaneously reveals a real distinction of essence and *esse* in being. This becomes clearer if we keep in mind the fundamental difference between the act by which the intellect knows extra-mental being (the real order of knowing), and the act by which the intellect knows itself (the order of self-awareness). In the act by which extra-mental being is known, the intellect first knows the essences of things through simple apprehension, a process combining sense perception, abstraction, and adequation. However, since essence is not *esse*, *esse* cannot be known in this way. *Esse*, rather, must be known through the judgment, or what Thomas calls composition and division, a process determining a whole hierarchy of judgment forms ultimately grounded in basic judgments of existence. The

---

22. Thus for example, were we to replace "truth" and "good" with "being" in the following passage from the same article, we would not at all alter the meaning of the passage. The terms in the original passage here appear in parentheses. "Being (true) and good include one another, for being (true) is something good, otherwise it would not be desirable; and being (good) is something true, other wise it would not be intelligible. Therefore, as the object of the appetite may be being (something true) as having the aspect of good, for example, when someone desires to know being (truth), so the object of the practical intellect is being (good) directed to operation, and under the aspect of truth. For the practical intellect knows being (truth), just as the speculative, but directs being (the known truth) to operation" (reply to obj. 2).

process, then, by which *esse* is known must be distinguished from the process by which essence is known—though it must be understood that the former cannot be separated from the latter, at least insofar as simple apprehension is the pre-condition, or occasion, for judgment. Hence simple apprehension and judgment together constitute the intellect's act of knowing material being. And insofar as material being is a unity, not only of form and matter, but of essence and *esse*, both speculative and practical reason are actuated, or perfected, in that act. Yet it is precisely through this actuation that the intellect is also brought to a knowledge of itself.

Consequently, though things are known primarily via their essences in the real order of knowing, in the order of self-awareness, however—that is, in the order by which the intellect knows itself—this priority is reversed. As Aquinas avers in his *Summa Theologiae*, Q. 87, art. 1, the intellect knows itself not by its essence, but by its own act. This is because the human intellect is, essentially speaking, only a capacity or potency in the genus of intelligible beings. It is not actually intelligible until it is actuated by some intelligible form. It has, in effect, essentially the power or capacity to understand, but not to be understood until actuated by an intelligible form other than itself. This means that in the order of self-awareness, the first thing that the intellect knows is its own act of understanding. In the order of awareness, that is, of the reflexive turn of the mind upon itself, the first thing that the intellect understands is its own being, for the intellect only actually (as opposed to potentially) has being when it is actuated, or informed, through some intelligible nature. It is only later, through a second critical reflection that the intellect begins to work out an epistemology. The intellect *initially* understands itself through its own actuation—that is, the intellect initially understands that it has been actuated or perfected, that it has being, and that its being (actually speaking) is its awareness. Only later does it ask *how* it knows its own being.

Now in knowing its own act, its own being, the intellect immediately understands that its being is contingent, that it is a participation of that which perfects it. The intellect knows this implicitly; that its being is contingent is only made explicit through secondary reflection. But the intellect also immediately and implicitly understands that there is a real relation of dependency not only on secondary causes extrinsically perfecting it as final ends, but also on a secondary final cause ultimately perfecting it as an intrinsic end, namely, as its own being. As we know, because God is the last end, He is in every other end. Therefore, insofar as any being knows its own act of being, that being implicitly seeks the last end, or implicitly desires to possess the last end, since it implicitly understands the relation of its own being to that of the First Being. Given that it is *esse* that primarily perfects as end or good, and the good is what is apprehended by practical reason, practical reason implicitly and at least indirectly directs every action to that end. In seeking actualization, we necessarily seek God.

Interestingly enough, Thomas likens the process of becoming explicitly aware of our desire for God to a reduction of conclusions to first principles. In *Summa Theologiae*, I-II, Q. 94, art. 2, for example, Aquinas says that the precepts of natural law are to practical reason what the first principles of demonstration are to speculative reason, and that both are self-evident principles. Of course, the first of these indemonstrable principles is based on an apprehension of being—a notion included in all that we apprehend, and first revealed to speculative reason. Yet here Aquinas is referring to being apprehended under the aspect of truth, or intelligibility. Being as good, however, is apprehended by practical reason. In other words, in the real order of knowing, an understanding of being as truth (known via speculative reason) takes priority, while in the order of awareness, an understanding of being as good (known via practical reason) takes priority. In the order of awareness, we first understand *esse* through our own *esse*, our own actuation, which is to say that we first understand the good (or the desirability of being) by understanding the desirability of our own being.

But as we may now safely assert, this priority is merely relative, and involves no derivation of the practical from the speculative, or of the speculative from the practical, for being and good form a unity that is reflected in the very unity of the intellect's act. It is not that the intellect first knows being and the indemonstrable first principles of being obtained through the power of speculative reason, and *then* knows the good and the self-evident precepts of natural law in a second but separate apprehension obtained through the power of practical reason. Rather, the apprehension of being as this takes place simultaneously in the real order of knowing and the order of awareness is the immediate foundation for both.

The implication, then, is that for Thomas there is no problem of deriving evaluative conclusions from non-evaluative premises, of deriving "ought" from "is," given that for Aquinas the good is implicitly contained in being. Being, in other words, presupposes causality. That is, to say of things that they are, and that they are good insofar as they are perfective of others and themselves, and therefore seek ends (both extrinsic and intrinsic) by virtue of the fact that they are caused to be, is the same as to say that being is inconceivable apart from causality. And, since being and good are convertible, and since a being's goodness is derived from its *esse*, the claim "all things seek the good" carries the weight of a law, of an *a priori* or self-evidently true principle—a principle that is universally and necessarily true—which first comes to light in the intellect's knowledge of its own being. This is a rule, then, which commands our obedience, since it is a principle of our being. But the causality presupposed by being (including our own), of course, is a causality hierarchically conceived, and ending in an ultimate, Final Cause. An ultimate Final Cause, however, implies intention, or design. Thus being is from the start shot through with value, for things "are" only by virtue of the intention of the ultimate Final Cause. Consequently, one cannot separate facts from values. For Aquinas, no being is an object in the first sense, for the *esse* of all being, including our own, is by participation of the last end. That last end, of course, is unlimited *esse*, and hence inherently free *esse*. Everything in creation is thus the result of a free act. That things are, that they are good, and that each implicitly desires to possess the last end (each in its own way), is the consequence of a free act proceeding from a genuinely free being. Of course, insofar as we participate in the Last End, that end is in us by similitude or likeness. That "Good is to be done and evil avoided," then, is simply commanded of us by virtue of the fact that "All things seek the good." In sum, the reformulators who miss this, end up trying to excise goodness from Thomas's metaphysics in order to make of the good and/or ethics something autonomous. As one leading theorist has said recently, "The initial impulse for an ethical question is not an awe-inspiring confrontation with being itself, but rather practical experience.... [T]he starting point of any science of human affairs is the experience of intentionally striving after a good that accompanies every human being," and, "The question about the 'ought' does not answer to the experience of being, but rather to the experience—the subjective experience—of the goal-directed nature of our striving, choosing, and doing. Moral philosophy arises from the systematic reflection upon this experience."[23] For these thinkers, the metaphysical and the ethical represent two different orders (an order of being and an order of goodness) known, or apprehended through two different intuitions (an intuition of being through simple apprehension and judgment, and an intuition of the good as that after which we intentionally strive), given in two different operations having two different ends (an operation of speculative reason directed toward truth, and an operation of practical reason reflecting upon the subjective experience of the goal-directed nature of our striving), giving rise to two different kinds of judgment having to do either with what is apprehensible, or what

---

23. Martin Rhonheimer, *Natural Law and Practical Reason*, trans. Gerald Malsbary, (New York: Fordham University Press, 2000), p. 23.

is appetible as the object of our striving. Because we are talking about two distinct orders, the first principle of practical reason, they say, cannot be reconstructed from the first principles of theoretical reason. As this paper has made clear, however, this position simply misrepresents Thomas, because for Aquinas being and goodness do not constitute two distinct orders, but rather form a fundamental unity. Consequently, when it comes to being and goodness (and thereby metaphysics and ethics), we are not talking about two distinct intuitions, operations, or judgments. They are one in reality, different in reason, or reflection alone.

Thus, both reason and being are the measure of right action. Yet the measure is not taken from an apprehension of essence, but rather from an apprehension of *esse*, for it is the *esse* of beings, and most importantly our own *esse*, that is understood by practical reason to be good, i.e., perfective.

III

Thomas's personalism, his philosophy of the person and the common good, rests on this foundation of the metaphysics of *esse*, for only a metaphysics that gives priority to the act of being and participation enables us to see that "the human person is ordained directly to God as the ultimate end."[24] As Maritain correctly pointed out, this truth lies at the very heart of Christian wisdom. As participations of the highest goodness, our goodness (degree of perfection or actualization) has being only in relation to the Final End, Whose very essence is His *esse*, or goodness. As such, our ordination transcends every created common good. Because we are extrinsically and intrinsically perfected beings, we understand that our being is necessarily caused by, and is dependent on, Infinite, or Unlimited Being, and we understand this precisely in our acts of critical reflection on our own being. Our being, therefore, and hence our goodness, is known to consist of a real relation of dependency on God, and this means that there is in us, insofar as we know this truth, an image of God shared by no other creature. Our very being, in other words, is relational—it is that degree of perfection made possible by the whole series of ends perfective of us both extrinsically and intrinsically, and culminating in the Highest Good. In a very real sense, our perfection, and thus our being, is realized only in the other. We seek our perfection in the perfection of God, the ultimate Final End. And, because

24. Maritain, *The Person and the Common Good*, p. 15.

the Last End is in all of its secondary ends, the freedom found in the Last End is also found in us, albeit in a participated way.

But as Maritain also pointed out, because this freedom is necessarily the freedom of spirit, it is also eminently personal. This means that our being is unlike the being of other creatures, for our being is a spiritual existence, a self-possession made possible through intellect and love. Unlike individuality, which is turned toward matter, personality is turned toward the highest dimensions of being. As a real dependency on that which perfects us as our ultimate final cause, our being, as person, has its roots in the Last End. Therefore, as a reflection of that original self-giving, the person is also a self-giving, a reaching out to, and a desire for, the other, as well as a dependency on the other. The subjectivity or interiority of the person is dialogic—the person only has being relationally, for the person is only actuated through the other. Indeed the "other" is the very precondition for the interiority of the person. Thus insofar as our free acts tend toward the Highest End, we desire that uncreated common good which (as origin and source of all goodness) informs every other common good by way of participation. Quoting Maritain, "Personality tends by nature to communion."[25] The implication, of course, is that pursuit of the Highest Good entails pursuit of the lesser, created common goods, such as the life of the family, and life in society. The person cannot reach perfection apart from the other, and so must pursue his perfection in and through the other. The person must, in other words, pursue the common good. Only in this way can the person reach his ultimate perfection. Yet as Maritain says, this good is common in that it is "common to both the whole and the parts into which it flows back, and which in turn, must benefit from it." [26] The common good, in effect, is the good of human persons—not the good of the mere individual, nor the good of the whole collection of individuals. This notion of the common good presupposes the human person as the very condition for its possibility, and can only be realized in persons.[27]

25. Ibid., p. 47.
26. Ibid., p. 51.
27. Maritain makes an analogy with the Persons of the Trinity to clarify this relation. For the Divine Persons, each one is in the other through infinite communion, such that their common good is the good proper to each. Yet because human beings are individuals as well as persons, the common good that we are called to pursue is not absolutely identical to the good of each person. Rather, the common good for man is superior only if it benefits persons and flows back to them. On the hand, the spiritual value, or good of the person transcends the whole of the common good, in material terms.

Finally, just as the person is a participation of the Highest Good, and thus is subordinated to it, so the common created good of persons is a participation of the Highest Good, and therefore also subordinated to it. Hence the extent to which the person pursues the common good is the very extent to which he also pursues his own perfection, and vice versa. In conclusion, it is clear that Thomas's philosophy of the human person and the common good, which lies at the very heart of his moral philosophy, presupposes a metaphysically grounded notion of practical reason. But it is also clear that the metaphysics in question must be a metaphysics that gives priority to *esse* and participation, rather than essence, for when practical reason apprehends the good, it apprehends *esse*, either the *esse* of its own being or the *esse* of some other being, which stands in a real relation of dependency necessarily on an ultimate, Final End. This recognition, in turn, becomes the foundation for a moral philosophy based on an understanding of the human being as person, whose good is inseparable from that of the common good. If, on the other hand, we attempt to ground practical reason in a metaphysics of essence, we are forced to either accept the criticism of having attempted to derive values from facts, or to reformulate Thomas's philosophy in such a way as to excise his ethics from his metaphysics. The first result is philosophically untenable, and the second result leads to the destruction of Thomas's philosophy of the person and the common good. Only the metaphysics of *esse* and participation enables us to avoid being impaled on the horns of this dilemma. By embracing the metaphysics of *esse* and participation, as both Aquinas and his great interpreter, Maritain, envisioned it, we avoid the first by demonstrating that the fact/value distinction does not hold in a metaphysics where priority is given to *esse*, and we avoid the second by showing that because the distinction does not hold in the metaphysics of *esse*, there is no need to reformulate Thomas's system, and hence no need to sever the link between his ethics and metaphysics. Most importantly we also show, thereby, that the foundation for Thomas's personalism is sound.

The Naturalistic Fallacy and Natural Law Methodology

W. Matthews Grant

It is customary to divide contemporary natural law theorists—at least those working broadly within the Thomistic tradition—into two main camps. In one camp are those such as John Finnis, Germain Grisez and Robert George, who deny that a natural law ethics need base itself on premises supplied by a methodologically prior philosophical anthropology. According to these thinkers, practical reason, when reflecting on experience and considering possible ends of action, grasps in a non-inferential act of understanding certain basic goods that ought to be pursued. Since these goods are not deduced, demonstrated, or derived from prior premises, they provide a set of self-evident or *per se nota* primary precepts from which all other precepts of the natural law may be derived. Because these primary precepts or basic goods are self-evident, natural law theorizing need not wait on the findings of anthropologists and philosophers of human nature.[1]

A rival school of natural law ethicists, comprised of such thinkers as Russell Hittinger, Ralph McInerny, Henry Veatch and Anthony Lisska, rejects the claims of Finnis and his colleagues for the autonomy of natural law

1. For major statements and defenses of this position see John Finnis, *Natural Law and Natural Rights* (Oxford: Oxford University Press, 1980); Germain Grisez, *The Way of the Lord Jesus*, vol. 1, *Christian Moral Principles* (Chicago: Franciscan Herald Press, 1983); Robert P. George, "Recent Criticism of Natural Law Theory," *University of Chicago Law Review* 55 (1988), pp. 1371-1429.

ethics over and against the philosophy of human nature.[2] According to these thinkers, to deny the dependence of natural law theory on philosophical anthropology would be to take the "natural" out of natural law.[3] Such critics are highly skeptical concerning the purported self-evidence of Finnis's basic goods, and they contend that Finnis and his colleagues are driven to such dubious claims primarily because of their acceptance of the naturalistic fallacy, which once accepted, is thought to preclude one from adopting the sounder method of deriving the natural law from conclusions drawn from the philosophy of human nature.

Although the term "naturalistic fallacy" was originally coined by G.E. Moore to refer to what he took to be the error of defining "goodness" in terms of some natural property such as "pleasure," "happiness," or "that which is conducive to evolutionary survival," the term has most often been used by contemporary philosophers to refer to the different claim, at least as old as Hume, that there is a fundamental logical distinction between *is* and *ought*, *fact* and *value*, *description* and *prescription*, such that one cannot validly deduce the latter from a set of premises consisting only of the former. So understood, the naturalistic fallacy is just a case of the more general logical rule that a valid conclusion cannot introduce something not in the premises. Opponents of natural law theory have relished (while its defenders have worried over) the fact that natural law theory might be vulnerable to the naturalistic fallacy insofar as it claims to derive ethical norms from a purely theoretical or descriptive account of human nature. Indeed, in a well-known section of his landmark book, *Natural Law and Natural Rights*, Finnis recognizes the naturalistic fallacy as the most common objection to natural law theory. He considers whether natural lawyers have shown that they can derive ethical norms from facts and responds in the negative: "They have not, nor do they need to, nor did the classical exponents of the theory dream of attempting

2. See Russell Hittinger, *A Critique of the New Natural Law Theory* (Notre Dame, Indiana: University of Notre Dame Press, 1987); Ralph McInerny, "The Principles of Natural Law," *American Journal of Jurisprudence* 25 (1980), pp. 1-15; Henry Veatch, "Natural Law and the 'IS' – 'OUGHT' Question: Queries to Finnis and Grisez," in *Swimming Against the Current in Contemporary Philosophy* (Washington, D.C.: The Catholic University of America Press, 1990), pp. 293-311; Anthony J. Lisska, *Aquinas's Theory of Natural Law: An Analytic Reconstruction* (Oxford: Oxford University Press, 1996).

3. Hence, Veatch asks "How can the enterprise of natural law ethics be anything other than an effort to find some sort of basis for morals and ethics in nature itself, and thus in the facts of nature?" see "Queries to Finnis and Grisez," p. 294. And Hittinger asserts, "Natural law ... obviously entails a commitment to law as in some way 'natural,' and nature as in some way normative." See *Critique of the New Natural Law Theory*, p. 8.

any such derivation."[4] He goes on to insist, "It is simply not true that any form of natural law theory of morals entails the belief that propositions about man's duties and obligations can be inferred from propositions about his nature."[5]

Finnis's critics have taken these passages as evidence that he espouses the self-evidence of the basic goods primarily because he accepts the naturalistic fallacy and believes that it rules out deriving the natural law from a methodologically prior philosophical anthropology.[6] In response, these critics have argued that the naturalistic fallacy itself rests on a mistake—that there is, in fact, no genuine fallacy in deducing an *ought* from an *is*, a *prescription* from a *description*. Hence, there is no need to resort to the claim that the basic goods are self-evident, since one can quite validly derive them from a true theoretical account of human nature.

The following discussion examines the naturalistic fallacy and its relevance to natural law methodology. Section One distinguishes two different kinds of *oughts* that one might attempt to derive from an *is*, and two different kinds of natural law theories, distinguished by reference to the kinds of *oughts* that make up the natural law precepts of those theories. Section Two argues that, although this point is seldom noticed, whether or not there is a genuine fallacy in deducing an *ought* from a set of exclusively descriptive premises depends on what kind of *ought* one seeks to deduce. One can quite easily deduce a *conditional ought* from a set of exclusively descriptive premises, but attempts by McInerny, Veatch and Lisska fail to show how one can deduce a *categorical ought* from such premises. Finally, Section Three draws out the implications of this conclusion for natural law methodology, arguing that, although acknowledging the naturalistic fallacy has significant consequences for natural law, it does not, as is often assumed, preclude one from inferring the content of natural law from a methodologically prior philosophical anthropology.[7]

---

4. Finnis, *Natural Law and Natural Rights*, p. 33.
5. Ibid.
6. See Veatch's "Queries to Finnis and Grisez," esp. pp. 294-95. See also Lisska's *Aquinas's Theory of Natural Law*, esp. pp. 157-63.
7. As intimated above, the chief participants in this discussion take themselves to be working in the Thomistic tradition—indeed, both camps take themselves to be the true heirs of Aquinas. Consequently, their treatments of these matters oftentimes include interpretation of Aquinas's texts alongside analysis of the issues for their own sake. The temptation is always there to interpret Aquinas's intentions according to one's own views or to substitute Aquinas's authority where one's own arguments need further development or precision. In what follows, I resist the temptation to engage in Thomistic exegesis, and concentrate solely on the philosophical questions at hand.

Two Kinds of *Oughts*

The *locus classicus* for the naturalistic fallacy are some remarks by Hume in Book III of his *Treatise of Human Nature*:

> In every system of morality, which I have hitherto met with, I have always remarked, that the author proceeds for some time in the ordinary way of reasoning, and establishes the being of a God, or makes observations concerning human affairs; when of a sudden I am surprised to find, that instead of the usual copulations of propositions, *is*, and *is not,* I meet with no proposition that is not connected with an *ought*, or an *ought not*. This change is imperceptible; but is, however, of the last consequence. For as this *ought*, or *ought not*, expresses some new relation or affirmation, 'tis necessary that … a reason should be given, for what seems altogether inconceivable, how this new relation can be a deduction from the others, which are entirely different from it.[8]

What is this "new relation" or "affirmation" expressed by the words *ought* or *ought not*, yet absent from propositions stating what *is* or *is not* the case? Hume neglects to tell us. But I will offer the following suggestion: Most generally it seems that these words, *ought* and *ought not*, express the *necessity* that some action be undertaken by the agent or agents to whom the *ought* is addressed.

So far so good. But a moment's reflection makes us realize that there are different ways in which an action can be necessary for an agent to perform. A teenage boy announces to his father that he wishes to take his girlfriend to the prom in a limousine. The father advises his son, "Boy, you *ought* to start saving your allowance." Clearly, the necessity of the action expressed by this *ought* is conditioned on the teenager's antecedent desire to take a limousine to the prom. Take away the desire and you take away the *ought*. Such conditional *oughts* express the necessity of a means to an end. Sometimes, as in the example above, there are a variety of means for accomplishing the same end; sometimes there is only one means of accomplishment. In the former case, no single action will be *the* one necessary means, although some action will be necessary, and if we knew all the possible means for achieving the end desired, we could express disjunctively what the agent in question ought to do. For example, the father could tell his son that he ought to save his allowance, *or* get a part-time job, *or* ask for the limousine rental as a birthday gift, etc.

---

8. David Hume, *Treatise of Human Nature* (Buffalo, New York: Prometheus Books, 1992), p. 469.

Our example of a conditional ought is trivial, but it need not be. In fact, it would be possible to develop a natural law theory in which all the precepts of the natural law had the *ratio* of conditional oughts. In a series of lectures in which she aims to defend the Church's ban on artificial contraception, for instance, Janet Smith gives a "three-minute course" on natural law in which she presents the natural law approach to ethics as follows: "Natural law says that if you want things to prosper, you have to use them in accordance with their nature."[9] She then goes on to examine, in more detail, human nature and, in particular, the nature of human sexuality and marriage. She employs a variety of different techniques, ranging from an analysis of the two-fold purpose of the conjugal act and the inevitable consequences of thwarting or severing those purposes, to citing statistical data showing the relationship between pre-marital sex and subsequent divorce rates and between the use of natural family planning and marital longevity; from asking her audience to engage in a number of thought experiments, to recounting as anecdotal evidence stories from her personal experience or the experience of friends and acquaintances. In the end, she concludes that engaging in sex before or in artificial contraception within marriage is inimical to the prospering and happiness of marriage. The moral is clear. If you want a happy marriage, you *ought not* engage in premarital sex or in artificial contraception. Such activity is, according to the natural law, inimical to the flourishing of the marital enterprise.

Smith's presentation of the natural law in general and her defense of the prohibition on artificial contraception in particular construe natural law precepts as having the character of conditional oughts. One ought not use artificial contraception, if one desires a happy marriage. Take away the desire and you take away the ought. One can imagine a systematic derivation of natural law precepts that moves from the fact that all human beings by nature desire happiness, to the demonstration that, in order to be happy given the natures we have, human beings must pursue certain activities and refrain from others, to a whole list of things that human beings ought and ought not do. The precepts on such a natural law theory would have the character of conditional oughts. Notice, however, that this fact by itself would not make such precepts subjective or merely relative to personal interests. Unlike the desire of the teenager who wanted to ride in a limousine, the desire to be happy, as well as the means of achieving it, would be universal and necessary. Such precepts would, therefore, be universal and necessary—and hence they would

9. Janet E. Smith, "Contraception, Why Not" (One More Soul, 1999).

enjoy two properties that many moralists have thought essential to any maxim that could count as a genuine moral law. The challenge for such a natural law theory, however, would be to show that it could generate precepts proscribing all those things that we know to be unjust. On an ethics comprised of strictly conditional oughts, the only reason I ought to do or refrain from doing anything is because it is a necessary means or obstacle to *my happiness*, which *I desire*. It is fairly easy to see how premarital sex and artificial contraception could be obstacles to a happy marriage, and hence, that I ought not engage in such activities given my desire to be happy.[10] But there are other acts that we normally take to be wrong where it is not clear how the performance of them would be inimical to my happiness. What happens, for example, when that required for my own happiness conflicts or seems to conflict with that required for the happiness of another? Suppose that one of the activities in which we need to engage in order to be happy is the pursuit of knowledge, and suppose I am a doctor, curious about the effects of certain toxins on the human immune system. Assuming that I can get away with it (perhaps the government will even fund my research), is there any reason I ought not test the effects of such toxins on some of my patients? In order to proscribe such activities, a natural law theory comprised of conditional oughts would have to show that one of the ends I must pursue in order to attain my own happiness is the happiness of others. While not necessarily impossible, such would be a difficult task, particularly without recourse to revelation.

But apart from this difficulty, some will not be satisfied with a natural law theory comprised of conditional oughts, because they believe a genuine moral law or obligation cannot be conditioned on any prior desire of the agent, regardless of whether that desire happens to be the universal desire for happiness and irrespective of the fact that such oughts would direct one to universal and necessary means of attaining that happiness.[11] On the contrary, some will seek in a natural law theory to discover certain acts which ought to be done or ought to be avoided regardless of the agent's

---

10. My point is not that such activities are just obviously inimical to a happy marriage—that Smith's claims are uncontroversial. Rather, my point is that it is clear how such activities might have a bearing on my marriage and hence could be related negatively to my own happiness. There are other activities we take to be immoral, however, where it would appear more difficult to show how they might be obstacles to my own happiness, even if they are clearly obstacles to the happiness of another.

11. "Ought nots" on such a theory would, of course, direct one *away from* activities incompatible with the happiness one desires.

desires. Some will want to say, for example, that one ought not engage in artificial contraception, irrespective of whether one desires a happy marriage. What such a theory seeks, therefore, is a set of oughts expressing a different kind of necessity—the unconditional necessity that the agents to whom they are addressed perform or refrain from performing certain actions. We might call these *unconditioned* or *categorical oughts*, since they express a necessity to act, unconditioned by antecedent desire.

Contemporary natural law theorists have lacked sufficient clarity concerning whether they seek conditional or categorical oughts as natural law precepts. This situation is unfortunate not only because one's choice in this regard makes for a significantly different natural law theory with significantly different logics, challenges, and implications, but because the methodology for deriving natural law precepts will have to be different in each case. This point can be appreciated only when we have come to realize that whether one can deduce an *ought* from an *is* depends on which kind of ought one seeks to deduce.

Deducing *Ought* from *Is*

McInerny and Veatch have criticized Finnis and Grisez for the scrupulous care they take to avoid committing the naturalistic fallacy. According to McInerny, such scruples have "a certain dated charm" about them,[12] while Veatch chalks up this concern to their understandable, if unfortunate, "Oxbridge superstitions."[13] Both McInerny and Veatch attempt to deflate Finnis and Grisez's concerns about the naturalistic fallacy, McInerny by offering examples of what he takes to be a valid inference from *is* to *ought*, and Veatch by developing the account of human nature that he thinks would make such an inference possible. As we shall see, the proposals of both McInerny and Veatch remain ambiguous.

McInerny suggests that the following inference is valid:

1) Joe weighs two hundred and fifty pounds.
2) It is not healthy to be overweight.
3) Therefore, Joe *ought* to go on a diet.[14]

However, all we need do is ask whether McInerny intends the conclusion to be a conditional or categorical ought to realize that something is missing in

12. McInerny, "Principles of Natural Law," p. 8.
13. Veatch, "Queries to Finnis and Grisez," p. 295.
14. McInerny, "Principles of Natural Law," p. 12.

the premises. To generate a conditional ought, McInerny needs the additional premise "Joe desires to be healthy." On the condition that Joe desires to be healthy and assuming that Joe needs to go on a diet to satisfy this desire, Joe ought to go on a diet. Take away the desire and you take away the ought. Notice that we generated this conditional ought from exclusively factual, descriptive or *is* premises: "Joe weighs two hundred and fifty pounds," "It is not healthy to be overweight" and "Joe desires to be healthy."

If McInerny intends his conclusion to be a categorical ought, however, he will need a different additional premise, such as "One ought to pursue one's health." And if we should ask whether this new premise is a conditional or categorical ought, the answer is clear. It must be a categorical ought in order to yield a categorical ought in the conclusion. For if "Joe ought to pursue his health" only on the antecedent condition that, for instance, Joe desires happiness, then that "Joe ought to go on a diet" would also be conditioned on that desire. But the whole point of a categorical ought is that it is not so conditioned. It follows that one cannot deduce a categorical ought except from a set of premises that itself contains at least one categorical ought. Is there a fallacy involved in deriving an ought from a set of exclusively factual or descriptive premises? That depends on whether you want a conditional or categorical ought as your conclusion.[15]

While McInerny attempts to show us by example that an *ought* can be deduced from an *is*, Veatch attacks the naturalistic fallacy by arguing that a proper, teleological understanding of nature renders unproblematic such inferences. In a more recent book, Anthony Lisska seconds Veatch's strategy. According to Veatch and Lisska, proponents of the naturalistic fallacy tend to conceive of an essence or nature geometrically, as a static collection of properties, complete in and of themselves. As a consequence, any value or ought would have to be understood as relating to such an essence extrinsically, as an addition imposed from the outside, as it were. Given this understanding of essence, it is no surprise that philosophers have thought it a fallacy to deduce oughts from a list of the properties making up human nature, for there are no oughts within the ontology itself.[16]

15. It might be argued that McInerny's premise (2) above, "It is not healthy to be overweight," is not simply an *is* or *factual* premise, but is already *evaluative*. It is not my concern to debate whether or not "health" should be considered an evaluative concept. The question is whether premise (2) is sufficient to generate an "ought" and if so, what kind? The fact that the question "what kind?" arises suggests that premise (2) is not sufficient of itself to generate an "ought." Rather, one needs a premise concerning the desires of the agent or a premise asserting that health ought to be pursued regardless of antecedent desire.

16. See Veatch, "Queries to Finnis and Grisez," pp. 301-02. See also Lisska, *Aquinas's Theory of Natural Law*, pp. 161-63, pp. 195-201.

Veatch and Lisska propose, by contrast, that human nature be conceived of, not statically, but dynamically, as a set of dispositional properties tending toward certain natural ends or completions. These ends are then identified as the goods proper to human nature. As Joseph Koterski explains, describing our nature in terms of dispositions towards a set range of goods "does not involve adding any value to a fact, but only of finding values already in the natural outcome of the fact that is the disposition itself." Since human nature "already includes potentiality and development within the ontology, ... there already is an *ought* within the *is*."[17] Consequently, so Veatch and Lisska argue, there is no fallacy involved in inferring an ought from the content of human nature thus understood.[18] In Veatch's words,

> With this, then, is it not clear that an "ought" has been directly introduced into our very account of man and of human nature? ... Just as it is impossible to determine what a human being, just as a human being, really is in fact, without determining what he might be or could be—i.e., without taking account of a man's potentialities and the actualities toward which those potentialities are oriented—so also it is no less impossible to determine, or really even adequately to state, what a human being is, without making reference to what he ought to be—i.e., without making reference to that natural end or fulfillment or good which it is incumbent upon any human being (by nature) to try to become. Here, clearly, there is no dubious inference from "is" to "ought" ... the very "is" of human nature already has its "ought" contained within it.[19]

Veatch's use of "incumbent" suggests that it is a categorical or unconditioned ought that he believes to be contained within the very facts of human nature. But have Veatch and Lisska shown that a teleological conception of nature enables us to circumvent the naturalistic fallacy? In my estimate, their solution turns on an ambiguous or equivocal use of the word "good." "Good" can be defined to mean either

> 1) The "end" of a natural potency, appetite, inclination, tendency or process of development;
>
> or,
>
> 2) that which ought to be done or pursued.

17. Joseph Koterski, S.J., "A Recent Controversy in Natural Law Theory," (paper presented at a conference entitled "Degrees of Truth: Current Controversies Concerning Aquinas," New York University, April 30, 1999).
    18. See Veatch, "Queries to Finnis and Grisez," pp. 302-05. See also Lisska, *Aquinas's Theory of Natural Law*, pp. 195-201.
    19. Veatch, "Queries to Finnis and Grisez," p. 303.

In developing their teleological accounts of human nature, Veatch and Lisska define "good" in terms of the first meaning. Hence, Lisska argues that "the 'good' is nothing more than the development of the process structured by the nature of the set of dispositions," and that "it is incoherent to ask about an end, as an actualized disposition, whether or not it is good. It is good analytically, because that is the definition of the concept of 'good.'"[20] And Veatch proclaims that "good" should be understood "as just the actuality toward which a given potentiality is ordered, as to its proper fulfillment or completion or actuality."[21] So Veatch and Lisska, at any rate, start off explicating "good" according to the first definition, and in this sense they appear entitled to say that the "good" is contained within the very facts of human nature as they understand it.

Yet to say of something, for example, knowledge, that it is good according to the second definition of "good" clearly adds something to saying that it is good according to the first definition. Veatch and Lisska appear to want to argue that because knowledge is good in the first sense, by being an end or actualization of a natural human potency or inclination, we can validly deduce that human beings ought to pursue knowledge. But this reasoning is fallacious.[22] How can we move from the recognition that

a) knowledge is the actualization or end of a natural human potency or inclination
to
b) human beings ought to pursue knowledge?

If we want to deduce (b) from (a) we need an additional premise in the form of a categorical ought such as "Human beings ought to pursue those ends to which they are naturally inclined." Alternatively, we could move from (a) to (b) not discursively, by way of deductive inference, but through an additional, non-discursive, non-inferential act of insight or understanding that enables us to grasp knowledge, a good in the first sense, as also a good in the second sense, namely, something that ought to be pursued. This latter method, involving an act of insight or understanding rather than a deductive inference from prior premises, is the one favored by Finnis and Grisez. Neither method, however, would be guilty of the naturalistic fallacy.

20. Lisska, *Aquinas's Theory of Natural Law*, p. 199.
21. Veatch, "Queries to Finnis and Grisez," p. 309.
22. Alasdair MacIntyre, in his review of Lisska's book, offers a similar critique. See Alasdair MacIntyre, "Natural Law Reconsidered," *International Philosophical Quarterly* XXXVII, no. 145 (March 1997), pp. 95-99.

Notice, also, that our rejecting Veatch and Lisska's strategy for circumventing the naturalistic fallacy does not in any way commit us to denying Veatch's contention that one cannot adequately state what a human being is without making reference to what he (categorically) ought to be. We need only deny that one can reach this knowledge about what he ought to do or be by way of deductive inference from premises that do not include a categorical ought.

Consequences for Natural Law Methodology

The concern not to infer from *is* to *ought* is not "a symptom of over-fastidiousness," as McInerny suggests, nor is it "due to one's taking the terms 'deduction' and 'inference' in a somewhat straitened and overly technical sense," as Veatch proposes.[23] The concern to avoid the naturalistic fallacy does not *by itself* reflect an aversion to authentic metaphysics, much less to a teleological conception of nature. Rather, it reflects an interest in self-consciously articulate and careful argumentation, argumentation that makes explicit its premises and how those premises support a conclusion. Insofar as natural law theory seeks to be articulate in its argumentation, it behooves natural law theorists to consider the relevance of the naturalistic fallacy to natural law methodology.[24]

The naturalistic fallacy pertains to logic, and as such, it is relevant primarily to the logical and epistemological question confronting any natural law theory, namely, how to justify or derive the natural law precepts. As intimated above, a crucial decision to be made at the outset is whether one's precepts will consist of conditional or categorical oughts. In neither case, however, does recognition of the naturalistic fallacy prevent one from deriving the primary precepts or basic goods from a methodologically prior philosophical anthropology, as many have supposed. The impression that it does results, I suspect, from Finnis's acknowledging the naturalistic fal-

---

23. See McInerny, "Principles of Natural Law," p. 12, and Veatch, "Queries to Finnis and Grisez," p. 298.

24. McInerny derides the problem of moving from *is* to *ought* as "one of the most pointless controversies of modern moral philosophy." The logic of McInerny's solution to the problem, however, is clearly based on conditioning the oughts of the natural law on every agent's antecedent desire for fulfillment. Although there is much to be said for McInerny's approach, I think he overlooks the fact that many (whether rightly or wrongly) want their "oughts" to be of the unconditioned variety, in which case concerns about the naturalistic fallacy are far from pointless. See Ralph McInerny, *Ethica Thomistica* (Washington, D.C.: The Catholic University of America Press, 1997), p. 37.

lacy in Chapter Two of *Natural Law and Natural Rights* together with his overly sweeping proscriptions against deducing "ethical norms from facts" or "man's duties and obligations … from propositions about his nature," along with his subsequent choice to arrive at the basic goods through insight rather than inference.[25] We have seen, however, that if one seeks conditional oughts for one's precepts, the naturalistic fallacy is completely irrelevant: one can deduce a conditional ought from a set of exclusively factual or descriptive premises. Hence, one can base these precepts on a philosophical anthropology, deriving them from propositions about necessary means to or constituents of human happiness together with the assertion that happiness is something all men desire. The most serious challenge for such a natural law theory will be to show how many of those actions which the natural law has traditionally been thought to prohibit, such as stealing, can be reduced to negative conditions on the happiness each agent antecedently desires for himself. But one need not worry about inferring an *ought* from an *is*.

The naturalistic fallacy does become relevant, however, if one seeks categorical oughts for one's natural law precepts. We have seen that one cannot deduce a categorical ought except from a set of premises that itself contains a categorical ought. Yet even this realization does not prevent us from inferring our precepts from premises supplied by a teleological conception of human nature. The following is a valid argument, deducing a categorical ought *from* an anthropological premise *together with* a categorical ought:

> 1) Human beings ought to pursue those ends to which they are naturally inclined.
> 2) Knowledge is the actualization of a natural human potency or inclination.
> 3) Therefore, human beings ought to pursue knowledge.

Clearly, the argument never gets off the ground without the philosophy of human nature. The conclusion is based directly on the findings of a methodologically prior philosophical anthropology.

In a subsequent essay, Finnis and Grisez do a better job of clarifying (although in language somewhat different than my own) the precise consequences of acknowledging the naturalistic fallacy:

> We have never said that one cannot pass from metaphysical and/or factual truths *together with principles of practical reasoning* to normative conclusions. Our point rather was that there can be no valid deduction of a normative conclusion without a

25. Finnis, *Natural Law and Natural Rights*, p. 33.

normative principle, and thus that *first* practical principles cannot be derived from metaphysical speculations.[26]

This last point raises an important consideration for any natural law theory that seeks categorical oughts for its precepts. If one cannot inferentially justify a categorical ought except by means of deduction from a set of premises that itself contains a categorical ought, it follows that there must be at least one first categorical ought that does not receive its justification by means of deductive inference from prior premises. This ought would have the character of a first principle, and as such, it would have to be self-evident—"self-evident" meaning not that it is intuitively manifest or clear and distinct, but that given sufficient reflection, it could be understood to be true without being formally demonstrated.

Acknowledging the naturalistic fallacy has the following consequence, therefore, for the methodology of any natural law theory seeking categorical oughts as precepts: such a theory will need to propose at least one self-evident and indemonstrable first categorical ought as a first principle. As far as the naturalistic fallacy or the question of validity goes, it does not matter what that first categorical ought is. Finnis and Grisez propose a whole list of basic goods to play the role of first principles. Because these basic goods, precisely in order to play this role, must be self-evident and indemonstrable, Finnis and Grisez deny that they are inferred from premises supplied by philosophical anthropology.[27] But as far as the naturalistic

---

26. John Finnis and Germain Grisez, "The Basic Principles of Natural Law: A Reply to Ralph McInerny," *American Journal of Jurisprudence* 26 (1981), p. 24.

27. To say that the basic goods are not inferred from premises supplied by philosophical anthropology is to make an epistemological claim about how we come to know these goods, not a metaphysical claim. Indeed, that the goods are what they are may be grounded in or explained by human nature, even if we do not come to know them by way of inference from premises supplied solely by a descriptive account of human nature. On this view, what is prior in the order of being is not necessarily prior in the order of knowing. In fact, if we agree with Veatch that an adequate account of human nature includes what human beings ought to be or do, we might say that the non-inferential act of understanding by which we come to know the basic goods is part of the process by which we come to our account of human nature. That is to say, rather than deducing the basic goods from an already worked out and completed philosophical anthropology, it may be that we develop our philosophical anthropology on the basis of our non-inferential insight or understanding that certain goods ought to be pursued. For a defense of this possibility, see Robert P. George, "Natural Law and Human Nature," in *Natural Law Theory: Contemporary Essays*, ed. Robert P. George (Oxford: Oxford University Press, 1992), pp. 33-6. See also John Finnis, "Natural Law and the 'Is'—'Ought' Question: An Invitation to Professor Veatch," *Catholic Lawyer* 26 (1981), pp. 270-72.

fallacy goes, one could postulate a different first categorical ought, whereby the basic goods *were* derived from the philosophy of human nature. One might, for example, propose the above premise (1) as one's first principle: "Human beings ought to pursue those ends to which they are naturally inclined." In either case, it will be incumbent upon the natural law theorist to offer a non-inferential justification of the proposed first principle, one which will most likely follow the normal procedure of showing that rejecting the principle leads to absurd consequences.[28]

It is not my purpose here to adjudicate between these two alternatives, nor even between the choice of a natural law theory based on conditional versus categorical oughts. I merely intend to show what the logically viable alternatives are for working out a natural law methodology. There has been less clarity than one might wish within contemporary discussion of the naturalistic fallacy and its relevance to natural law theory. This paper will have achieved its aim if it has left these matters less confused than it found them, even if it does so by more clearly exposing the errors of those, like myself, who think there is still something left to Hume's warnings about *is* and *ought*.

28. For a discussion of how this justification might proceed, see George, "Recent Criticisms of Natural Law Theory," pp. 1410-14.

Capital Punishment or Prudential Execution?

James P. Mesa *and* John R. Traffas

The photograph of Pope John Paul II sitting in an Italian prison cell with Mehmet Ali Agca, his would-be assassin, is a powerful image and example that invites us to reflect on how we are to live the Gospel. How concretely are we to follow Jesus' admonition to forgive those who trespass against us and to pray for those who persecute us? Is a will to forgive significant only for those directly involved, victim and assailant; or is there an implicit public and political meaning in such an offer of reconciliation? The Pope's personal experience with an attempted assassination and his life-long concern with defending the dignity of each person have produced a new challenge.

The Holy Father's appeals for mercy for capital offenders are forms of personal intervention into the realm of public policy on criminal justice, yet they do not lay down a thorough theoretical challenge to the fundamental right of political authority to employ the death penalty. However, the encyclical *Evangelium Vitae* (1995), certain episcopal pronouncements, and relevant revisions of the *Catechism of the Catholic Church* (1997), all present an apparent radical departure from the Church's centuries-old defense of the death penalty. Such a shift can be the cause of confusion for many Catholics who may see a relativist onslaught on fundamental, unchanging moral principles. Thus it is important to get a sense of the nature of this change and explore the possible conditions that justify it.

The recent thorough scholarly work of Steven A. Long and the widely discussed article by Avery Cardinal Dulles, provide a reasonable basis for claiming that the change is not a foundational shift from traditional basic moral principles, but a reconsideration of how they apply in the world today.[1] We do not intend to give an unassailable defense of the change nor to engage in a "text-war," citing Scripture, Church Fathers, or Councils in defense of the change. Our purpose is limited to suggesting ways of understanding the reasonableness of the Church's prudential focus.

We need to keep in mind the profound difference between moral absolutes prohibiting acts that are inherent violations of human dignity and those prohibitions that are conditional.[2] Some prohibitions are conditional because they involve matters that are by their nature good but inappropriate under certain conditions. Thus the marital embrace is a noble and worthy good, but it would certainly be out of order for the newlyweds to exercise their right with gusto on the altar steps after the priest has just declared them man and wife.

Indeed, the new restriction of the use of the death penalty is breathtaking in its sweep, but it is clearly not an absolute condemnation and prohibition of it. The revised teaching maintains that because of new "concrete conditions," the licitness of its *use* is admitted though limited to very rare cases.[3] Thus the Church's teaching on the death penalty deals with a *permissible* act. This is in marked contrast with the teaching concerning abortion and contraception, which are intrinsically evil and must be prohibited absolutely. But the death penalty is not described as intrinsically evil and therefore cannot be prohibited absolutely. Because fundamental principles are not being rejected, those who have urged the Church to accommodate her teaching on abortion and contraception to changing concrete conditions in the modern world, will find no comfort in this accommodation.

Sin is first and foremost an offense against God. All such offenses merit punishment, but only God truly knows the seriousness of the offense and its proper punishment. Judgment and punishment are properly God's alone. The Christian Faith traces the true gravity of sin to that moment in pre-history when the penalty of death was placed on us all. This profound character of sin and its effects sets the stage for the drama of Redemption. And though primarily an offense against God, sin also offends persons— the sinner himself and others. The natural good of each individual person and the common good require stable, orderly community life. And so every

1. Steven A. Long, *"Evangelium Vitae, St. Thomas Aquinas, and the Death Penalty,"* *The Thomist* 63 (1999), pp. 511-52; and Avery Cardinal Dulles, "Catholicism and Capital Punishment," *First Things*, 112 (April 2001), pp. 30-5.

2. At *Summa Theologiae* I-II, 94, a. 4 and 5, St. Thomas says that secondary precepts of natural law may apply only *"ut in pluribus"* (in most cases), and that they may be changed under rare circumstances.

3. *Catechism of the Catholic Church* (London: Geoffrey Chapman, 1997), 2267, p. 488. Hereafter *CCC*.

sin has a community dimension at least in that it harms others directly or indirectly. In the latter case, a so-called private sin corrupts the character of the individual and weakens his ability to promote the common good as he ought.

Further, it is a given that the good order of any society requires persons with authority to govern and to legislate. The Church has always understood that public officials ultimately have their authority from God. In a truly just civil society, only those sins that offend public order would be designated crimes, that is, come under the scrutiny of its law and its public officials. Even so, not all offenses against public order would be crimes, for to include all such sins would require an impossibly vast and intrusive policing system. As such, the practical determination of what is to be prohibited to and required of its citizens is among the most difficult matters facing civil society.

Good order need not be, nor can it be, perfect order. The judgment of those who govern must constantly engage a welter of changing conditions—economic, technological, cultural and so on—which at best render such decisions as reasonable but never certain.

Certainly not all sins are crimes in civil law. And given human fallibility, not all defined crimes are indeed sins: many a good citizen claims that he has done no wrong when cited by an officer of the law. But when they are crimes, sins merit punishment through the system of penal law. The seriousness of sin as such, however, is neither diminished nor increased because it is also a crime. An unfortunate soul may be among the damned for an unrepented sin that was not treated as a crime. But when a sin *is* a crime, the judgment of its seriousness and the determination of the punishment for it must be made in *concrete conditions* by those who have responsibility for the governance of the community. The Final Judgment is indeed God's, but public officials, who have their authority from God, must exercise it for the common good here and now. It is important to be reminded of these simple points in order to appreciate the modification in the Church's teaching on the administration of the death penalty.

Further, we need to affirm what may be offensive to the modern ear— *punishment is a good.* Punishment for crime is a good not only for the community but also for the sinner. However, its *societal efficacy* as means to remedy, rehabilitation, and reconciliation is dependent upon the good will of all involved. As a member of the community who seeks to redress the evil he has done, the criminal should acknowledge his guilt, accept the punishment, and resolve to amend his life. For their part, the members of the community should accept the judgment and actions of the authorities, and to the extent determined by them, be reconciled with the criminal. Punishment, which is directed to redressing the disorder caused by crime, is dependent upon the proper will of all those concerned. This unity of good will is more likely to occur where civil authority is respected, the laws are seen to be just, and the administrators of justice are held to be virtuous—character, like truth, also matters.

Aquinas's synthesis of the Catholic tradition on capital punishment in the *Summa Theologiae* and the *Summa Contra Gentiles* has stood intact since the thirteenth century. Again, it is not our purpose to review the particulars of that tradition. But there is an element in his thinking that should be noted. Aquinas takes the death penalty seriously because he views civil society to be an exact analogy to the society of the blessed and of the *viatores* (those on the way). Each society has its own informing principle: charity is that of the society of the blessed;[4] concord is the common good that informs human society.[5] Some offenses against charity or concord are remedied by ordinary punishments: the temporal punishment of Purgatory makes the sinner fit company for the blessed, while fines, imprisonment, or corporal disciplines aim to restore the offender to civil society.

But sometimes, something more radical is required—if you will, something very anti-radix: an uprooting, a total banishment from society. Natural equity, according to Aquinas, demands "that each person be deprived of the good against which he acts."[6] Thus, "he who sins against the ultimate end and against charity, whereby the society of the blessed exists and also that of those on the way toward happiness, should be punished eternally,"[7] while "according to civil justice, he who offends against the state is deprived completely of association with the state, either by death or by perpetual exile."[8] Imprisonment should be seen as either temporary or permanent exile from the community though the offender still remains under its power. If the offense merits banishment from one's community but does not render the offender totally unfit for human association, exile to a foreign land could serve as remedy. But it would be irresponsible to burden another society with one who has been judged unfit for human association; the death penalty is the ultimate social banishment. Banishment from the garden was the primordial exile and hell is the final one.

4. *On the Truth of the Catholic Faith. Summa Contra Gentiles. Book III: Providence, Part II*, trans. Vernon J. Bourke (New York: Image Books, 1956), 144, 4, p. 215. Hereafter *SCG*.
5. *SCG*, III, 146, 4, p. 220.
6. Ibid., III, 144, 4, p. 215.
7. Ibid.
8. Ibid.

Thomas Aquinas's commonly accepted stating of the argument for capital punishment is challenged in the modern era when the very understanding of human nature shifts. The first thorough theoretical attack on the moral permissibility of capital punishment came in 1764 from Cesare Beccaria.[9] His position was predicated on a thoroughly Hobbesian theory of society, according to which humans leave the danger and instability of the state of nature by surrendering some of their claims to the civil state, wherein they find protection from nature. As the right not to be killed is an inviolable natural right, according to Beccaria, it may never be infringed by civil society through the invoking of the death penalty, even in the case of a murderer or other grave offender.

Beccaria and his progeny have an understanding of human nature and the nature of the state that is clearly irreconcilable with the Christian teaching about moral responsibility, the social nature of man, and the common good. Replacing the *common good* with *natural rights* as the principle informing civil society, they abandon the connection and continuation of civil society with its transcendent foundation and end in God. Thus they lose any sense of "manifesting the truth regarding the transcendent order of justice and the wickedness of the offense"[10] against it. In the latter half of the twentieth century, even the Church will adopt rights-based language, while attempting to give such language a thoroughly different meaning.

With Pope John XXIII and Vatican II, the tenor of the Church's social teaching changes significantly. Previously popes had dealt with and addressed aristocratic or monarchical rulers; after World War II and the demise of colonialism, the movement of equality and democracy was sweeping the world. At Vatican II, the Church asserts the naturalness of human sociality, consistent with the tradition of Aristotle through Aquinas. However, it anchors its social teaching, usually addressed "to all men of good will," not directly on the Word of God (which has authority only for those with religious faith), but on the teaching that the human person is "the origin, the subject and the purpose of all social institutions."[11] The common good is instrumentally "the sum of those conditions of social life which allow so-

9. For a discussion of Beccaria, see Walter Berns, *For Capital Punishment. Crime and the Morality of the Death Penalty* (New York: Basic Books, Inc., 1979), pp. 18-21.

10. Long, "*Evangelicum Vitae*, St. Thomas Aquinas, and the Death Penaly," p. 251. Commenting on *Summa Theologiae* I-II 87, a. 3, ad.2, Long (pp. 520-2) finds more than a deterrent effect in punishment: it may inspire many to recognize sources outside their wills which make intelligible not only the reason for avoiding punishment, but for acting virtuously.

11. *Pastoral Constitution on the Church in the Modern World* (*Gaudium et Spes*), in Walter M. Abbott, S.J., general editor, *The Documents of Vatican II* (New York: Herder and Herder, 1966), no. 25, p. 224. Hereafter *GS*.

cial groups and their individual members relatively thorough and ready access to their own fulfillment."[12] However, the common good "consists chiefly in the protection of the rights, and in the performance of the duties, of the human person,"[13] upon whose dignity as image of God all rights are ultimately based.[14]

The Vatican II shift to the human person is neither a shift to the isolated human individual, nor to an acceptance of a politics that looks only to the sum of individual wills. Pope John Paul II has attempted to correct aberrations in contemporary liberal democracies by referring to the common good as centered on the serving of the dignity of the human person. Thus in the encyclical *Centesimus Annus* (1991), he challenges the claim "that agnosticism and skeptical relativism are the philosophy and the basic attitude which correspond to democratic forms of political life."[15] The Church does not deny *"the legitimate autonomy of the democratic order"*[16] when it calls for political decision-making to be based upon the truth about man and the common good. The common good "is not simply the sum total of particular interests; rather it involves an assessment and integration of those interests on the basis of a balanced hierarchy of values; ultimately it demands a correct understanding of the dignity and rights of the person."[17]

The Pope's treatment of the death penalty in *Evangelium Vitae* (1995)[18] is different from Aquinas's, especially in its sense of the relevance of historical factors. The Pope notes[19] three historical changes that qualify the discussion of the death penalty. First, there is the fact of increasing opposition to its use both in the Church and in civil society. Second, there have been such "improvements in the organization of the penal system"—presumably, technological and juridical advances that make more successful the quarantining of vicious criminals from society—that cases absolutely requiring use of the death penalty "are very rare, if not practically nonexistent." Third, the Pope implies that the modern conception of the limited state, with an accompanying narrowly conceived end—public order (not

12. *GS*, 26, p, 225.

13. Declaration on Religious Freedom (*Dignitatis Humanae*), in Abbott, *The Documents of Vatican II*, pp. 683-84, no. 6. Hereafter *DH*.

14. Ibid. 2, p. 679.

15. *On the Hundredth Anniversary of Rerum Novarum* (*Centesimus Annus*), (Washington, D.C.: United States Catholic Conference, 1991), no. 46, p. 89. Hereafter *CA*.

16. *CA*, 47, p. 92.

17. Ibid.

18. *The Gospel of Life* (*Evangelium Vitae*), (New York: Times Books/Random House, 1995). Hereafter *EV*.

19. Ibid., 56, pp. 99-100.

the comprehensive common good)—might not justify an act as definitive as capital punishment.

Especially as interpreted by John Courtney Murray, S.J., the Vatican II *Declaration on Religious Freedom* had justified restrictions on religious freedom by government only in its defense of the public order.[20] Murray[21] distinguished government and civil society with respect to their varying ends and competencies. While civil society has as its end the common good, government exists for the care of the public order. The end of public order is justice (the safeguarding of human rights), the preservation of public peace (social harmony), and the promotion of public morality (respect for law and generally accepted mores). Constitutionally limited government is not a valid arbiter in questions of religious truth, according to Murray, because it simply lacks the competence to investigate such matters. Accordingly, it may not deny to the human person—the one whose human dignity lies in the inherence of the image of God—the freedom to pursue religious truth and other most profound human ends. Only if the practice of that pursuit harms the rights of others to pursue religious truth, or to live in social harmony, may the government restrict the actions of a citizen. Government may not dictate internal belief or religious practice; it may only guard against the harming of other citizens' rights to such immunity.

In *Evangelium Vitae*, Pope John Paul II implies that the death penalty violates the dignity of the human person, and is thus an overreaching on the part of limited government. The death penalty "must be viewed in the context of a system of penal justice ever more in line with human dignity and thus, in the end, with God's plan for man and society."[22] And further, given "the concrete conditions of the common good"[23] that obtain today, nothing should be done, even in the name of justice, to obscure the vision of that dignity.

It is well to ponder what might lie behind the Pope's phrase, "the concrete conditions of the common good." Conceivably the Pope has in mind especially the moral component of the common good, and especially the capacity—or incapacity—of contemporary humans to be aware of moral

    20. *DH*, 7, pp. 685-7.
    21. See, for example, Murray's discussion in, "Preface" and "The Declaration of Religious Freedom. A Moment in its Legislative History," in John Courtney Murray, S.J., ed., *Religious Freedom. An End and A Beginning* (New York: Macmillan and Company, 1966), pp. 7-11; 15-42.
    22. *EV,* 56, p. 99.
    23. Ibid., p. 100.

good and moral evil. While there was in Machiavelli and Nietzsche, for instance, a concerted philosophical effort to counter the very discrimination between good and evil, the Holy Father seems to be addressing the increasingly distorted popular moral imagination that concretely pervades the culture of death. Moral imagination is a rich but vague concept that was promoted especially by the late Russell Kirk. He warned against the modern tendency to reduce moral judgment to mere cold propositional thinking and recommended attending to the significant role of memories, emotions, appetites and habits that shape our moral perceptions. Moral imagination points to "a power of ethical perception which strides beyond the barriers of private experience and momentary events."[24]

A similar suspicion of mere propositional thinking is also found in Aquinas's accounts of the moral virtue and the role of prudence, a judgment of practical reason.[25] Prudence is reason's application of moral principles to concrete cases. The truth of the prudential judgment is grounded in the reality of the person in the existential situation. It is a properly-discerning-reason-in-action. Prudential insight requires the proper fusion of reason, appetites, and senses. The simultaneously properly-oriented-appetites provide focus for correct discernment of the situation and give impetus for proper action. This is in marked contrast with imprudence, and its distorted imagination, which fails to comprehend the real conditions of moral action. When moral imagination is disordered, reason is blinded and unable to receive the sweet clarity of reasoned argument.

In applying Kirk's understanding of moral imagination to the question of punishment, one must insist that an action or deprivation *must be seen as a punishment* to serve as punishment. Given the distortion in modern imagination, natural death is not seen as a penalty; nor is it seen as the tragic consequence of sin. The moment of death is not fraught with the anxiety of facing final judgment, since in the opinion of many contemporary humans there is none. When Christians sing "O death, where is thy sting," the dread of final judgment is tempered only by the hope in Christ's victory over

24. Russell Kirk, "The Perversity of Recent Fiction: Reflections on the Moral Imagination," in *Reclaiming a Patrimony: A Collection of Lectures by Russell Kirk* (Washington, D.C.: The Heritage Foundation, 1982), p. 46. William Kirkpatrick, in his work *Why Johnny Can't Tell Right from Wrong* (New York: Simon and Schuster, 1992), builds on this notion of moral imagination as it applies to moral education. Cf. esp. pp. 206-10. For a connection of moral imagination to the thought of Jacques Maritain, see James P. Mesa, "The Good, the Bad, and the Ugly: The Aesthetic in Moral Imagination," in *Beauty, Art, and the Polis*, ed. Alice Ramos, American Maritain Association (Washington, D.C.: The Catholic University of America Press, 2000), pp. 237-44.

25. See esp. *ST*, II-II, 47, 51.

death. But in the culture of death, imagination is being formed to see death as a solution. Abortion and euthanasia are the final solutions to inconveniences; one's own death, too, might be seen as a solution to the burden of existence. The death penalty is in danger of becoming the final solution to crime. The sting of death is washed away not by flowing waters of grace, but by a stream of words and images promising sweet oblivion. The sense of the transcendent, the holy fear of the numinous, is so reduced that the gravity of death is obscured and the true meaning of the death penalty loses efficacy. The general society no longer views the sinner/capital offender as banished from the community he has offended and returned to God to be dealt with as accords with divine justice or mercy.

There is one aspect in which the Church could be accused of contributing to the impoverishment of the moral imagination's sense of capital punishment. The Church's current teaching in the *Catechism*[26] associates the death penalty more with the principle of physical defense against threat than with the idea of punishment and the application of a transcendent standard of justice to concrete acts. In itself the use of defensive force is justified by the presence of an imminent threat to some fundamental good. It does not require a determination of the state of mind of the aggressor; it is not concerned with making judgments about the aggressor's personal guilt or sinfulness. Force is not so much punishment as that means which is necessary for reasonable defense. The principle of defense is a matter of natural law; it is very nearly an intuitive, self-evident principle that is accepted even by reasonable persons who reject the death penalty.[27]

The restricting of licit use of the death penalty strictly to situations of physical defense appears to be grounded in the concern to maintain reverence for life, even the life of a criminal, whenever possible. However, when the death penalty is justified only on the basis of its defensive service against physical harm, it might appear to be used strictly for utilitarian purposes. Authoritarian regimes especially are prone to using force internally because their legitimacy is open to such broad challenge. Further, authoritarian regimes are typically relatively impoverished, thus lacking in those "steady improvements in the organization of the penal system" which Pope John Paul II finds to militate against the need to employ the death penalty. Accordingly, whether in non-repressive liberal democracies which lack the imaginative means to view the death penalty against a transcendent horizon, or in repressive regimes which opportunistically use force to defend

26. *CCC*, 2263-7, pp. 487-88.
27. Ibid., 2264, p. 487.

the individual or group ruling for their own self-interest, it would perhaps be more accurate to dispense with language of capital punishment and speak rather of *prudential execution.*

Even in the few situations seen by *Evangelium Vitae* as justifying use of the death penalty, a prudential calculus is presupposed, inasmuch as there is an inverse relationship seen between occasions for the licit use of the death penalty and the aforementioned improvements in the organization of the penal system. The wealthier the nation, and the greater its ability to construct secure prisons for the worst offenders, the less it can justify employing the death penalty, according to this calculus.

Fyodor Dostoevsky's *The Brothers Karamazov* contains a scene in which punishment is discussed. During the Karamazovs's meeting with Fr. Zosima, it comes out that Ivan Karamazov authored a magazine article challenging a book on the relationship between Tsarist Russian ecclesiastical and civil courts. Ivan's motives in writing the article are suspect. While he appears to be a Westernized intellectual in many respects, perhaps even an atheist, his article is quite maximalist in its understanding of the Church. "Thus," Ivan says in explaining his article,

> it is not the Church that should seek a definite place for itself in the state, like "any social organization" or "organization of men for religious purposes" (as the author I was objecting to refers to the Church), but, on the contrary, every earthly state must eventually be wholly transformed into the Church and become nothing else but the Church, rejecting whichever of its aims are incompatible with those of the Church.[28]

Ivan himself applies his principle to the matter of punishment. "If everything became the Church, then the Church would excommunicate the criminal and the disobedient and not cut off their heads."[29] For a prisoner with faith, this excommunication would more compellingly lead him to confession of his guilt and reform than would the threat of execution. Fr. Zosima follows the thrust of Ivan's argument:

> If it were not for Christ's Church, indeed there would be no restraint on the criminal in his evildoing, and no punishment for it later, real punishment, that is, not a mechanical one ... the only frightening and appeasing punishment, which lies in the acknowledgment of one's own conscience.... If anything protects society even in our time, and even reforms the criminal himself and transforms him into a different

---

28. Fyodor Dostoevsky, *The Brothers Karamazov*, trans. and annotated Richard Pevear and Larrissa Volokhonsky (New York: Vintage Books, 1990), p. 62.

29. Ibid., p. 63.

person, again it is Christ's law alone, which manifest itself in the acknowledgement of one's own conscience.[30]

Father Zosima, the most revered elder of an Orthodox monastery, does not make programmatic statements which lay out plans and timetables.

> And there is no need to trouble oneself with times and seasons, for the mystery of times and seasons is in the wisdom of God, in his foresight, and in his love. And that which by human reckoning may still be rather remote, by divine predestination may already be standing on the eve of its appearance, at the door.[31]

Pope John Paul II has a different ministry than that of Dostoevsky's Elder Zosima. From its start, his papacy has proceeded programmatically from a central insight: "only in the mystery of the Incarnate Word does the mystery of man take on light.... Christ ... *fully reveals man to himself* and brings to light his most high calling.... Human nature, by the very fact that it was assumed, not absorbed, in [Christ], has been raised in us also to a dignity beyond compare."[32] It is only in contrast to this profound dignity of the person that the tragic character of death—and the true gravity of the death penalty—can be seen. One might not be doing the greatest violence to the Holy Father's words in suggesting that civil society today is not good enough to authorize the use of the death penalty. Unlike the prisoners of whom Father Zosima spoke—"for Russian criminals still have faith"[33]— many, whether within or outside today's courtroom dock, not only lack faith, but also are deficient in moral imagination.

At the start of his papacy, Pope John Paul II was not hesitant in high-lighting the extent of the Gospel's reach even into our understanding of justice: "The redemption of the world ... is, at its deepest root, the fullness of justice in a human Heart—the Heart of the First-born Son—in order that it may become justice in the hearts of many human beings, predestined from eternity in the First-born Son to be children of God and called to grace, called to love."[34] Yet, the path to the civilization of love follows a route of innumerably many discrete judgments and acts. Individually and corporately, prudence must be employed in concrete circumstances to seek what Aristotle and Thomas Aquinas called legal justice, whereby "man is in

30. Ibid., p. 64.
31. Ibid., p. 66.
32. *Redeemer of Man* (*Redemptor Hominis*), Washington, D.C.: United States Catholic Conference, 1979), no. 8, p. 24 (quoting *GS*, 22). Hereafter *RH*.
33. Dostoevsky, *Brothers Karamazov*, p. 65.
34. *RH*, 9, pp. 25-6.

harmony with the law which directs the acts of all the virtues to the common good."[35]

Those charged with authority within the Church must prudentially judge how best to present the truths entrusted to them and to exercise their unique authority within its proper scope. The Church's teaching is for the long run. The Pope has hope, but hope is not idle; it is proactive and keeps in mind future generations. Pope John Paul II is profoundly aware that the Church's teaching is not mere pronouncement, but also a shaping of culture and moral imagination. Catechesis is not directed to the heads of university professors but to the heart of all humanity. In no case should those entrusted with the transmission of Catholic teaching be negligent in distinguishing between the intrinsic evil of abortion and the possible evils of capital punishment. A good teacher should avoid confusing his or her charges.

35. Aquinas, *Summa Theologica*, trans. Fathers of the English Dominican Province (New York: Benziger Brothers, Inc., 1947), II-II, 58, 5, resp., p. 1438.

Respect For Persons As A Guide To Genetic Enhancement

Katie Hollenberg

I. Introduction

Is it possible that someday it will be considered unethical for parents not to enhance their unborn child with the best characteristics modern genetics can make possible? With the approach of genetic enhancement, what will happen to individuality and diversity? Will those who are considered imperfect individuals become less valuable in society than those with optimal characteristics? And, if we rid humanity of all our imperfect characteristics, thus taking away the struggles and difficulties of normal functioning, what will happen to the work ethic and determination of persons?

The goal of the Human Genome Project, as stated by Dr. Louis Sullivan, is "to locate and describe the activity of human genes, to dispose for new treatments and cures for diseases, as well as to develop a deeper understanding of all biological processes."[1] But it follows that along with the illness-treating technologies of the Genome Project, other kinds of applications also will occur. Understanding the biological processes more thoroughly does not necessarily mean that this knowledge will be used solely for the ethical well-being of persons. In some cases, the knowledge gained concerning an individual's genetic makeup could be used to that person's detriment. Consider the case of those individuals who have preexisting diseases resulting from their genetic abnormalities. These examples raise many ethical questions regarding the potential benefit or harm of genetic enhancement.

1. French Anderson, "Human Gene Therapy," *Science*, 8 May 1992, p. 810.

The concept of eugenics, however, is at the forefront of these issues, particularly when many physicians and medical professionals throughout the world hold the notion of health as a state of optimal physical or cognitive functioning.[2] The difficulty arises when we try to distinguish between defective gene repair and the enhancement of normally functioning genes. The repair of abnormal genes may restore health and thus help to restore equal opportunity to unequal individuals within the natural limits of humanity. On the other hand, genetic enhancement may be used to increase the ability of normally functioning genes or to change the genetic makeup of individuals in order to enhance their skill to an elite level.

Numerous ethical problems arise regarding the science of genetic enhancement when we seek to understand what separates it from outright eugenics. Where does one draw the line between what procedures are and are not morally acceptable? It is clear that enhancement can help to create a better physical being, but this does not necessarily mean that a better person will result. As Jacques Maritain notes in his book, *The Person and the Common Good*:

> Because it is ordained to the absolute and is summoned to a destiny beyond time, or, in other words, because of the highest requirements of personality as such, the human person, as a spiritual totality referred to the transcendent whole, surpasses and is superior to all temporal societies.[3]

Maritain emphasizes the important intrinsic value of each individual human person, not merely as a being with certain "good" qualities that will increase his or her usefulness in society. The affirmation of this intrinsic value encourages an ethics that focuses on respect for persons as its fundamental principle. Since respect for persons involves the avoidance of harm to human beings, as well as the active promotion of their well-being, genetic enhancement should only be used if the enhancement benefits the whole person. Moreover, respect for persons demands that all human beings are treated justly. And so if genetic enhancement is made possible to only those who have adequate health care, then they will have an unfair advantage over others who could not afford to endow their children with such improvements.[4] Some would say that society already encourages en-

---

2. Phillip Sloan, ed., *Controlling Our Destinies: Historical, Philosophical, Ethical, and Theological Perspectives on the Human Genome Project* (Notre Dame, Indiana: University of Notre Dame Press, 2000), p. 217.

3. Jacques Maritain, *The Person and The Common Good* (Notre Dame, Indiana: University of Notre Dame Press, 1966), p. 61.

4. Sloan, *Controlling Our Destinies*, p. 221.

hancement through activities such as private schools, athletic camps, or music lessons. This form of natural enhancement, however, does not drastically alter the genetic makeup of the individual. These improvements seem tame in relation to changing the genetic code of the unborn to enhance their skill, ability, or beauty.

Beyond these concerns, two additional problems arise. First, it is obvious that certain physical changes will allow individuals to feel healthier and better about themselves, such as reduced weight, lowered blood pressure, and increased beauty. However, these individuals may overlook the emotional changes or stresses that might occur as they seek to approach perfection. Secondly, environmental influences remain regardless of any genetic changes that take place. Whether or not children are genetically enhanced, they will still be influenced by the values and moral principles instilled in them by their social environment. If one's environment is negative, it is unlikely that genetic enhancement alone would be able to take the place of the love and nurturing needed for that child to grow within his or her community. These examples raise many ethical questions regarding the benefit of enhancement and its potential for harm.

II. Eugenics and Genetic Enhancement

The direction of genetic enhancement today is challenged by the concept of eugenics. Is it aimed solely at helping those who seem to be lacking optimal functioning, or is its goal that of creating vain perfection? Traditionally, eugenics concerned races and societies, not individuals only. Within the eugenics movement, there are two distinct approaches: positive and negative. Positive eugenics encourages reproduction, but only among those who are fit. This movement encourages "fit" people to have more children so as to create a better genetic society. Negative eugenics, on the other hand, promotes the sterilization or elimination of any person thought to have undesirable genes. This would stop reproduction of the unfit genes by simple extermination.

In Germany during World War II, the world saw attempts at both types of eugenics. Negative eugenics programs were occurring throughout concentration camps, with the goal of developing "racial hygiene" within the country.[5] But the attitude of Hitler did not stop at the Jewish prisoners. Rather, Hitler wanted to purify all of Germany. Thus, the Germans wanted to control

5. Arthur Caplan, "What's Morally Wrong With Eugenics?" in *Controlling Our Destinies*, p. 211.

the offspring of the citizens and eventually wipe out the characteristics viewed as undesirable within the Nazi state. Negative eugenics programs such as these were aimed at eliminating the undesirable genes through strictly enforced prohibitions in the areas of sexual relationships, marriages, and sterilization of "unfit" women. At the same time, however, positive eugenic programs were also in full effect throughout Germany. Those who satisfied the specific characteristics desired by the government were urged to have more children. If they were successful, rewards and benefits were offered for ideal gene pool reproduction.[6]

And so, in theory, both positive and negative eugenics can enhance the genetic makeup of a specific population. However, we must be cautious; the idea of population enhancement is often presented as having only positive results because of the apparent good that it will provide society in the future. Eugenicists generally share a common belief: "Concern for human betterment through selection - - that is, by taking measures to ensure that the humans who do come into existence will be capable of enjoying better lives and of contributing to the betterment of the lives of others;"[7] such is their motivation for enhancing individuals. Allen Buchanan points to this and several other dangers in his book *From Chance to Choice: Genetics and Justice*, which explains very clearly the dangers of the appeal of the genetic enhancement movement. One example is that many eugenicists tend to believe that a person's rank in society is solely a reflection of his or her capabilities, meaning that social standing is one factor that could be used as an indication of the genes which should be passed down to later generations. Another danger is that acceptance of the eugenics ideology diminishes the ability of members within a society to recognize the originality and uniqueness of others. For example, with instruction in eugenics introduced into Nazi-era German medical schools and practices, physicians became numb to the idea of individuality and genetic differences in their treatment of patients and family members.[8] Instead, they began to revel in their new discoveries and continued to perform disastrous surgeries and medical procedures, paying no attention to the consequences or ethics of experimenting on human persons. Thus, the focus of eugenics on population enhancement is fraught with danger. It violates the ethical norm of respect for persons by ignoring the importance of individuality and the unique characteristics and inherent value of the person.

6. Ibid, p. 210.
7. Allan Buchanan et al, *From Chance to Choice: Genetics and Justice* (New York: Cambridge University Press, 2000), p. 33.
8. Ibid.

III. Individual Enhancement

What is sometimes overlooked however, is that both positive and negative eugenics also can be performed at an individual level, influencing the direct offspring of the parent.[9] Those who desire genetic enhancement for their children are not aiming for the good of a race or society, but rather for the betterment of their progeny concerning specific characteristics they deem important. This idea of enhancing specific traits in an individual seems to be more controversial in the current debate over genetic engineering, because it is a revised form of eugenics, though now on an individual basis.

It is important to reflect on the implications of this contrast between racial and social eugenics versus individual enhancement. When enhancing a trait for the betterment of society by attempting to rid the population of a defective gene, the goal is less focused on the good of the few, and aimed more directly at helping society as a whole. Efforts to enhance certain properties of large-scale populations look, at first glance, to be beneficial for all persons involved. The treatment is not harming anyone physically, but actually embodies the opposite aim: to make the lives of future generations better. Today, governments tend to avoid direct involvement in genetic enhancement efforts, because of the moral repugnance directed towards the memory of Hitlerian eugenics. If this is so, why does it now seem to be acceptable, even noble, for individual couples to desire the same thing for their unborn children? If the world has rejected racial eugenics as immoral, why are similar choices, made at the individual level, viewed so differently?

The difference in attitude between eugenics and individual enhancement among geneticists is coupled with a shift in focus on the contemporary scene. What once aimed at the removal of harmful genes causing defects and abnormalities in children has now turned towards improving the characteristics inherent in every person that may not be deemed "desirable." Symbols of beauty such as attaining a certain height now have the chance to become one of the many alterable characteristics available to every person. This new form of enhancement is not merely for the purpose of treating disease; the goal is to take seemingly normal persons and attempt to improve both the mental and physical traits with which they were born.

9. Caplan, "What's Morally Wrong with Eugenics," p. 213.

There is a long list of problems regarding this type of individual enhancement, but a few are especially notable. The first is the problem of having the capability of knowing in advance your probable genetic future. As Leon Kass asks in his article, "The Moral Meaning of Genetic Technology," "will and should we welcome knowledge ... that genes will definitely produce at an unknown future time a serious but untreatable disease?"[10] If a patient discovers that he carries the gene for Huntington's disease, will he live the rest of his life in fear and unhappiness, not knowing when it will become active? It is possible that foreknowledge of your condition will be helpful in determining treatment or prevention? And finally, what if the condition is untreatable? Tensions arise when we are faced with difficult questions such as these, because previously they did not exist. At some point, it may have been better to consider the opinion that ignorance is bliss, and that we should continue living our lives the way we would even if these options were not available at all. The psychological and social implications of this issue lead to many more problems than solutions, and they lead one to question whether or not this is responsible medicine and science.[11] This problem is heightened by the fact that we know about many more diseases than we can treat. Is such knowledge "beneficial" or "harmful?"

A second problem concerns the payment and cost of determining the specific characteristics of a person's genome. It is probable that the average person will not be able to pay for genetic testing on his or her own, but, with the help of insurance companies, everyone may be eligible. There are serious implications that follow from this, however. If the insurance company pays for the procedure, it should have access to the results as well. With this information, the company could discontinue providing medical coverage for a person found to have a serious condition (or the predisposing gene) that could require future expensive medical attention. This hardly seems ethical, as this type of situation challenges our normal sense of privacy and justice. It defies the purpose of insurance as a support system that helps those in need, and takes away our rights to receive treatment even while we continue to pay for coverage.

A third problem regarding genetic enhancement is the ability of the individual or geneticist to "play God." Some critics dismiss this concern as a theological matter, but the issue is valid whether or not the interpreter has a religious orientation. Geneticists play the role of "creator" when they

10. Leon Kass, "The Moral Meaning of Genetic Technology," *Human Life Review* (Winter 2000): p. 79.
11. Ibid, p. 80.

determine, through their own beliefs, who and what characteristics are worthy of existence in this world. Kass notes, "Not only are they [geneticists] creating life, but they stand in judgment of each being's worthiness to live or die."[12] The problem arises because these scientists are judging worthiness not on moral grounds, set by each individual and his or her beliefs, but rather on genetic ones, given inherently to each person. Although we are only capable of "playing" the role, the implications are still the same: we are using our human reason and limited capabilities to determine the worth of another individual. In the future, the power we have over one another will only grow and this may increase our willingness to make decisions for people without their input.[13]

A final problem worth noting is the depersonalization of bringing children into the world that have been genetically enhanced before birth. Moreover, if the characteristics of the unborn may be more desirable after enhancement, many will have less chance of being born with a defect or abnormality. But doesn't this strike at the heart of what it means to be human, with true flaws and individual characteristics that were given to us naturally? In Pope John Paul II's Apostolic Exhortation "On the Family," he explains the need for compassion towards children in our society. "Concern for the child, even before birth, from the first moment of conception and then throughout the years of infancy and youth, is the primary and fundamental test of the relationship of one human being to another."[14] This increasing control over our offspring runs the risk of making the process of having a child become similar to a mere manufacturing operation.[15]

On the other hand, after explaining the negative aspects of genetic enhancement and the ethical implications surrounding it, some would argue that we also should acknowledge the positive aspects of enhancement for all members of society. Not all instances of enhancement raise ethical questions. On the contrary, some geneticists are working diligently to map the human genome and determine which genes carry specific defects and abnormalities that create lifelong problems for their carriers. As a society, we have an obligation to give our children the best possible care and opportunities available to them at the time. This has always been a primary goal of medicine, one that respects persons. Beyond simply working to remove harmful defects, however, the concept of enhancement also allows for

12. Ibid, p. 82.
13. Ibid.
14. John Paul II, Apostolic Exhortation, "On The Family," (Washington, D.C.: United States Catholic Conference, 1982), p. 24.
15. Kass, "The Moral Meaning of Genetic Technology," p. 82.

creating new capacities and standards of goodness for humanity as a whole.[16] This includes such possibilities as improving our children's memory capacity, intelligence level, and physical characteristics - - the list is truly endless. Some would even say that if we were all given the chance to enhance the characteristics of our offspring, diversity would increase because not everyone will want the same characteristics for his or her child.[17] The argument is that different people with different values and beliefs will not all want the same characteristics for their children, and thus it will depend solely on what each parent values. This could be viewed as beneficial to the future well being of humanity.

IV. Respect For Persons As A Guide To Genetic Enhancement

The moral problem arises when we face this question: what lines do we draw regarding ethics and enhancement, and how do we protect ourselves from losing personhood and inherent dignity? These are key issues surrounding the controversy.

To resolve the problem of where the line may be drawn, it is necessary to explain "personhood." The concept of "personhood," especially as it is used on the contemporary scene, is lacking. It does not give us any concrete indication as to how we should follow through with the dilemmas that genetic enhancement has presented to society. This does not mean that we can ignore the moral obligations that are attached to the concept of "personhood." Instead, it is helpful to once again turn to Maritain for insight:

> Because each soul is intended to animate a particular body, which receives its matter from the germinal cells, with all their hereditary content, from which it develops, and because, further, each soul has or is a substantial relation to a particular body, it has within its very substance the individual characteristics which differentiate it from every other human soul.[18]

This explains precisely what it means to be an individual person; not only does it include the importance of unique physical characteristics, but also a reference to the "soul" of the individual, which encompasses personhood in a spiritual way. Thus, when dealing with the notion of "personhood" in relation to each individual, it is necessary to make a simple transition. Whatever our notion of personhood, we must shift our under-

16. Ibid, p. 77.
17. Matt Ridley, "The New Eugenics," *National Review* 31 (July 2000), p. 14.
18. Maritain, *Common Good*, p. 36.

standing of respect for persons from that of the abstract notion regarding personhood as a concept, to that of respect for persons on an individual level for each human being. The general idea of "respect for persons" is embodied in concrete acts of respect for each individual human being.

This relates directly to the question of genetic enhancement because it challenges the motives behind developing medical technology. The reasoning behind genetic enhancement, particularly the Human Genome Project, is to improve the physical characteristics of human beings by altering their genetic makeup. This goal seems to aim at the good of society, particularly by aiding those who carry genes that are prone to disease or illness that would have been previously untreatable. Leon Kass highlights another important point in his article when he explains the danger of these procedures: "Enhancement is a soft euphemism for 'improvement,' and the idea of improvement necessarily implies a good, a better, and perhaps even a best."[19] From this explanation comes a glimpse into just how far genetic enhancement can extend: that although its first goal is preventing disease and helping individuals, there is also the ability to "improve" those who are not prone to disease and have normal functioning.

It is a part of human nature and modern society to want to improve individual characteristics, which is shown through such trends as dieting and plastic surgery. What makes us think that this will be any different with the availability of genetic enhancement? With the capabilities of genetic enhancement, why would people deny themselves and their children the hope for an easier, happier life? This kind of thinking is the main part of the problem. Many people do not realize that if we are not careful, this altering of genetic makeup could be the beginning of a downward spiral leading to the destruction of individuality and uniqueness. This is not to say that all genetic enhancement is bad. Using genetic enhancement as reparation to rid individuals of defective genes is a noble cause. Enhancement as an extension of medical practices or as a part of medical therapy is both moral and ethical because it follows the principle of respect for persons. But unless enhancement stays within the confines of medicine as a way of correcting abnormal genes, problems are sure to arise.

It is also necessary to realize the risks involved with genetic enhancement because of unknown future repercussions. "Until certain knowledge of the real risks and benefits associated with human genetic engineering has been obtained, the potential risks to all of the future descendants of the patient outweigh any benefit to a very small number of persons who might

19. Kass, "The Moral Meaning of Genetic Technology," p. 79.

benefit."[20] The notion that parents today are choosing the fate of their descendants is a frightening one, not to mention that we are still unsure what consequences these alterations will have on future generations. With these concerns looming over such a controversial issue, it is necessary to step back and evaluate the real benefit that will come out of such procedures.

The time to consider the ethical issues of enhancement is now, while we are still on the doorstep of such monumental changes that have the potential to alter human society dramatically. Returning to Jacques Maritain, he states:

> Historical conditions and the still inferior development of humanity make difficult the full achievement of the end of social life. But the end to which it tends is to procure the common good of the multitude in such a way that the concrete person gains the greatest possible measure, compatible with the good of the whole, of real independence from the servitudes of nature.[21]

To the extent that genetic enhancement can further our "independence from the servitudes of nature," it would seem worthwhile; to the extent that genetic enhancement would seek to further our own individual (or our children's) variety, it does not. True respect for the human person transcends mere physical enhancement and affirms the intrinsic dignity and sanctity of the whole person, body and spirit.

20. Bernard Gert, "Genetic Engineering: Is It Morally Acceptable?" *USA Today*, January 1999, national ed., p. 30.
21. Maritain, *Common Good*, p. 54.

Plate XXVII Sunt lacrimae rerum...

Lacrimae Rerum—Tears at the Heart of Things: Jacques Maritain and Georges Rouault

Bernard Doering

In his *Journal d'un Théologien*, the famous Dominican (later Cardinal) Yves Congar recounts his memories of the meetings of the *Cercle Thomiste* at Jacques Maritain's home, first in Versailles and later in Meudon. He describes the attitudes that predominated at the early meetings in which he participated. There was, he wrote, a kind of intrepid and absolute faith in the slightest detail of a text of St. Thomas. Everyone seemed sympathetic to *Action Française* and more or less shared in its massive over-simplifications, its solid disdain for others, its brutal conviction of being right and of possessing the truth, in sum, a group spirit completely lacking in any nuance whatsoever. To one degree or another, Maritain, the recent convert, shared in this attitude. It was, says Congar, the Maritain of *Théonas,* of *Antimoderne,* of *Three Reformers* and *The Dream of Descartes.* There was a prevailing orthodoxy that was literary, philosophical and political as well as dogmatic and religious. There was general agreement that Henri Ghéon was the greatest playwright, del Sarte the greatest sculptor, Maurice Denis the painter who had no equal.

But, to tell the truth, says Congar, Maritain was bigger than all this. There was within him another Maritain, the real Maritain, the artist, the revolutionary, the friend of Péguy, the Dreyfusard, the free spirit which corrected and went beyond the Maritain of the early meet-

The illustrations from the "Miserere" which is a gift of Mr. Leonard Scheller are reproduced with permission of the Notre Dame Snite Museum of Art. The photography was made possible by a generous grant from the Notre Dame Institute for Scholarship in the Liberal Arts.

ings of the *Cercle Thomiste*, the Maritain, says Congar, of *Art and Scholasticism*, of the *Réponse à Jean Cocteau*, of *Integral Humanism* and all that followed.[1]

So *Art and Scholasticism*, seems to have been the first sign of his breaking away from the intransigent zeal of those years. Raïssa wrote in *Les Grandes Amitiés* that it was in thinking of Georges Rouault that Maritain composed *Art and Scholasticism*.[2] And concerning Rouault, Jacques himself wrote that "a philosopher could study in him the virtue of art as in its pure state, with all its demands, its mystery and its purity."[3] His friendship with Rouault seems to have been one of the first influences that helped free him from the conservative constraints imposed by the spiritual directors at the early meetings of the *Cercle*.

I was first introduced to Rouault by Maritain's essay "Three Painters" and another essay by Wallace Fowlie, and, after I viewed his paintings in museums and consulted a number of art books, he became one of my very favorite painters. One of the greatest pleasures of my research visits to Kolbsheim was the opportunity to view the "Miserere" series. Rouault had given to Maritain a complete set of the 58 black and white engravings that make up the collection, and once Antoinette Grunelius learned that I loved and admired Rouault, she would set up at each visit the complete set in the immense foyer of her chateau for me and my wife, Jane, to view at our leisure.

The "Miserere" gets its title from the first word in Latin of one of the penitential psalms that is used most often in the liturgies of Lent and at funerals: Miserere mei deus, secundum magnam misericordiam tuam ("Have mercy on me, O God, according to thy great mercy"). It is a plea for forgiveness. Rouault had his own understanding of this psalm. In addition to its being a plea for the forgiveness of the sins of individuals against God which were the cause of the sufferings and death of Christ, for him it was also, and especially, a plea for forgiveness for the sins of society against the poor and the weak.

The title of this essay derives from the subtitle of plate XXVII of the "Miserere:" *Sunt lacrimae rerum*. These words themselves come from a famous line in Virgil's *Aneid*. When Aeneas arrives at Carthage and, in a temple there, sees a frieze depicting the fall of Troy and the deaths of the Trojan heroes, his family and his friends, he exclaims with profound

---

1. Yves Congar, *Journal d'un Théologien* (Paris: Cerf, 2000), p. 35ff and footnote 94.
2. Raissa Maritain, *Les Grandes Amitiés* (Paris: Desclée De Brouwer, 1962), p. 169.
3. Jacques Maritain, *Frontières de la Poésie* (Paris: Rouart, 1935), p. 133.

sadness: "Sunt lacrimae rerum et mentem mortalia tangunt" (There are tears at the very heart of things, and the mortal nature of those things troubles the mind of man).

Who was this great intimate friend of Maritain? Georges Rouault was born of a working-class family in the Belleville *faubourg* or suburb of Paris, in the cellar where his parents had taken refuge to escape the bombardment by government troops during the uprising of the Commune in 1871. A Parisian suburb was not like our suburbs, full of green lawns and large houses where we live to escape the crowding and the grime of our city centers. The "faubourgs" were the dingy areas encircling Paris where the poor lived in crowded tenements and dirty hovels next to the factories where they worked. (*Rue des solitaires*—Street of the lonely people).

In Rouault's family there reigned an extraordinary artistic and cultural atmosphere, closely related to working with material—creating art—the opposite of the bourgeois mentality of buying art for decoration. As a child he spent hours making chalk drawings on the floor of his poor home. On Sundays he took frequent walks with his grandfather along the quays of the Seine searching the book stalls for prints, especially of Manet and Courbet. He was proud of his humble beginnings and of his artisan heritage. He was a poet too. He wrote:

> In the *faubourg* of toil and suffering,
> In the darkness I was born.
> Keeping vigil over pictorial turpitudes,
> I toiled
> Miles away from certain dilettantes.

[Plate X: *Au vieux faubourg des longues peines* (In the old suburb of long sorrows).]

His father was an *ébéniste*, that is, a skilled craftsman, a maker of fine furniture, who worked at the Pleyel piano company. He tells of his father wincing when his wife opened a drawer too suddenly or too violently. Wood suffers too, he would say to her.

In 1895, at the age of 14, Rouault was apprenticed to a stained-glass restorer. It was at this work that he developed what he called his "passionate taste" for bright colors and his love for ancient stained-glass windows. He had a deep admiration for and an almost mystical affinity to the anonymous artisan-workers of Romanesque times and the early Middle Ages. This work marked him for life.

Rouault had a very difficult career at the beginning. He was disparaged by art critics who completely misunderstood him. They ridiculed his

Plate X Au vieux faubourg des longues peines

"déformations," his "gribouillage" (scribbling or doodling). They had no way of classifying him. Was he a Primitive like Rousseau *le douanier*? Was he a Fauve like Derain?

Maritain, however, did understand him. His first text on art, and well before any article he published on philosophy, was an introduction to the catalogue of the first exposition of Rouault's works at the *Galerie Druet* in February and March of 1910, and which was published under the pseudonym "Jacques Favelle." In his *Carnet de Notes* Maritain tells us that Rouault asked him to choose a name for his signature that would suggest a connection with the workers who built the cathedrals of France. "Favelle" was a good find as a working-class name; it concealed Jacques's identity as the grandson of Jules Favre.[4]

To a self-portrait Rouault gave the title *L'Apprenti* (The Worker-apprentice). In his introduction, Maritain called Rouault a true primitive who was a popular or people's artist, for his frank and naïve inspiration is very close to that of the happy artisans of days gone by, those of Romanesque and early medieval times. He spoke of Rouault's "naïve images, made by a patient workman who loved his tools and the matter he was working on," who loved his craft "with a serious and obstinate passion and with a constant need to perfect his technique." Already in 1910 Maritain seemed to foresee in an uncanny way the central inspiration of the great "Miserere" collection. He wrote that Rouault "finds his inspiration, not in some abstract system or some literary emotion, but in what life itself, the life of [his own] time and of [his own country], makes him, so to speak, touch with his finger."[5]

There seem to have been three great influences on Rouault the artist: the painter Gustave Moreau, the author Léon Bloy, and the philosopher Jacques Maritain.

In 1900 Rouault left his apprenticeship to study painting at the *Académie des Beaux Arts*, first under Robert Delaunay, then under Gustave Moreau. Moreau was a Catholic who distrusted all forms of dogma and ecclesiastical hierarchy. He had a deep attachment to his Faith, especially as an iconographic storehouse. Rouault admired Moreau's interior sentiment of humility before the spiritual dimension of all reality, before the sacramentality of the universe. He loved the sacramentals of Catholic liturgical tradition: bread, wine, water, fire, candles, oil, palms, ashes, incense, etc. He was radically independent from all artistic schools and encouraged his students

4. Nora Possenti-Ghiglia, *Cahiers Jacques Maritain* (Publication of the *Cercle d'Etudes Jacques et Raïssa Maritain*, Kolbsheim, France) 12 (November, 1985), p. 10, n 12.

5. Jacques Maritain, "G. Rouault," *Cahiers Jacques Maritain*, 12 (November, 1985),p. 24.

to develop their own particular styles and to guard ferociously their own independence. During this time, Rouault himself came to conceive of faith as a profoundly religious sentiment, which, though not articulated, demanded absolute abandon.

As for Bloy, Rouault knew him before Maritain did. It was at Bloy's home that Maritain first met Rouault; they both were frequent visitors.[6] Jacques wrote that "What [Bloy] revealed to them cannot be expressed: the tenderness of Christian brotherhood and that kind of trembling pity and fear before a soul ... marked by the love of God."[7] They were astounded by his practice of voluntary poverty and by his all-consuming love of the poor. Bloy did not understand or appreciate Rouault's art. He "accused him, affectionately, but without much consideration for his feelings, of falling into a demonic form of art and of finding delight in ugliness and deformity. [Rouault] would listen, motionless, ashen and silent."[8] Bloy's writings and conversations were filled with fulminations against the complacent and indifferent rich. He insisted on the centrality of the "Cross" in the life of the Christian and on the role of suffering in the life of the entire Mystical Body of Christ. Maritain was impressed enough to list in his writing on Bloy a series of quotations on the subject of suffering.

> —Suffering passes away—to have suffered does not.
> —A heart without affliction is like a world without revelation. It sees God by a feeble glimmer of light.
> —Man has places in his heart which do not yet exist and into which suffering enters so that they may come to be. I would never finish if I wanted to describe the marvelous effects of suffering on man's faculties and on his heart. *It is the handmaiden of creation.*
> —Our hearts are filled with angels when they are filled with affliction.[9]

The influence between the painter and the philosopher was mutual. In a wonderfully perceptive essay "Jacques Maritain and Rouault. At the fountain-head of a fruitful friendship" Nora Possenti-Ghiglia wrote:

> It is difficult, for anyone who was not a part of this friendship, to grasp the value of the exchange between the philosopher and the painter "in the inexpressible regions

6. Raïssa Maritain, p. 167.

7. Jacques Maritain, *Quelques pages sur Léon Bloy, Ã uvres Complètes,* vol. III, p. 1022.

8. Jacques Maritain, *Frontières de la Poésie,* p. 135.

9. Jacques Maritain, "In Homage to Our Dear Godfather Léon Bloy," in *Untrammeled Approaches* (Notre Dame, Indiana: University of Notre Dame Press, 1997), pp. 37-39.

of the heart" (as Maritain put it), but everything leads us to believe that this exchange was as fruitful for one as for the other. And perhaps the dialogue which resulted from the contact between their personal sensitivities and experiences was less noticeable in explicit allusions in their writings, than in the very sensitivity with which Maritain approached the problems of art and of poetry, and in the way in which Rouault gradually emerged from that "abyss of sorrow and of infinite melancholy" which he bore within himself.[10]

In 1909 the Maritains moved to Versailles and the Rouaults followed two years later. There they met frequently, and the Rouaults took meals with the Maritains on an almost weekly basis and held long conversations together.[11] They discussed religion, mysticism, social justice, the philosophy of beauty and the practice of art. Rouault found in Maritain an understanding and sympathetic listener with whom he could escape from his solitude, to whom he could speak of himself and of his art before a lively and open intelligence. It was in thinking of Rouault that Maritain, as mentioned, wrote *Art and Scholasticism* and he made frequent references to his artist friend in *Creative Intuition in Art and Poetry*. This "grand philosophe" even babysat the four Rouault children,[12] whom their father listed in a little poem which Maritain affectionately cites in "Three Painters" (from *Frontières de la Poésie):*

Geneviève mon gros bourdon	Genevieve my bumble bee
Isabelle ma colombelle	Isabelle my little dove
Michel faible pilier de la maison	Michel feeble pillar of the household
Agnès petit pigeon	Agnes my little pigeon

On one occasion Jacques took the six year old Geneviève and her little sister Isabelle to the doctor to have them operated for tonsils and adenoids. As they walked to the Clinic Geneviève held the hand of this "grand philosophe" and Isabelle rode on his shoulders. Jacques had given up a whole day of work, Geneviève wrote later, to replace her parents who were "too impressionable" to assist at the operation.

The two friends shared a profound respect for the common people and the poor. In his essay "Exister avec le peuple" Maritain wrote:

10. Possenti-Ghiglia, p. 9.
11. Ibid.
12. Genevieve Nouialle-Rouault, "Maritain, Rouault et Nous," *Cahiers Jacques Maritain,* no. 4-5 (November, 1982), pp. 79-84.

> If we love that living human thing which we call the people ... we will want first and foremost to exist with them, to suffer with them and remain in communion with them.
>
> Before "doing good" to them and working for their benefit, before practicing the politics of one group or other ... we must first choose to exist with them, and to suffer with them, to make their pain and destiny our own.[13]

Maritain wrote of Rouault: "What he sees and knows with a strange pity, and what he makes us see, is the miserable affliction and the lamentable meanness of our times, not just the affliction of the body, but the affliction of the soul, the bestiality and the self-satisfied vainglory of the rich and the worldly, the crushing weariness of the poor, the frailty of us all."[14]

Maritain was not disturbed by the "distortions," the "déformations," the "gribouillage," that Bloy so insensitively ridiculed. He wrote that Rouault seeks to "reproduce as much as he possibly can the truth of the things that move him," with a kind of "naïve frankness" or "frank naïvete." "He knows that truth is never found in the copy." He does not see things in their banality. "He has an imaginative vision of things, he contemplates them in the world of their greater reality and it is in this world that he paints them."[15] In *Creative Intuition in Art and Poetry,* Maritain wrote:

> Saint Thomas insisted that art imitates nature *in her operation*—not in respect to natural appearances, but in respect to the ways in which nature herself operates.... Such a genuine concept of "imitation" affords a ground and justification for the boldest kinds of transposition, transfiguration, deformation, or recasting of natural appearances, in so far as they are the means to make the work manifest intuitively the *transapparent* (emphasis mine) reality which has been grasped by the artist."[16]

At this point in his text Maritain cites Rouault expressly.

What exactly was this world of Rouault, which his creative intuition turned into a *transapparent* reality? It was principally a world of human beings, of suffering and solitude, all victims of sin and evil. We might categorize them, and then consider each individually, as follows: the Poor and their oppressors, Clowns, Prostitutes, Refugees, and Christ. At Rouault's funeral Abbé Morel said that Rouault "touches evil with the greatest profundity, but also with the clearest purity."

13. Jacques Maritain, *Raison et Raisons: Essais détachés* (Paris: Egloff, 1947), chap. XI.
14. *Cahiers Jacques Maritain*, no. 12 (November, 1985), p. 24.
15. Ibid., p. 26.
16. Jacques Maritain, *Creative Intuition in Art and Poetry* (New York: Pantheon Books, 1953), pp. 224-5.

Poor and Their Oppressors

First, we see the injustices perpetrated by the legal system, the judges and the lawyers:

Plate LII: *Dura lex, sed lex* (The law is hard, but it is the law)

Some of the engravings in the "Miserere" were made in series, often as illustrations of one of Rouault's poems. The following is just such a case: (This is my translation of the poem)

> The condemned man went away
> Indifferent and weary.
> His lawyer in hollow
> Pompous phrases
> Proclaimed his total innocence.
> A red-robed prosecutor
> Held society blameless
> And indicted the accused man
> Under a Jesus on the cross
> Forgotten there.

Plate XVII: *Le condamné s'en est allé* (The condemned man went away).

Plate XIX: *Son avocat en phrases creuses clame sa totale innocence* (His lawyer in hollow pompous phrases proclaimed his total innocence).

Plate XX: *Sous un Jésus en croix, oublié là* (Under a Jesus on the cross, forgotten there).

There is no red-robed prosecutor here, but elsewhere Rouault did paint some red-robed judges. In the case of these judges and lawyers, Rouault's intention seems to have been, not so much to condemn, as to lament the situation and point out the complicity of us all (see *Ne sommes-nous pas forçats?*—Are we not all condemned to hard labor?). It is the same with the next group of Rouault's oppressors, the complacent rich and the self-satisfied bourgeoisie.

Plate XVI: *Dame du haut quartier croit prendre pour le ciel place réservée* (A lady from a chic neighborhood thinks she has purchased her reserved seat in heaven).

Plate LII Dura lex, sed lex

Plate XVII La condamné s'en est allé

Plate XIX Son avocat en phrases creuses
clame sa totale innocence...

Plate XX Sous un Jésus en croix oublié là

Plate XL: *Face à face* (Face to face).

See also *Des ongles et du bec* (With beak and claw), *Nous croyant rois* (Believing ourselves kings), *Plus le coeur est noble, moins le col est roide* (The more noble the heart, the less stiff the neck), and *Loin du sourire de Reims* (A far cry from the smile at Reims). The *Sourire de Reims* refers to the smile on the face of an angel in the Cathedral of Reims.

Then there are "the poor" themselves—in their helplessness, suffering and loneliness:

Plate XXV: *Jean-François jamais ne chante alleluia* (Jean-François never sings alleluia).

And the working poor: on one occasion, the sight of a poor butcher at work in his butcher shop on wheels as it passed down the street sent Rouault back to his studio to paint. See also *Le dur métier de vivre* (The hard job of just getting through life) and *Vie d'embûches et de malices* (Life is full of ambushes and acts of malice).

In the next plate we encounter the destitute who survive only through comradeship and compassion:

Plate LV: *L'aveugle parfois console le voyant* (Sometimes the blind console those who see).

Maritain wrote that there was in Rouault, "like a spring of living water, an intense religious sentiment, the stubborn faith of a hermit ... which made him discover the image of the divine Lamb in all the abandoned and rejected for whom he felt a profound pity."[17] By identifying with the poor, as Maritain suggested in "Exister avec le people," Rouault identifies with their sufferings.

Plate XXXII: *Seigneur, c'est vous, je vous reconnais!* (My Lord, it's you, now I recognize You!).

Clowns

The next general category is clowns. Individual paintings were often the result of a single moving experience. Maritain says that the basis of Rouault's painting is "the most profound and severe emotion," a "primitive

17. Jacques Maritain, *Frontières de la Poésie*, p. 132.

Plate XVI Dame du haut quartier croit prendre
pour le ceil place réservée

Plate XL Face á face

Plate XXV Jean-François jamais
ne chante alleluia ...

Plate LV L'aveugle parfois a consolé le voyant

emotion" in the face of "the truth of the things that move him," as in the case of the butcher. In this case, it was the sight of a traveling circus entering town. Later he took to spying on the circus people as they set up in the *Place Grenelle* after the parade or as they prepared to move on after the show. It was the world of Puccini's *Pagliaccio,* of Fellini's lonely circus strongman in *La Strada,* a world that led the great American clown, Emmet Kelly, to declare that the profession of the clown is the saddest profession in the world.

Plate VIII: *Qui ne se grime pas* (Who of us does not put on whiteface). See also Rouault's paintings *Le vieux clown* (*The Old Clown*), and *Clown.* As with the poor, clowns too often survived only through companionship and tenderness.

Prostitutes

The third general category is the prostitutes, or as the French say "Filles de joie," (daughters of joy), a term that comes from the Old Testament. Prostitution was a legally sanctioned enterprise in France at this time, and in the "Maisons closes" or legal brothels, the daughters of joy had to submit periodically to degrading medical examinations to protect the clients. In the Realist School of painting, prostitutes were often portrayed with a kind of cynicism and complicity, as in Manet's *Olympe* and Toulouse-Lautrec's *Examen médicale.* To Toulouse-Lautrec's cynicism, Rouault opposed tears of rage. In Rouault's nudes there is no sensual relish in decadence for its own sake. Again, it was often a single moving experience that drove him to paint. A single glance was enough to open for him an entire universe of emotional reality. He knew of the poor street-walkers in his *faubourg* who, in winter, posed for artists in the nude without pay, solely for the privilege of warming themselves in the painters' studios. The moving experience in this case was an encounter with an older, shop-worn prostitute, grotesquely made up, who, with a forced smile, propositioned him from a doorway near his home.

Plate XIV: *Fille dite de joie* (A daughter of joy, as the expression goes).

Rouault's prostitutes are not objects of man's desire, but debased, suffering creatures made in God's image. There is no joy. For him there were no "happy hookers" who succeeded in marrying their rich clients to live happily ever after, like Julia Roberts in the film "Pretty Woman." He portrays,

Plate XXXII Seigneur, c'est vous, je vous reconnais!

Plate VIII Qui ne se grime pas

Plate XIV Fille dite de joie

Plate LIV Debout les morts

not the error of sin, but the pain of sin. There is a kind of hardness and resentful resignation in the faces of his brutalized prostitutes. See also his paintings *Filles au fourneau* (prostitutes in the"display" room) and his other paintings of prostitutes.

Refugees

The next category is refugees—the victims of war, poverty and famine.

Plate LIV: *Debout les morts* (Up on your feet, you dead).

See also *Les ruines elle-mêmes ont péri* (The ruins themselves have perished), *Bella matribus detestata* (Wars detested by mothers), and *Mon doux pays, où êtes-vous?* (My sweet homeland, where are you?).

Christ

Finally there is the category of Christ—the human Christ rather than Christ in his divinity. The painter seems preoccupied with the sufferings and the eternal presence of Christ in the person of the poor, rather than with His death. Here is another series meant to be viewed together. The three subtitles make up one sentence.

Plate II: *Jésus honni ...* (Jesus, mocked ...).
Plate III: *Toujours flagellé ...* (Forever scourged ...).
Plate IV: *Se réfuge en ton coeur, va nu-pieds de malheur* (Takes refuge in your heart, oh barefoot waif of misfortune).

In all his portrayals of the Redeemer, what stands out is the impassivity of Christ's face. There seems to be a total lack of aggressiveness. See also *C'est par ses meurtrissures que nous sommes guéris* (It is by His wounds that we are healed), *Et Véronique au tendre lin passe encore sur le chemin* (And Veronica with her tender linen still passes along the way), and *Il a été maltraité et il n'a pas ouvert la bouche* (He was mistreated and He never opened his mouth).

William A. Dyrness noted that when Rouault painted his Christs in color, he painted them in the same colors as his clowns and prostitutes.[18]

18. William Dryness, *Rouault: A Vision of Suffering and Salvation* (Grand Rapids, Michigan: Wm. B. Eerdmans Publishing Co., 1971), p. 185.

Plate II Jésus honni ...

Plate III Toujours flagellé ...

Plate IV Se réfuge en ton coeur
va nu-pieds de malheur

Plate XXXV Jésus sera en agonie jusqu' á
la fin du monde ...

Dyrness noted also that whatever the outward aspects of Christ's earthly identification as human may be (see his painting *Ecce homo*—Behold the Man), this identification finds its "basis and justification for Rouault [in] Christ's espousal of human suffering ... Christ's presence is a presence of suffering in and with our suffering," [19] especially with the sufferings of the least of His brethren. "Whatsoever you do unto these the least of my brethren, you do unto me." Consequently:

Plate XXXV: Jésus sera en agonie jusqu'à la fin du monde (Jesus will be in agony until the end of the world).

See also *Aimez-vous les uns les autres* (Love one another), and *Le juste comme le bois de santal parfume la hache qui le frappe* (The just man like sandal wood perfumes the axe that strikes him).

Georges Rouault has been called the last painter of Icons because of his simplicity of forms, the heavy but luminous colors, the gravity of tone, the eschewing of exact representational realism and the indistinctness of contours. Dyrness says of Rouault that, "if the image is less clean, it is more alive with a kind of spiritual energy."[20]

The tone is indeed grave, but it is not one of all pervasive gloom. What is everywhere present is what Maritain called his "stubborn faith of a hermit," his Bernanosian tenacious hope against hope. This hoped-for ideal is always there, either directly or by suggestion. See *Il arrive parfois que la route soit belle* (At times the road turns out to be beautiful), *Il serait si doux d'aimer* (It would be so sweet to love) and his paintings *Evasion* (Escape), *Paysage biblique* (Biblical landscape), *Paysage tragique* (Tragic landscape) and *le Christ et deux disciples* (Christ and two disciples).

Plate XXIX: Chantez matines, le jour renaît (Sing matins, for the new day is aborning).

It was an unwavering hope and an unshakeable faith in his Christ and in his artistic vision of a deeper spiritual reality, masked by the ugliness, horror and brutality of the sensible world around him, that led Rouault " a galley slave, [to row] hard, like a poor fisherman, against the currents on the ocean of human and pictorial turpitudes. ...To tell the truth, I painted in order to open, day and night, the eyelids of the sensible world, but closing them from time to time to better see my vision blossom fully and become

19. Ibid., p. 186.
20. Ibid., p. 183.

Plate XXIX Chantez matines, le jour renaît

more ordered." This is what led his daughter Isabelle to say: "The ultimate feeling that Rouault had about his own person and the sign by which he recognized its reality seems to me to have been joy." "It is also the joy of having endowed disinherited beings with beauty and power."[21] So like Gerard Manley Hopkins, Rouault could sing Matins with each daybreak:

> ... though the last lights off the black West went
> Oh, morning, at the brown brink, eastward springs—
> Because the Holy Ghost over the bent
> World broods with warm breast and ah! bright wings.
>   (God's Grandeur)

Rouault was a "loner." The profound joy he experienced came from his intimate association with his family and a very few fast friends like André Suarès and Jacques Maritain. If he cultivated very limited relationships with his contemporaries, it was not out of disdain, but because of the impossibility to communicate with them except on the level of a profound artistic and human solidarity,[22] and this was precisely the level on which he could communicate with Maritain. The two shared many things: a kind of pristine, childlike innocence, an enlightened sensitivity to beauty, a profound solidarity with the poor, the downtrodden and the disinherited of the earth, a thirst for justice, and a profound religious sentiment. On all of these matters they could communicate on an intimate basis and they did so.

What Maritain brought to Rouault was intimacy, warmth, understanding and encouragement. But it is doubtful that Rouault would have painted differently had he never met Maritain. What Rouault brought to Maritain was a sharpening of his artistic sensitivity, an intellectual liberation from the smothering constraints of his spiritual and intellectual guides at the time of his conversion. Without Rouault, we may never have known *Art and Scholasticim* and all the luminous works that followed.

21. *Giuseppe Marchiori,* Georges Rouault (Paris/Lausanne: Bibliothèque des Arts, 1965). From the last unnumbered pages of commentary on the illustrations included in the book.
22. Ibid., p. 30.

Vera Icona: Reflections on the Mystical Aesthetics of Jacques Maritain and the Byzantine Icon[1]

Cornelia A. Tsakiridou

For centuries Christianity pondered the question of her God's image, the challenge of representing Him in forms that she found ready made in a pagan world, bound to its gods and myths. The philosophers, Plato first among them, tied the image to a transcendent origin and made verisimilitude the criterion of its virtue and vice, intimating that, like Janus, art could turn a face either toward the absolute or toward the vulgar and depraved world of desire and illusion. By contrast, then, what is Christian art? It is the "art of humanity redeemed," answers Jacques Maritain, an art that belongs to man by virtue of a nature touched by God, a creative impulse not unlike that of a bee, we are told, but with one difference, our freedom to reject it and look elsewhere for inspiration.[2] This suggests that art must make redemption evident objectively either in its content or in its form or in both. It must in a definitive, distinct way, be *Christian* art. But what constitutes a Christian work of art as such? For Maritain "the work will be Christian in proportion as the love is alive."[3] Love is related to Christ's presence, experienced by the artist in a way that af-

---

1. In loving memory of Father William (Bill) J. Krupa, O.S.A.
2. Jacques Maritain, *Art and Scholasticism*, trans. J. F. Scanlan (New York: Charles Scribner's Sons, 1935), pp. 68-69.
3. Ibid., p. 71.

fects the work's creation and its visible form. There is no doubt that this form is beautiful, characterized by virtuosity but also by an inner brilliance, attributed to an "intrinsic super-elevation," a movement in the form that distinguishes Christian from ordinary beauty.[4] It is difficult to visualize what is described here and Maritain does not give compelling examples in *Art and Scholasticism*. It is clear though that what makes art Christian is not a "right" content defined by some correspondence to certain truths of faith e.g., in a didactic sense.

The modality of truth in Christian art is determined by contemplative communion, sacramental love that unites artist, world and work of art with Christ. For this love to arise in the artist and find expression in art, a particular relationship to Christ must be in order. Maritain quotes Fra Angelico: "... to paint the things of Christ, the artist must live with Christ."[5] This is a vital relationship not left to abstract intellection or the imagination. Life with Christ consists of full participation in the mysteries of His cross and sacrifice. In *Art and Scholasticism* Maritain refers Christian art to *ascesis*, a discipline of life and sensibility nourished freely within the mystical body of the Church. His sources are the intense, purgative sensibility of Carmelite spirituality evident in the poetry of St. John of the Cross, and Thomist contemplation infused with love. Desire for God energizes and transfigures the artist's intellectual vision.[6]

Ascesis (spiritual exercise) and art also converge in the Byzantine icon, painted by an artist who fasts and prays, rooted in sacramental life. Maritain is opposed to the model of Christian art that has evolved out of the Byzantine tradition and to art in general that is ecclesiastically regulated. In *Art and Scholasticism* and in *On the Grace and Humanity of Jesus* he provides arguments for a mystical aesthetics that is free, sacramental and rooted in the Cross. For Maritain, Christian iconography is vitally ordered to Christ's Passion. This is best expressed in a concept that appears only in passing in his essay on painter Georges Rouault, the concept of the *vera icona*, known in the tradition as the *Veronica* (*vera icona* or true icon), the image-relic of Christ's face impressed in cloth. Art is Christian to the extent that *vera icona* defines the aesthetic object. To that we must add another element, that of experience. Christian art is art that is constituted in a way that makes prayerful contemplation possible. Maritain prays and contemplates

4. Ibid., pp. 70-71.
5. Ibid., p. 71.
6. Thomas Aquinas, *Summa Theologiae*, II-II (New York: Benziger Bros., 1948), vol. IV, pp. 180-81.

the art of Rouault in a manner analogous to *lectio divina* (prayerful reading), in *visio divina* (prayerful seeing). His mystical aesthetics is consistent
with those of the Byzantine icon with the difference that Maritain reasserts
the significance of an ascetic subjectivity and therefore a certain plasticity
in the aesthetic range of the Christian image and art.

I

Images and statues of living things, whether worshipped as divine or
not, were forbidden in the Hebrew Bible under the charge of idolatry. A
God heard in human voice but not seen or encountered in the natural
world and the human form cannot be "aesthetic," in the literal sense of
the word. If we must speak of sensibility in this context, it is one in
which the ear but not the eye is sanctified, so that of the world one seeks
only the form and order of the letter, the semiotic, to which the somatic,
the carnal and tangible, must conform. Here there is no "art" since there
is no freedom to let the form speak for itself, out of its own being, without restriction or regulation. This is why Christ, the *theanthropos*
(God-Man), emerging out of human flesh mysteriously, without the aber-
ration implied by miracle, was so scandalous. That He was a Son rather
than a Messiah speaks to a profound kinship with nature, a kinship that
affirms but also transfigures the natural bonds of family, making Him
everybody's son and brother. Thus He instructs Mary and St. John from
the Cross: "*ecce filius tuus ... ecce mater tua*" (behold your son ... behold
your mother) (John 19:26). This call to communion, spoken on the verge
of death known until then to be final and irreversible, is rarely viewed
aesthetically. Yet it is not difficult to see in it an invitation to "circumscription" (*perigraphe*) and a revelation of form that begins from the
moment that Pilate utters "*Ecce homo*" (behold the man). For with this
utterance the audience is invited to see and behold (*idou*) the one that he
presents, a presence taken all the way to the Cross (John 19:5). For all
that man is and can be to his fellow man is revealed on the Cross to which
not only the Incarnation, itself a drafting of flesh from within, but also
the Resurrection, the exposition of flesh intact and immaculate, are drawn.

The Cross marks and projects the periphery of Christ's body. It is a
topos (place) of sin and death that *lifts* man and nature to the Resurrection.
The frame made of hard wood on which flesh is stretched to its limit is not
accidental to the Incarnation. It is part of its hidden substantiality and Passion. In the drama of human sin, nature too is a participant. There is here
no historical accident of a crucifixion. Into this aesthetic of death and the

spectacle that constitutes it, God enters for His own sacrifice after which being is never the same—even if man, having denied the Cross, wills it to be. To this literal apotheosis of human sin, God comes as victim and savior. The sight of the Crucified inverts its own spectacle (the staged drama of His public torture and execution), for against it and around it forms the sight of the Resurrection, the conversion of death to life. Having lived within the imaginary, within an illusory world of which Christ, in death, was the end and, having also anticipated in the presence of ephemeral beauty the death of his body and senses, man is now free to rediscover in form the presence of life. Thus, in Matthew, Jesus likens those caught in loveless piety and devotion to white washed tombs that "look beautiful (*oraioi*) but are filled inside with dead bones and every kind of filth," an image that speaks to the aesthetic of illusion and death shattered by the Cross (Matthew 23:27-35). For in the presence of the Cross, man cannot anymore be silent, as one is in front of the lifeless statue or sign of God—what happens also when the cross does not bear the Crucified—but must speak to his own abandonment of God and fellow man. Before the utterance of redemption is heard, *He is risen*, all forms must rupture first in the cry of guilt and sin, then in the joy of the new life.

The Crucifixion is the essential iconographic moment of Christianity and as such defines its art. Hans Urs Von Balthasar has noted that *after Christ* art springs from an abundance of being; form comes to the artist not from the imagination or from culture, but "from beings themselves," awakened to the love of the Trinity.[7] Brought to utterance through Christ's sacrifice, this new Adamic being is no longer the object of human "representation," since, now sanctified, it is *free* to be itself and to be "presented" as such, its itinerary open, though not without anguish, to the post-Resurrection artist.[8] Thus, for Von Balthasar, modern subjectivist aesthetics, where expression is appropriated by the human voice and sensibility (so that only man speaks for being and represents it), is problematic because it violates the freedom that Christ in his Passion bestowed on all things. There is another caveat. Being that is ordered to Passion cannot be apathetic. Inert, stylized form does not belong to Christian art. The art of beauty, the form within which there is no "nonform" (*Ungestalt*) and in which therefore the void or *kenosis* of the Cross is erased, either precedes or ignores the Incarnation.[9] What undermines aestheticism for Von Balthasar is the fact that it

7. Hans Urs von Balthasar, *Theo-Drama, Theological Dramatic Theory*, vol. II, trans. G. Harrison (San Francisco: Ignatius Press, 1990), pp. 26-27.

8. Ibid., p. 31.

9. Ibid., p. 27.

refuses to recognize our world as a place of horror and loss—the same recognition that it denies to the Cross.[10] It is only by a misconception of the Resurrection that art glorifies either God or man. Von Balthasar's warning is scriptural to the core. Paul's mystical vision of the body as a *topos* (place) of perpetual Passion invites us to de-aestheticize art. For we are called to embody not only Christ's dying (*nekrosis*) but also as *periferontes* (carrying) suggests, to bear that unique death in its promise of life—a circumscription where flesh once again contains Him, lives and breathes, dies and rises with Him (2Corinthians 4:10). The Latin translates Paul's Greek better than the English: *semper mortificationem Iesu in corpore circumferentes ut et vita Iesu in corpore nostro manifestatur* (always carrying in the flesh the dying of Jesus so that the life of Jesus may be shown in our flesh clearly). One need not doubt a Marian modality in this passage, by which, what has been called "aesthetic," is now ordered to her person and mystery. Art is to carry being as Mary did, by an act of surrender, adoration and perpetual union with her Son that culminates in her sharing the self-emptying of the Cross.[11]

In his mystical study of Christ, *On the Grace and Humanity of Jesus* (delivered as a series of lectures in 1964), Maritain, like Von Balthasar, objects to a triumphalist Cross on which Christ suffers in divine isolation, apart from human suffering.[12] The example he gives is the crucified Christ *Pantocrator* (all-powerful) of the Orthodox tradition, the Christ reigning victorious over all creation, even in death. For Maritain, this conception of Christ undermines human participation in the crucifixion: "the crucifix bearing the *Pantocrator* becomes the symbol of a common consciousness in which the sense of the Cross is still very insufficiently developed."[13] For the Cross to be complete, it must issue an invitation to communion; according to Maritain, it must become a Passion jointly suffered by God and man. Otherwise, Christ's mystical body stands apart. In His isolated divinity, Jesus suffers what man can only view from a distance—a divine spectacle to be imitated but not shared.[14] The difference here is one between imitation and participation, contemplation and radical communion. The Orthodox *Pantocrator* also represents an abandonment of Jesus and

10. Ibid., pp. 29-30.
11. John Paul II, *Encyclical Letter: Redemptoris Mater (Mother of the Redeemer)*, March 25, 1987, #18.
12. Jacques Maritain, *On the Grace and Humanity of Jesus*, trans. Joseph W. Evans (New York: Herder and Herder, 1969), pp. 30-34.
13. Ibid., p. 31.
14. Ibid., p. 32.

a rejection of human complicity, Maritain argues: "Jesus *has received no aid* from others in order to suffer and in order to accomplish the work of which He alone was capable."[15] In the same context we read an objection to another extreme often encountered in Spanish art: dolorism, the reduction of the Cross to an instrument of torture and that of Christ to its human victim. Thus if on the one hand, Christ is in His most human moment only a reigning God rising in glory against the backdrop of a fallen humanity, on the other hand, He is in His most divine moment only a ravaged servant. Either position, being extreme, disrupts and distorts the economy of the Cross that is centered on its *mesotes* or *mediocritas* (mean). From Maritain's standpoint, the Cross is the *locus mysticus* (mystical place) of communion, the intersection and union of God and man, in which the *theanthropic* mystery is both finalized and opened to humanity. But essential in this union is the presence of the man of history, a condition to which Christ himself on the Cross is subjected: "Each one indeed carries his own cross," Maritain writes, "but … this cross is, *in reality*, a tiny little portion of the Cross of Jesus. There is but one Cross, that of the Savior—that Cross, *Spes unica* (sole hope), which is the primary end of the Incarnation, and in which we are called to participate."[16]

In emphasizing the communal nature of Christ's Passion, Maritain opens the mysteries of the Cross to human history. He calls it a place of "horror and dereliction" in the presence of which most would be tempted to close their eyes. The desire to see only Christ's love and redemption—the "gentleness of His heart which passes to the instrument of His torment"—makes it easy to forget that the Cross is also "hard, abominably hard."[17] This "naked" hardness is at the center of human history and sin, where man allows or causes his fellow man and child to suffer degradation, excruciating pain, or death.[18] It makes present for all to see what is most difficult to accept: that man should so suffer as his God did and that as long as man allows and causes others to suffer, so suffers his God, so suffers he, so is the Cross raised and Christ crucified. God, writes Maritain, "has sent His Son in order to make Him suffer in all plenitude—a certain day where all the times are gathered together—that which is *inadmissible to man*."[19] Thus gathered in the Crucified, from the

---

15. Ibid.
16. Ibid., pp. 30-33.
17. Ibid., p. 36.
18. Ibid., pp. 34-37.
19. Ibid., p. 37.

beginning of history, are the sins of humanity that find there their redemption. The Cross is alive. Man in his sin and need, God in His love and
abundance meet there. The absence of this vitality is the reason that Maritain
finds the *Pantocrator* concept and image problematic.

II

Knowing that Maritain has written repeatedly about suffering and art, particularly with reference to modernism, it is reasonable to find his meditations on
the Cross aesthetically challenging. If the Christian artist is to stand with eyes
open to the divinity and humanity of Christ's Passion, he or she must resist the
temptation to avoid the torment of the Cross either by idealizing it or making it
culturally salient – as Von Balthasar also cautions.[20] There is a beautiful passage
that deserves to be quoted in full as its aesthetic and mystical sensibility show
well how Maritain understood and experienced the relationship between redemption and art. It also makes clear why the image of the Cross raised against
a heavenly rather than an earthly world (the former traditionally favored by
Orthodox iconography), would be incomplete from his standpoint.

> Jesus has taken on Him[self] all the *sufferings* at the same time as all the
> *sins*, all the *sufferings* of the past, of the present, and of the future, gathered
> together, concentrated in Him as in a convergent mirror, in the instant that
> by His sacrifice He became,—in a manner *fully consummated* and through
> the sovereign exercise of His liberty and of His love of man achieving in
> supreme obedience and supreme union the work which was entrusted to
> Him—the Head of humanity in the victory over sin.[21]

This "convergent mirror," at once opaque and luminous, is the Cross and
Corpus of the Crucified. Maritain discerns in this mirror the darkest of human passions and sins and the loving acts of sacrifice of all those that partake
of Christ (His life and death) and stand transfigured in His mystical body.
Suffering humanity is vitally present in the Cross; it is not merely imaged or
simulated. This notion shapes Maritain's aesthetics, as we shall see later. In
the ancient Christological hymn, recalled by Paul in his letter to the Colossians,
all things of heaven and earth, living and dead, gather, rest and find their
peace *per sanguinem crucis eius* that is, in and through the blood of Christ's
Cross. (1Colossians:13-20). For Maritain too Christ crucified cannot be a

20. Von Balthasar, pp. 26-27.
21. Maritain, *On The Grace and Humanity of Jesus*, pp. 41-42.

man empty of other men, of the visceral and carnal modalities that constitute human agony and desolation and bring to the cruelty of the Cross the devastation of life and nature that has marked human history. He cannot be shown in the form of a type, a formulaic figure, empty of emotion. He must be fully man and fully God, as we are taught by the mystery of the Incarnation. Thus, in the midst of the light of Resurrection, we encounter the darkness of the abominable pain of the Cross in which all human suffering from the beginning of time is gathered. It is from the midst of this darkness that man is finally free to utter with Christ *Deus meus, ut quid dereliquisti me* (my God, why have you abandoned me)? We may think here of an absence, retraction and silence of being in the very midst of its plenitude and abundance, an offering of itself that leaves it empty, bearing only the form of love—a concept difficult but not impossible to visualize.

Now, if we consider these ideas in the context of his rejection of the *Pantocrator* Christ, they give additional reasons for finding that type problematic, especially from an aesthetic point of view. The dialectic of light and darkness, of *plerosis* (filling or fulfillment) and *kenosis* (emptying), is central to the Byzantine icon whose form defined Christian art in the West until the time of Giotto. For Maritain, this dialectic is important and remains a central part of his definition of Christian art. What is missing from the icon, Maritain would suggest, is a particular kind of physicality, the presence of sacrificed and sanctified flesh, flesh common (vulgar) but also set apart, transfigured. Maritain wants art that fasts and feasts, delights and devastates, judges and redeems, and belongs, as does Christ Crucified, to the fullness of hell and the fullness of heaven. Here the coordinates of the Cross are central; art must take artist and viewer to the depths and heights of the human spirit, the darkness of the tomb and the light of the Resurrection. Maritain calls these modalities "scandalous" and his description vividly recalls the rhythm and iconography of St. Bonaventure's *Lignum Vitae* (*The Tree of Life*). The imagery is vivid and intense: "God made flesh, God in agony, God condemned, God spit upon and scourged, God crowned with thorns, God nailed to the Cross, God dead, God buried and risen?"[22] The question mark at the end is appropriate since the Cross has a time in the future, it remains open; death does not seal it just as the Resurrection does not annul it. Thus for art, the form that disintegrates in matter, that is

---

22. Ibid., p. 38. Compare especially with two stations in *Lignum Vitae*, "Jesus Nailed to the Cross" and "Jesus Given Gall to Drink." St. Bonaventure, *Bonaventure: The Classics of Western Spirituality*, trans. E. Cousins (New York: Paulist Press, 1978), pp. 148-53.

broken to its death, must also, within the same image or object, be reconfigured, saved and redeemed. It must be shown with an intimation of wholeness, to which it is open and yielding.

In his essays on Carmelite mystical theology in *The Degrees of Knowledge*, Maritain distinguishes ontological from mystical suffering. In the latter the soul, in self-surrender, dies a death that "does not obliterate sensibility, it refines and makes it more exquisite; it does not harden the fibers of being, it softens and spiritualizes them, it transforms us into love."[23] We find a brief mention of the Dominican (Thomist) and Carmelite aesthetic in a comparison of the works of Fra Angelico and El Greco. Unity of truth defines Fra Angelico's Thomist vision whereas a unity of love orders the Carmelite passion visible in El Greco's elongated figures that stretch in darkness transfigured toward the invisible horizon of God's presence.[24] For Maritain, the two are not mutually exclusive. Drawn out of contemplation, love mystically unites the human soul to God, a notion shared by both St. Thomas and St. John of the Cross.[25] Reconciliation and order belong to contemplation, but to the heart belongs disparity which only love can vanquish. Contemplation and rupture, delight and agony are joined in the mystical death of God on the Cross. Having first lost everything in a darkness or night of the senses, the poet recovers there the luminous and subtle forms of transfiguring love, as did St. John in his *Spiritual Canticle*.[26] Thus the artist who senses mystically does so with his or her senses dead to the world, but not in the ontological sense that impoverishes and destroys nature or that empties art of beauty. Here we see why both St. Thomas and St. John are relevant. Writes Maritain, "the perfection, not only moral, but metaphysical, of the human creature was never and will never be more fully achieved than when the most beautiful of the children of men was immolated upon the wood of the cross."[27] In his short essay on the painter Georges Rouault, Maritain applies this notion to art in a most compelling way. Its language is passionate and intense, very similar to that of *On the Grace and Humanity of Jesus*. This is where we shall see clearly Maritain engage in *visio divina* (prayerful seeing), praying and living the art that he

---

23. Maritain, Jacques, *The Degrees of Knowledge*, trans. G. B. Phelan (Notre Dame, Indiana: University of Notre Dame Press, 1995), p. 353.
   24. Ibid., p. 378.
   25. Ibid., pp. 340-44, 388.
   26. Ibid., pp. 378-79.
   27. Ibid., p. 355.
   28. Ibid., pp. 382-83.

contemplates. At work are the philosopher's intellect and the mystic's sensibility. For Maritain, Rouault's art shows the vital unity of contemplation and love lived by the artist and offered graciously and mystically by his work, exactly as they are offered by the poetry of St. John of the Cross.[28] Viewed in this context, his important distinction between ontological and mystical sensibility and his Thomist and Carmelite understanding of the latter, proposes a new type of Christian art that is both profane and sacred. From Maritain's perspective what he is offering as an alternative is meant to cancel two dominant views of art in Christian tradition and life that he considers problematic.

The first is suspicion of nature and carnality and therefore of art to the extent that it brings both to attention in its object and experience. Especially in the East, where this suspicion has survived eighth and ninth century iconoclasm, the Orthodox Church responded by regulating content and expression and limiting Christian art to an auxiliary, didactic and liturgical role, as a *lingua sacra* (sacred language) in images. Thus in the East, the separation of sacred and profane art is clear and not likely to be revoked any time soon. Extreme measures prescribed by both Byzantine and Reform opponents of art have been consistently rejected by the Orthodox on the basis of philosophical and theological arguments against iconoclasm based on the Incarnation, dated to St. John Damascene and St. Theodore Studite. In the West, the legacy of Reform iconoclasm, transplanted successfully in America, is benign neglect with intervention occurring only when the work of art is expressly anti-Christian or vulgar ("offensive"). The second view is related to this aesthetic of indifference but emphasizes unconditional freedom of expression essentially determined by the artist's subjectivity. Thus art that purports to be "Catholic" or "Christian" is such by the artist's will and intention and by a consensus of taste in clergy and laity that essentially concedes the irrelevance of sacred art in worship and that of theology and spiritual life in forming aesthetic experience.

Maritain believes that there is no need to either contain Christian art within a single canonical aesthetic language, as argue the advocates of the Byzantine type, or to separate it entirely from mystical theology, prayer and *ascesis*, as happens in most instances with "Christian" art today. It is clear from his reflections on Rouault and the arguments of *Art and Scholasticism* that the Byzantine canon is not entirely dismissed. Its apophatic, purgative qualities are central to his aesthetics even as what he perceives to be its formalism and lack of vitality are rejected. In Rouault especially, Maritain finds a compelling example of the transfiguration of beauty that issues from the union of Thomist contemplation and Carmelite love.[29] But Rouault, it is worth noting, in his abstraction and rejection of naturalism, is in many instances closer to the Byzantine form than Maritain perhaps would admit. Maritain's problematic is that he wants to maintain artistic freedom though conditionally, arguing as we shall see, that it is possible for art to be both free and ordered mystically to the person of Christ.

In what follows, we shall look in some detail at the Byzantine icon and contrast its theological and aesthetic principles with those proposed by Maritain. His critique of modernism will be addressed in that context with reference to *visio divina* and the *vera icona*. With Rouault's art as a prototype for both, Maritain is embracing what is actually a Byzantine art but in a modality that seeks to be consistent with subjective, esoteric expression and certain modernist forms that emphasize abstraction. His idea of an ascetic sensibility, formed by the sacramental and spiritual life of the Church, reiterates the Byzantine solution to the relationship between art and Christ but, contrary to Byzantine practice, assumes a spirituality centered on the exploration of inner life. Thus, Maritain's ideal is an artist who masters the icon but who is also open to expanding its aesthetic range without compromising its ascetic discipline and apophatic character

III

For Orthodox Christianity, the very existence of a Christian art is a testament to the triumph of true faith over heresy, represented most poignantly in the final victory in 843, in Constantinople, of the *iconolatres* (defenders of images) against their detractors or *iconoclasts*. It was in that period that art acquired a theology and the Church sanctified the senses in what Jaroslav Pelican has aptly termed "the rehabilitation of the visual."[30]

Belief in the poverty of the senses and the reduction of art to utility, implicit in all iconoclasm, then and now, reflects the absence of *charis* (grace) for which the Greek preserves, in the sense of ingratitude (*acharistia*), the opposite of what is preserved for us in the Eucharist (*eucharistia*). Von Balthasar reads *charis* in its total sense when he reminds us that *chara* and *chairomai*, joy and enjoyment or delight are

---

29. Georges Rouault, *Georges Rouault,* Text by Jacques Maritain (New York: Harry N. Abrams, 1969), pp. 5-6.

30. Jaroslav Pelikan, *Imago Dei: The Byzantine Apologia for Icons* (Princeton: Princeton University Press, 1990); see especially pp. 99-119, the chapter under the same title.

essential to the nature of grace.[31] Thus, when being is subject to utility, it is not only graceless but also ungrateful, as are those who so order it. For where grace is absent so is enjoyment, as Puritanism amply shows in its sterile and morbid forms. To the iconoclast, the image is not a *corpus* (we could think of it only as a corpse); it has no inherent passion or begging frailty that Christ can transfigure. Its pagan origin and carnality condemn it. It is a semblance to be crushed. The idea that in Christ, man, nature and man's works are redeemed and can, in the freedom that He has gained for them, now bring forth their own goods, their own Eucharistic forms as sacrifice, however poor or vulgar they may be, is incomprehensible.[32] This is why verisimilitude becomes so important in the iconoclastic argument. In verisimilitude, the modality of the imaging itself is determined externally, its truth given by *representation* rather than by presence. For the latter, viewed exclusively in pagan terms, as an epiphany of a deity in the object of cult, is precisely what is being feared. But that fear is possible only because for the iconoclast the mystical union of Incarnation and Resurrection on the Cross, by which being is transfigured (not transcended), replenished and redeemed (and therefore too is art), is yet invisible.

Recent attempts to approach the Orthodox icon philosophically have emphasized its "eucharistic realism."[33] By realism in this context is meant the presence of Christ in the Eucharistic mystery carried as a concept to church iconography, assigned, through human agency, the same function of presenting Christ to the faithful. Thus the icon operates analogically to the Eucharist. In two studies that examine the Byzantine icon as art, in terms of its composition and unique features in comparison to Western art, Yiannis Kordis, has attempted to present it as an aesthetic object par excellence, that is independent of nature or of any effort to simulate it.[34] At the same time, as aesthetic object, the icon participates in the Eucharistic mystery analogically and dynamically by assuming a key liturgical role. Its

31. Von Balthasar, *Theo-Drama*, p. 24.
32. The separation of senses and art from the divine is a commonplace of iconoclasm as early as the third century. See the writings of Eusebius, Bishop of Caesarea (265-340) and Epiphanius, Bishop of Salamis (d. 403) in Mango, Cyril, *The Art of the Byzantine Empire, 312-1453: Sources and Documents* (Englewood Cliffs, Prentice-Hall, 1972), pp. 16-18, 41-43.
33. Yiannis Kordis, *Ta Portraita tou Fayum kai e Byzantine Eikona* ["The Portraits of Fayum and the Byzantine Icon"] (Athens: Armos, 2001), p. 64, #26.
34. Ibid., p. 69.

dynamism rests in the absence of depth by which objects, instead of re-treating in a space that distances itself from the viewer (as in perspective), take the opposite direction and meet him on the surface of the painting. It is clear, from Kordis' account that this dynamism is by no means related to an expressive form since the icon is essentially "clean" of emotion.[35] Thus on this point, we know immediately that we have a key difference with Maritain who will insist on expressiveness though not without certain conditions, as we shall see more specifically below.

It is worth spending some time on the composition of the icon in order to make clear its peculiar dynamism. Arranged according to height rather than depth, items in the icon that would otherwise be placed in the back-ground of an image are moved to the upper part of the composition forming a vertical hierarchy. Through a frontal projection of surface, objects appear to be shown from above, in full rather than partial view. Linear and sche-matic, these figures move toward the viewer out of their two-dimensional frame, entering liturgical space and time, a sacred, ecclesiastical domain in which their place is not different from that of the words and sounds that constitute the Byzantine liturgy. Thus what is distinct about the Orthodox liturgical experience, if we may use that term, is that, though polymor-phous, it remains ordered to Scripture, essentially to the Word, as surrogates of which sound and image preach and sanctify. The latter is especially important to stress since otherwise the Byzantine icon would assume the function given to art by Reform theology. What sanctifies the icon is that being detached from the natural world, it is also exempted from the com-munication of character and personality or of the carnal vitality associated with physical form. Kordis insists that were the icon geared toward nature, as in the art of the Renaissance, it would draw attention away from the mysteries taking place in church. As he sees it, if that were the direction of the aesthetic object in sacred art (i.e., beyond the image and toward the object depicted), the eye would direct the mind to seek truth in either the natural or secular realm, a move that is essentially anti-ecclesial. Another fundamental problem with this shift in the aesthetic object is the confusion of secular and soteriological function. For especially with regard to the latter, we can explain the austerity and economy of the Byzantine form. In the icon, facial features are emphasized separately (delineated as eye, nose and mouth), thus undermining the vital unity that one typically experiences

---

35. Ibid., pp. 71, 43. See also Yiannis Kordis, *En Rythmo, To Ethos tes Grammes ste Byzantine Zografike* ["In Rhythm: The Ethos of the Line in Byzantine Painting"] (Athens: Armos, 2000), p. 72.

in a face. As a result, the entire figure is marked by an express lack of interior life—it is by design "empty" and "cold."[36] As Kordis points out, the Byzantine solution to art's liturgical function is to establish an aesthetic dynamism based on compositional principles rather than a dynamism that is inherent in form and emphasizes expression—what Von Balthasar and Maritain would support.[37]

St. Theodore the Studite's insistence that "substance" (*hupostasis*) in sacred art should only be rendered in the modality of a thing's appearance explains the expressive emptiness of the icon. Jesus, Mary and the saints may be shown as human beings but they may not be rendered in their distinct particularity, in the *fullness* of a human person.[38] The icon presenting Christ is only presenting a certain man and it does that through similitude or semblance—the main sense of *eikon* in Greek—refusing to present him in his inner and outer vitality since art, it is reasoned, cannot render substance. Thus we have in this view the persistence of the Neoplatonic semblance for which the image remains defined by the basic meaning of *eikon*, always a reflection, never an object in its own right. Kordis' move to make the icon aesthetic, an *eikon par excellence,* that is independent of verisimilitude, avoids rather than answers the question. Instead of a suffering *man* we are shown a suffering *type* who *stands for* the man and in this sense *re-presents* him; it does not make him present, even though that is the very point on which Orthodox iconography is supposed to differ from its western counterparts.[39]

---

36. Kordis, *Ta Portraita,* pp. 43, 67.

37. Ibid., pp. 63-73.

38. Ibid., pp. 56-57. For St. Theodore Studite, art and the image specifically cannot reveal anything about the human soul. See also Cyril Mango, *The Art of the Byzantine Empire, 312-1453: Sources and Documents* (Englewood Cliffs, New Jersey: Prentise-Hall, 1972), and Hans Belting, *Likeness and Presence, A History of the Image before the Era of Art,* trans. E. Jephcott (Chicago: The University of Chicago Press, 1994) for original texts, commentary and discussion of Orthodox theology on this subject and on iconoclasm in general. According to Mango, iconoclastic debate was largely theological. Questions central to artistic theory and judgment were of little concern. Truth in art was relegated either to tradition or to conventions associated with the type and labeling of an image. See Mango, pp. 149-50.

39. The idea, as Kordis explains, is that the icon's point of reference is not the objects or figures it depicts (as in Western art) but the viewer in liturgical space with whom presumably it enters in communion. The image, qua image, or object that is aesthetically constituted, belongs to the liturgy exclusively. The truth and presence of what it depicts are never of interest and their consideration is at best a distraction. See especially Kordis, *Ta Portraita,* pp. 76-71.

Despite the existence of works in which typology and expression are intertwined (most successfully in the Cretan and Macedonian schools), the Byzantine icon continues to be regulated in both content and manner of composition by a strict typology. Outside the context of liturgy and Scripture—to which this typology is ordered—figures and objects cannot stand on their own, freely. Their being is derivative and their connection to subjectivity (either the artist's or the viewer's) is at best subtle with stylistic differences centering mostly on line and illumination.[40] Within the form itself, the absence of expressive movement in most instances complements the existence of this sacred vocabulary that any pious Orthodox iconographer (the name appropriately is "haghiographer," painter of holy things) must master.[41] Thus, the icon can be viewed as a staged narrative of Christ's life, ordered to distinct episodes or scenes. Icons are illustrative of the sacred text (and its liturgical extension), but seem to share little of its inherent passion, the hidden Paschal event that permeates the life of Christ—and of which Mary is the first station. Only forms that function mnemonically or semiotically, by insertion in scriptural and liturgical language, can participate in the economy of redemption. Thus the faces of the saints, of Christ and His Mother, appear empty and purged of passion, as if the Paschal mystery is already over and the viewer looks at the icon as a window to the world of Resurrection and Christ's glory.

With their schematic figures forming against an illuminated screen, icons are symbolically infused with divine light but remain immobile and silent, insinuating but not presenting their passion. Ascetically formed, in certain cases emaciated, they seem to have transcended all carnal modalities, death included. They show no expressive urge, no extension and rupture of flesh toward the Word, away from its own finality and sin, with that anguish that Maritain found in Rouault or that Von Balthasar insists that art can and should realize. Thus, what is called "eucharistic" does not contain the full humanity of Christ's Passion; rather, what the icon is trying to convey is that what Christ offers of himself, he offers from the direction of the Father namely, his divine nature in which the

40. It was not until the sixteenth century and even later that icons were inscribed with the name of the painter and donor. For a brief history of Byzantine haghiography, see Athanasios A. Karakatsanis, *Treasures of Mount Athos* (Thessaloniki: Museum of Byzantine Culture, 1997), p. 49.

41. The classic example of a haghiographer's manual is Dionysos of Fourna, *Ermeneia tes Zografikes Technes* ["Interpretation of the art of painting"]. See Greek translation by K.C. Spanos, (Athens 1997) of Russian edition; *Manuel D'Iconographie Chretienne*, ed. A. Papadopoulos-Kerameus (St. Petersbourg: Imprimerie B. Kirschbaum, 1909).

mystery of Communion is contained. The *charisma* (given and gift) that places the Cross as body and blood within the center of the Eucharist, are not directly, literally depicted. This is a sensibility that approaches radical asceticism in which man can be saved only if he loses his physical vitality and if nature follows him in that loss.

Maritain's objection to this view is that love and the rupture that brings form to utterance (confession) cannot be present without that vitality. The contrast therefore between the Byzantine icon and what he is proposing is that the icon insists on strict regulation of form and expression and resists rupture on an individual basis, even if that individual is Christ Himself. For Maritain, as one who has the benefit of an aesthetic vision formed by Thomistic and Carmelite mysticism as well as by his own profound love for art, this restriction is unnecessary. Still, to make the contrast sharper, we must point out that what characterizes the best of Byzantine painting is inner tension and restraint. Tension rather than expression, introverted rather than extroverted dynamism is clearly visible in its forms. One of the best examples is the *Man of Sorrows* type, associated thematically with the deposition of Christ and historically with end-of-eleventh century Byzantine Hymns on the Lamentations of the Virgin on her son's Passion. In an icon titled *Deposition of Christ* (c. 1400), we have an excellent case of Byzantine introversion and interiority.[42] The silent communication between the dead Christ and His sorrowful mother is at once mystical and intimate suggesting that his death is only physically present, as the rendering of his body makes plain. In fact this is the silent dynamism of form that Maritain will admire in Rouault but in the context of a different aesthetics and theology.

IV

Maritain, as we have seen, finds the idea of a "confessional" or "clerical" Christian art deeply problematic[43]. From his perspective, the grace and mercy of the Cross make any external restriction of art's form redundant, a regression to a time before Christ's advent. Grace "heals the wounds of nature," making art's redemption and liberation possible.[44] Art is "freed by

---

42. Anastasia Drandaki, *Greek Icons: 14th-18th Centuries, The Rena Andreadis Collection,* trans. J. Avgherinos (Milan: Skira 2002), pp. 20-21. See also, a variety of examples from the best of Cretan, Macedonian and Athonite icons in Karakatsanis, *Treasures of Mount Athos,* pp. 64-70, 104-105, 164.

43. Maritain, *Art and Scholasticism,* pp. 68-69, 137.

44. Ibid., p. 69.

grace" to create beyond illusion, to be genuinely "inspired."[45] This means that its ontology is mystically formed and awaits recognition. Maritain seems to suggest that art's freedom precedes that of the artist and that the artist enters art not unlike we enter the Church through the sacraments. Already, he notes, the Church has more than one liturgy, and that because she has as "her sole object ... worship and union with her Savior, and from this loving worship an excess of beauty overflows."[46] For Maritain, this activity of love in which the Church is mystically formed is the same activity that, by analogy, forms art. It is not by design but by gift that art escapes the monotony of norm or the uniformity of principle. Just as in liturgy there is no one exclusive rite, no need for regulation and uniformity, so too in art there is no one canonical sacred language or "religious technique."[47] Where the qualities of sacred art are prescribed, notes Maritain, it becomes isolated from the human community, losing not only its relevance to its age but also its expressive vitality. "Confine it," he cautions, "and it becomes corrupted, its expression a dead letter."[48] Given totally to Christ, art, like being, finds its own inherent measure to which the artist freely and vitally responds. This vitality is profoundly ecclesial and mystical. A Christian art, Maritain explains, will "emerge and impose itself only if it springs spontaneously from a common renewal of art and sanctity in the world"—as happened in the Middle Ages.[49]

Writing about the art that we now classify as "modernism," Maritain uses language that suggests his Carmelite view of the Cross. Like modern man, art is called from Golgotha to bear witness to its own predicament, to suffer its own testimony to its age. Here the Greek *marturion* (*martur*: suffering witness) is appropriate; not used by Maritain, it is nevertheless implicit in what he expects of art. The artist that is called to see and testify will live through her art; the artist will be part of it, impressed by it, called to communion, even against his or her will. Artists, we are told, are called to God in "an age far removed from Christ," and, in that unwanted vocation, face "excruciating" difficulty.[50] Ironically (but providentially) those who come to art in a "simple-minded idolatry" that worships the self and its works, are bound to suffer even more.[51] For Maritain, the disposition of

45. Ibid., pp. 68-69.
46. Ibid., p. 72.
47. Ibid., p. 143.
48. Ibid., p. 142.
49. Ibid., p. 73.
50. Ibid., p. 69.
51. Ibid., p. 117.

art, any art, is toward the recesses of being so that the artist, even when unaware and unprepared—perhaps especially then—is touched and broken by its mystery and hidden realities. From this silent communion, sanctified by Christ, art leads man to *ascesis* and redemption. This is why the artist that seeks to possess and order form to his subjectivity stands exposed in that very act, for the work, like the wood of the Cross, openly bears his (and our) failure. In being preoccupied with the Self, the artist violates a plenitude that is offered to him freely and therefore risks in that rejection of love for the sake of one's Self and will, the unbearable truth of Christ's judgment shown in the artist's work. In one of his essays on St. John of the Cross, Maritain reminds us that the liberty availed by Christ is not ordered to the flesh but to the "Holy Spirit who sanctifies and sacrifices."[52] Thus the artist, seeking her liberty in the opposite direction finds, through an exercise of divine mercy, the path to the Cross. Here, in this turn or conversion—something that Maritain sought and nourished in his artist friends but also experienced in his own life—lies the redemptive nature of art, its *charismatic* being.

Drawing on our "essential creative weakness," art reveals human sin: "the work of art always ends by betraying, with infallible cunning, the vices of the workman," as the Cross betrays our vices, then and now.[53] Thus, we may speak of a transparency that the work of art has, not just to the moral disposition of the artist, but also to the artist's sensibility, to the way that is, that her senses approach and constitute the world. Writes Maritain: "All that is most real in the world escapes the notice of the darkened soul."[54] What in being is transcendental, its goodness, beauty and truth, withdraws in the presence of sin from the artist's sensibility so that in the *kenosis* that follows, the artist encounters only a haunting absence that the work makes unbearably bare. Maritain's insight is profound, considering that in modernism the artist was to be finally emancipated from rules and norms, and emerge as a master of her own creative destiny. The agony that he calls "excruciating," comes from the failure of that hope, from a loss of self against all expectations; a loss of the artist to art—the work "is made by art alone."[55] Like a disoriented and abandoned child, "simple-minded" man stands deceived, unloved by his own creation. In

---

52. Maritain, *The Degrees of Knowledge*, p. 387.
53. Maritain, *Art and Scholasticism*, pp. 117-18.
54. Ibid., p. 118.
55. Ibid., p. 132.

response, art comes to speak the strange truth, a truth so relevant to today's art: having denied the gift of grace, we stand wounded, absent from our own creations—the idol now rising and effacing man. This conclusion is interesting because it assumes an initial rejection of Christ and the Church typical of art in the recent centuries. It thus situates the artist with an illusion of freedom for which he ultimately has to confront a meaningless and impersonal art and thus the failure of expression. From the Orthodox perspective, this may be a predictable outcome, accepted on faith by those who submit in obedience to the *lingua sacra* of the Byzantine icon and its sensibility. At the same time, the implicit distinction of a sacred and profane art, with which the Orthodox seem quite comfortable, is problematic for Maritain who seems to want a convergence of all art, even if in an ideal time, to Christ.

"Christ crucified draws to Himself everything there is in man." Modern art "must be converted to find God again," Maritain writes. In modernism and what follows it, there is, even for those that cannot see it, a dark night of the soul, an aridity of spirit and absence of love at the end of which art will finally recognize its true mission.[56] Converted, art is an "ascetic discipline," a spiritual exercise intent on transfiguring matter by making it "resplendent with a dominating intelligibility."[57] Here *claritas* (radiance) exists not formally—on the surface of the design—but vitally since as Maritain notes in a different context, the work brings to life a "a new creature, an original being capable in its turn of moving a human soul."[58] This is possible only because the artist, having found in things a sacred plenitude, a generosity that cannot be possessed and to which she is called not only to respond but to reciprocate by an open commitment to Christ—ultimately by love—brings form to utterance. Maritain writes movingly of Rouault's painting that it "clings, … to the secret substance of visible reality" and therefore its "realism" does not refer to matter but to the "spiritual significance of what exists (and moves, and suffers, and loves and kills)." Describing a profound communion between being and subjectivity, he calls Rouault's art "transfigurative, … obstinately attached to the soil while living on faith and spirituality."[59] The connection to Carmelite spirituality is direct and explicit. In all great artists, Maritain notes, we find a "unity of creative emotion and working reason." But that in itself is not sufficient to result in great or

56. Ibid., pp. 118, 116, 139.
57. Ibid., p. 130.
58. Ibid., p. 63.
59. Rouault, *Georges Rouault*, pp. 21-22.

properly Christian art. What is "native privilege" must be perfected and that requires purgation, the model of which is the luminous darkness of the Cross. The work of art is the culmination or "final victory of a steady struggle inside the artist's soul, which has to pass through trials and "dark nights" comparable, in the line of the creativity of the spirit, to those suffered by the mystics in their striving toward union with God." "Such," Maritain concludes, "was the case with Rouault."[60]

These observations are not forced. Studying Rouault's work, we may easily see that texture, line and color have a fluid and graphic solidity, a sort of spiritual *gravitas* that defies the flatness of the canvas on the one side and the superficiality of an arbitrary subjectivity on the other. It is indicative of this *gravitas* that light has been thoroughly internalized and integrated with color and texture so that it is not external or accidental to the figures and objects present but an inimical part of their vitality and being. It is light rendered silent, pensive, solitary, desolate, contemplative and penitential, exactly as we suggested for the icon titled *The Deposition of Christ*. In lithographs like Rouault's *Veronica's Veil* (1930), this subtle illumination of flesh and matter that turns into utterance even as nothing and no one speaks, is even more pronounced; it recalls again the Byzantine icon and its often dramatic linearity. The same with *The Funeral* (1930) in which light, set deeply within the outlines and textures of things, brings the dark procession into an other day and time, the end of death and the beginning of new life. Especially in *Veronica's Veil* the degree of abstraction and intense illumination within the forms themselves that eliminates detail, recalls the emotional and expressive emptiness of faces and figures in the Byzantine icon. Kordis refers to it as the *neptic* path (vigilance, watchfulness), by which artist and public, being faithful Christians, engage in a *catharsis* of mind and heart.[61] What is different though in Rouault, that a Byzantine icon would never show, is the expansion of the line itself into an expressive object. In the icon the delineation of objects, figures and their constitutive parts is imperative. The boundaries that separate them are clear and distinct. As a result, the inner tension of forms is subject to internal and external restraint and the line serves that purpose.

For Maritain, Rouault's art is itself a sign of grace and redemption, a response to the artist's confession: "I was not made to be so terrible."[62] Studied without theological assumptions, Rouault's paintings do present a

60. Ibid., p. 16.
61. Kordis, *En Rythmo*, p. 80.
62. Rouault, *Georges Rouault*, p. 28.

unity of spiritual, moral and natural life that resonates with what we may call an aesthetic communion. This is how we can best describe it. What is ugly, tormented and desolate but also redeeming in man is shared by everything around him. There is no marked domain of ugliness and beauty, vice and virtue. In *Christ Mocked by Soldiers* (1932), Christ's body is outlined in the same harsh lines and colors that make up the vulgar faces of His tormentors. Conversely, his isolation and solitude keeps them vitally close but also apart as if in their mockery they too are alone and abandoned, just like He is, a transcending humanity present in their communion of hatred and love. Thus the painting enters the Cross; it belongs to the mystical body that gathers those that sin—even against Christ Himself—and delivers them renewed in mercy. The irony of the soldiers' mockery is that they have been gathered, humanized and redeemed by the very One that they torment and reject. In the presence of Jesus, they cease to suffer their hatred. It is works like this that lead Maritain to approach Rouault's art as an invitation to prayer. Here it is not aesthetic empathy that moves him but encounter with art's mystical participation in the Cross. Elsewhere in that essay he notes Rouault's fascination with Veronica's veil, marked by Christ's face, as if "to imprint the divine mercy on human art."[63] In this phrase Maritain describes in almost epigrammatic form the mystery that unites art and Cross, a mystery that Rouault witnessed in his art as he himself confesses in the short poem that prefaces his *Miserere* (1922) etchings.[64]

Conclusion

From the standpoint of this brief remark, the impact of the *Mandylion* or *Veronica* on the Christian imagination can be understood in a way that radically departs from anthropological and art historical interpretation—especially of the kind that is theologically void.[65] Intimacy with Christ—in an impression that is not a semblance but rather, as that tradition has consistently perceived, a relic, a gratuitous extension of His living body—reiterates the mysteries of His person in which the ancient and contemporary Church find their uninterrupted vocation. More than the *acheiropoietos*, the image painted without human hands, the *Mandylion* perpetuates the moment where Incarnation and Cross transfigured the

63. Ibid., p. 34.
64. Ibid., p. 36.
65. On the Veronica and Mandylion, see Belting, *Likeness and Presence*, 1994, chapters 4 and 11.

senses having first, at the abominable sight of the Crucifixion, stripped them of meaning and relevance. In art that is ordered to the *vera icona* and is therefore, according to Maritain, Christian in the fullest sense of the word, truth is not that of a form or type matched to the object or person that it depicts—as in a similitude. It is rather, the truth of a *stigma*, a mark of blood and sweat directly deposited and impressed, in which, by analogy to the Passion, cloth, wound and agony are indistinguishable. This is not a mere mark. Like the stigmata of the saints, it is a *living wound* in which, in paradox, the redemptive and salvific mystery of the Cross is offered to the senses, as Christ first showed to Thomas. The wounds are Christ's but also the artist's who, nailed with Christ on the Cross, struggles, as Maritain wrote of El Greco, to convert and transfigure a world that, seduced by sin and drawn to illusion or to unredeemed sensuality, resists transfiguration.

In the work of art, the artist's communion with Christ's Passion is transferred to canvas, wood or any part of nature on which he or she works. The notion of *ascesis* to which Maritain refers the practice of art and the life of the artist finds fulfillment in the *vera icona*. For Maritain, Rouault's art bears the stigmata of redemption not in what it shows—its subject matter—but in the manner that it delivers form, in its lines, light, colors and texture, the artist's intimate spiritual and carnal language, true to Christ because it has been purified in His love. This is why in *Christ Mocked by Soldiers*, we do not see mockery or opposition but three figures united in a shared Passion, not in an intentional, designed manner but in a spontaneous translation of the artist's subtle vision and sensibility. This is art that is aesthetically, theologically and mystically significant, an example of what Maritain saw in some modern artists which led him to believe that their work should not be rejected by the Church as irreverent or put aside as irrelevant.

For Maritain, Christian art is art that is inextricably ecclesial and mystical and in so being has realized its ontological and theological vocation. In his view, it is possible for the artist to discover her vocation and also the unique path to Christ without conforming to any singular *lingua sacra*. This is a fundamental difference with the Orthodox view but not necessarily one that is irreconcilable. Ultimately, for Maritain, art that is vital to the human spirit and profound in the questions it poses about human existence and purpose in life and the order of things, leads to Christ. For the Orthodox too, the icon's inner tension and luminosity, cannot be achieved by a mere adherence to a typology or an iconographic manual. The best evidence for that, in an age where the commercial icon has proliferated, is the striking difference between that work of skill and the work that is properly *haghiographic*, i.e., where the artist's hand is guided by God and trained in an *ascesis* of spirit and sense. In the end, the languages of Christian art may converge in the tense, restrained and luminous silence of the Byzantine icon, infused perhaps with the expressive dynamism that Maritain admired in many of Rouault's works. For the reader who is eager to see icons that presage this convergence, the fourteenth century icon *John the Baptist* in Vatopedi Monastery, Mount Athos, is a good example.[66]

66. Karakatsanis, *Treasures of Mount Athos*, p. 84.

"No Literary Orthodoxy": Flannery O'Connor, the New Critics, and Jacques Maritain

Sarah J. Fodor

Flannery O'Connor could be as ferocious a defender of the integrity of the literary work as the leading "New Critics" of the 1950s and 60s: John Crowe Ransom, Allen Tate, Cleanth Brooks, and Robert Penn Warren. In the O'Connor Collection in Milledgeville, Georgia, is a videotape of O'Connor's 1955 television interview with *New York Times* reporter Harvey Breit. The segment preceded a dramatization of her short story, "The Life You Save May Be Your Own." Breit asks sweetly, "Flannery, would you like to tell our audience what happens in [the rest of] that story?" and O'Connor retorts, "No, I certainly would not. I don't think you can paraphrase a story like that. I think there is only one way to tell it and that's the way it is told in the story."[1]

Many critics have concluded that O'Connor is a "New Critical" writer. One has only to consider her carefully crafted fiction, in which every detail counts to construct a meaningful whole, to see how her stories reward the close reading advocated by New Critics. O'Connor wrote her first stories while at the State University of Iowa's Writer's Workshop during the late 1940s, when New Critics had begun to wield great power within American universities. She published her tales in journals affiliated with New Critics,

1. Rosemary Magee, ed., *Conversations with Flannery O'Connor* (Jackson, Mississippi: University Press of Mississippi, 1987), p. 8.

such as *The Kenyon Review*, where Ransom was editor. Finally, O'Connor herself acknowledged that she was a member of "'that literary generation whose education was in the hands of the New Critics or those influenced by them, and with these people the emphasis was on seeing that your thoughts and feelings—whatever they were—were aptly contained within your elected image.'"[2]

Even as O'Connor acknowledges this influence, her statements about the New Critics are ambivalent. Her wording—"in the hands of ... these people"—suggests she wants to distance herself from New Critical aesthetics even as she embraces them. She does not so much claim that the New Critics—"or those influenced by them"—educated her personally as that they influenced her "literary generation." While acknowledging the pervasiveness of the New Critical aesthetic during her formative years, she maintains a separation from it.

O'Connor admired and maintained friendly contacts with Ransom, Tate, and Warren, but she was skeptical about the value of literary theory for guiding writing. Less than a decade after graduating from Iowa, she does not hesitate to mock it. In a 1953 letter to Sally Fitzgerald, she describes a talk given by poet Robert Lowell, who suffered from manic-depressive disorder: "Toward the end he gave a lecture at the university that was almost pure gibberish. I guess nobody noticed, thinking it was the new criticism."[3] Later, on a more serious note, during a 1960 lecture on "Some Aspects of the Grotesque in Southern Literature," O'Connor locates her fiction at the confluence of several literary traditions:

> ... this tradition of the dark and divisive romance-novel has combined with the comic-grotesque tradition, and with the lessons all writers have learned from the naturalists, to preserve our Southern literature for at least a little while from becoming the kind of thing Mr. Van Wyck Brooks desired when he said he hoped that our next literary phase would restore that central literature which combines the great subject matter of the middlebrow writers with the technical expertness bequeathed by the new critics and which would thereby restore literature as a mirror and guide for society.
>
> For the kind of writer I have been describing, a literature which mirrors society would be no fit guide for it, and one which did manage, by sheer art, to do both these things would have to have recourse to more violent means than middlebrow subject matter and mere technical expertness.[4]

2. Frederick Asals, *Flannery O'Connor: The Imagination of Extremity* (Athens, Georgia: University of Georgia Press, 1982), p. 130.

3. Flannery O'Connor, *The Habit of Being: Letters,* ed. Sally Fitzgerald (New York: Farrar, 1979), p. 74.

4. Flannery O'Connor, *Mystery and Manners: Occasional Prose,* ed. Sally Fitzgerald and Robert Fitzgerald (New York: Farrar, 1969), p. 46.

O'Connor disparages New Critics as focusing on "mere technical expertness" while she implicitly claims for herself the difficult marriage of mimetic and didactic goals ("mirror and guide") and claims the "violent means" that characterize her *oeuvre*.

O'Connor's statements in her letters, essays, and interviews indicate that her literary aesthetics *was* New Critical in important ways, but only to the extent that techniques valued by New Critics, like narrative objectivity and symbolism, enabled her to write fiction that provides "a mirror and guide for contemporary society," and that, in particular, reflects her Catholic faith. She never hesitated to acknowledge the orthodoxy of her faith but, at the same time, insisted on the freedom of the artist: "There is no literary orthodoxy that can be prescribed as settled for the fiction writer."[5] She preferred to ground her practice in the example of other writers, in her own experiences, and in Thomistic aesthetics. These three sources form an integrated core of O'Connor's aesthetics.

Previous scholars have ably demonstrated how O'Connor found models for her use of sensory detail and symbolic imagery not only in New Critical aesthetics, but also in the fiction of authors such as Henry James and Joseph Conrad and in Christian sacramentalism. Our sense of the New Criticism today, however, typically foregrounds the "technical expertness" that O'Connor belittled while overlooking the role of intuition in artistic creation that is emphasized by New Critics such as Brooks and Warren as well as Thomist philosopher Jacques Maritain who, like the New Critics, was a formative influence on O'Connor.[6]

As is abundantly clear in the TV interview, O'Connor's concept of the literary work parallels the New Critical view that the work of art is complete in itself—autonomous, unique, and organic. She shares the New Critical dictum that though the literary work embodies meaning, a paraphrase can never fully account for the work. Like the New Critics, O'Connor prefers fiction that "shows" rather than "tells." In the tradition of Gustave Flaubert and Henry James, the New Critics insist that poetry and fiction, like drama, should be presentational. In their respective fiction textbooks, Brooks and Warren as well as O'Connor's mentor Caroline Gordon and her husband,

5. O'Connor, *Mystery*, p. 32.
6. O'Connor had read Maritain's *Art and Scholasticism* by 1950 when she stayed with Sally and Robert Fitzgerald in Connecticut to work on *Wise Blood*. By 1952, when she had been diagnosed with lupus and had returned home to Georgia, she asked that Sally Fitzgerald send her Maritain's book, which she had left behind. By 1955 she had developed the habit of reading St. Thomas's *Summa Theologica* every night before going to bed (O'Connor, *The Habit*, p. 93).

poet-critic Allen Tate, privilege the dramatized scene, objectively rendered. O'Connor sounds stereotypically New Critical in a 1956 letter when she pans Frances Newman's novel, *The Hard-Boiled Virgin* (1926): "dear Lord, it's all reported; the most undramatic fifty pages I have been exposed to since [Pater's] *Marius the Epicurean*."[7]

O'Connor's descriptions of the writing process reflect her belief in the organic inter-relation of character, plot, and theme, discoverable by creative intuition rather than imposed. She advises her friend "A" in December of 1956:

> When you have a character he will create his own situation and his situation will suggest some kind of resolution as you get into it. Wouldn't it be better for you to discover a meaning in what you write than to impose one? Nothing you write will lack meaning because the meaning is in you. Once you have done a first draft then read it and see what it says and then see how you can bring out better what it says.[8]

This advice seems based on O'Connor's own experience in composing. She once told an audience of student writers that she began writing "Good Country People" with "a description of two women I knew something about" who became Mrs. Hope and Mrs. Freeman. The idea of having the salesman steal Hulga's prosthetic leg didn't occur to her, she claimed, "until ten or twelve lines before he did it." O'Connor took pleasure in experiences where the story seemed to wrest control away from the author. The best stories, she said, are those that surprise the writer as well as the reader.[9]

O'Connor felt that she was writing best when she was least aware of technique. She explains to "A:"

> I have also led you astray by talking of technique as if it were something that could be separated from the rest of the story. Technique can't operate at all, of course, except on believable material. But there was less conscious technical control in GCP than in any other story I've ever written. Technique works best when it is unconscious, and it was unconscious there.[10]

O'Connor goes so far as to question Caroline Gordon's emphasis on technique—Gordon, the lifelong mentor whom, according to biographer

---

7. O'Connor, *The Habit*, p. 128.

8. Ibid., p. 188. The identity of this correspondent was kept anonymous in the publication of the letters, but has since been revealed as Betty Hester.

9. O'Connor, *Mystery*, p. 100.

10. O'Connor, *The Habit*, p. 171.

Sally Fitzgerald, "Flannery never felt ... she had outgrown."[11] Thanking editor Catharine Carver for her responses to the manuscript of *The Violent Bear It Away*, O'Connor writes, "Caroline read it but her strictures always run to matters of style. She swallows a good many camels while she is swatting the flies—though what she has taught me has been invaluable and I can never thank her enough."[12]

Gordon and Tate claimed as a "master-piece,"[13] "Good Country People," the story that O'Connor says she wrote intuitively, almost unconsciously. Allen Tate went so far as to telegraph editor Robert Giroux from Italy, urging him to make room for the story in O'Connor's first collection, *A Good Man Is Hard to Find*, then in press. Perhaps O'Connor had absorbed Gordon's technical exhortations thoroughly enough to attend to them automatically. In any case, Tate and Gordon value a story whose technical elements seem effortlessly controlled—organic.

Contrary to today's typical view of the New Criticism, Brooks and Warren also show an openness and flexibility about technical strictures. In *Understanding Fiction*, their short-story anthology that has come to represent New Critical teaching, they provide an "Appendix: Technical Problems and Principles in the Composition of Fiction," designed as an aid for student writers. Their title promises that they will focus on technique and provide rules for writing. But its opening sentence cautions, "If one learns anything about fiction from reading a limited number of short stories and novels, it is that there is no single, special technique or formula for writing good fiction."[14]

When O'Connor described her composing process, she cited everyday experience more often than theory. Although she placed her stories in the romance tradition, she also thought in terms of literary realism, taking into account probability, believability, *vraisemblance*: as she quotes one of her readers, "how some folks *would* do."[15] Likewise, Brooks and Warren explain that an appropriate question for any story concerns the believability of the characters: "Are they 'real'? ... Do their actions logically follow

11. Sally Fitzgerald, "A Master Class: From the Correspondence of Caroline Gordon and Flannery O'Connor," *Georgia Review* 33 (1979), p. 846.

12. O'Connor, *The Habit*, p. 328.

13. Caroline Gordon, letter to Flannery O'Connor, 19 February 1955, O'Connor Collection, Ina Dillard Russell Library, Georgia College and State University.

14. Cleanth Brooks and Robert Penn Warren, eds., *Understanding Fiction*, 2nd ed. (New York: Appleton, 1959) p. 570.

15. O'Connor, *Mystery*, p. 90.

from their natures?"[16] O'Connor thought of her characters as realized individuals. She writes to "A" in 1960:

> There doesn't have to be any connection between Enoch [in *Wise Blood*] and a criticism of humanism. As a fiction writer, I am interested first in Enoch as Enoch and Haze as Haze. …when I wrote it my mind was not primarily on … abstract things but only on what would Haze and Enoch do next, they being themselves."[17]

She does not deny that characters can be symbolic; rather, she sets aside such analyses while composing.

A workshop in which O'Connor participated with Robert Penn Warren in 1959 provides an extended example to compare how she and this author at the center of New Critical circles describe the writing process. Both were guests at the annual Vanderbilt University Literary Symposium. That year, the second edition of *Understanding Fiction* was published, including O'Connor's short story, "A Good Man Is Hard to Find." Vanderbilt could be seen as the birthplace of the New Criticism, as the meeting place in the early 1920s of the then-called Fugitives (a group that included Ransom, Tate, and Warren, and later, Brooks). Given the location and gender of the symposium participants, who included twelve men and one woman, the atmosphere might have overwhelmed a young woman (O'Connor was 34) on a panel with Robert Penn Warren, a famous writer, critic, and author of a text she had used as a student. There is no indication, however, that O'Connor is a bashful proselyte echoing the older, wiser mentor, or that theory dictates how she writes or describes experience. Often, she answers questions first, and Warren follows, echoing her response.[18]

O'Connor and Warren speak as writers, not theorists. Their comments communicate their sense of the intuitive nature of writing, of writing as a process of discovery and shaping. Asked about the value of outlining before writing, O'Connor states flatly, "I just don't outline." Warren adds, "I had an outline once, and it took me two years to pull out of it. You think you've got your work done." When O'Connor acknowledges that she "anticipated" the ending of "A Good Man Is Hard to Find," a student asks, "Do any of you begin with the theme first, and hunt for the story, or do you do it the other way around?" O'Connor says she begins with the *story*, "Be-

---

16. Brooks and Warren, *Understanding Fiction*, 1st ed. (1943), p. 28.
17. O'Connor, *The Habit*, p. 403.
18. Magee, *Conversations with Flannery O'Connor*, pp. 19-36. The O'Connor Collection in Milledgeville also holds a tape recording of this session.

cause the theme is more or less something that's in you, but if you intellectualize it too much you probably destroy your novel." Warren agrees with O'Connor: "I think people can freeze themselves by their hasty intellectualizing of what they are up to."[19]

Despite the prevalent view today of New Critical writing as rigidly controlled, Warren describes the writing process as intuitive, even emotional. At one point, professor and critic Walter Sullivan presses Warren to account for the technical coherence of his work: "Red, to get back to this novel business: your books are awfully well put together. The opening sequences contain so many images of the book as a whole, and prepare for so many things to happen. You've got to know a whole lot or you couldn't write that way." Warren points out, "There's no law that makes you put the first chapter first, though ...," distinguishing drafting from revising. Elaborating on his answer, he defers to O'Connor:

> I don't think it's knowing how the story comes out that's the point. As Flannery just said, you know what you want it to feel like.... You may have your big scenes in mind before you start.... You don't know whether they will jell out or not jell out. But it seems to me the important thing is to have enough feeling envisaged and prefelt, as it were, about the way the book's going to go ... as long as it is there, you have something to guide you in this automatic process of trial and error.[20]

Sullivan can't quite believe this; he insists: "This is wonderful talk, and I certainly don't want to minimize what you and Flannery have said. I think it is absolutely true, but I am speaking among company here which I know perhaps more intimately than you. I am afraid we might get a little too far off into a romantic notion of the muse." But O'Connor concurs with Warren, explaining, "When you write the thing through once, you find out what the end is. Then you can go back to the first chapter and put in a lot of those foreshadowings."[21] Jacques Maritain is not mentioned in this conversation, but he anticipated its conclusions in *Art and Scholasticism* (1920), a book O'Connor owned, annotated, and kept in her library: "Aesthetics must be intellectualist and intuitivist at one and the same time."[22]

Both O'Connor and Warren express wariness about beginning a story with "belief," with any abstract theme or idea. Asked whether belief inter-

19. Ibid., pp. 19-20.
20. Ibid., p. 21.
21. Ibid., p. 23.
22. Jacques Maritain, *Art and Scholasticism and the Frontiers of Poetry*, trans. Joseph W. Evans (New York: Charles Scribner's Sons, 1962), p. 164.

feres with writing, O'Connor replies, "I don't think a theological point of view interferes in any way unless it becomes so dominant that you're so full of ideas that you kill the character." Warren spins out this idea, asking: "Flannery, would this be true about theology or anything else: that by the sort of deductive way of going at it—illustrating the point—you're a dead duck before you start?" O'Connor agrees, fervently: "You don't begin a story with a system. You can forget about the system. These are things that you believe; they may affect your writing unconsciously. I don't think theology should be a scaffolding."[23] Again, Maritain's previous formulation resonates in O'Connor's. Discussing "The Purity of Art," he explains, "every thesis [an intention extrinsic to the work itself] whether it claims to demonstrate some truth or to touch the heart, is for art a foreign importation, hence an impurity."[24]

More often than not in her letters and essays, O'Connor cites theologians and authors rather than literary theorists to explain her aesthetics. Like the New Critics, Maritain believes that true art is not utilitarian or propagandistic. The "habit" or *habitus* of art is an inner virtue. The Christian artist can best develop this *habitus* by striving to make the best work rather than by trying to mold art into a dogmatic expression of faith.[25] In his chapter on "Christian Art," Maritain advises:

> Do not *separate* your art from your faith. But leave *distinct* what is distinct. Do not try to blend by force what life unites so well. If you were to make of your aesthetic an article of faith, you would spoil your faith. If you were to make of your devotion a rule of artistic activity, or if you were to turn desire to edify into a method of your art, you would spoil your art.[26]

Jacques Maritain was not a New Critic, but his ideas about the autonomy of art are congruent with New Critical principles. One does not have to *try* to write as a Christian, because faith and art are ultimately inseparable. Faith—like literary technique—works best in art when the author is least conscious of it. While O'Connor's stories reflect her faith, she did not write as an apologist for the faith. Instead, she concentrated on reflecting in a well-made work what she saw in the world.

23. Magee, *Conversations with Flannery O'Connor*, p. 29.

24. Maritain, *Art and Scholasticism*, p. 62.

25. O'Connor cites Maritain's concept of the "habit of art," and St. Thomas's focus on the "the good of that which is made," for example, in "The Nature and Aim of Fiction," a composite of her lecture notes published in *Mystery and Manners*, pp. 64-65.

26. Maritain, *Art and Scholasticism*, p. 66.

Maritain first published *Art and Scholasticism* in 1920, before the rise of the New Criticism. He completed its third and final revision in 1935, shortly before teaching at Princeton University in the early 1940s. During this period, he developed a friendship with Caroline Gordon and Allen Tate. In his Mellon Foundation lectures, published in 1953 as *Creative Intuition in Art and Poetry*, Maritain chooses the poetry of Tate and Ransom to illustrate certain points. Developing an argument that reflects O'Connor's and Warren's experience of composing, Maritain explains that intuition is the heart of the creative process: "Poetic intuition ... is born in the unconscious, but it emerges from it; the poet is not unaware of this intuition, on the contrary it is his most precious light and the primary rule of his virtue of art."[27]

Similarly, O'Connor's views on symbolism, which scholars have traditionally linked to the New Criticism, also reflect Thomistic aesthetics. Discussing the composition of "Good Country People," O'Connor insists that she did not choose Hulga's wooden leg as a symbol; rather, the leg "accumulated ... meaning" as she wrote the tale.[28] For O'Connor, symbolism is not a technique that one uses to add resonance to fiction. Instead, it reflects the layers of meaning that exist in the world and that one perceives while "staring" at it.[29] Maritain also praises this kind of symbolic layering that reflects one's perception: "the more the object of art is laden with signification (but with spontaneous and intuitively grasped signification, not with hieroglyphic signification), the greater and richer and higher will be the possibility of delight and beauty."[30]

O'Connor found support in both New Critical theories and Thomist aesthetics for her sense that literature should not be designed to prove a point. Yet despite her wariness about didacticism, she wanted her art to reflect what she saw as the realities of God's world, and for readers to perceive these realities. In order to communicate this view without slipping into propaganda, she combined violent characters and events with an understated narrative style, relying on her belief, grounded in Thomistic aesthetics, that the realities of the created universe will pass through the artist's being into the work of art.

Many of O'Connor's aesthetic principles coincide with those of the New Critics: her sense of the organic nature of the art work; her experience that

27. Jacques Maritain, *Creative Intuition in Art and Poetry* (New York: Pantheon, 1953), p. 91.
28. O'Connor, *Mystery*, p. 99.
29. Ibid., p. 77.
30. Maritain, *Art and Scholasticism*, p. 55.

writing is a process of discovering that organic whole; her view that belief informs art, but art does not serve belief; and her practice of incorporating details with symbolic resonance in an objectively rendered narration. But O'Connor distrusted theory. Instead of citing New Critical experts to explain her aesthetics, she refers to writers or theologians. The works of writers like Flaubert, James, and Joyce, whom O'Connor names approvingly, also serve as a foundation for much of the New Critical aesthetics. Thus, O'Connor's aesthetics integrated literary and religious principles.

It might seem odd that a writer with strong and orthodox religious beliefs found congenial a literary theory that distrusts didacticism and limits the role of statement in literature. I believe, on the contrary, that it was precisely this aesthetic that allowed O'Connor to respect both her art and her religion. She felt that a utilitarian art that existed to serve religion would be a perversion of art. She wanted her fiction to represent sin and doubt and yet express faith. The Thomistic aesthetic formulated by Jacques Maritain and the literary theories of the New Critics, as expressed in modern literature, enabled Flannery O'Connor to maintain a vital faith and a vibrant art.

CAN JACQUES MARITAIN SAVE LIBERAL DEMOCRACY FROM ITSELF?[1]

Raymond Dennehy

Maritain enthusiastically supported liberal democracy with all its pluralism. He also vigorously argued that democracy depends on society's
acceptance of several truths about God and the human person. Practically speaking, how compatible are these two positions, the one requiring
society's affirmation of specific truths, the other guaranteeing its members as much freedom of thought, conscience, speech, and behavior as is
consistent with the maintenance of democratic institutions? This essay
inquires into this question by addressing the following topics: (1) Maritain's
enthusiasm for liberal democracy; 2) the challenge of liberal democracy;
(3) Maritain's two fundamental proposals for simultaneously preserving
truth and liberal democracy: the "Concrete Historical Ideal" and the "Democratic Secular Faith;" and (4) an evaluation of those proposals in relation
to current movements in the United States.

---

1. I use the term "liberal democracy" here in its broadest sense to mean a society
committed to allowing its members as much personal freedom as is consistent with the
maintenance of democratic institutions. I accordingly stay clear of the admittedly crucial
but, for my purposes, irrelevant Marxist claim that there is another sense of "liberal
democracy"—"the democracy of a capitalist market society"—that is inconsistent with my
use of the term. For the Marxist view see C. B. MacPherson, *The Life and Times of Liberal
Democracy* (Oxford: Oxford University Press, 1977), p. 1.

Maritain's Enthusiasm for Liberal Democracy

Two basic reasons fueled Maritain's enthusiasm for liberal democracy. First, he regarded it as testimony to the dignity of the human person, especially as that dignity pertained to freedom of conscience; second, he saw liberal democracy's separation of Church and State as the embodiment of the distinction drawn in the Gospels between "the things that are God's" and "the things that are Caesar's."[2] Yet it is important to note that this enthusiasm was for the *idea* of democracy rather than for any existing democracy. Even the lavish praise he bestowed on American democracy and its people, a praise bordering on hagiography, springs from the promise held by existing institutions and traditions, not their reality.[3] The attributes that he identifies as the components of democracy—personalist, communal, pluralist, and Christian or theist[4]—are not descriptive properties but normative criteria: a political society is democratic *if* it embodies them. The question is, what are the odds of it embodying them?

The Challenge of Liberal Democracy

If these four criteria are essential to democracy, how does Maritain propose to defend the truths they embody when confronted by the dynamism of the freedom of thought, speech, and action that liberal democracy espouses? For example, Maritain clearly regards the requirement that society be theist or Christian as primary; it suffuses the other three with the distinctive meanings that allowed the emergence of democracy in the modern world.[5] Besides being non-negotiable, these truths are seminal to what Maritain calls the "democratic secular faith."[6] This faith embraces a "moral charter, a code of social and political morality ... the validity of which is implied by the fundamental compact of a society of free men...."[7]

Because liberal democracy is committed to allowing its members as much freedom of belief, speech, and action as is consistent with the public

2. Jacques Maritain, *Man and the State* (Chicago: The University of Chicago Press, 1951), p. 108.
3. Jacques Maritain, *Reflections on America* (New York: Charles Scribner's Sons, 1958); see the book's final chapter, "America Is Promise," pp. 193-200.
4. Jacques Maritain, *The Rights of Man and Natural Law*, trans. Doris M. Anson (New York: Charles Scribner's Sons, 1947), pp. 20-22.
5. Ibid., pp. 22-24.
6. Maritain, *Man and the State*, p. 108f.
7. Ibid. p. 112.

welfare, its greatest challenge is the reconciliation of pluralism with unity. However, the commitment to pluralism is more than a commitment to tolerate viewpoints that are merely divergent. As John Courtney Murray observed, pluralism acknowledges "... the coexistence within the one political community of groups who hold divergent and incompatible views with regard to religious questions—those ultimate questions that concern the nature and destiny of man within a universe that stands under the reign of God. Pluralism therefore implies disagreement and dissension within the community."[8] John Rawls cast the problem in starker terms when he wrote that no one of these "incompatible yet reasonable comprehensive doctrines ... is affirmed by citizens generally."[9] The imperatives of pluralism not withstanding, however, there can be no political community without unity;[10] colliding viewpoints pose a problem just because they exist in a community. This means that beneath all the "incompatible comprehensive doctrines," there must be (*pace* Rawls) some commonly held truths regarding fundamental propositions. Otherwise the public discourse that makes democracy work will be impossible since such discourse or "argument" will be constructive only if grounded in shared truths.[11]

Richard Rorty advances a pragmatic principle of unity, agreeing with Rawls that "democracy precedes philosophy." As a philosophical relativist who insists that an incorrigible ethnocentrism excludes the possibility of objective truth, Rorty would appeal to majority opinion on all civil issues: the members of a democratic society vote on the principles and institutions they think should be in place. Rorty echoes Rawls in advocating that people, such as Ignatius of Loyola and Nietzsche, who are unwilling to compromise their principles, should be banished from the political community. He thus locates the heart of democracy in majority opinion.[12] In contrast, Ronald Dworkin rejects "the majoritarian premise" " and with it the majoritarian conception of democracy. It is not a defensible conception of what true democracy is, and it is not America's conception."[13] Dworkin appeals instead to a "moral reading of the Constitution," that, briefly stated, is a

---

8. John Courtney Murray, *We Hold These Truths* (New York: Sheed and Ward, 1960), p. x.

9. John Rawls, *Political Liberalism* (New York: Columbia University Press, 1993), p. xvi.

10. Murray, *We Hold These Truths*, p. x.

11. Ibid., pp. 27-23.

12. Richard Rorty, "The priority of democracy to philosophy," *Objectivity, Relativism, and Truth* (Cambridge: Cambridge University Press, 1991), pp. 175-96.

13. Ronald Dworkin, *Freedom's Law* (Cambridge, Massachusetts: Harvard University Press, 1996), p. 31.

consistent application of legal precedents as seen, for example, in the Supreme Court's movement from decisions pertaining to sterilization and contraception to abortion.[14]

Clearly, Maritain would not accept the principles of public unity defended by Rawls, Rorty, or Dworkin. Instead, Maritain offers two theories for preserving truths while allowing for maximum personal freedom, and reconciling plurality with unity. The first is his "concrete historical ideal,"[15] and the second is the "democratic secular faith."[16]

Maritain's Proposals for Saving Democracy

THE CONCRETE HISTORICAL IDEAL

Maritain's adoption of Sorel's "concrete historical ideal" serves as a brilliant model for displaying how the fundamental truths of Christendom analogously apply to modern secular culture. Although remaining essentially unchanged despite its incarnation in the institutions and sensibilities of a given culture in the latter's historical setting, the concrete historical ideal allows for progress.[17] Implicit in this use of the concrete historical ideal is a metaphysics of progress. Change in itself is no guarantee of progress. Progress presupposes both permanence and change. The concept of change is broader than the concept of progress in that while all progress is change, not all change is progress. Aging, for example, constitutes change, but from a biological standpoint, it is regress; equally regressive is the change from a democratic to a tyrannical government. Thus progress occurs when change builds upon and perfects what already exists, as the unfolding of a rose seed into a rose bush. Here we have a harmony of both permanence and change. In an important sense the rose bush is in the seed. No constitutive part from the outside has been added to the process; the blossoming of the roses is but the actualization of the seed's natural potentialities.[18] Thus it is crucial to the concrete historical ideal that it expresses the truths it embodies *analogically*, not univocally or equivocally: truths remain the same while expressing themselves differently according to each historical situation.

14. Ibid., pp. 53-54.
15. Jacques Maritain, *Integral Humanism*, trans Joseph W. Evans (Notre Dame, Indiana: University of Notre Dame Press, 19730), pp. 121ff.
16. Martain, *Man and the State*, p. 108.
17. Maritain, *Integral Humanism*, pp. 127-32.
18. Jacques Maritain, *A Preface to Metaphysics* (New York: Books for Libraries, 1979), pp. 2-3 and 12-14.

In contrast, reactionaries entertain a univocal conception of the truths essential to culture, a conception that leads them to condemn significant changes in social, economic, or political institutions as an erosion of those truths. For example, during the 1920s and 30s Maritain's critiques of traditional socio-economic institutions put him in bad odor with conservatives who believed that institutional change threatened order. His riposte appears in early editions of his book, *The Things That Are Not Caesar's*,[19] which bore the motto on its frontispiece, "There is order even among the demons." And it is eminently plausible that Maritain's socio-political theories halted Brazil's movement toward Fascism in the 1930s as the entrenched privileged classes sought increased authoritarian political rule to thwart the masses' march towards socialism in their demand for justice. Maritain's theories halted this polarization by offering a rationale for progressive change in society while preserving traditional cultural and socio-economic truths.[20]

THE DEMOCRATIC SECULAR FAITH

Not a religious faith, the democratic secular faith rather consists of a set of truths that the majority of the members of society must hold if democracy is to endure. Unlike the sacral world of the West in the Middle Ages, a world unified by a Catholic Christianity, the modern world is secular. This wrecks any realistic hope of finding philosophical or theological agreement on the theoretical level. Maritain's solution to the problem of finding consensus lies in what he calls "practical points of convergence:"[21] people can agree on a law or public policy while entertaining differing theoretical justifications for doing so. Given the pluralistic environment, Maritain is persuaded that this practical approach is the only way to preserve freedom of thought, discussion, and conscience, all of which are at the heart of democracy.[22] Some writers balefully regard the open society of liberal democracy, especially its free press and electronic media, as a fatal weakness,[23] whereas Maritain, as though taking a page from John Stuart Mill's *On Liberty*, regards "the freedom of expression and criticism" as the mainstay of the people's political liberties.[24]

19. Jacques Maritain, *The Things That Are Not Caesar's*, trans. J. F. Scanlon (New York: Charles Scribner's Sons, 1931).

20. Ibid.

21. Jacques Maritain, *Man and the State* (Chicago: The University of Chicago Press, 1956), pp. 108-11 and 176-78.

22. Ibid., p. 112.

23. Jean-Francois Revel, *How Democracies Perish*, trans. William Byron (Garden City, New Jersey: Doubleday, 1984).

24. Maritain, *Man and the State*, p. 146.

Maritain emphasizes, however, that, despite the centrality of that particular freedom, the democratic faith must nevertheless be handed down and inculcated. The family is primarily responsible for doing that, but, because it lacks the resources needed to complete the task, the public schools must take over at an early stage: "the educational system and the State have to provide the future citizens not only with a treasure of skills, knowledge, and wisdom—liberal education for all—but also with a genuine and reasoned out belief in the common democratic charter, such as is required for the very unity of the body politic."[25] The fulfillment of this project demands personal conviction and commitment from teachers: "Those who teach the democratic charter must believe in it with their whole hearts, and stake on it their personal convictions, their consciences, and the depths of their moral life. They must therefore explain and justify its articles in the light of the philosophical or religious faith to which they cling and which quickens their belief in the common charter."[26] The teachers sign an oath to the effect that if they arrive at the stage where they no longer believe in what they are teaching, they will ask to be reassigned to other teaching duties without incurring any professional penalty.

Maritain warns that democracy must remain vigilant for, and ready to act against, intellectual subversives, those who advocate doctrines and practices inimical to democracy. Maritain denominates them "political heretics."[27] Because he regards freedom of conscience as the indispensable mark of human progress, he insists that it must be preserved. At all events, he tells us, it is not the government's job to impose truth on the members of society.[28] So what to do in the face of the "political heretics? Maritain finds the answer in what he calls the "prophetic shock-minorities." Its members are not "*the people*" but those he designates as the "*inspired servants or prophets of the people.*"[29] They are not the rulers or elected representatives— although that is the ideal—but instead consist of "small dynamic groups freely organized and multiple in nature, which would not be concerned with electoral success but with devoting themselves entirely to great social and political ideas and which would act as a ferment either inside or outside the political parties."[30] The "prophetic shock-minorities" are called upon to exert their greatest influence in times of "crisis, birth, or transformation."[31]

25. Ibid., p. 120.
26. Ibid., p. 121.
27. Ibid., p. 114.
28. Ibid., pp. 117-18.
29. Ibid., p. 39.
30. Ibid., p. 140.

Examples of such people that Maritain cites are the fathers of the French or the American constitutions, men such as Thomas Jefferson and Tom Paine or John Brown.[32]

The primary task of the "inspired servant of the people is to *awaken* the people, to awaken them to something better than everyone's daily business, to the sense of a supra-individual task to be performed."[33] Maritain's use of the word, "shock" is appropriate, for the prophetic shock minorities must rouse the people from a somnambulistic state: "The people are to be awakened—that means that the people are asleep. People as a rule prefer to sleep. Awakenings are always bitter. Insofar as their interests are involved, what people would like is business as usual: everyday misery and humiliation as usual. People would like not to know that they are *the* people."[34] "Shocked," "awakened," but not disrespected. In a democracy, the first precept is to trust the people "even ... while awakening them." This is to respect their human dignity and to foster the growth of the democratic mind. The Rousseauist principle "to force the people to be free" impeded the growth of the democratic mind and fed the illusion "of the mission of the self-styled enlightened minorities."[35]

The Fragility of Maritain's Proposals

It was noted at the outset of this essay that Maritain's enthusiasm for liberal democracy must be understood as an enthusiasm for its *idea*; it is an enthusiasm for a possibility rather than for an any assurance that it would be realized. How great the distance between the idea and it's realization reveals itself in the following considerations.

First, the concrete historical ideal, although a brilliant model for explaining how the essential truths of democracy may be preserved while assuming diverse historical and cultural incarnations, relies on the analogical nature of the truths the ideal asserts. Were the assertions of those truths *equivocal* rather than *analogical,* the model would collapse. But this is

31. Ibid., p. 140.
32. Ibid., p. 141.
33. Ibid.
34. Ibid., p. 142; It seems that Maritain himself had a bit of the shock-troop in him. He published his first article, "La Science Moderne et la Raison," in June, 1910 in the *Revue de Philosophie*. According to his wife, his intention was to "'break window-panes' and annoy the reader." Raïssa Maritain, *We Have Been Friends Together* and *Adventures in Grace: The Memoirs of Raïssa Maritain*, trans. Julie Kernan (Garden City, New York: Image Books, 1961), p. 335.
35. Maritain, *Man and the State*, p. 143.

exactly what Maritain's theory of liberal democracy must confront when he writes that democracy is open to people of diverse philosophical and religious outlooks, including atheism, as long as they accept the values of freedom, rights, justice, and human dignity.

This accommodation is laudable for its generosity but it fails to take into account the mercurial nature of terms such as "liberty," "justice," and "rights," all of which require specification if they are to avoid equivocation and persuasive manipulation. "Freedom" lends itself to uses that are mutually contradictory.[36] For example, proponents of negative freedom construe "freedom" as the absence of external restraint whereas proponents of positive freedom construe it as the capacity to attain one's self-perfection by acting in accordance with some objective standard whether it be the law of human nature, society, or the State.[37] Maritain, on the contrary, entertains a specific understanding of "freedom," as is clear in a number of his writings.[38] He rejects interpretations of freedom, such as Rousseau's, which hold that humans enjoyed an idyllic freedom in the state of nature, only to have that freedom corrupted by civilization; Maritain argues, on the contrary, that freedom must be conquered and the conquest can occur only in political society.[39] This view of freedom embraces both the negative and the positive versions but gives pride of place to the latter. The freedom to choose is a necessary condition of the higher "freedom of independence or autonomy," which is the freedom of self-perfection attained by actualizing the potencies of human nature as one identifies oneself increasingly with the Absolute.[40]

Accordingly, if the democratic secular faith requires acceptance of the freedom of the person, the question of which notion of freedom one embraces becomes paramount. Clearly, the social and political structures presupposed by freedom construed as "The only freedom which deserves the name is that of pursuing our own good in our own way, so long as we

36. See Isaiah Berlin, *Two Concepts of Liberty* (Oxford: Oxford University Press, 1963).

37. For the *locus classicus* of negative freedom, see John Stuart Mill, *On Liberty* (New York: The Liberal Arts Press, 1956), pp. 16-17; for positive liberty, see T. H. Green, *Lectures on the Principles of Political Obligation* (London: Longmans, Green and Co. 1960), pp. 2-3, 8.

38. "*Spontanéité et Indépendance,*" *Mediaeval Studies*, vol. 4, 1942; *Scholasticism and Politics*, trans. and ed. Mortimer J. Adler (New York: Doubleday and Company, Inc., 1960), chap. 5; "The Conquest of Freedom" *Contemporary Philosophy*, ed. James L. Jarrett and Sterling M. Murrin (New York: Henry Hold and Company, 1957) p. 509.

39. Maritain, "The Conquest of Freedom."

40. Maritian, *Scholasticism and Politics*, p. 136.

do not attempt to deprive others of theirs or impede their efforts to obtain it"[41] are different from those, such as Maritain's, which construe such a notion of freedom as only the necessary condition of a higher freedom that is based on objective, universal standards.

If the notion of "freedom" runs the constant risk of becoming a merely persuasive term, the notion of "right or rights" fares no better. The meaning of rights has changed radically since the start of our nation, going from the moral claims of the people against the government to a subjective moral claim, a belief that rights are a kind of aesthetic license to live one's life according to subjective assessments.[42] Maritain himself observed "a tendency to inflate and make absolute, limitless, unrestricted in every respect, the rights of which we are aware, thus blinding ourselves to any other right which would counterbalance them."[43]

Such understandings of "freedom" and "right" nullify the concrete historical ideal. If the univocal allows of no change and the analogical allows of change while keeping permanent the essential nature of the truths in question, the *equivocal* represents complete change. The materializing of the human person, the subversion of freedom as subjective option, the State as the final arbiter of human life and destiny, the denial of God's existence, either in theory or practice, all are devolutions that are inimical to the concrete historical ideal.

But the more serious concern about the efficacy of Maritain's democratic secular faith is its wellspring. For him such problems as cited above can be ameliorated significantly and thus the democratic secular faith more perfectly realized to the extent that the people are "imbued with Christian convictions and [are] aware of the *religious* faith which inspires it...." All along Maritain has insisted that democracy approaches its fulfillment only as it becomes more Christian.[44] As noted earlier, this does not mean that he thereby advocates a theocracy or that the Church should be permitted to rule political society.[45] Rather, he means that the ideals of modern democracy are Christian in origin and, hence, that the values of Christendom must energize its social and political institutions: "This world was born of

41. John Stuart Mill, *On Liberty*, ed. Currin V. Shields (Indianapolis: The Bobbs-Merrill Company, Inc., 1956), pp. 16-17.

42. Russell Hittinger, "Liberalism and the Natural Law Tradition," *Wake Forest Law Review*, (1990), pp. 429, 486-99; see also, Mary Ann Glendon, *Rights Talk: the Impovrishment of Political Discourse* (New York: Free Press, 1991).

43. Maritain, *Man and the State*, p. 103.

44. Ibid., pp. 52, 109.

45. Ibid., pp. 110-14.

Christendom and owed its deepest living strength to the Christian tradition.... Its ultimate error lay in believing that man is saved by his own strength alone, and that human history is made without God."[46] Maritain is persuaded that the chief characteristics of modern democracy—respect for the dignity and rights of the person, universal suffrage, the equality of all human beings, etc.—were inspired, and thus became cultural forces, in the West by the Gospels.[47]

The cash value of Christianity's influence on democracy expresses itself in the crucial notion of freedom. Christianity brought to light the person's transcendence over political society by calling attention to his ultimate destiny—union with God.[48] Absent this theological ground of social and political freedom, no argument for the freedom of innocent men and women from social or state control can be absolutely binding. Given that the classic utilitarian defense of that freedom is based on "the greatest good for the greatest number of people," it should not be surprising that a prominent utilitarian, Peter Singer, takes the position that "an infant with severe disabilities should be killed."[49] The moral of this story is clear: an ethic devoid of a metaphysical or theological grounding in the nature of the human person is incapable of offering any philosophical or theological defense of democracy insofar as it lacks ontological grounding in the nature and finality of the human person. Unlike Christian ethics, an ethic without content does not originate in the notion of Creation,[50] but rather in the self-interest of the individuals and the groups that control them.

Despite the reasonableness of Maritain's argument for democracy's origin and dependence on Christian doctrine, the process of secularization in our society since the eighteenth century when the Continental Congress "called upon the fledgling nation to observe days of 'publick (sic) humiliation, fasting and prayer, as well as days of 'thanksgiving'"[51] has proceeded unabated. Consider the view of Rawls, which construes Christianity as only one of several conditions for the formation of the modern West rather than as the most important cause sustaining force. He confines the influ-

---

46. Jacques Maritain, *Christianity and Democracy,* trans. Doris C. Anson (New York: Charles Scribner's Sons 1944), p. 21.

47. Ibid., p. 44.

48. Maritain, *Man and the State*, pp. 148-49.

49. Helga Kuhse and Peter Singer, *Should the Baby Live?* (Oxford: Oxford University Press, 1985), p. v.

50. St. Paul, *Epistle to the Romans*, chap 1.

51. Ellis Sandoz, *A Government of Laws: Political Theory, Religion, and the American Founding* (Baton Rouge, Louisiana State University Press, 1990), p. 87.

ence of the Christian religion to "the Reformation and its consequent religious pluralism."[52]

The above considerations force one to wonder how feasible is Maritain's reliance on the public school teachers to transmit the democratic secular faith. Given the widespread influence of "political heretics," such as Rawls, Rorty, Dworkin, and Singer, on today's academic culture, one has to ask how many public school teachers can be found to teach, with conviction, the democratic charter? The universities and colleges from which they graduate abound with professors and required readings that propose a view of democracy quite different from that espoused by Maritain or the Founding Fathers. Postmodernist rejections and various neo-Marxist critiques of the presuppositions of objective knowledge presented in the Declaration of Independence exert great influence in the university classrooms. Thus in the current climate, public school teachers cannot be counted upon to share Maritain's vision of the democratic charter. Indeed, many of them hold philosophies that contradict it.

This concern about the dependability of the public school teachers to transmit and defend the democratic secular faith only intensifies the dubiety about the efficacy of Maritain's notion of the "practical points of convergence." It is one thing to persuade people of differing theoretical views on matters of shared practical concern to come together; it is quite another to try to persuade people whose differing theoretical views demand practical policies and laws that are mutually incompatible.[53] Consider, for example, the current "hot-button" topic of abortion. Pro-abortion advocates, supported by the U.S. Supreme Court, argue that the Constitution demands abortion's legalization; opponents argue that this legalization strikes at the very heart of the Constitution, which document is an affirmation of the intrinsic and inalienable dignity of all human beings. What happens to the "practical points of convergence" when the number of people who are against abortion, if only even for practical reasons, becomes a minority?

These points of concern reveal the vulnerability of Maritain's democratic secular faith to the political heretics. Because he regards freedom of conscience as the indispensable mark of human progress, he argues, as noted earlier, that government must not try to impose truth on the members of society. This confronts the "prophetic shock-minorities" with a Herculean demand to defend the truths on which democracy rests. The contemporary American scene displays a new diversity, one that confers a dramatically

52. John Rawls, *Political Liberalism*, pp. xxii-xxiii.

53. See, for example, R. M. Dworkin, *Life's Dominion: An Argument about Abortion, Euthanasia, and Individual Freedom* (New York: Knopf, 1993).

different reference and hence meaning on the term "pluralism" as well as demanding a more urgent need to formulate a common theological and philosophical viewpoint that can serve as a foundation for a democratic community. Non-Christian religions, a secular philosophy that repudiates the need for any advertence to God and personal immortality,[54] the postmodernist challenge to the objectivity of knowledge that underpins the Enlightenment philosophy embraced by the framers of American democracy,[55] a demand for a multicultural curriculum in the schools, a revisiting of the question "Who is an American?,"[56] freedom of speech vs. pornography, hate-speech, and campus speech codes, the right to life vs. the death penalty, abortion, physician-assisted suicide, and human cloning, not to mention, the traditional, legal understanding of marriage as a union of male and female vs. the demand for legalized same-sex marriages, all these, and more, come together, with the mounting force of a river fed by tributaries, to collide with the traditional understanding of the public philosophy.

Still, the prospects are not all dark. Somewhere, now lost to my memory, Maritain speaks of the "spiritual power" of truth and justice, using the example of Martin Luther King and the Civil Rights Movement of the 1960s. King's assassination did not defeat the movement, just as Ghandi's did not defeat his nationalist movement. But the spiritual power of the prophetic shock-troops can continue to exert its influence for centuries afterwards without having saved the societies in which its shock-troops lived. The power-brokers of Athens brought Socrates to trial on trumped-up charges that led to his execution. To be sure, the power of his public witness lived on. Almost no one can now recite the names of his murderers: whatever celebrity Meletus, Anytus, and Lycon enjoyed went into the grave with them, whereas today, 2500 hundred years later, the example of Socrates continues to inspire college students the world over. Socrates won by the superior power of truth and justice, but that is the verdict of a long history. The Athens of his day, a first-rate power, continued to thrash about in its moral and intellectual confusion until, by the third century B.C., it had declined to become a fifth-rate power.

The lesson to be drawn from the above examples is that truth unifies, but not until it first divides. In Gethsemane, Christ prayed to the Father that

54. John Dewey, *A Common Faith* (New Haven, Connecticut: Yale University Press, 1934); Corliss Lamont, *The Philosophy of Humanism* (New York: Ungar, 1965), pp. 12-13.

55. *The Debate on Modernity*, ed. Claude Geffre and Jean-Vierre Jossua (Glen Rock, NewJersey: Concilium Press, 1992).

56. See Michael J. Sandel, "America's Search for a New Public Philosophy," *The Atlantic Monthly*, March, 1996, pp. 57-74.

all men might be one; yet on another occasion he warned that truth is divisive: indeed, He had entered human history to bring the sword, so that brother would fight brother, father, son, and mother, daughter; he warned the apostles that people would hate them because they hated him. In our country, the Civil War is perhaps the greatest and most dramatic example of this. The hatred and loss of human life and property were enormous. But in the end, the house divided became the house unified. Is it reasonable to count on this happening again, especially in light of the aforementioned contemporary challenges? America's success in abolishing slavery offers reasonable hope, but what are the odds? After all, how many profound crises can a nation survive? One can agree that Maritain was correct in holding that (1) given the secularization of culture, liberal democracy is the only form of government worthy of the human person and his freedom; 2) the notions of the "concrete historical ideal" and "democratic secular faith" are the correct models for liberal democracy; and that 3) the "prophetic shock-minorities" are the only hope for defending that model against the "political heretics" and thereby saving liberal democracy. But one must not forget that these three positions are *criteria* for the existence and survival of democratic society, and not descriptions of an existing democracy. Can Maritain's enthusiasm for liberal democracy be translated into a realizable, sustainable political society? One recalls Socrates' answer to the question about where the ideal Republic was to be found: "It is only an idea," he replies, "and exists nowhere."[57]

---

57. Plato, *Republic*, IX, 592a; see also Maritain, *Reflections on America*, for Maritain's application of the concrete historical ideal to American democracy.

Jacques Maritain and Emmanuel Mounier On America: Two Catholic Views

William J. Fossati

As Catholic intellectuals, Jacques Maritain and Emmanuel Mounier were part of that Catholic renaissance which took place in France in the early twentieth century. Drawing initial inspiration from Pope Leo XIII's encyclical *De Rerum Novarum* (1891), a generation of young French men and women devoted their intellectual powers to fashioning a rational Catholic response to the challenges of industrialism, materialism, and collectivism.[1] Others who dedicated themselves to giving Catholicism a new voice which would challenge the dominant ideologies of the late nineteenth century included Gabriel Marcel, Teillard de Chardin, Simone Weil, and Charles Peguy. The Catholic reawakening in France stressed the theology of St. Thomas Aquinas. Aquinas's insistence on approaching the sensible world within a framework of rational thought struck both Maritain and Mounier as the perfect means of combating what they perceived as the materialist and irrational worldview against which Leo XIII had inveighed.

---

1. *Encyclical Letter of Pope Leo XIII on the Condition of the Working Class* (*Rerum Novarum*), New translation authorized by the Holy See (Washington, D.C.: Apostolate of the Press, 1942), p. 13. See also Gordon Wright, *France in Modern Times*, 5th ed. (New York: W.W. Norton and Co., 1995), p. 287.

What is more, the partisans of the Catholic revival were not content simply to withdraw from a world gone mad with an unquenchable desire for material gain. In keeping with the papal encyclical, they believed themselves called upon to mount an offensive against the forces of scientism and positivism. They would make use of their considerable intellectual gifts and their ability to order their ideas in the form of the written word. Thus, the Catholic revival in France always had about it the quality of an active force; a dynamic counter thrust to joust with the spiritually dead conceits of the modern world.

The writings of Jacques Maritain and Emmanuel Mounier are indicative of this spirit of intellectual activism. Both men sought to bring a vigorous exposition of the Catholic alternative to the *Weltschmerz* of twentieth-century life. In regard to Maritain, his writings are generally characterized by an aggressive explication of Thomistic philosophy, not as something out of the Middle Ages, but as a vibrant mode of ordering one's life. Maritain was perfectly willing—eager is a better word—to show the philosophy of St. Thomas as one which has immediate applications to human life in the age of science. As an example, there is his essay, *Court Traité de l'Existence et de l'Existant* (1947). Written at the height of the "Sartrean Revolution," when Jean-Paul Sartre, Simone de Beauvoir, and Albert Camus brought the grimness of war-torn Europe into the realm of philosophy with their existentialist description of humanity, the *Court Traité* clearly—and forcefully—offers a salutary alternative. Maritain was not content simply to rail at the twentieth-century existentialists as godless nay-sayers. Rather, he offered his own version of existential philosophy that was founded on a Thomistic understanding of the human condition.

Maritain begins his consideration of existentialism by recalling St. Thomas's existential realism.[2] He then develops his views on human existence employing the ideas of St. Thomas, ideas which Maritain had "developed around some of the philosophic themes which he held closest to his heart and upon which he meditated for a long time...."[3] Having established the basis for his consideration of existential thought, he proceeds to make his case for St. Thomas Aquinas as the only true exponent of existentialism. Describing the thought of St. Thomas as "... the only authentic existentialism ...,"[4] he moves immediately to demonstrate that far from being a part

2. Jacques Maritain, *Court Traité de l'Existence et de l'Existant* (*Œuvres Complètes*) (Paris: Éditions Saint-Paul/Fribourg: Éditions Universitaires Suisse,1990), vol. IX, p. 12.

3. Ibid.

4. Ibid., p. 13.

of history, the thirteenth-century Dominican speaks to the twentieth century as vigorously as ever. Noting that in the hands of twentieth-century thinkers, the term "existentialism" has been reduced to just another word, Maritain points to the durability of St. Thomas because of his avoidance of labels. "St. Thomas does not proclaim himself as either an existentialist or a realist; for that matter, he never called himself a Thomist. These terms are subsumed in his thought."[5] Maritain's intent is not to offer St. Thomas Aquinas as a voice of authority beyond question, but to propose Thomism as a dynamic alternative to the erroneous thinking into which twentieth-century philosophy had fallen.

Beyond his critique of existentialism, Maritain applied his Thomistic insights to speculative philosophic matters as well as matters of practical affairs. In 1947 he rendered a critique of the United Nations Educational, Scientific, and Cultural Organization's (UNESCO) Universal Declaration of Human Rights. The starting point for UNESCO's declaration was the concept of human rights which had come out of the eighteenth-century Enlightenment. The declaration depended heavily on the Enlightenment's opposition to the divine right of kings and the theory that God had bestowed certain unquestionable powers on the Church.[6] The *philosophes* of the eighteenth century constructed their doctrine of the rights of man in that curious sort of rationalist argument peculiar to the Age of Reason. To the eighteenth-century philosophers, human rights rested on natural law. Their natural law was similar to Newton's mechanical laws; however, it existed outside of humanity and, like the law of gravity, exerted its effect. Maritain might just as well have thundered forth against the mechanistic perception of reality held by these Enlightenment thinkers. Yet, he did not. Rather, he offered a more flexible description of natural law, one that was based on St. Thomas's understanding. Maritain described natural law as *interior* to human beings. It was not just another physical law to be applied. He pointed out that the Thomistic understanding of natural law considered it the wellspring from which all human laws emanated.[7] He criticized the eighteenth-century thinkers; by glibly interpreting natural law as physical law, he insisted, they had granted human beings near god-like status. As the only rational creatures in the universe, humans were able to perceive natural law—physical laws included—and utilize them to their own desires.

5. Ibid., p. 15.

6. Jacques Maritain, *Sur la Philosophie des Droits de l'Homme* (*Œuvres Complètes*) (Paris: Éditions Saint-Paul/Fribourg: Éditions Universitaires Suisse, 1990), vol. IX, p. 1082n.

7. Ibid., p. 1083.

No reactionary, Jacques Maritain gave the framers of the Universal Declaration of Human Rights a gentle tug on the sleeve. "Do not be blind to the complexities of humanity or humanity's need for rational order," he seemed to be saying. Viewed through the lens of Thomistic rationality, the question of human rights took on the aspect of a multipurpose tool; a tool for the greater understanding of how laws might benefit the human condition. As Maritain expressed it, "... a sane notion of natural law allows us to understand the intrinsic differences which differentiate natural law itself from the law of man, positive law."[8] This was his imaginative suggestion for UNESCO. Natural law, properly understood, could provide a meaningful expression of the world body's concern for human dignity and freedom. He was not content to take an intransigent stance in regard to the organization's identification of human rights with the eighteenth century. Maritain had no interest in pitting Thomist dogma against twentieth-century liberalism. His concern was to explore ways of improving upon modern concepts of justice by way of demonstrating the timelessness of Catholic philosophy.

Like Maritain, Emmanuel Mounier was part of the French-Catholic intelligentsia which took inspiration from the Catholic renaissance in the opening years of the twentieth century. Mounier, like his confreres, was convinced that the Catholic faith, reinvigorated, offered a saving alternative to the age of materialism. In Mounier's eyes, "the age of materialism" was a many-headed hydra; it was made up of a number of components, all of which he saw as threats to the human spirit. He was distrustful of those products of the modern era which he labeled "individualism" and "liberalism."[9] For Mounier, these twin evils were at the heart of popular twentieth-century democracy. Certainly the French Third Republic had undergone a number of unsettling periods: the Dreyfus Affair, the Great War, and the Depression. Also, Mounier was keenly aware that much of the Third Republic was dedicated to that virulent anticlericalism which had grown out of the French Revolution. The nineteen-thirties must have been especially galling to him; it was a decade that brought both the Great Depression and the Popular Front Government of Léon Blum. The economic, social, and political turbulence of the time served as an indictment, in his view, of everything that was wrong with the materialist, liberal, and democratic regime in France.

8. Ibid., p. 1084.
9. Seth D. Armus, "The Eternal Enemy: Emmanuel Mounier's *Esprit* and French anti-Americanism," *French Historical Studies* 24, no. 2 (Spring, 2001), p. 271.

Thus convinced, Mounier proceeded to organize a counter-movement through which he could arouse the faithful to the perils of liberal democracy. In 1932, he established a monthly journal, *Esprit*, which would serve as a forum for the dissemination of his ideas. During the thirties, *Esprit* became a well-respected intellectual journal in France.[10] As the editor, he encouraged Catholic writers to weigh in with articles not only supportive of the Faith, but which were also critical of the whole range of evils that had arisen from the age of materialism. From the beginning, Mounier presented his agenda for moral reform with the trappings of a revolutionary movement. Even as the Catholic renaissance in France had always attracted young people, Jacques and Raissa Maritain were examples, Mounier sought to continue this trend and present his point of view as new and vigorous over against the decadence of the Third Republic.

At the heart of his "revolutionary movement," was his philosophy of *personalism*. Personalism as Mounier used the term was a means by which the individual would maintain his individuality, but at the same time remain part of the body of Christ in the Catholic community. Such individuality was certainly not to be confused with that willfulness of the individual that Mounier identified as a legacy of the popular democratic movement. On the contrary, he saw what passed for the emphasis on the individual or the "person" in twentieth-century society as "… a variety and a vagueness which risk bringing to the metaphysics of the individual rather peculiar obligations. In fact, every day an unrepentant individualism renews itself in forms of a 'personalism' which is an easy consciousness of the self. We are thus able to see this inexhaustible 'person' stand out as a complaisant devil …"[11] Mounier placed his understanding of the individual's role in society on his reading of St. Augustine and St. Bonaventure, both of whom he viewed as insisting on a direct connection (a "sort of spiritual short circuit") between God and man.[12] Thus, his notion of the "person" as described in his philosophy of personalism was the traditional Catholic insistence on God's unique relationship with every human being carried out through the good offices of the Church.

In his public utterances, in his writings, and in the pages of *Esprit*, Emmanuel Mounier called on Catholics to heed this unique relationship and to turn away from the evils of modernism. He called for a revolution of the spirit; a militant opposition not only to the Third Republic but also to all of

---

10. Ibid., p. 271.
11. Emmanuel Mounier, *Liberté sous Conditions* (Paris: Éditions du Seuil, 1946), p. 13.
12. Ibid., p. 21.

the modernist trappings associated with it and with the twentieth-century West as well. His call was for the rejection of "mass democracy" which was for its citizens "... the most cunning and cruel hoax of all."[13]

Though his personalism was couched in terms of the Catholic renaissance and he often spoke in the idiom of revolutionary change and moral revival for France, Mounier was an unregenerate reactionary. Taking inspiration from Maurice Barrès and Charles Maurras, he despised the political and economic accomplishments which had taken place in France since 1789. The neo-Thomism which energized the thinking of Jacques Maritain after 1906 became a bludgeon to be used against modernism by Emmanuel Mounier. The moment that brought the full extent of his reactionary inclinations to light was the fall of France and the Occupation in 1940. Mounier and those close to him greeted the German victory as a beneficial purgative to the decadence of the Third Republic.[14] In the months after the defeat, Mounier hailed the events of June 1940 as the overture to a new era of liberation from everything which he had abhorred about the Third Republic. It is not the purpose of this essay to indict Mounier as a collaborationist. Perhaps he was, perhaps he was not. Nonetheless, while Maritain was in the United States and Canada lending his talents to the Allied cause, Mounier was speaking and writing on behalf of the Catholic supporters of the Vichy Government.[15]

Yet, to label Emmanuel Mounier as a fascist is to fail to understand the complexity of his views on Catholicism and twentieth-century culture. Of *petite bourgeois* background, he was the son of a pharmacist's assistant from the provincial city of Grenoble. As a young man, he took up the study of medicine only to abandon it in favor of philosophy. His philosophy professor at the University of Grenoble was Jacques Chevalier, a prominent Catholic thinker with pronounced Bergsonian tendencies. Like his mentor, the young Mounier embraced a Catholicism predicated on action rather than contemplation. Before leaving Grenoble for the Sorbonne in Paris in 1927, he was active in the Society of Saint Vincent de Paul in which he performed charitable work among the region's depressed working class.

Once at the Sorbonne in pursuit of a university teaching degree, he found that the Bergsonian intellectual formation which he had received through Chevalier had inculcated in him an aversion to the idealist philosophy then dominant at that institution. For him philosophy was a mode of

13. Ibid., p. 218.
14. Armus, "The Eternal Enemy," p. 272.
15. Ibid., p. 273.

action, not just an exercise in abstract thinking. By the time he had completed his studies in Paris, he had taken on an enduring realism which was driven by a keen sense of spirituality.[16] As one of the founders of the journal *Esprit* in 1932, he strove to dedicate the new publication to a nonpolitical voice which would indict modernism's two dominant forces: Marxist socialism and capitalism.

Mounier's philosophy of personalism can be seen as existentialism baptized into the Church. Mounier's human being was a spiritual being; one that constantly struggled to know or experience the divine. Mounier, by descrying modern societal and political barriers to human spirituality, set himself the task of battling modernism by declaring his enmity to the ideologies which he identified as those fueling twentieth-century political and economic movements. By the time of the founding of *Esprit*, this meant opposition to capitalism and Marxism. Tormented by the Great Depression, the world seemed divided in its desire to embrace one or the other of these two credos as a means of cure. Mounier warned in the prospectus for the first issue of *Esprit* that relief from human misery was to be found in neither system.[17] Both were materialist, both without spiritual content.

For Mounier, the great bastion of capitalism was the United States. Even before the founding of *Esprit*, Mounier had identified the United States as the modernist monster whose "… worship of the machine suffocates all life, spontaneity, initiative, [and] grace …."[18] At the heart of his distrust of the United States was his belief that its liberal heritage—as well as that of France—had come out of the Jacobin experience of the late eighteenth century. His critique went on. Mass democracy had grown out of the period of the French Revolution. Majority rule that is at the core of liberal democracy was, for Mounier, inimical to the spiritual robustness of the population. In fact, he went on, the rule of the majority had become the tyranny of the majority; more oppressive "than tyrants are,"[19] the masses had become the new dictators. While he was careful not to appear as an apologist for the fascist dictatorships of Mussolini and Hitler, he insisted that the spirit-killing majority-rule of the United States was equally bad. Unlike Maritain, who was concerned with the matter of sincere, devout Catholics versus those who were casual and nominally Catholic, Mounier

16. Jean-Louis Loubet del Bayle, *Les Non-Conformistes des Années 30* (Paris: Éditions du Seuil, 1969), p.127.

17. Armus, "The Eternal Enemy," p. 272n.

18. Ibid., p. 278.

19. Ibid., p. 281.

viewed *all* Catholics in *all* democracies, especially the United States, as victims. For him, the same materialist, individualist, and tyrannical societies against which he had set himself victimized them.[20]

Esprit was suppressed in 1941 by the Vichy government. Mounier was arrested and briefly jailed as a subversive in 1942. Even so, he continued to insist that the Vichy government was the only legitimate voice of the National Revolution. The right wing was convinced that the defeat of 1940 was a new beginning for France. In 1944, he denounced the Americans for having invaded North Africa and General Henri Giraud, the Free-French leader, for cooperating with them.[21]

With the end of the war, Mounier published *Esprit* once again. Although most of the pre-war right wing in France had been dismantled, Mounier continued to fear American democracy and American capitalism. However, after 1945 his traditional anti-Americanism took on a different form. Before the war, Mounier and *Esprit* had been apolitical. His interests and energies had lain in the areas of philosophy and religion. After the end of hostilities, Mounier and his journal ventured into French Marxist politics!

While most French men and women celebrated the Liberation, Mounier complained that the Americans had prevented "the brilliant Free French" from scoring a final victory over Germany. Odd that he should have made this remark. Prior to his arrest by Vichy authorities in 1942, he had predicted that forces of the National Revolution would one day have to battle the Free French.[22] Consistency of thought was not his objective. Rather, he was searching for a new method by which to rejuvenate his philosophy of personalism. He understood that the events of 1940-45 made it unwise to continue to be anti-republican. The right in France had been far too discredited. Yet he was still convinced of the efficacy of his personalist *melange* of spiritualism, action, and revolution. Articles in *Esprit* during the late forties seldom missed a chance at pillorying the United States for a broad range of sins—all having to do with American capitalism. In the issue published in April 1947, the journal took up the matter of Moroccan independence from France. While this was not a subject that occupied a major spot in American foreign policy, the editorial staff strongly suggested that a serious problem in French-Moroccan relations was the fact that the Americans

20. John Hellman, *Emmanuel Mounier and the New Catholic Left, 1930-1950* (Toronto: University of Toronto Press, 1981), p. 197.

21. Ibid., p. 189.

22. Armus, "The Eternal Enemy," p. 293.

had occupied Morocco during the war. While in the French protectorate, according to *Esprit*, the Americans had attempted to inculcate the culture with their noxious brand of "yankee" commercial aggressiveness. This, according to the article, had an unsettling effect on the simple, yet ancient culture of Morocco. As the article expressed it

> Here again, it is not for Morocco to be ruled by the basic measure of "time is money" which is [for Americans] the master, but by the humanist principle: "action is the only joy of the spirit" and this is the principle of the settler and the nationalist, it is the principle of initiative and responsibility which is not used to draw insane profits from an accelerated economy, but to regulate harmony and an economic tempo according to the guidance of human rhythm."[23]

This statement encapsulates *Esprit*'s post-war anti-Americanism. America was to be seen as the capitalist villain; the Americans' sole interest was material wealth and the by-product of this greed was the destruction of a spiritual and pastoral culture. Maintaining his pre-war commitment to personalism, Mounier sought to make of the United States a paradigm of everything which personalism loathed. In another *Esprit* article published after the war, the subject was the Allied occupation of Germany. In an otherwise thoughtful treatment of the problem of the de-nazification and rebuilding of Germany, the article took a gratuitous shot at the American occupation forces. The criticism was essentially a rehash of his earlier remarks. The piece contended that the American zone of occupation was characterized by "G.I. brutality, failure to understand Europeans, insolent luxury, etc. ..."[24] Noticeable in all of these articles is the absence of any pronouncements even mildly critical of the Soviet Union.

Beginning in June 1947, the state of European-American relations offered Mounier an opportunity to attack America and to present himself as a convert to the increasingly popular *Marxisant* impulse in French intellectual circles. This movement was related to but not part of the large communist party in post-war France. With the pre-war right wing in shambles, Mounier searched for some issue which would revitalize his journal and his philosophy of personalism. The post-war United States was made to order. It was still the perceived materialist, modernist monolith which Mounier had attacked during the thirties. Only now, French resentment of America began to take on a political cast which it had not formerly had. As the Allied powers divided into the mutually hostile camps of the capitalist west and

---

23. André de Peretti, "Maroc et France," *Esprit*, N° 132 (April, 1947), p. 549.
24. J. Baur, "Complainte d'Occupé," *Esprit*, N° 134 (June, 1947), p. 977.

the communist east, political forces in France mirrored world political tensions. The communist party emerged from the war more powerful than ever. Able to point to a major role in the resistance, the communists presented themselves as the true saviors of France and the only hope for a working class which had been treated poorly for over a century. The French communist party took its cue from Moscow and became more hostile to America as the Cold War deepened. Many members of the party in France were youthful and intellectual. Mounier's anti-Americanism seemed to have ready appeal for them. Certainly no communist himself, Mounier could, nonetheless, court those on the left by clothing his traditional anti-Americanism in revolutionary garments. He saw, and he was correct, that the issue of anti-Americanism in France had appeal to revolutionaries on the left as well as to reactionaries on the right. Latterly, he detected similarities between Marxist ideology and personalism. Both, he argued, pointed out the alienation which capitalism had brought to the human race; both called for a revolutionary counter thrust to the powers of industrial wealth.[25] This was the basis for his Marxist inclinations; he styled himself a revolutionary struggling for the same ends as the communists, but insisted on dedicating his revolution to God.

The summer of 1947 saw the advent of the Marshal Plan, an ambitious American program for the rebuilding of war-ravaged Europe. Immediately denounced by the Stalin regime, the French communist party took up the cudgels and also condemned it as American imperialism.[26] *Esprit* saw the American program as a sort of Trojan Horse. The Americans were willing to pay for the rebuilding of Western Europe, but included in their generous offer was a demand for a European commitment to rearm, with the Soviet Union as the target. Here was the catch, according to Mounier and the editorial staff at *Esprit*: the demand for French public expenditure for rearmament would offset the economic benefits of the Marshal Plan.

But it is on the economic level that is here introduced a new and deadly inconsistency. Even as I, André Véron, write this, the United States is training and equipping ten armored divisions in France including all the attendant expenses. Thus will the cost in tanks and guns crush under its heel that which we are trying to build. The inflationary gulf that will not fail to perpetuate inequality and place French industry in so dangerous a situation that without doubt it will be forced to call upon new investment funds from Wall Street and thus bring on its own economic subservience.[27]

25. Armus, "The Eternal Enemy," p. 276.
26. Hellman, *Emmanuel Mounier and the New Catholic Left, 1930-1950*, p. 211.
27. André Véran, "Visages Américains du Plan Marshall," *Esprit*, N° 144 (April, 1948), pp. 551-52.

From the distance of fifty-five years it seems incredible that someone with Mounier's intelligence could see anything but benefit for France in the Marshal Plan. Yet, that is to ignore his sense of history. During the thirties, he attacked the Third Republic unrelentingly; in 1940, he was convinced that the National Revolution had been effected. The years from 1940 to 1944 were both agonizing and disillusioning for him. At war's end, he was determined to be on the "right" side of history for a change. Ever the revolutionary (personalism had always called for a revolution of the spiritually active), he thought that he had spotted the ground swell of revolution in the left. He did not want to be left behind again.[28]

Perhaps it is fair to say that Emmanuel Mounier was a thinker who found himself tossed by the tides of history. At one point in his career, he criticized Jacques Maritain for what he understood as Maritain's inflexible distrust of progress as evidenced in *Antimoderne* and *Trois Réformateurs*. At the heart of his reproof of Maritain was his conviction that Christianity had to express itself and act in the coin of the time. To Mounier, Maritain was hopelessly stationary in his thinking and unable to consider a Catholicism that would provide spiritual substance in a world which prized modernity.[29]

But was Mounier correct in his reading of Maritain regarding his remarks on the matter of progress? True, *Antimoderne* is a critique of Cartesian and Kantian science. It is not a diatribe against either progress or modernity. As was his mode of instruction, Maritain offered a reminder of what modern science was. Unlike Descartes or Kant, Maritain refused to assign metaphysical weight to the physical sciences. His distrust of modernity as spoken through science lay in the demand of some proponents of the scientific method that they be given absolute freedom to interpret their findings in any way they pleased. Beneath the banner of freedom of thought, what they really were clamoring for was a freedom from *responsible* thought. "What they are asking for in reality is not the freedom of reason or the freedom to reason. It is freedom from reason, the freedom to reason without rule or measure, the freedom to deceive themselves as they wish, as much as they wish, wherever they wish without any control of themselves."[30]

---

28. Paul A. Gagnon, *France Since 1789* (New York: Harper and Row, 1972), p. 488.

29. Tony Judt, *Past Imperfect: French Intellectuals, 1944-1956* (Berkeley: University of California Press, 1992), p. 87.

30. Jacques Maritain, *Antimoderne* (*Œuvres Complètes*) (Paris: Éditions Saint-Paul/ Fribourg: Éditions Universitaires Suisse, 1990), vol. II, p. 950.

Maritain's quarrel with science did not arise from any distrust of progress or modernity in itself; rather, the conflict lay with his perception of science conducted without any rational guide. True to his Thomistic persuasion he insisted that physical science, like all other human endeavors, must be governed by rationalism. As he points out in *Antimoderne,*

"Science in general is as *historical* as *rational.* But science in its qualified sense, that is, physical and mathematical science, is primarily a part of *rational* science which concerns itself not with all of created nature, but with the lesser natures of the material world; that is, by an object that is not revelatory to us. In fact it ought to deal with a number of very limited truths. Secondly, it concerns itself with these natures not by attempting to penetrate the essence of their reality but with attempting to translate certain of their exterior relationships into a language, the language of mathematics. This is particularly serviceable for the human intellect and the convenience of man."[31]

In his *Trois Réformateurs,* Maritain taxed modern western culture for its self-centeredness and its nearly hysterical demands for the rights of the individual.[32] In his denunciation of the culture of neuroses fostered by moderns such as Luther, Kant, Freud, and Nietzsche, it was as though he were attacking Mounier's philosophy of personalism directly. He was critical of the modern impulse to break away from the message of the Church.

Maritain was never blinded by what some Europeans denounced as American "materialism." In fact, he saw European criticism of American materialism as a handy fable by which participants in a culture with far too many of its own failings could shift their dissatisfaction to others. This was, as Maritain described it, "an old prejudice which confused spirituality with an 'aristocratic' misunderstanding of improvements which material life could bring (especially the material life of others)."[33] Maritain recognized the material accomplishments of the United States for what they were; a potential for the betterment of human existence. One of his intellectual strengths was his critical approach to any question. For Maritain, the matter of American materialism was no exception. It was not his intent to play the cheerleader for American material wealth. He remarked on Americans' tendency, like the populations of the other industrialized nations, to be seduced by "the corruption that emanates from

31. Ibid., p. 951.
32. Jacques Maritain, *Trois Réformateurs (Œuvres Complètes)* (Paris: Éditions Saint-Paul/Fribourg: Éditions Universitaires Suisse, 1990), vol. III, p. 451.
33. Jacques Maritain, *Réflexions sur l'Amérique* (Paris: Arthème Fayard, 1958), p. 30.

the framework and the liturgy of our modern civilization."[34] Here was neither an *apologia* for American materialism nor a recrimination of American worldliness. It was a comment on his conviction that human failings do not respect national boundaries.

Maritain's critique of the human condition was framed in his concern that man tended to search for facile alternatives to God's grace. In the United States, he observed that a common substitute for the God of Holy Scripture was the god of man and nature as gathered under the rubric of the Enlightenment. He noted that "with a remarkable frequency" Americans tended to cling to the eighteenth-century article of faith that if humanity followed nature's lead and its own inclinations, all would be in harmony.[35] The false prophecy of the Enlightenment was its denial that "in our nature there is not a hidden root of evil."[36]

Yet, this does not brand Jacques Maritain as an opponent of modernity *qua* modernity. While he was censorious of the ideas of Luther, Descartes, and Rousseau, the thrust of *Trois Rèformateurs* can hardly be called a wholesale indictment of the modern age. This is evident in his approach to Blaise Pascal: "Saints have their empire, their glitter, their victory, their luster, and they have no need of fleshly or spiritual splendor for they neither acquire anything nor take it away: they are seen by God and the angels and not by carnal forms nor inquisitive spirits. God is their satisfaction."[37] The fact that Maritain would quote Blaise Pascal, like Descartes, a seventeenth-century figure—and a scientist, undermines Mounier's criticism regarding Maritain's distrust of progress. His referral to Pascal illustrates the importance he placed on devotion to God; for Maritain, the issue was not the era during which an individual lived, nor was it his or her activities during that period. Rather, that Maritain would look to the inventor of the calculating machine as a source of spiritual inspiration surely gives the lie to Mounier's contention that Maritain had difficulty accepting modernity.

However, unlike Mounier, who doggedly clung to the one and only idea he ever had, Maritain showed through his public utterances and his writing that he, in fact, did appreciate the historical forces that affected and shaped society. In *Man and the State*, it is clear that Maritain, far from seeing the United States as the contradiction of everything that championed the spirit

34. Ibid., p. 31.
35. Ibid., p. 139.
36. Ibid., p. 140.
37. Maritain, *Trois Rèformateurs*, p. 457.

and freed the human species, recognized the healthfulness of democratic principles in America:

It is a fact that in democratic nations, like France and the United States, which have had a harsh historical experience of struggles for freedom, each one would be ready to give its assent to all the articles of such a [democratic] charter. Having been given the virtue of universality with which they have been endowed, as [Arnold] Toynbee and others have reminded us, the civilization inherited from Christianity and its natural power of influence, there is good reason to hope that in all the areas of civilization the people (I say people as they are represented by their governments) would be well disposed to give a similar assent.[38]

Written during his sojourn in the United States, *Man and the State* is Maritain's summation of his reflections on democracy and its role in the post-war world. As the passage above suggests, Maritain was a thoughtful admirer of American democracy. Moreover he believed that democracy as it had evolved in the United States and France could serve as a model to those parts of the world which had yet to experiment with democratic government.

Maritain and Mounier had much in common regarding their devotion to Catholicism, yet each saw in the twentieth century a different set of dynamics. Emmanuel Mounier was tortured and, in the end, defeated by his perception of modernity. Jacques Maritain founded his view of the modern age on his reading of the *philosophia perennis*. In so doing, he came to the conclusion that no culture in any era ought to be condemned by definition, but that all cultures can be burnished by striving to adhere to universal truth.

38. Jacques Maritain, *L'homme et l'Etat* (*Œuvres Complètes*) (Paris: Éditions Saint-Paul/Fribourg: Éditions Universitaires Suisse, 1990), vol. IX, p. 613.

The Quest for Truth and Human Fellowship in a Pluralist Society

Henk E.S. Woldring

Democratic societies are characterized by a complex plurality. In this essay I will show that Jacques Maritain accounts for this complexity by distinguishing five types of plurality: a) the plurality of worldviews (religions and philosophical theories), b) the plurality of associations, c) the plurality of human beings, d) the plurality of cultural contexts, and e) the plurality of creative minorities. Moreover, these types of plurality are interconnected. The significance of each plurality falls into two categories. First, the label of plurality can be used in a descriptive sense, i.e. simply as a way of acknowledging its existence as a fact. Second, this label can be used in a normative sense or as a means of advocating for diversity in itself as a desirable state of affairs. This essay will explore Maritain's description of the characteristics of the five types of plurality by contrasting his ideas with those of other thinkers. The conclusion will answer three questions: first, how does Maritain describe and consider these five types of plurality, both in themselves and in their interrelations? Secondly, does the advocacy of one type of plurality as a desirable state of affairs imply moral relativism, i.e. does it imply that moral values are relative and a claim of truth is impossible? Thirdly, would it be possible to achieve human fellowship in a society that is characterized by such complex plurality?

Plurality of Worldviews

Wilhelm Dilthey, one of the first philosophers who systematically investigates the phenomenon of a worldview, argues that there is a relationship between a worldview and metaphysics. He is critical of metaphysics because of its claim to universal validity without, in his view, employing a scientific method capable of establishing such validity. On the other hand, however, he argues that metaphysics is not without value because it embodies a worldview, a basic response to the totality of life and the world. A close study of metaphysics reveals its worldview. However, Dilthey argues that each worldview grasps a single aspect of reality and, as such, it is not able to form a complete concept of reality in an objective way.

Dilthey does not have an attitude of indifference towards worldviews but he relativizes their exclusive claims of truth. He proposes a "philosophy of philosophies" that will clarify the meaning of worldview perspectives as reflected in a diversity of philosophical theories which compete with one another. He attempts to overcome the exclusive claims of truth of worldviews by his comprehensive "philosophy of philosophies" which does not have the character of a worldview since he does not want to relativize his own philosophy.[1]

Dilthey's criticism of the exclusivity claims of worldviews is certainly correct if it results in arrogance, ethnocentricity, or the creation of a spiritual ghetto. A worldview is not a goal in itself. It means literally a "viewed world," which itself means that different worldviews have one thing in common: human beings live in the same public world, they are part of humankind, they deal with the same riddle of life and the same world. This world includes a challenge for human beings to think about human origin and meaning, to develop their potential and possiblities, and to act responsibly. Although people make practical choices regarding their worldviews, moral values, and thought, they do this not only in confrontation but also in communication with others. Since all people live in the same world, they possess the possiblity of dialogue and cooperation.

Unlike Dilthey, Max Weber argues that worldviews that contain different systems of moral values do not complement each other; instead, they struggle with each other and that, essentially, they do not have anything in common.

---

1. See Wilhelm Dilthey, *Weltanschauungslehre: Abhandlungen zur Philosophie der Philosophie, Gesammelte Schriften*, Vol. VIII (Leipzig/Berlin: Treubner, 1931), in particular the chapter "Die Typen der Weltanschauung," (pp. 75-118) that has been translated by William Kluback and Martin Weinbaum as *Philosophy of Essence* (New York: Bookman Associates, 1957).

The confrontation of moral values, in the end, never has anything to do with mere alternatives, but it deals with an irreconcilable life-and-death struggle, like between "God" and "the devil." There is no place for relativizing or compromises, at least, not about what concerns their ultimate meaning. However, as everyone experiences the factuality and, consequently, the outward appearances of life, the relativizing and compromising of moral values are common; in almost every important situation in which a real human being determines his point of view, the various spheres of moral values intersect. This is precisely the numbing aspect of the daily grind in its most essential form: the person who is trapped in a daily routine is not aware of this mixture of fatal hostile moral values that are partially determined by psychological, and partly by pragmatic, factors. Moreover, he does not want, strictly speaking, to become aware of it.[2]

Weber argues that at the level of worldviews and systems of moral values there is a continuous struggle with no compromises and relativity. He acknowledges that in everyday life, systems of moral values partially overlap. However, if a human being takes this situation for granted, and if he chooses to ignore this struggle, then it will have a numbing effect. Although Weber discusses an irreconcilable struggle between worldviews, he argues that if human beings chase after the ultimate good of their worldviews following the maxim of an ethic of absolute ends without accounting for the possible destructive consequences of their actions, then these ends may be damaged and discredited for generations. He disqualifies them as politically irresponsible human beings. They endanger social peace and security. Although one should be aware of the struggle of worldviews, Weber also argues that "what is decisive is the trained relentlessness in viewing the realities of life, and the ability to face such realities and to measure up to them inwardly."[3] Human beings should not take a partial overlap of moral values in practical life for granted, but by virtue of their worldviews and moral values they "would have done better in simply cultivating plain brotherliness in personal relations. And for the rest—they should have gone soberly about their daily work."[4]

2. Max Weber, "Der Sinn der 'Wertfreiheit' der soziologischen und ökonomischen Wissenschaften" (1917) ["The Meaning of 'Value-Neutrality' of Sociological and Economic Disciplines"], in *Methodologische Schriften* (Frankfurt: Fischer, 1968), pp. 246-47. (my translation).

3. Max Weber, "Politics as a Vocation" (1919), in H.H. Gerth and C. Wright Mills, (eds.), *From Max Weber: Essays in Sociology* (London: Routledge and Kegan Paul, 1948), pp. 126-27.

4. Ibid., p. 128.

By contrast with both of these thinkers, Maritain argues that in a pluralist democratic society, citizens belong to very different philosophical and religious creeds (worldview plurality), and that, at the same time, they should cooperate for the common good. He argues that a plurality of worldviews does not mean that different worldviews complement each other. In the public debate, representatives of different worldviews advocate different social and political ideals, and they employ different arguments. Notwithstanding these different ideals and arguments, Maritain claims that various worldviews have moral values and central tenets in common when he writes that

> men possessing quite different, even opposite metaphysical or religious outlooks, can converge, not by virtue of any identity of doctrine, but by virtue of an analogical similitude in practical principles, toward the same practical conclusions, ... provided that they similarly revere, perhaps for quite diverse reasons, truth and intelligence, human dignity, freedom, brotherly love, and the absolute value of moral good.[5]

Maritain argues that there are deep divisions between opposing worldviews, and that there is no doctrine or a "philosophy of philosophies" to reconcile or to overcome these divisions. Yet, he argues that very different worldviews can converge because of similar moral values that work toward the same practical outcomes: "There are a certain number of moral tenets—about the dignity of the human person, human rights, human equality, freedom, law, mutual respect and tolerance, the unity of mankind and the ideal of peace among men—on which democracy presupposes common consent."[6]

Representatives of various worldviews should revere those moral tenets, because "without a general, firm, and reasoned-out conviction concerning such tenets, democracy cannot survive."[7] They have to give account of their worldviews and of the similarity of moral values which underlie practical conclusions and which make these conclusions possible. For this reason he argues that we need "theoretical justifications, the conceptions of the world and of life, the philosophical or religious creeds which found, or claim to found, these practical conclusions in reason."[8] Theoretical justifications from diverse worldviews cannot be reduced to private life

---

5. Jacques Maritain, *Man and the State* (Chicago: The University of Chicago Press, 1951), p. 111.
6. Jacques Maritain, *On the Use of Philosophy: Three Essays* (New York: Atheneum, 1965), p. 12.
7. Ibid.
8. Maritain, *Man and the State*, p. 111.

since they have a legitimizing function for democracy and, therefore, a legitimate place in public life.

Since Maritain argues that a democratic society is characterized by a plurality of worldviews, and since he wants to consider all citizens as responsible moral human beings whatever worldview they hold, he not only highlights the fact of this plurality but also defends this plurality as a desirable state of affairs. This position does not lead him to a position of relativism as some authors suggest.[9] Within this worldview plurality, Maritain maintains his commitment to the Gospel and the truth of its message. At the same time he acknowledges the right of those who deny this truth, because he "respects in them human nature and human dignity and those very resources and living springs of the intellect and of conscience."[10] Maritain wants to do justice to other religious or philosophical worldviews, not by borrowing from them or exchanging certain ideas with them, but by getting a clearer view of his own worldview thanks to them, and by enriching it from within and extending its principles to new fields of inquiry.[11] Human beings who adhere to different worldviews can cooperate because of "intellectual rigor and justice."[12] Maritain does not discuss cooperation between worldviews, because they are abstract sets of ideas. He advocates cooperation and brotherhood between human beings founded on an intellectual duty to understand and respect each other's point of view in a genuine and fair manner. This intellectual duty is strengthened by intellectual charity: the love for each other's ideas in order to take great efforts to discover what truths they convey.[13]

Unlike Dilthey, Maritain neither relativizes differences of worldviews, nor considers them complementary to one another. Like Weber, he considers worldviews in essence as very diverse and even as opposite to each other. However, like Dilthey, he acknowledges that representatives of various worldviews have to cooperate in the same public world, and that different worldviews have moral values in common. Like Weber, Maritain argues that human beings should be aware of the struggle between worldviews. Moreover, they should justify their practical conclusions and their underlying moral values by pointing out similarities in diverse worldviews.

---

9. Richard J. Mouw and Sander Griffioen, *Pluralisms and Horizons: An Essay in Christian Public Philosophy* (Grand Rapids, Michigan: Eerdmans, 1993), p. 18.

10. Maritain, *On the Use of Philosophy*, p. 24.

11. Ibid., p. 28.

12. Ibid., p. 25.

13. Ibid., p. 29.

Plurality of Associations

Two founding fathers of the social theories that concern the plurality of associations are Johannes Althusius (1557-1638) and Alexis de Tocqueville (1805-1859). The German philosopher, Althusius, discusses the nature of the relationship between the state on the one hand, and other associations of public law (cities, provinces) and private citizens (families, guilds), on the other. He defines the state as "an imperium, realm, commonwealth, and people united in one body by the agreement of many symbiotic associations and particular bodies, and brought together under one right. For families, cities, and provinces existed by nature prior to realms, and gave birth to them."[14] Next, his central claim is that every association makes its own laws by which it ought to be ruled: "Proper laws (*leges propriae*) are those enactments by which particular associations are ruled. They differ in each specie of association according as the nature of each requires."[15]

According to the universal principles of natural law, which are clarified by the Ten Commandments, the government ought to restrict the activities of citizens and associations by law, in order to defend the fundamental rights of every human being. These rights include: a) the right of natural life, including the liberty and safety of one's own body, b) the right of a good reputation, honour and dignity, and c) the right of property.[16] When discussing social and economic policy, Althusius argues that the government should have the right and responsibility to regulate public commerce, contracts, and business on land and water. It should also have the right to maintain a monetary system, a common language, and the public duties and privileges.[17] By employing these rights the government should not pursue a policy of social welfare, but it should create conditions in its laws and policies so that associations can exercise their rights and responsibilities.

Althusius opposes the idea of the absolute state in which private associations are considered as parts of the state as the supreme and all-embracing community. He advocates a horizontal social order in which both the state and private associations have their own rights and responsibilities. However, there is a hierarchic social order between the state and the variety of associations insofar as they lie within a system of law created by the government.

---

14. Johannes Althusius, *Politica* (1604, 1610, 1614), an abridged edition by Frederick S. Carney (Indianapolis: Liberty Fund, 1995), p. 66.
15. Ibid., pp. 21-22.
16. Ibid., p. 80.
17. Ibid., pp. 84-85.

In sum, Althusius defends four important characteristics of the plurality of associations: 1) every association makes its own laws by which it ought to be ruled; 2) the legal power of the state is restricted regarding non-state associations on the basis of their own authority; 3) the government should defend the fundamental rights of every human being, and 4) it should create conditions for socio-economic welfare.

The French philosopher, Alexis de Tocqueville, also discusses extensively the plurality of associations. He observes that many people see the state as a danger to their freedom, but acknowledges at the same time that individuals can counterbalance state-power. They can form private associations in which they can unite their strengths and realize moral values like human dignity, freedom and responsibility. These associations can be founded in every sector of society: industry, education, healthcare, and amusement.[18]

In Tocqueville's view, exercising democratic freedom would be threatened not so much by governmental centralization, but rather by administrative centralization. He acknowledges that governmental centralization is necessary for the existence and survival of each state: the central government, maintenance of the public legal system, enactment of laws, and foreign policy. However, there are private interests as well. These should be promoted by private associations like industries, commercial enterprises, schools and churches. If the government desires to centralize and control these interests then Tocqueville speaks of administrative centralization. In that case the government would take away many responsibilities of citizens. It would teach citizens and adminstrators of private associations that they have no authority and, consequently, it would undermine the vitality of society.[19]

Administrative centralization should be feared for the sake of protecting private associations, which, according to Tocqueville, have proper rights and duties that are not reducible to those of the state. Like Althusius, he advocates a horizontal social order. However, if industries and other free associations strive only for their own interests and do not take into account the interests of the whole society then they endanger public safety. The government has the task of limiting the freedom of free associations for maintaining a stable state and the public order, for respecting laws, and for promoting welfare.[20] Thus, there is a hierarchic order of associations within the state only insofar as it is within a system of law where the government

18. Alexis de Tocqueville, *Democracy in America*, 2 vols. (1835/1840), edited by J.-P. Mayer (New York: Harper and Row, 1988), vol. II, pp. 513-17.

19. Ibid., vol I, p. 88.

20. Ibid., vol. II, pp. 520-24.

creates conditions so that these associations can exercise their own rights and responsibilities.

In sum, both Althusius and Tocqueville argue that on state territory there can be various types of associations who have their own rights and responsibilities that are different from the institutions of the state. The idea of the plurality of associations serves as a model of the social and moral design of society: it is related to social design in the sense of creating spheres of life in which people can exercise their responsibility for their private associations; it is related to moral design in the sense of actualizing moral values which enable citizens to live with dignity, freedom and responsibility.

Maritain also describes the plurality of associations by identifying this plurality as characteristic of the idea of civil society itself: citizens who belong to a variety of autonomous associations and institutions participate in this type of society. In this context "autonomy" means that every social association governs itself, and carries out duties according to its own rights and responsibilities. He does not describe associational plurality as a fact only, but, like Althusius and Tocqueville, he advocates this plurality as a good that contributes to the vitality of civil society.[21]

Maritain argues that the state comprises the associations on its territory, that it is superior to them, and that it is an agency with the power to use coercion in the service of its citizens. There is a hierarchic ordering of the state and these associations.[22] The state has, in particular, the task of maintaining laws, promoting public order and public interest. However, the state should acknowledge the autonomy of associations but can, if it is in the public interest, provide assistance subsidiarily if these "lower" associations cannot fulfill their tasks. The presupposition of the idea of subsidiarity is that associations should be able to accomplish their rights and responsibilities. Maritain advocates, like Althusius and Tocqueville, for a horizontal ordering of the mutual relationships between those associations. However, if those associations cannot adequately fulfill their tasks the state should, ultimately, take over their tasks for the sake of the common good.

Maritain characterizes his theory of the state as an "instrumentalistic" one, in order to make clear that the state is not a goal in itself but a means to promote the common good, and a means to protect itself against totalitarian threats. He characterizes the modern state also as a "juridical machine," with its laws, its power, and its organization of the social and economic life

21. Maritain, *Man and the State*, pp. 12-13.
22. Ibid., pp. 13-15.

as "part of normal progress." However, a degeneration of this progress may occur if the state becomes identified with the totality of associations. In that case, one could speak of an "absorbing," and sometimes of a totalitarian state. This is a state that regulates the common good not only through political means but also by controlling and organizing science, the economy, and other social sectors.[23]

Maritain argues that not only the state can degenerate by transcending its bounds, but associations themselves can degenerate as well.[24] The reason for the degeneration of associations is that they can be oppressive for their participants and for other associations.

Concerning the former, Maritain argues that an important reason for the failure of modern democracies to realize democracy is "the fact that this realization inevitably demanded accomplishment in the social as well as in the political order, and that this demand was not complied with."[25] A constitutional democracy should be complemented by a democratization of associations. This social democracy is not only a manner of organizing associations, but it serves first and foremost as a moral design to enable citizens to live with dignity, freedom, and responsibility.

On the other hand, if associations transcend their rights and freedoms by oppressing other social associations, Maritain contends that they will threaten the vitality of society. Industries can impose requirements that threaten the interests of families, groups of employees and consumers. They could misuse their autonomy and become more or less oppressive. The rules of the market and commercialization that determine the economic sector of society should not play a decisive role (perhaps an accidental role) in families, schools, universities, churches or hospitals. On the other hand, love, education, faith and care are not determinative ideas in economic affairs (although they too may have an accidental role).[26]

The important idea about associational plurality is not simply that societies are socially differentiated; rather, it is the meaning of this differentiation that matters: associational plurality decentralizes power, and promotes citizens' freedoms and a way of life in accordance with their human dignity. The decentralization of power means that differentiated associations rule their own affairs without being controlled by other communities.

23. Ibid., pp. 19-20.
24. Ibid., pp. 18, 20-23.
25. Jacques Maritain, *Christianity and Democracy & The Rights of Man and Natural Law* (San Francisco: Ignatius Press, 1986), p. 19.
26. See Maritain, *Man and the State*, pp. 19-25.

Moreover, associational pluralities also have a valuable contribution to make to their individual members since they are the sources of their social identities, moral values, and virtues. Furthermore, they promote the commitment of their members to participate in the society at large.[27]

Since Maritain's view of an associational plurality is not only descriptive but in essence normative (he advocates for this plurality), he criticizes the state and those associations which transcend their rights and responsibilities, thus endangering the associational plurality itself and, consequently, the health and vitality of a good society.

Plurality of Human Beings

Hannah Arendt distinguishes three fundamental human activities: labor, work, and action. In particular, action is the activity that occurs directly between human beings. It corresponds to the human condition of plurality: we all are human beings but no two persons are ever alike.[28] To act, in its most general sense, means: to begin, to take an initiative, or to set something into motion. Moreover, action is closely related to speech which is the effect of the human condition of plurality: one can communicate and disclose oneself as a unique human being among equals. Without speech, human beings could not understand each other. The meaning of action becomes relevant only through the spoken word announcing what one does, has done, or intends to do.[29]

Those distinguishing characteristics of action and speech imply that human beings depend on the continuous presence of others in their plurality.[30] Arendt argues that the capacity to begin something new implies freedom in its authentic meaning, i.e. to show one's unique personal identity, and to excel. However, she does not interpret freedom of action in an individualist manner but always closely connects it with plurality and solidarity, and, consequently, with collective action to form social relationships and associations.[31]

Although Maritain does not discuss Arendt's theory, there is no reason in principle why he would not agree with it. He discusses the plurality of

27. Maritain, *The Rights of Man and Natural Law*, pp. 103-05; Maritain, *On the Use of Philosophy*, p. 32.
28. Hannah Arendt, *The Human Condition* (Chicago: The University of Chicago Press, 1958), pp. 176-77.
29. Ibid., pp. 178-79.
30. Ibid., pp. 9, 22, 179-80.
31. Ibid., pp. 187-88.

human beings in a way that complements Arendt's theory. He recognizes Arendt's idea of human freedom which is to show one's unique personal identity, and to excel. He calls this plurality the "freedom of autonomy" of human beings. This means that one's free will must develop a psychological and moral attitude that makes a person someone "having dominion over [his] own acts and being to [himself] a rounded and a whole existence."[32] A person should rule his acts and should have the power to overcome and to hold in control those impulses and passions that otherwise could easily enslave him.

Acquiring a psychological and moral attitude does not occur naturally. It is an achievement indeed to bring a person to maturity as a morally responsible agent. Fr. James Schall describes freedom of autonomy as the "freedom that comes when, through discipline, asceticism, habit and purpose, a person can rule his acts to choose what in fact is true."[33] Since discipline, asceticism and habits differ from one person to the other, freedom of autonomy may be achieved in different degrees in different human beings.[34]

Through the analysis of freedom of autonomy Maritain gives an account of his view of the plurality of human beings. He highlights this plurality as a fact but also defends it as a desirable state of affairs. He often discusses the need for education for the development of various human possibilities and potentials, but he acknowledges that human beings in this respect are not equal. There are human beings who have the capacity to excel, but he wishes to do justice to others with different qualities.

Moreover, persons achieve their freedom of autonomy in concrete social, economic, juridical and moral actions. These actions are conditioned by the variety of associations in which they occur. A person's freedom of autonomy in various fields of action can be achieved only within differentiated associations. These associations are permanent frameworks of human actions that transmit moral values, norms, discipline, asceticism, habit and purposes of action. In short, within associations human beings learn their freedom of autonomy and how to become morally responsible persons.

32. Jacques Maritain, *Freedom in the Modern World* (1936; reprint, New York: Gordian Press, 1971), p. 30.

33. James V. Schall, *Jacques Maritain: The Philosopher in Society* (Landham, Maryland.: Rowman and Littlefield, 1998), p. 130.

34. Jacques Maritain, "The Conquest of Freedom," in *The Education of Man: The Educational Philosophy of Jacques Maritain*, ed. by Donald and Idella Gallagher (Notre Dame, Indiana: Notre Dame University Press, 1962), pp. 165-68.

Plurality of Cultural Contexts

Contextual plurality refers to a variety of cultural patterns of beliefs and practices or ways of life that people share. Practices and beliefs are part of the overt cultural framework or context and, as such, they are more or less fully known to the participants in society. The social scientist uncovers a covert cultural pattern by analyzing social, juridical and moral imperatives. This empirical analysis of the social scientist may indicate more or less universal normative rules. However, these rules have an abstract character and they do not eliminate concrete cultural differences. On the contrary, each cultural and subcultural context has something particular that should be taken seriously in its own right.

Richard Rorty, a postmodern philosopher, acknowledges this contextual plurality. He argues that this plurality is characterized by contingency; it is caused by accident in the course of history. It does not make sense to ask philosophical questions on what and how it happened in the course of history. It happened as it happened. Human beings who participate in a cultural context watch reality from this contextual framework and they make statements about it. Whether others may judge their statements as true or objective does not matter. Their statements are true or objective if they are in correspondence with reality as human beings see and experience it from their contextual framework. This plurality of opinions and statements is also contingent. Rorty argues that no philosophy can clarify this contingency, and no philosophy could judge those statements as right or wrong. However, according to him, this reflection does not lead to a moral relativism, because contextual plurality does not exclude the "conversation of mankind." Rorty interprets truth and objectivity as intersubjectivity, or as solidarity: agreement with others. This means that human beings should be in search of solidarity, not as an abstract idea but as a concrete experience of listening to outsiders who are suffering and to others who have new ideas. In his view, solidarity is not a given phenomenon to acknowledge, but something to create. However, solidarity is also characterized by contingency.[35]

Maritain does not acknowledge contextual plurality as a fact only; he also advocates it as a good state of affairs. However, he does not advocate this plurality uncritically, and he rejects the idea of its contingency. He holds that culture is:

---

35. Richard Rorty, *Philosophical Papers*, vol. I: *Objectivity, Relativism, and Truth* (Cambridge: Cambridge University Press, 1991), pp. 13, 21-34.

[T]he expansion of the peculiarly human life, including not only whatever material development may be necessary and sufficient to enable us to lead an upright life on this earth, but also and above all moral development of the speculative and practical activities (artistic and ethical) peculiarly worthy of being called a human development.[36]

Next, he argues that to speak of culture is to speak of the common good of human beings. "In the sense of our definition there is no culture that is not humanist."[37] To denounce a spiritual deviation of culture does not mean to condemn this culture, it means that Maritain employs certain criteria to evaluate it. These criteria are the ideas of progress and regress. In relation to these ideas, Maritain discusses the "consciousness of self," that is "the growth in awareness of an offended and humiliated human dignity."[38] This growth in awareness appears as a historical gain; it means the rise toward liberty and a morally responsible personality. He argues that all forms of progress of the modern age, of art, science, philosophy, or politics, exhibit this growth of awareness.

There is a progressive movement of societies as they evolve in history. Maritain argues that this movement depends on "the double law of the degradation and revitalization of the energy of history, or of the mass of human activity upon which the movement of history depends."[39] This means that while the wear and tear of time and mental passivity degrade the moral energy of human beings, the creative forces, which are characteristic of the spirit of human dignity and liberty and which normally find their application in the efforts of the few, constantly revitalize the quality of this energy. Society advances thanks to the vitalization of moral energy springing from this spirit and liberty. This means that progress will not take place by itself but by the ascent of consciousness that is linked to a superior level of organization: a civilized community. This community cannot be achieved through compulsion but only by the progress of moral consciousness and relationships of justice and brotherhood—the "essential foundations" of this community.[40]

Although this progress may be achieved in different cultural contexts in different ways, it will never be achieved easily nor without conflicts. It can be achieved only by great political vigilance stimulated by a process of

36. Maritain, *Freedom in the Modern World*, p. 82.
37. Ibid., p. 83.
38. Jacques Maritain, *Integral Humanism: Temporal and Spiritual Problems of a New Christendom* (Notre Dame, Indiana: University of Notre Dame Press, 1973), p. 231. See also Maritain, *Christianity and Democracy*, pp. 36-37.
39. Maritain, *The Rights of Man and Natural Law*, p. 113.
40. Ibid., pp. 114-15, 118, 121.

education.[41] This political vigilance and educational process should be initiated by the rightful authority of the rulers.[42] However, sometimes the political leaders have become morally bankrupt. Then the time has come "to call upon the moral and spiritual reserves of the people, of common humanity—the last reserves of civilization. These moral and spiritual reserves are not a tool in the hands of those with authority, however; they are the very power, and the source of initiative, of men cognizant of their personal dignity and their responsibility."[43]

Plurality of Creative Minorities

For better or worse, Maritain held that the great historical changes in society have been brought about by the "efforts of the few," those who incorporate and revitalize forces of society and who are themselves characterized by a spirit of human dignity and liberty. Moreover, he argues that a democratic society needs "inspired servants or prophets of the people" who form "prophetic pioneering minorities."[44] These minorities have a mission that contains a promise for society: they are prophets of political and social emancipation and the basic transformation of social structures.[45] In this context, political emancipation means to achieve a personalist democracy. Social emancipation and the basic transformation of social structures refer to a social democracy as discussed above.

Maritain argues that those prophets are not elected representatives of the people. The vocation of prophetic leadership "should normally be exercised by small dynamic groups freely organized and multiple in nature, which would not be concerned with electoral success but with devoting themselves entirely to a great social and political idea, and which would act as a ferment either inside or outside the political parties."[46] He has in mind Christian minorities in particular, but also other worldview minorities as well—minorities which are characterized by a prophetic or a peculiar style of thought. However, he is aware that there may be false prophets who are not characterized by a spirit of human dignity and liberty, but rather who want to dominate others.

41. Maritain, *Christianity and Democracy*, p. 26.
42. Ibid., pp. 41-42.
43. Ibid., p. 64.
44. Maritain, *Man and the State*, pp. 139, 141.
45. Ibid., pp. 139-46.
46. Ibid., p. 140.

Maritain highlights the existence of the plurality of those prophetic or creative minorities and he finds them congenial. However, he does not discuss the origin of these minorities. To clarify their origin, a free interpretation of Karl Mannheim's analysis of groups which are characterized by a peculiar style of thought may suffice.[47] First, Mannheim discusses a general worldview of a culture in a given era. For instance, the worldview of the Enlightenment in France in the eighteenth century was characterized by its belief in reason and in scientific, technical, and moral progress. Another example is the general worldview of the Romantic era that may be characterized by some dominant factors: creativity of the individual human being within the context of a historically experienced identity of the nation. The general worldview of contemporary Western culture may be characterized by a thorough individualism of human beings who arbitrarily make their moral choices, who have a materialist-consumerist life-style, and who participate in the process of technological globalization.

Second, there are also particular worldviews: Catholicism, Calvinism, Islam, Socialism, Libertarianism, and Liberalism. Of course, mixtures of these particular worldviews may occur in human life; for instance, there are Catholic socialists, Calvinist libertarians and Islamic liberals. Particular worldviews always endure beyond the influence of the general worldview. It can also happen that a particular worldview opposes a general worldview; groups of Christians, Socialists, and Muslims may criticize the general worldview of contemporary Western culture.

Third, people who adhere to a particular worldview want to achieve something in practice. All those particular worldviews are characterized by certain general intentions which are subdivided into special strivings: these may be economic, political, moral, or philosophical.

Fourth, those strivings attempt to achieve certain goals. If those economic, political, moral or philosophical strivings have an engagement with concrete social goals, Mannheim speaks of certain styles of thought: conservative, revolutionary, emancipatory or pragmatic.

Fifth, and this is the crux of Mannheim's analysis: human beings who adhere to a certain worldview, who share certain general intentions and philosophical strivings, and who are engaged with certain social goals form an intellectual stratum that is characterized by a peculiar style of thought. Moreover, a sociological analysis of this intellectual statum may clarify that a grouping that is characterized by a peculiar style of thought may be called a social stratum.

47. Karl Mannheim, *Essays on the Sociology of Knowledge* (London: Routledge and Kegan Paul, 1952), pp. 184-89.

These groups may exist within and across associations, and they may attempt to achieve social or moral changes within those associations or society at large. Maritain has precisely those groups in mind when he discusses creative or prophetic minorities: action groups of cooperating human beings who share a certain worldview, general intentions, philosophical strivings, who have an engagement with social and political goals, and who have an emancipatory style of thought in common.

Conclusions

The first question that was posed in the introduction, "how does Maritain describe and consider these five types of plurality, both in themselves and in their interrelations?" can be answered as follows. Maritain does not only accept a plurality of worldviews, associations, human beings, cultural contexts and creative minorities as a fact, he also advocates for this plurality as a desirable state of affairs. However, he does evaluate this plurality critically.

First, a plurality of worldviews means that they may not be complementing each other but rather they may be quite different, competing or even opposed to one another. Yet, he acknowledges that human beings who adhere to different worldviews may have moral values and practical tenets in common.

Secondly, a plurality of associations ought to be autonomous to achieve their own rights and responsibilities, and to actualize moral values like human dignity, freedom and responsibility. Ideally, they should complement and cooperate for the sake of the common good. However, if the state or associations transcend the bounds of their competences, they can cause social oppositions, struggle, and social degeneration.

Thirdly, a plurality of human beings entails the development of the freedom of autonomy and/or the psychological and moral attitude of human beings. Maritain argues that this attitude may be achieved in different degrees in different human beings. Consequently, human beings are competitive in certain fields of action while they may need to cooperate and complement each other in other social areas.

Fourthly, a plurality of cultural contexts means primarily differentiation. Although Maritain does not discuss the nature of this plurality, he is not indifferent to it. He argues that the development of a culture should be evaluated according to the ideas of progress and regress.

And finally, a plurality of creative minorities means that there are various groupings which are characterized by their own style of thought.

Although their styles of thought may be very different, groupings with emancipatory styles of thought may complement each other, and in this case they may cooperate to achieve common goals.

Thus, the mutual relationships between these types of plurality focus on human beings who are adherents of worldviews, and participants of social associations, cultural contexts and creative minorities. By virtue of one's worldview and its moral values, a person develops his or her psychological and moral attitudes, and participates in social associations which belong to a (sub)cultural context. Also creative minorities need autonomous moral human beings who incorporate and revitalize the moral and spiritual forces of the people, and who struggle to achieve certain emancipatory goals.

The second question posed in the introduction: "Does an advocacy of one type of plurality as a desirable state of affairs imply moral relativism, i.e. does it imply that moral values are relative, and a claim of truth is impossible?" would be answered by Maritain in the negative. He maintains the truth of his worldview, moral values, and anthropological and socio-philosophic ideas. From this perspective, he is in search of communication and cooperation with adherents of other worldviews on the basis of common moral values. From the standpoint of these moral values, he criticizes deficiencies of associations, a lack of development of the psychological and moral attitude of human beings, cultural degeneration, and oppressive minorities.

And lastly, the third question posed in the introduction "Would it be possible to achieve human fellowship in a society that is characterized by such complex plurality?" can be answered as follows: Maritain acknowledges that human beings who adhere to different worldviews and who have different social positions may share common moral values that make it possible to achieve human fellowship across religious, social, and cultural bounds. Moreover, he also acknowledges that there is a real and genuine tolerance and human fellowship "only when a man is firmly and absolutely convinced of a truth, or of what he holds to be a truth, and when he at the same time recognizes the right of those who deny this truth to exist, and to contradict him, and to speak their own mind, not because they are free from truth but because they seek truth in their own way, and because he respects in them human nature and human dignity."[48]

---

48. Maritain, *On the Use of Philosophy*, p. 24.

"… A Truth We May Serve"
A Philosophical Response To Terrorism

John G. Trapani, Jr.

There is a humorous story about a meeting between French and American business leaders.

> The French devoted themselves darkly to the discussion of ideas while the Americans blithely and relentlessly kept bringing the discussion down to the practical level. Things didn't go well. They went so badly, in fact, that in a moment of exasperation one of the French representatives turned to an American colleague and exclaimed,"Well! That may work in practice but it will *never* work in theory!"[1]

Beyond humor, however, the relationship between theory and practice does pose serious philosophical concerns. For example, the *practical* problem of terrorism in America today ought to involve us in serious reflection on the interrelated *theoretical* ideas about peace, democracy, tolerance, and truth. Specifically, these philosophical reflections pass through the crucible of that natural tension between the theoretical, passionate adherence to the foundational truths of democracy (e.g., the dignity of all human persons and the universality of human rights) on the one hand, and, on the other hand, the (practical) necessity of sustaining, within a pluralist, multicultural, democratic society, a mutual tolerance for certain ideas which otherwise might menace that society's pursuit of peace.

---

1. As quoted in *Boston College Magazine*, Spring 2001, p. 6.

All theoretical discussions of truth involve a host of distinctions and presuppositions about the nature of reality, human nature, the human mind (or intellect), and the metaphysics of human knowing. Upon these presuppositions, conclusions about the very possibility of attaining truth depend and alternatives abound. For example, from a realist metaphysical and anthropological perspective, truth is attainable, and it in turn provides the theoretical ground for one vision of American democracy; on the other hand, from a post-modern perspective, human beings do not and cannot attain any ultimate or absolute truths and, as such, a different vision of democracy results. Though some may argue against the realist position today, it was that position nonetheless that supported the claim of the framers of the Declaration of Independence and the U.S. Constitution that American democracy is founded upon immutable truths ("We hold these truths"); the system of governance that they established, and the fruits of which we continue to enjoy today, is rooted in those truths. Any attempt to deconstruct those claims is a form of "Monday morning quarterbacking"—it assumes that the historical and political results that have unfolded over these past centuries could have been the same even if a softer position on truth had been embraced. But, of course, as in all such conjectural second-guessing, accuracy is impossible. On the contrary, the historical facts being what they are, it is reasonable to assert that the realist assumption that the metaphysical truths that under gird democracy are not only real and possible but also, that true tolerance, political fellowship, and the sustenance of human rights and freedoms are impossible without them.

To test this claim about philosophical realism and its practical consequences, we might begin by considering two perspectives on truth, and then, subsequently, by asking whether philosophy has anything to say about America's present engagement with terrorism. After all, one might object, isn't our present situation really a form of war (a new "cold war") that simply requires the physical strength of "homeland security?" In both cases, the insights of Jacques Maritain reveal the salutary practical implications that result from his theoretical discussions about truth and democracy; they pertain to the political and religious pluralism in contemporary American society in general, and to the threat posed to our democracy by international terrorism specifically.

Two Perspectives on Truth

From one perspective, truth has a supreme utility; it supplies the goal of knowledge that is the accumulation of what Maritain calls the "truths that serve us."[2] Discovered by the empirical, natural and social sciences, we learn the truths about objective reality so that we may use this knowledge in order to solve human problems and to further the quality of human life. This legitimate (though limited) conception of truth, easily leads to a world-view where the universe exists for us to explore, manipulate, and do with what we will; we are the source of our own solutions to the problems which confront us, regardless of whether these problems are of natural or human origin.

From a broader metaphysical or natural theological perspective, however, the universe can also be understood as ultimately dependent upon a divine creator who is the source of all truth, what Maritain refers to as "a truth we may serve."[3] While the former position, "truths that serve us," easily leads to an attitude of dominance over the world (a perspective of masculine power in its exploitation of nature, people, and things), the latter perspective, "a truth we may serve," by contrast, ought to lead to a sense of stewardship of the world (a perspective of feminine caring and nurturing for humanity and the natural world); if "truths that serve us" suggest a manipulation and objectification of the universe, "a truth we may serve" ought to lead to a reverence for and an empathy toward the universe and the human family, seen as the manifestation of the goodness of God's creation within which we are all bound in an ecological and spiritual interconnectedness. While "truths that serve us" may lead us to sing "I did it my way" (taking pride in our independence, knowledge, successes and triumphs), "a truth we may serve," by contrast, ought to lead us to proclaim "Thy will be done," reflecting the humility that derives from our enlightened ignorance of the vast, ultimately incomprehensible mystery of the universe and its Author, and our need to discover the natural law principles that alone enable us to live in ecological, political, and religious harmony. "Truths that serve us" would have us *stand* in honor and celebration of ourselves and our accomplishments; "a truth that we may serve" would have us *kneel* in homage and awe before the Lord and the majesty of all creation; "truths that serve us" yield useful truths; "a truth we may

2. Jacques Maritain, "The Majesty and Poverty of Metaphysics," *The Degrees of Knowledge* (Notre Dame, Indiana: The University of Notre Dame Press, 1995), p. 4.
    3. Ibid., p. 4.

serve" reveals that great and difficult paradox, what Maritain calls "useless" truth. As we shall see, the foundation of truth and that tolerance that alone enables us to live in mutual peace is in fact just such useless, transcendent Truth.

The ultimate importance of this theoretical discussion of truth is revealed dramatically in its practical consequences for political and religious thought by the events of September 11, 2001. And so we may ask: do theoretical philosophers have anything to say in the real, lived, and practical fight against terrorism? Maritain's position suggests an affirmative reply that requires two things: first, a steadfast devotion to truth, especially, in this case, concerning the foundational truths of human nature and democracy, and secondly, we need to establish a delicate balance in our ethical thinking by affirming and sustaining a subtle distinction which alone leads to true tolerance and human fellowship.

Fanaticism and Relativism

Maritain opens his essay, "Truth and Human Fellowship," with the proclamation of Madame Roland mounting the scaffold, "O Liberty, how many crimes are committed in thy name!"[4] In so doing, he is setting the stage by which the same may be said of Truth, or God, or any of the other ideals that fanaticism and terrorism have used as cloaks for their abominable acts of violence. Fanaticism, Maritain tells us, is that natural human tendency of "vicious inclinations"[5] "rooted in our basic egoism and will to power."[6] Terrorism, by extension, is thus the strategy of fanatics who seek to sanction their unspeakable cruelty and destruction as legitimate actions of the impotent combating the injustices of the powerful—actions which become all the more heinous when justified in the name of Truth or God or Allah. How remarkable that Maritain understood so many years ago an insight that is today so prophetically appropriate. And, while sometimes philosophers may argue about what truthfully can be known, splitting, as they do, theoretical hairs, Maritain quietly displays his immense practical compassion as a philosopher by emphasizing the significant impact that these distinctions have upon the lives of ordinary, innocent people who become the victims of the zealot's zeal.

---

4. Jacques Maritain, "The Philosopher In Society," *On The Use of Philosophy* (Princeton: Princeton University Press, 1961), pp. 6 - 7.

5. Maritain, "Truth and Human Fellowship," *On The Use of Philosophy*, p. 22.

6. Ibid., p. 21.

Though difficult to discern in this context, what really is at stake here is the tension between two real goods, tolerance and truth. Articulated as a question, the problem that this tension conceals may be expressed as follows: how is it possible for a diverse society to balance two essential but *seemingly* contradictory goods, both of which are foundational pillars of a just democracy? More specifically, how can the citizens of a pluralist society maintain a mutual respect and tolerance for the various and diverse ideas of their fellow constituents of the body politic *and* at the same time sustain a firm dedication to the fundamental truths of a healthy democracy—truths which include the essential inherent dignity of all human persons and their inalienable, universal human rights, which spring from and yet protect their integral, spiritual and political freedom? Should these positions fail to be balanced equally, the tendency for any society is to emphasize one of these goods to the detriment of the other.

On the one extreme, should the ideals of tolerance and respect, as the essentials of multiculturalism and post-modern diversity, be favored, a firm dedication to the foundational truths of democracy would be sacrificed. On this account, the moral extreme of Relativism results, and lovers of truth are seen as intolerant fanatics who are the enemies of democratic diversity. Swing the pendulum to the other extreme and, in order to emphasize the essential importance of inflexibly affirming the fundamental truths of an enduring democracy, it would appear that one must sacrifice an open tolerance for all ideas, including those which might subvert and undermine that democracy's very health and viability. This becomes the moral extreme of Fanaticism and, on this account, skeptical or multicultural relativists become the enemies of democracy's foundational truths. In the course of human history, at different times and places, human societies have suffered from one or the other of these moral extremes when they seek to assert either one at the expense of the other.

Maritain's solution to the errors that lie at the heart of Relativism and Fanaticism involves right thinking about both the objective order of "ideas" (that are either true or false when considered in themselves) and the subjective order of "persons" (who hold these ideas). When we think rightly in the objective order of ideas, we see that truth ought to reign and error ought to be eliminated. The intellect naturally desires to know the truth of things; we don't like it when people lie to us, and we quite naturally seek to correct errors when we observe them and can show the correction of them. On the other hand, thinking rightly in the subjective order of persons affirms the intrinsic worth and dignity of all human beings regardless of the political or philosophical ideas they may happen to hold.

This "right thinking" about the objective order of ideas and the subjective order of persons is essential for the proper and successful balancing of the tension between tolerance and truth. Shift that thinking improperly and the moral extremes result. Specifically, in the first case, the shift in right thinking about persons to ideas results in the following: instead of saying, correctly, that "all *persons* are to be loved and respected even when they may be in error," one could incorrectly conclude (in the name of mutual tolerance) that "all *ideas* are to be tolerated and respected, especially when our ability to know truth may be shrouded in doubt." In this way, the moral extreme of Relativism is born, and the right desire for the good that is a commitment to truth becomes its casualty.

On the other hand, the shift in right thinking about ideas to persons results in the opposite error: instead of saying, correctly, that "only those *ideas* that are true ought to be defended and proclaimed, and those *ideas* that are in error ought to be corrected or eliminated," one might mistakenly say (though in defense of truth itself) that "only those *persons* who embrace these "right" truths have legitimacy; those *persons* who are in error ought to be eliminated." In this way, the moral extreme of Fanaticism is born, and the right desire for the good that is mutual tolerance becomes its casualty.[7]

A Philosophical Response to Terrorism

In the face of the suffering of our present hour in history, Maritain's insights have the potential to renew our hope and help us, helpless philosophers that we may appear to be, to rededicate ourselves to the cause and importance of truth *and* mutual tolerance as the dual pillars of true democracy. By contrasting, as he does, the extremes of Fanaticism and Relativism—that the fanatic defends truth by eliminating those whom he or she believes to be in error, while the relativist seeks to protect human liberty and freedom by abandoning any adherence to truth altogether—Maritain shows that neither of these "moral extremes" is the answer. From this, we can discern a first hard truth of philosophy's response to terrorism: an ill-conceived notion of democracy that abdicates the affirmation of truth in favor of the rule of a skeptical majority cannot endure. Without truth, we would have nothing to live ... or die ... for.

But, we must be cautious. A pluralist democracy cannot be founded

---

7. Concerning this entire discussion, see ibid., pp. 22 - 23.

upon any obsessive dedication to truth alone, transcendent or otherwise. As we know, fanatical terrorists do that! Instead, a second hard truth of philosophy's response to terrorism lies in a concomitant commitment to true tolerance, the unconditional affirmation of the dignity and sanctity of each and every human person, even when in error. Combined, these hard truths may be summarized as follows: we must defend the truth of those foundational values of a healthy democracy, and we must also defend the precious sanctity of all human life, even in the face of those who may believe in ideals that are dramatically different from, and even opposed to, our own. In this, and this alone, resides true tolerance, true democracy, true human fellowship, ... and true peace.

Admittedly, this is not easy to do ... especially when the Other becomes that Fanatic and Terrorist who threatens our safety, our economic well-being, and our democratic way of life. Whether it be the Christian, the Jew, the Muslim, or the Atheist, the political conservative or liberal, the powerful rich or the powerless poor, Maritain makes clear that adherence to truth is difficult but necessary. In "Truth and Human Fellowship" he writes:

> There is real and genuine tolerance only when [we are] firmly and absolutely convinced of a truth ... and when [we] at the same time recognize the right of those who deny this truth to exist ... not because they are free from truth but because they seek truth in their own way, and because [we respect] in them human nature and human dignity."[8]

Nothing could be more essential at this time in our history, especially in these dark moments of violence, where violence is answered with ever-escalating rounds of more violence. A month after the World Trade Center bombing, *U.S. News* editor, Mortimer Zuckerman asked the question that brings all theoretical discussions crashing back to practical pavement: "how are we going to deal with an irrational, vengeful, and elusive global enemy?" he asks. His answer, for rational, common sense philosophers of truth and peace, is sadly chilling: "reason has no role with the irrational," he says. "We have to destroy them."[9]

A position such as this is a fanaticism of its own and it makes clear the necessity of a third hard truth: that is, the subtle, practical distinction between what Maritain calls the speculatively (or theoretically) practical, and the practically practical.[10] The former concerns the theorizing that we might

8. Ibid., p.24.
9. Mortimer Zuckerman, editor, *U.S. News and World Report*, 8 October 2001.

do about practical actions—everything from studying a magazine article in order to improve a golf swing, to discussions about the contents and merits of Just War Theory. The practically practical, on the other hand, concerns the realm of lived, concrete action—everything from going to the driving range and actually swinging the golf club, to the actual applications (both domestic and international) of those theoretical Just War principles. On the level of judgments about the principles of action, a reasonable claim to the truth of those principles may be sustained; on the level of judgments about the application of those principles in the cases of concrete action, we find ourselves in discussions within which men and women of good will may reasonably disagree.

This disparity of judgments concerning "appropriate" responses to terrorism is particularly evident in discussions in America today. A wide diversity of positions, with varying degrees of merit, can be argued, and certainty (about which position is "correct") is impossible to determine. Moreover, given the difference between the degree of certitude that legitimately can be expected from speculatively practical and practically practical judgments, we should understand this ambiguity as both normal and the best that can be hoped for. In his book, *The Time of Our Lives*, Mortimer Adler argues similarly when he distinguishes the three levels of ethical reasoning: on the level of universal principles (similar to Maritain's theoretically practical), a high degree of certitude may be argued and defended, while on the level of concrete judgments in particular cases (similar to Maritain's practically practical), a much lesser degree of truth (if any) should be expected.[11]

Asserting these distinctions, as intellectually subtle as they may be, is not the protestation of irrelevant philosophy; rather, they offer a perfect example of the need to reaffirm three of the many hard but essential truths of a decent and civilized humanity and an enduring democracy. With these truths in mind, we can see that our opening story is in fact inverted and yet strangely pertinent: our critics may whine that, while these philosophical ideals about truth, tolerance, and democracy, may work in *theory*, they will never work (i.e., are useless) in *practice*! To the contrary, we may exclaim in response: the ideas expressed in Maritain's essay do work in both theory *and* in practice ... though not a theory that is derived from truths that serve us alone. Rather, the veracity of Maritain's ideas derive from rational, philosophical analysis that clearly identifies those hard truths that are essential to

10. Maritain, *The Degrees of Knowledge*, pp. 330–35.

11. Mortimer J. Adler, *The Time of Our Lives* (New York: Fordham University Press, 1996), pp. 193–96.

the flourishing of any truly multicultural, pluralistic democracy that preserves human rights and freedoms. In the end, those who follow Maritain's ideas to their metaphysical conclusion will not be surprised to understand that these hard truths themselves ultimately depend upon a living and lived Gospel; they reminds us that we " ... do not live by bread, vitamins, and technological discoveries" ... or military might ... alone. Rather, in the world of our everyday experience, beyond any discussions about the useful and the useless, the theoretical and the practical, we " ... live by values and realities which are ... worth being known for their own sake; [we] feed on that invisible food which sustains the life of the spirit, and which makes [us] aware ... of [our] very reasons for living—and suffering, and hoping."[12] In this way, philosophy, when and only when it speaks these truths, has everything to say about our decently human and civilized response to terrorism. They alone are the truths that work in theory *and* in practice, because they all, ultimately, derive from and are rooted in the good news of "a truth we may serve."[13]

12. Maritain, "The Philosopher In Society," pp 6–7.
13. Maritain, *The Degrees of Knowledge*, p. 4.

Contributors:

Gavin T. Colvert is Assistant Professor of Philosophy at Assumption College in Worcester, Massachusetts. His areas of research include ethics, political philosophy, medieval philosophy, and philosophy of religion. He has a special interest in a dialogue between the work of St. Thomas Aquinas and contemporary philosophy. He has published articles on the work of philosophical figures such as Aquinas, William Ockham, Jacques Maritain, and Hilary Putnam, among others.

John A. Cuddeback is associate professor of philosophy at Christendom College. His teaching and research focus on themes in ethics, especially natural law, common good, friendship, and contemplation. He is the author of *Friendship: The Art of Happiness,* as well as several articles.

Raymond Dennehy is a former president of the American Maritain Association and is professor of philosophy at the University of San Francisco where he teaches epistemology, metaphysics, political philosophy, and social ethics. In addition to publications in journals, he has published *Reason and Dignity, Anti-Abortionist at Large: how to argue intelligently about abortion and live to tell about it,* and edited *Christian Married Love.* Dr. Dennehy is frequently invited to address contemporary ethical and social issues on television, radio, and university campuses.

Bernard Doering is Professor Emeritus of Romance Languages and Literature at the University of Notre Dame. He has published two books about Maritain: *Jacques Maritain and the French Catholic Intellectuals* (1983) and *The Philosopher and the Provocateur, the Correspondence of Jacques Maritain and Saul Alinsky* (1994). In addition, he has translated books by and about Maritain.

Desmond J. FitzGerald Professor Emeritus at the University of San Francisco. He attended the lectures of Fr. Gerald B. Phelan at St. Michael's, University of Toronto, as an undergraduate in the 1940s. He holds a B.A. and an M.A. from Toronto and an M.A. in political science and a Ph.D. in philosophy from the University of California at Berkeley. He taught at the University of San Francisco from 1948-1998.

Sarah J. Fodor is an independent scholar and associate director of foundation relations at Northwestern University. She has published essays on Flannery O'Connor in *Flannery O'Connor: New Perspectives* (ed. Sura P. Rath and Mary Neff Shaw, 1996) and in *Literature and Belief* and the *Flannery O'Connor Bulletin*. Her book reviews have appeared in the *Anglican Theological Review* and *The Christian Century*.

William J. Fossati teaches history at Rockhurst University in Kansas City, Missouri. He earned his B.A. and M.A. degrees in history from the University of Arizona. He holds a Ph.D. in modern European history from Kansas University. His area of specialty is French history after 1789. He has done extensive research in the area of the history of ideas. His specific focus is on the period of the Catholic revival in France in the early twentieth century.

W. Matthews Grant is an Assistant Professor of Philosophy at the University of St. Thomas in St. Paul, Minnesota. He received his Ph.D. in Philosophy from Fordham University. His research interests include philosophy of religion, medieval philosophy, natural law ethics and contemporary Thomism.

James G. Hanink is Professor of Philosophy at Loyola Marymount University, Los Angeles. His interests include Thomism and the personalist movement. He is also Associate Editor of the *New Oxford Review*, a Catholic journal of opinion.

Katie Hollenberg recently graduated from Rockhurst University with her B.A. in philosophy and psychology. She plans to pursue her Ph.D. in philosophy and become a professor. Her main areas of interest include medical ethics and the common good.

Gregory J. Kerr is Associate Professor of Philosophy at DeSales University. After receiving his B.A. and M.A. in philosophy from Boston College, he completed his Ph.D. at Fordham writing his dissertation on *Maritain's Receptive Intuition and the Benefits of Art*. He was former editor of the *Maritain Notebook*, the newsletter of the American Maritain Association.

312

James P. Mesa received his undergraduate and graduate degrees in philosophy from Saint Louis University and taught philosophy at Newman University in Wichita, Kansas from 1970 to 2002. His primary research interest was in ethics. He died on February 2, 2003, the Feast of the Presentation of the Lord.

Peter A. Pagan Aguiar teaches Philosophy at Aquinas College in Nashville, Tennessee. He received his B.A. from U.C. Berkeley and his Ph.D. from Fordham University. His publications include: "Natural and Supernatural Modes of Inquiry," in *Faith, Scholarship, and Culture in the 21st Century* (CUA Press, 2002) and "St. Thomas Aquinas and Human Finality" (*The Thomist*).

Matthew S. Pugh is Associate Professor of Philosophy at Providence College. He previously taught at Ohio Dominican College, Ohio State University, and the University of St. Thomas in Houston. His interests include Thomistic metaphysics, epistemology, and ethics. Dr. Pugh is the author of numerous articles in books and journals.

James V. Schall, S.J. is a professor of Government at Georgetown University. Among other books, he has written. *At the Limits of Political Philosophy, Another Sort of Learning*, and *On the Unseriousness of Human Affairs*.

Michael D. Torre is an Associate Professor of Philosophy at the University of San Francisco. He has contributed articles to several of the Maritain Association's series of volumes and was the editor for its *Freedom in the Modern World: Jacques Maritiain, Yves R. Simon, Mortimer J. Adler* (1989, with a second printing in 1990). He also has contributed to *Notes et Documents* of the Institut International Jacques Maritain, and recently served as one of its Vice Presidents.

John R. Traffas received his B.A. (Politics) and M.A. (Theology) from the University of Dallas. He has served as adjunct instructor of Theology at Newman University in Wichita, Kansas.

John G. Trapani, Jr. is a Professor of Philosophy and Chair of the Humanities Division at Walsh University in North Canton, Ohio. He received a B.A. from Boston College and a Ph.D. from St. John's University. A past President of The American Maritain Association (2000-2001), he has published many articles on various aspects of Maritain's philosophy and is the editor of *Truth Matters*. In addition, Dr. Trapani also is active as a professional musician and bandleader.

Cornelia A. Tsakiridou is Associate Professor in the Department of Philosophy, La Salle University and Director of the Diplomat-In-Residence Program since 1994. She holds a Ph.D. from Georgetown University. She has published numerous articles on aesthetics (visual art and poetics) and is editor and contributor of a Bucknell University Press volume on French artist Jean Cocteau titled *Reviewing Orpheus: Essays on the Cinema and Art of Jean Cocteau.*

Timothy S. Valentine, S.J. joined the Society of Jesus in 1988. With an S.T.L. from Weston Jesuit School of Theology (1994) and a Ph.D. in Philosophy from Columbia University (2000), he was as an Assistant Professor of Philosophy and Education at Fordham University from 2000-2003. Presently, he is with the U.S. Army, serving as the Battalion Chaplain for the 123rd Signal Battalion in Ft. Stewart, Georgia.

A. Leo White lectures at Morgan State University in Baltimore. He has published in the *Thomist,* the *Proceedings of the American Philosophical Society,* and he is the author of "Perception and Practical Reason in Thomas Aquinas," in *Aquinas on Being and Thought,* edited by Jerry Hackett, published by University of Binghampton Press.

Anne M. Wiles is Professor of Philosophy at James Madison University, Harrisonburg, Virginia. She has published articles in the areas of ancient Greek Philosophy, metaphysics, ethics, political theory, philosophy of education, and cross-cultural studies.

Henk E.S. Woldring is Professor of Political Philosophy at the Free University in Amsterdam and a member of the First Chamber (Senate) of the Parliament of the Netherlands for the Christian Democratic Party since 1999. He is the author of many books, including *Karl Mannheim: The Development of his Thought.*

Index